# Andrei Sannikov

# Tip of the day
## *A practical addendum to P6 manuals*

***Third Edition, Revised and Updated***

## Contents

About this book .......................................................................................................................... 4
Foreword .................................................................................................................................... 5
How to copy logical links ........................................................................................................... 6
Actual labor units incorrectly placed in time ............................................................................. 7
Why actual labor hours change after schedule updates ........................................................... 9
Incorrect float calculation with multiple calendars ................................................................. 10
How to add out-of-sequence flags to your schedule .............................................................. 12
How to check if activity and resource start/finish dates are aligned. ..................................... 16
    Part 1 ................................................................................................................................... 16
    Part 2 ................................................................................................................................... 18
How (and why) to change Global Calendars to Project .......................................................... 22
Why float values sometimes seem incorrect? ........................................................................ 26
Incorrect float calculation on paths with FF relationships ...................................................... 28
How to find driving "out-of-sequence" predecessors using the trace logic function ............. 30
How to filter in out-of-sequence activities .............................................................................. 33
How to change man-power loading on a portion of activity duration ................................... 36
How to merge multiple projects and how to maintain inter-project links after export/import ... 38
How to import actuals into your schedule .............................................................................. 45
How to group activities by start or finish dates ...................................................................... 49
How to display material quantities in a column ..................................................................... 51
How to remove subtotals from columns with user defined fields .......................................... 54
    Part 1 ................................................................................................................................... 54
    Part 2 ................................................................................................................................... 56
How to add code values to activity names ............................................................................. 59
How to display and correct activities with necks ................................................................... 61
How to split a schedule into separate projects ...................................................................... 65
How to generate schedule scenarios without using reflections ............................................. 69
Level of efforts – tricks and rules ............................................................................................ 74
    Part 1 ................................................................................................................................... 74
    Part 2 ................................................................................................................................... 78
How to make massive changes in logical sequence ............................................................... 80
    Part 1 ................................................................................................................................... 80
    Part 2 ................................................................................................................................... 84

| | |
|---|---|
| How and when to use resource leveling function | 92 |
| How to find all out-of-sequence relationships in a large network | 96 |
| Quick fix for late finish dates on completed activities | 98 |
| Time saving schedule updating techniques | 99 |
| How to check quickly the impact of different predecessors on completion milestones | 102 |
| How to find all external relationships in your schedule | 107 |
| What to do if P6 does not let you use the actual finish date of your choice | 111 |
| How to plot a rolling forecast curve straight from P6 | 113 |
| How to add mid-point target dates to your schedule | 118 |
| How to fix row height in your schedule | 121 |
| What to do with the driving flags on completed activities | 127 |
| How to check your schedule for driving external relationships | 131 |
| How to replace existing resources with new ones on activities with actuals | 135 |
| How to demote a code from Global to EPS and from EPS to Project | 139 |
| How to set up a filter for a period in the future | 144 |
| How to link your schedule to a progress tracking system | 148 |
| How to change week start day in weekly resource exports | 159 |
| How to place Completion Milestones after their predecessors when sorting by Finish | 163 |
| How to import contractors' schedules into your master plan | 167 |
| How to identify all UDFs and activity codes used in a schedule | 177 |
| How to link your schedule to a systems completion database | 180 |
| What to do if P6 does not let you de-actualize an activity start date | 186 |
| How to reinstate deleted activities from a baseline | 190 |
| Attachment – Planners' Frustration Corner | 198 |

About this book

This book is not a Primavera (P6) manual. It is a collection of various tips and workarounds for solution of common and not so common issues associated with the use of P6 software that the author put together during his career in planning and P6 support.

## Foreword

I have been working in different planning functions on various international projects for nearly 25 years and my duties often included support of planners working for me or contractors on our projects. In most cases, issues these planners encountered could be resolved by consulting one of the Primavera manuals – there many of them around - but sometimes I had to think out of the box and come up with a workaround that I used to capture in an email that I always called a "Tip of the day". This book represents a selection of these tips arranged in chronological order, I decided to keep the date and time stamp on most of them to give you an idea when a particular issue was brought to my attention and solved. Nothing is cast in stone and Oracle publishes new versions of P6 on a very regular basis; some of the issues that we ran into at that time might have been addressed in later releases of P6 software.

I hope you will find my tips useful.

Andrei Sannikov

24-Jul-13 08:14

## How to copy logical links

Sometimes, we need to copy all successors or predecessors from one activity to another. We can, of course, do it via export/import of activity relationships but this is a rather complicated process, which is reserved to massive logic changes and explained in detail in elsewhere in this book.

Say, you have Activity A and you want to copy all its successors into Activity B.

1. Copy and paste activity A, make sure you uncheck the "Only between copied activities" check box:

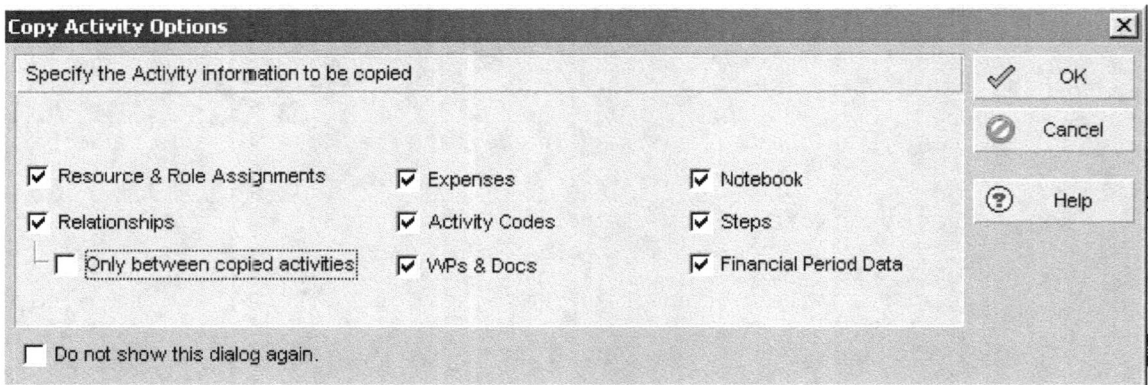

2. Now you have activity A1, which is an exact copy of activity A.

3. Assign A1 as successor to B.

4. Dissolve A1 using the Dissolve command in the drop down or Edit menu.

5. This will copy all successors from Activity A to Activity B.

**Notes**:
   a) If you want to copy all predecessors from Activity A to Activity B, assign A1 as predecessor to B in Step 3 above.

   b) If activity B is not a new activity and already has some logical ties, this process might results in circular references (a.k.a. loops), make sure you hit F9 each time you complete Step 4 above and clean up these loops if they appear.

Andrei Sannikov
Tip of the day

09-Aug-13 16:39

Actual labor units incorrectly placed in time

A recent review of one of the Contractor schedules showed that actuals were not displayed correctly - some activities were completed several weeks ago, however, the actual labor units in the resource profile appeared in the week following the data date:

You will notice that all these activities started and finished on the same day, and one would assume that their actual duration was 1 day.

P6 "thinks" in hours and for some strange reason when the dates are displayed without time (setting "Do not show time" in Edit > User preferences > Dates) and you apply actual start and/or finish the time of these events stored in the system is 0:00 (midnight), see the same table below with time displayed:

Therefore, the actual duration of each activity is 0h 0m and there is no time period the actual hours can be assigned to - P6 simply shifts them to the data date.

If you do display time during schedule update and apply actual start and/or finish, P6 will always display by default the first hour of the working day set in your calendar - e.g. 7 am - and as long as your actual duration is, at least 1 min long the actuals hours will be placed in the right time period.

When you review a schedule and notice some strange movement of the actual hours between schedule updates (as above) create/run a filter with the following conditions:

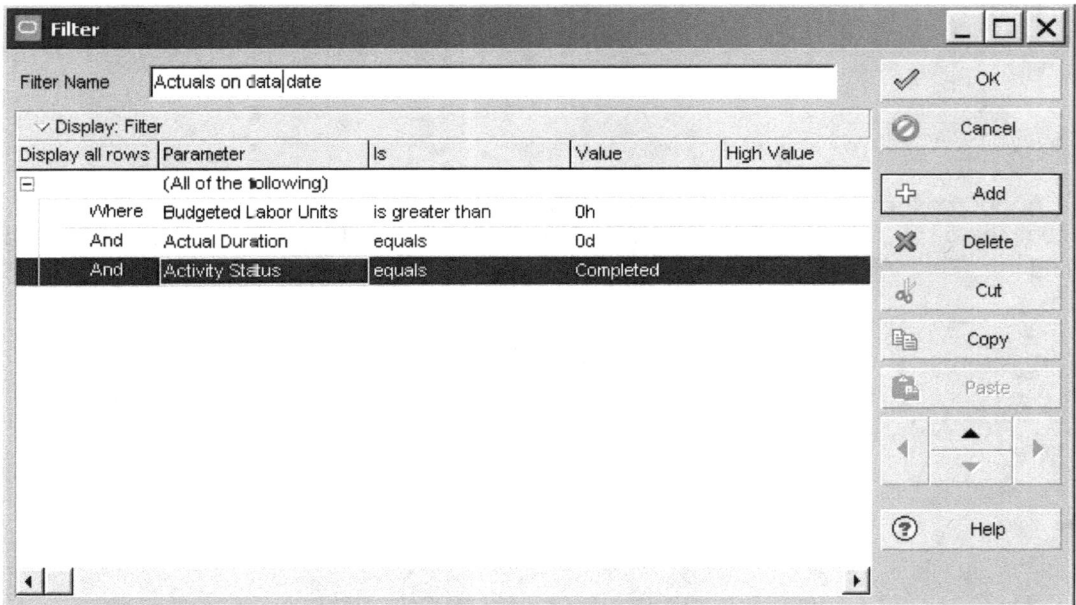

It might be a good idea to run this filter as part of your schedule review routine and share this finding with your counterparts in respective Contractor organizations as this "glitch" does not seem to be common knowledge.

A follow up note...

To fix this problem in an existing schedule:

- run the filter described above,
- display time,
- change the actual finish time on these activities to an hour during the working time period set in your calendar e.g. 8 am or later.

29-Aug-13 15:03

# Why actual labor hours change after schedule updates

As we all know all our contractors have substantial differences between the actual/earned hours in the schedules and the actuals in the weekly reports, which are generated by their progress management systems. Part of the problem is a wrong calculation setting used in almost all Contractor schedules.

In the project view go to Calculations tab:

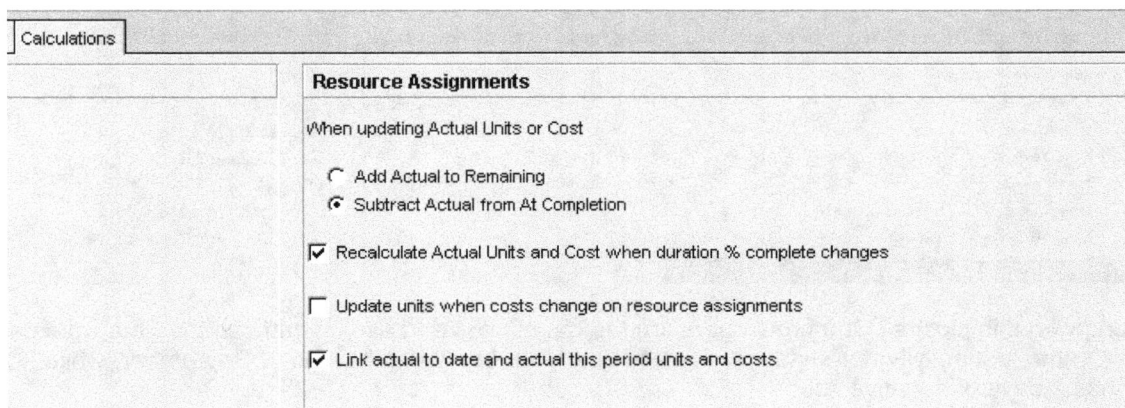

If "Recalculate Actual Units and Cost when duration % complete changes" (which is a default setting in P6) is enabled, the system changes actual labor hours when remaining and actual durations are modified during schedule updates. Bottom line changes can be very substantial, especially on high level activities loaded with lots of labor hours in some of the Contractor schedules. Some of our contractors load resources on level of effort type activities - against our advice - and since their duration changes automatically with each update so do the actual labor hours.

My advice is to disable this setting.

Andrei Sannikov
Tip of the day

21-Sep-13 15:13

## Incorrect float calculation with multiple calendars

I am sure some of you have noticed that P6 does not always calculate the late dates correctly on change of calendars and finish milestones and the late dates, as you know, determine your critical path and available float.

Below is a screen shot of a 15-day program with no constraints, very simple FS/0d lag logic and 15 days of negative float.

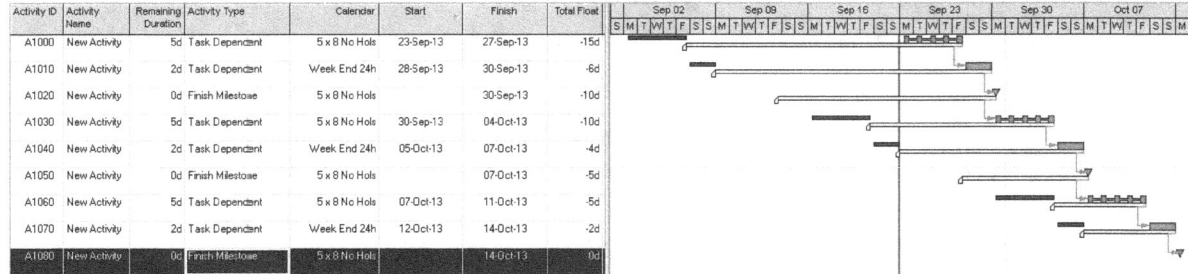

What is wrong with this picture? The brown bars are the Late Dates and as you can see the Late Date calculation is incorrect. On the last activity, for instance, the late dates are shown at the end of September, while it starts on Oct 12 and has 2 days of negative float.

When in P6 a Finish MS and activities driving it are on different calendars (typically with different workday durations) late dates/float calculation can be incorrect in some cases.

When you see something similar in your schedule, display the calendars in a column to make sure your float is indeed impacted by them and do one of the following:

1. If possible, change the calendar on your finish milestones to match the calendar of the activities driving it.

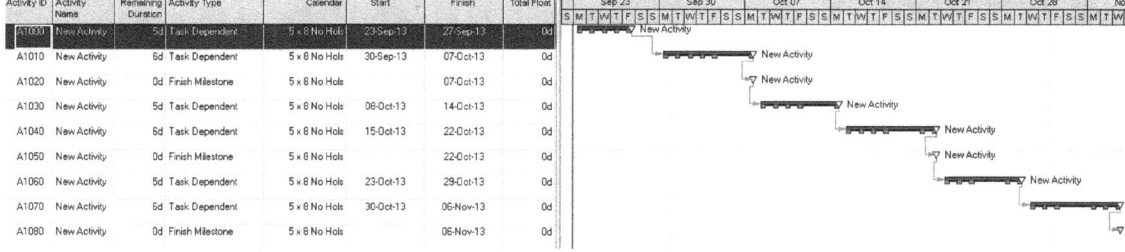

2. If this is not possible, change your Finish MS on this path to Start MS.

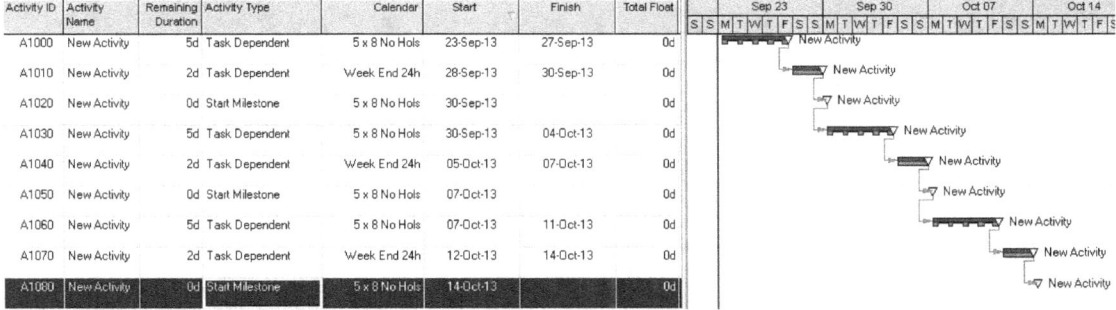

3. If you have multiple calendars with different workday durations in your network, consider changing all your Finish MS to Start MS with corresponding adjustments to the logic.

**A follow up note:**

This issue has been addressed in the latest versions of P6 and you will need to consider it only if you still have versions 8.2 or earlier on your machine.

11-Oct13 15:30

## How to add out-of-sequence flags to your schedule

When we use Retained logic mode for scheduling our projects, durations on some of the "in progress" activities can be impacted, as you know, if such activities started out of sequence i.e. before the dates set in their relationships. I could not find any built-in tools in P6 that would let us filter in such activities in the schedule and adjust the logic if necessary - let us create our own:

1. Set up a User Field similar to the one highlighted below:

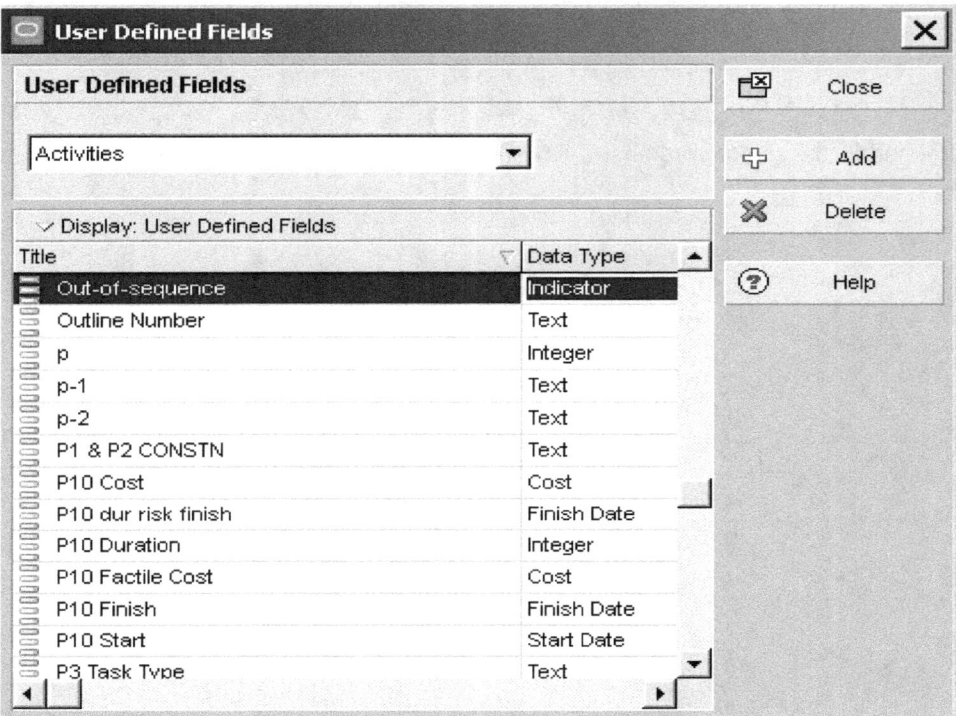

2. Schedule your project in Retained logic mode, make sure the log to file box is checked:

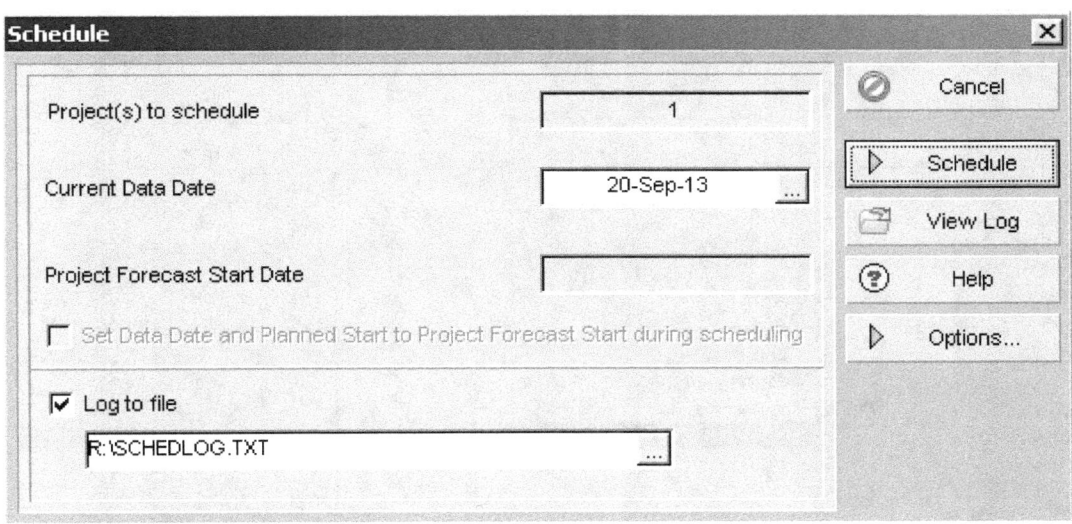

3. Open the resulting SCHEDLOG.TXT file, copy the Out of sequence section into an Excel spreadsheet - fields in this file are separated by Tab characters, which is fully compatible with Excel

4. In the resulting spreadsheet delete all the columns except the one with Activity ID - column F in our example:

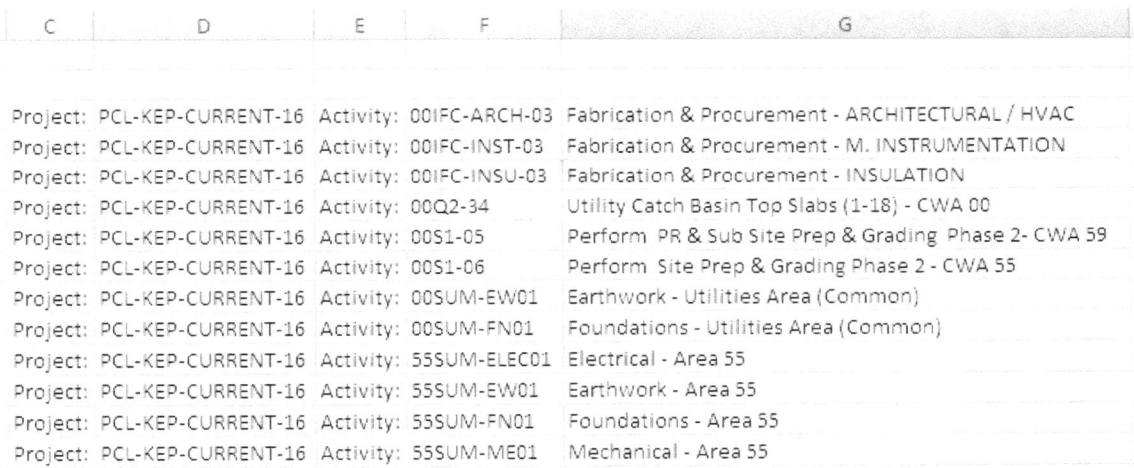

5. Type the word Red in the column next to Activity ID and copy it all the way down, save the file as, say, Out of sequence.xls

6. Go back to P6 and export your activities into Excel, choose the following fields in the Export Template dialogue :

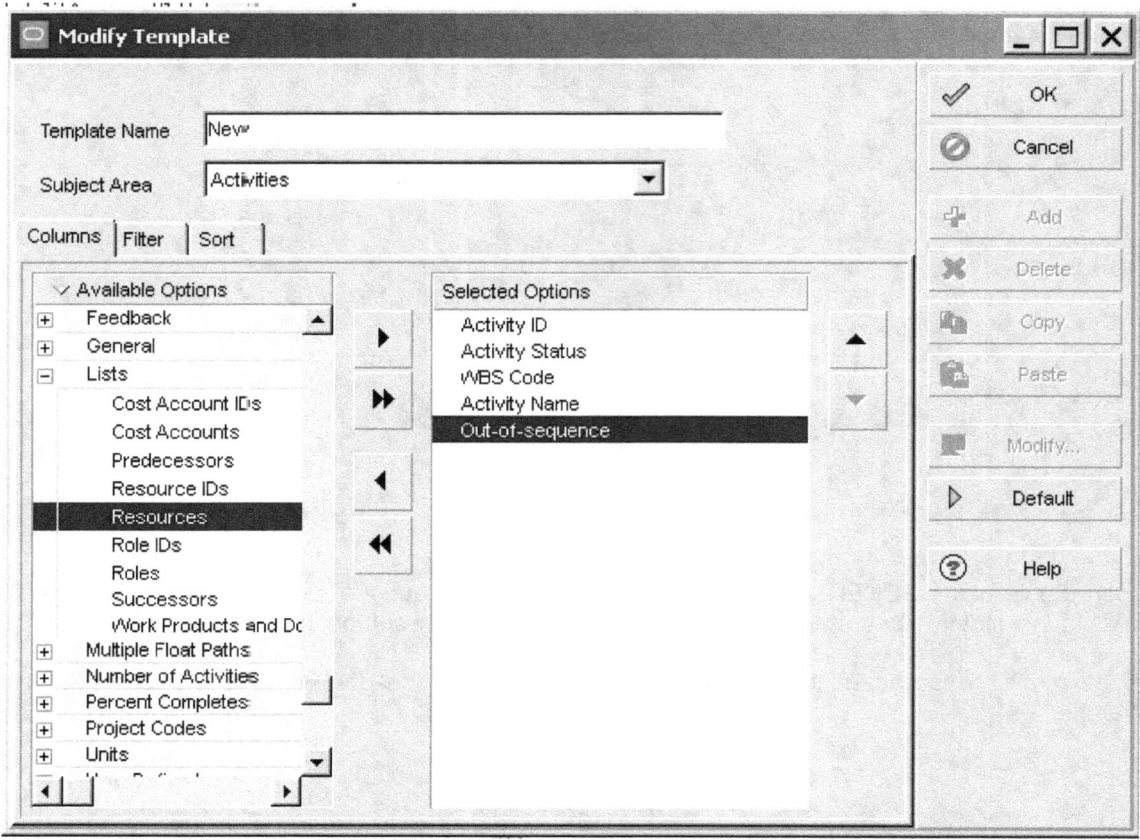

7. Add the data from your Out of sequence.xls under a separate tab in the export file P6 has generated.

8. Use a lookup function of your choice to populate the Out-of-sequence column; convert formulas into values and remove all the rows with #N/A - you will have something like that:

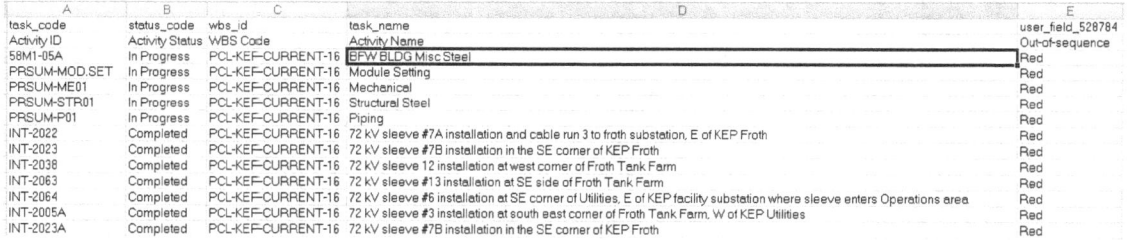

9. Import the file into your schedule, when you display the Out of sequence column in your layout you will see Red symbols on all the activities where durations could be impacted by the out-of-sequence logic:

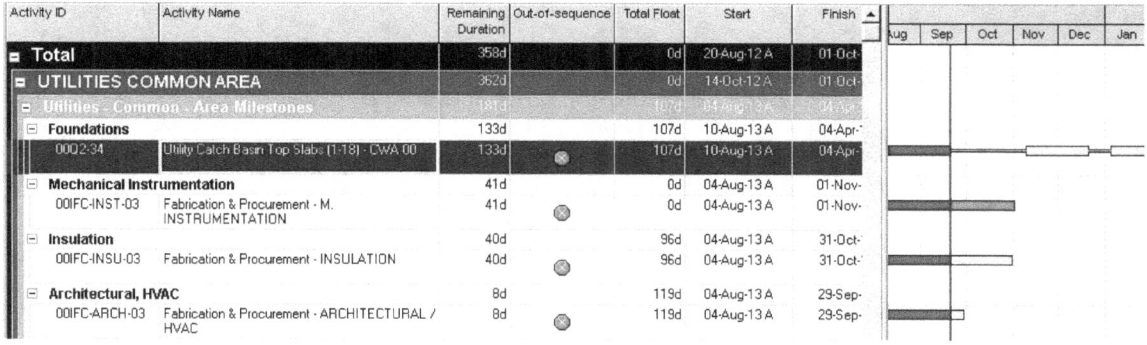

You can also set up a filter for out of sequence activities using the same out-of-sequence user field.

# How to check if activity and resource start/finish dates are aligned.

13-Oct-13 08:18

Part 1

I am sure all of us have been in situations when resources loaded on activities are not plotted correctly on our labor forecast or progress curves e.g., we know that there is no work planned beyond a certain date, but we see labor hours in the spreadsheet we downloaded from the schedule or the other way around. The most common reason for that is misalignment between activity and resource start and/or finish dates. It can be caused by operator or import errors, wrong Project settings (when Drive activity dates by default option is not checked):

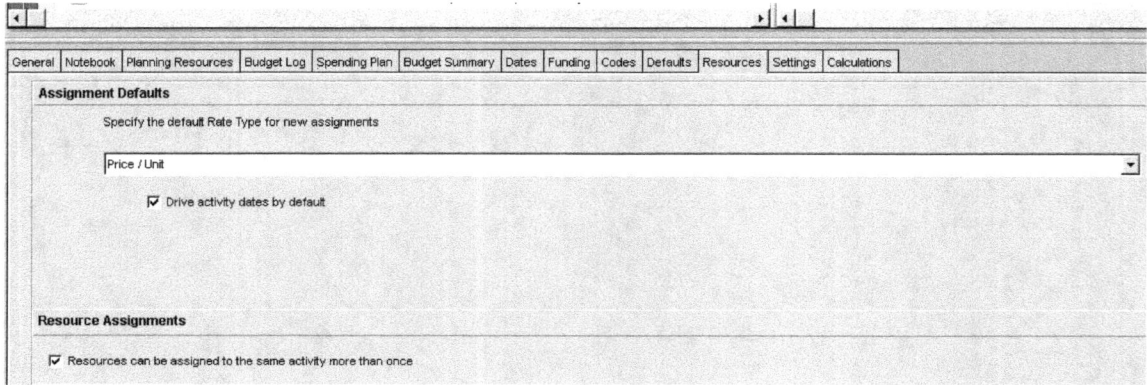

... or by some unknown program glitches.

This is how you can check your schedule:

1. Go to Reports > Add > New report

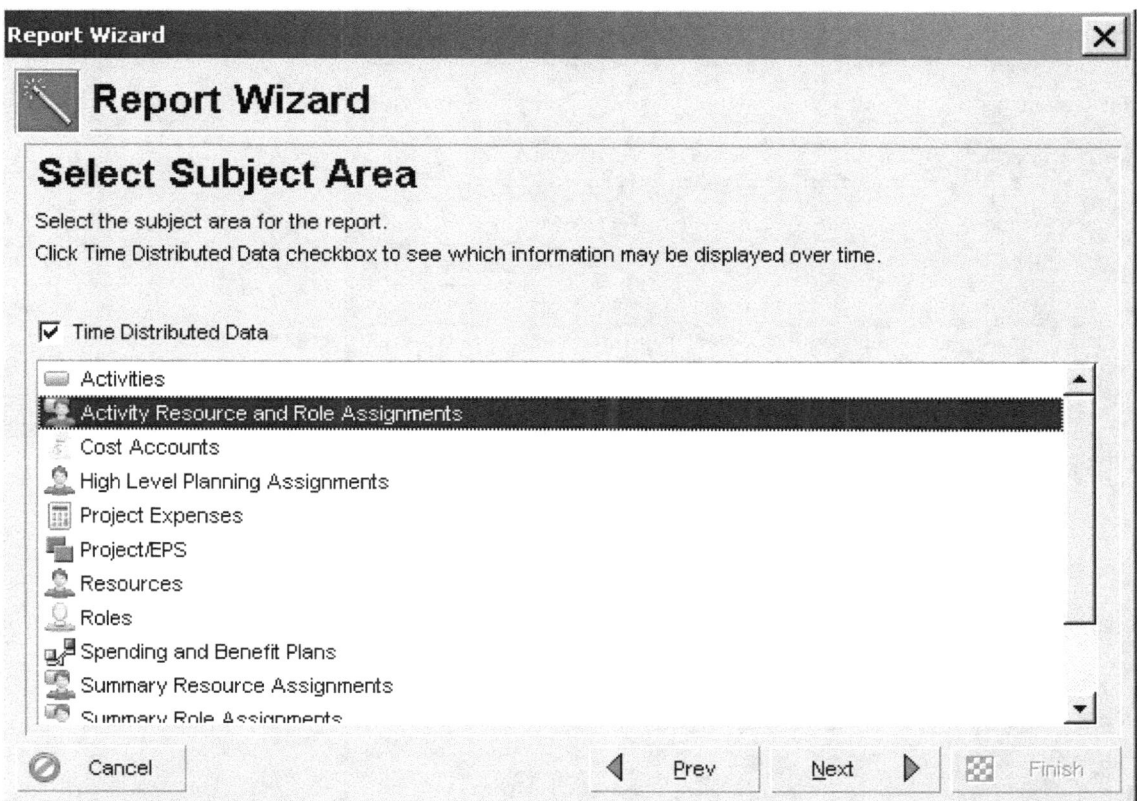

2. Select the following columns:

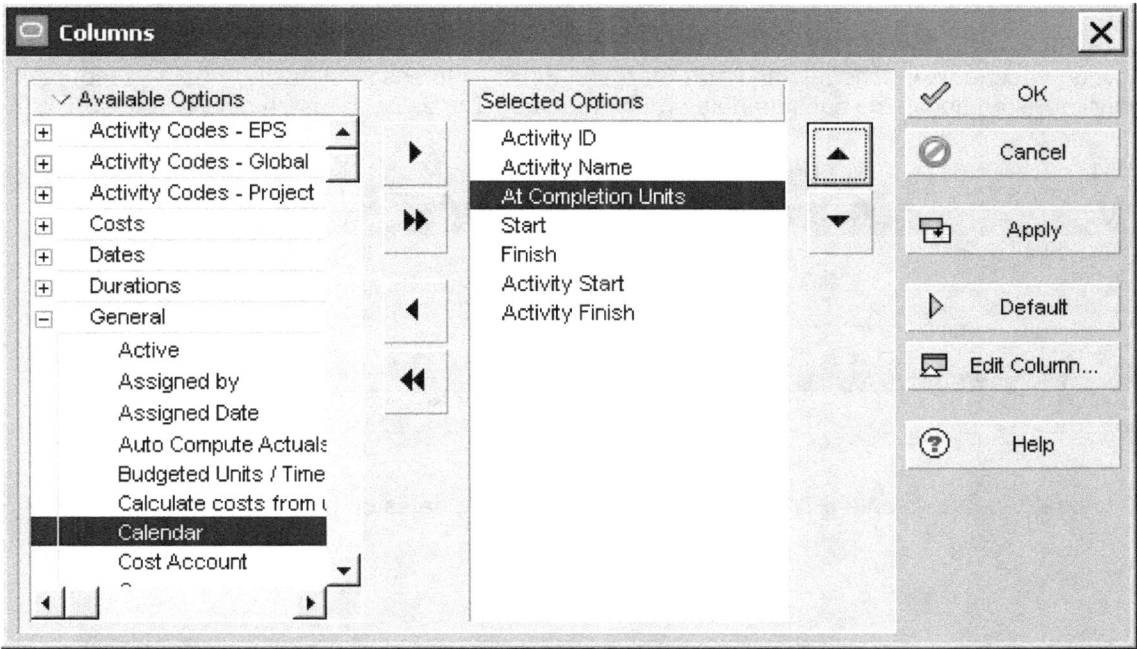

3. In the resulting spreadsheet remove asterix (*) signs from the activity dates:

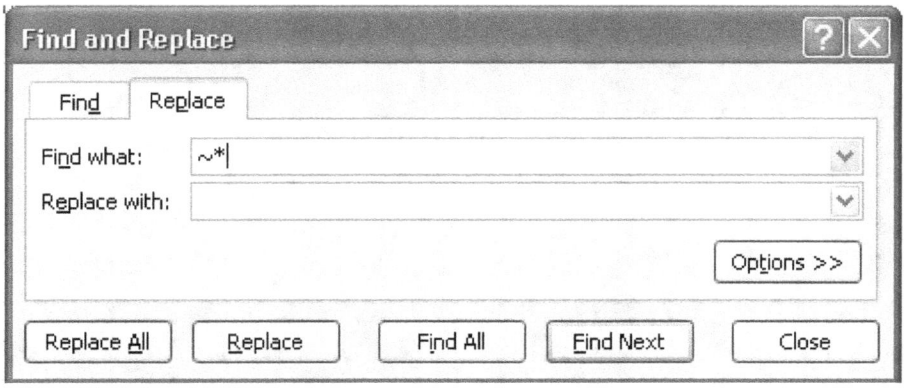

4. If you add 2 columns to your spreadsheet, you will be able to identify/filter in all the activities where activity dates do not match resource start finish dates:

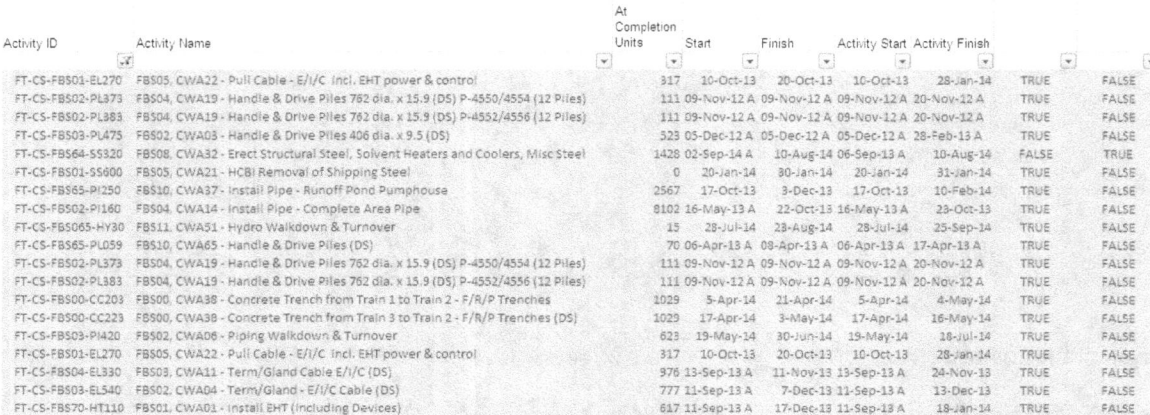

5. Now go back to your schedule and add Start and Finish columns in the activity detail, resources tab. Find activities listed above in your schedule and correct resource dates to match activity dates.

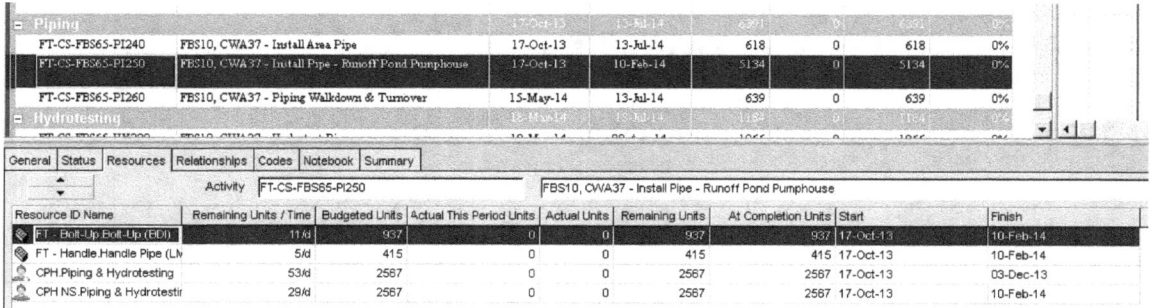

Unless, of course, resource availability has been restricted to these dates on purpose.

Andrei Sannikov
Tip of the day

24-May-15 14:25

Part 2

I am sure we all noticed that sometimes our resource profiles are not exactly aligned with our activity dates. If you display resource start and finish dates in the bottom view/resources tab you will see that in some cases your resource might finish before or after the finish date of your activity (start dates are usually the same - unless you manually changed them in the resources tab). See example below:

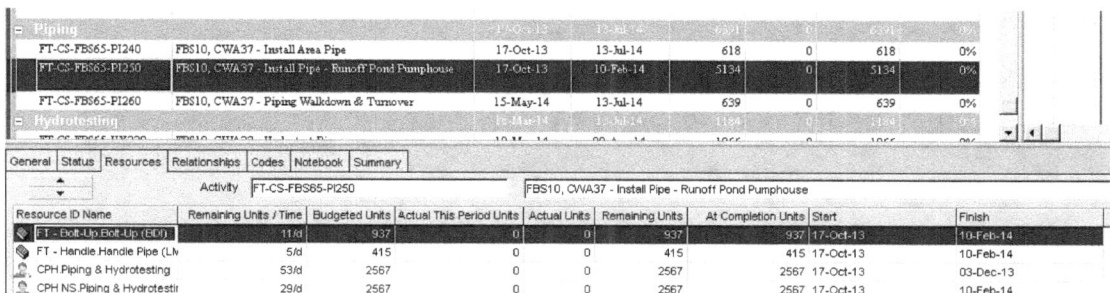

To understand the magnitude of the problem you can go to Resource Assignment view and create a layout with the columns shown below:

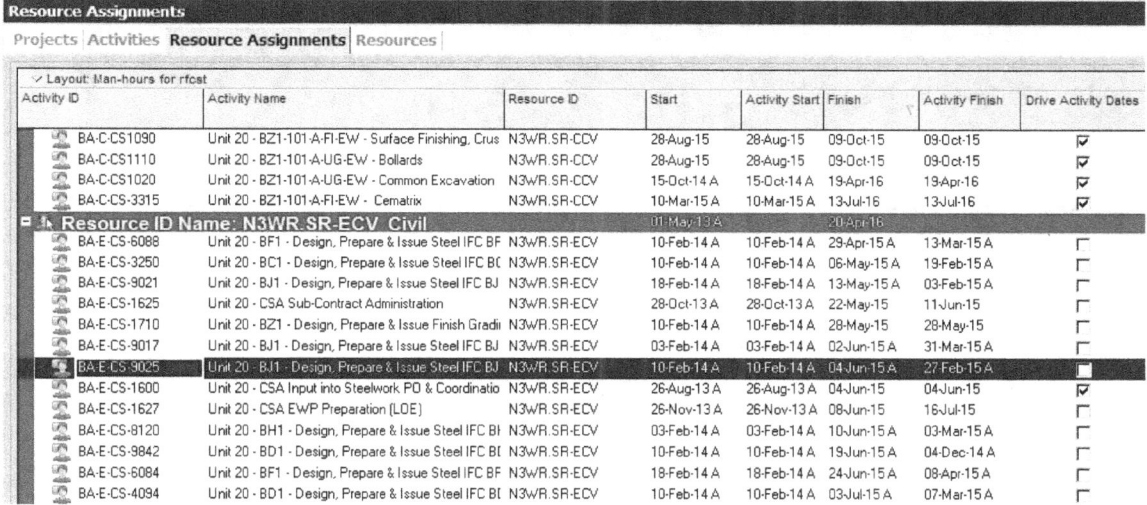

Copy/paste this spreadsheet into Excel and calculate the delta between Finish and Activity Finish columns. If you have a large network that has passed through many hands, chances are you will end up with a very long list of activities with different resource and activity finish dates, which would have a huge impact on resource histograms and planned progress curves.

If you look at the "Drive Activity Date" column in your spreadsheet you will notice that Not Started and In Progress activities that have different resource and activity finish dates will also have "No" in this column in most cases:

Andrei Sannikov
Tip of the day

| Activity ID | Activity Name | Finish | Activity Finish | Drive Activity Dates | Delta |
|---|---|---|---|---|---|
| BA-E-CS-1625 | Unit 20 - CSA Sub-Contract Administration | 22-May-15 | 11-Jun-15 | No | 20 |
| BA-E-CS-9772 | Unit 20 - BJ1 - Design, Prepare & Issue Stee | 14-Jul-15 | 30-Apr-15 | No | -75 |
| BA-E-CS-1900 | Unit 20 - BA1 - Design, Prepare & Issue Arch | 20-Jul-15 | 4-May-15 | No | -77 |
| BA-E-CS-1620 | Unit 20 - CSA Procurement Support | 1-Sep-15 | 11-Aug-15 | No | -21 |
| BA-E-CS-4210 | Unit 20 - BD1 - Design, Prepare & Issue Stee | 11-Jun-15 | 15-Jun-15 | No | 4 |
| BA-E-CS-9762 | Unit 20 - BH1 - Design, Prepare & Issue Stee | 20-Jul-15 | 30-Apr-15 | No | -81 |
| BA-E-CS-9792 | Unit 20 - BZ1 - Design, Prepare & Issue Stee | 30-Jul-15 | 15-Jun-15 | No | -45 |
| BA-E-CS-8126 | Unit 20 - BH1 - Design, Prepare & Issue Stee | 11-Aug-15 | 15-Jun-15 | No | -57 |
| BA-E-CS-9045 | Unit 20 - BJ1 - Design, Prepare & Issue Stee | 11-Aug-15 | 15-Jun-15 | No | -57 |
| BA-E-CS-9752 | Unit 20 - BZ1 - Design, Prepare & Issue Four | 25-Aug-15 | 28-Apr-15 | No | -119 |
| BA-E-PP-7730 | Unit 20 - BH1 - Generate, Yellow-off & Issue | 22-May-15 | 28-May-15 | No | 6 |
| BA-E-PP-6830 | Unit 20 - BD1 - Generate, Yellow-off & Issue | 22-May-15 | 28-May-15 | No | 6 |
| BA-E-PP-1228 | Unit 20 - Support to P&ID's Development/R | 15-Jun-15 | 30-Jul-15 | No | 45 |
| BA-E-PP-1370 | Unit 20 - Piping Material Control Isometrics | 3-Jul-15 | 28-May-15 | No | -36 |
| BA-E-PP-1350 | Unit 20 - Pipe Material Engineering Suppor | 11-Aug-15 | 17-Aug-15 | No | 6 |
| BA-E-PP-1228 | Unit 20 - Support to P&ID's Development/R | 15-Jun-15 | 30-Jul-15 | No | 45 |
| BA-E-PP-1370 | Unit 20 - Piping Material Control Isometrics | 3-Jul-15 | 28-May-15 | No | -36 |
| BA-E-EL-4800 | Unit 20 - BH1 - Prepare & Issue D.Vessels El | 13-Jul-15 | 14-May-15 | No | -60 |
| BA-E-EL-4810 | Unit 20 - BH1 - Prepare & Issue Module Elec | 20-Jul-15 | 22-May-15 | No | -59 |
| BA-E-EL-4515 | Unit 20 - BE1 - Prepare & Issue Module Elec | 20-Jul-15 | 5-Jun-15 | No | -45 |
| BA-E-EL-5030 | Unit 20 - Produce Wiring Diagrams to IFC / I | 23-Jul-15 | 15-Jul-15 | No | -8 |

Find these "misaligned" activities in your schedule, display the "Drive Activity Dates" column in the bottom view/resource tab, change the resource finish date or its remaining duration to align it with the activity dates, check the checkbox in the "Drive Activity Dates" column and you should not have this problem on the activities you have corrected in the future.

**Before**:

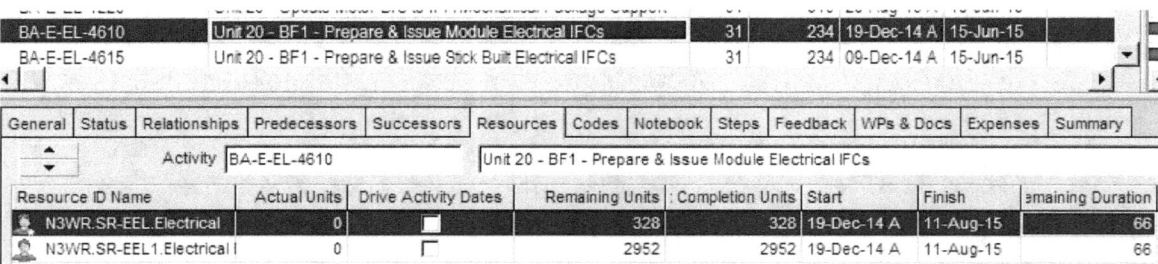

**After**:

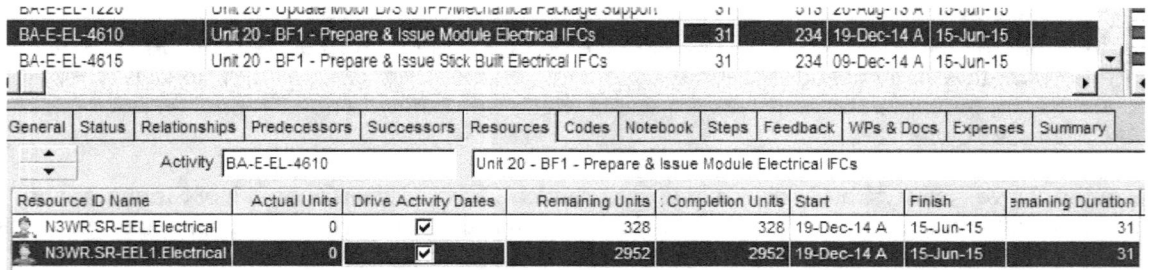

Even if we now change the remaining duration or finish date on the activity above the resource dates will move with it:

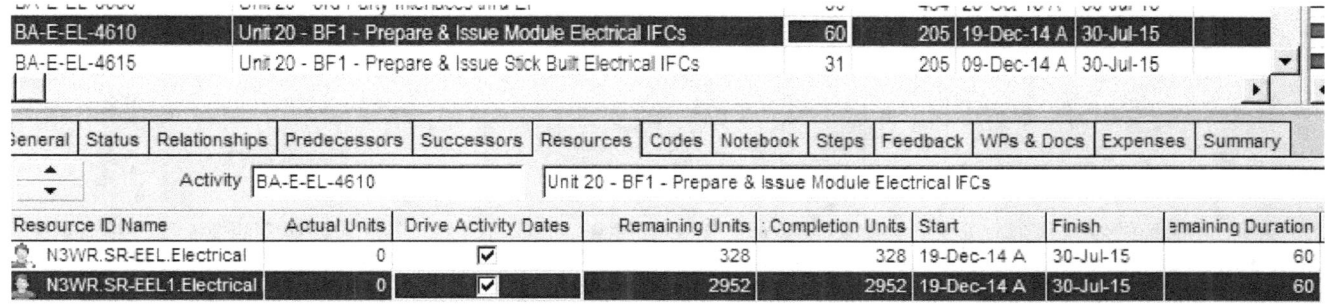

01-Nov-13 11:11

## How (and why) to change Global Calendars to Project

When we create a new project or add new activities to an existing project, we either use a default global calendar or pick up an existing calendar from the global calendar dictionary. Looks like normal routine and there is nothing wrong with this approach. Well, not quite...

There are two major problems associated with the use of Global calendars:

1. As opposed to projects Global calendars are accessible to all the users of a P6 database and although they cannot be deleted if they are used by another project they can be modified by anyone with appropriate access rights impacting your current and historical schedule data.

2. Default import setting in most systems is not to import calendars if a calendar with the same description already exists, which makes sense - otherwise your calendar dictionary would grow after each schedule import. However, if your contractor changes one or more of his calendars and you hit F9 after import your dates might be different from the dates on his computer and you will either need to re-import the schedule again with calendars - in which case these new calendars will be imported with a suffix - (and do it again after receiving each new update) or make corresponding changes to the calendars you already have in your system, which will impact your historical schedule data.

Solution? Use project calendars instead.

1. They are always attached to a project and regardless of the import settings your correspondent will upload them with your schedule.

2. To change them someone would need to open your project and chances of inadvertent modifications are close to none.

The only downside I can think of would be an extremely rare situation when you need to have a common calendar for several projects - you periodically modify this calendar and want these changes to be reflected in all the projects this calendar is used in.

If you agree with me and decide to switch from Global to Project calendars, here is what you need to do:

**New Project:**

Once you create your new project, setup your project calendars in > Enterprise > Calendars > Project , go to Project setting > Defaults for new activities and assign one of them as default for your project:

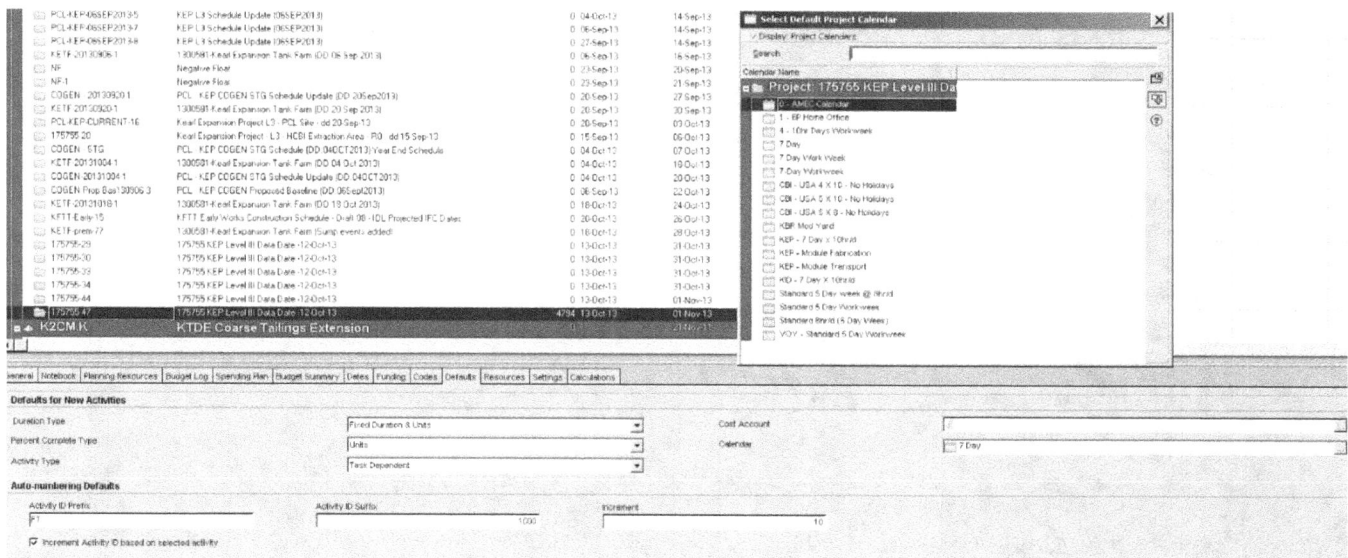

## Existing projects

There are several ways to convert Global calendars into Project Calendars in your existing project.

First, you need to need a list of calendars used in your project. The easiest way to create such a list is to Group and then summarize your schedule by calendar - View > Collapse to...

Then go to Enterprise > Calendars > Project. When you click on Add the system will display the list of available Global calendars, so you can choose a global calendar your new project calendar will based on. Add the calendars from the list you have prepared, I recommend using the same names + a prefix (like P- for Project).

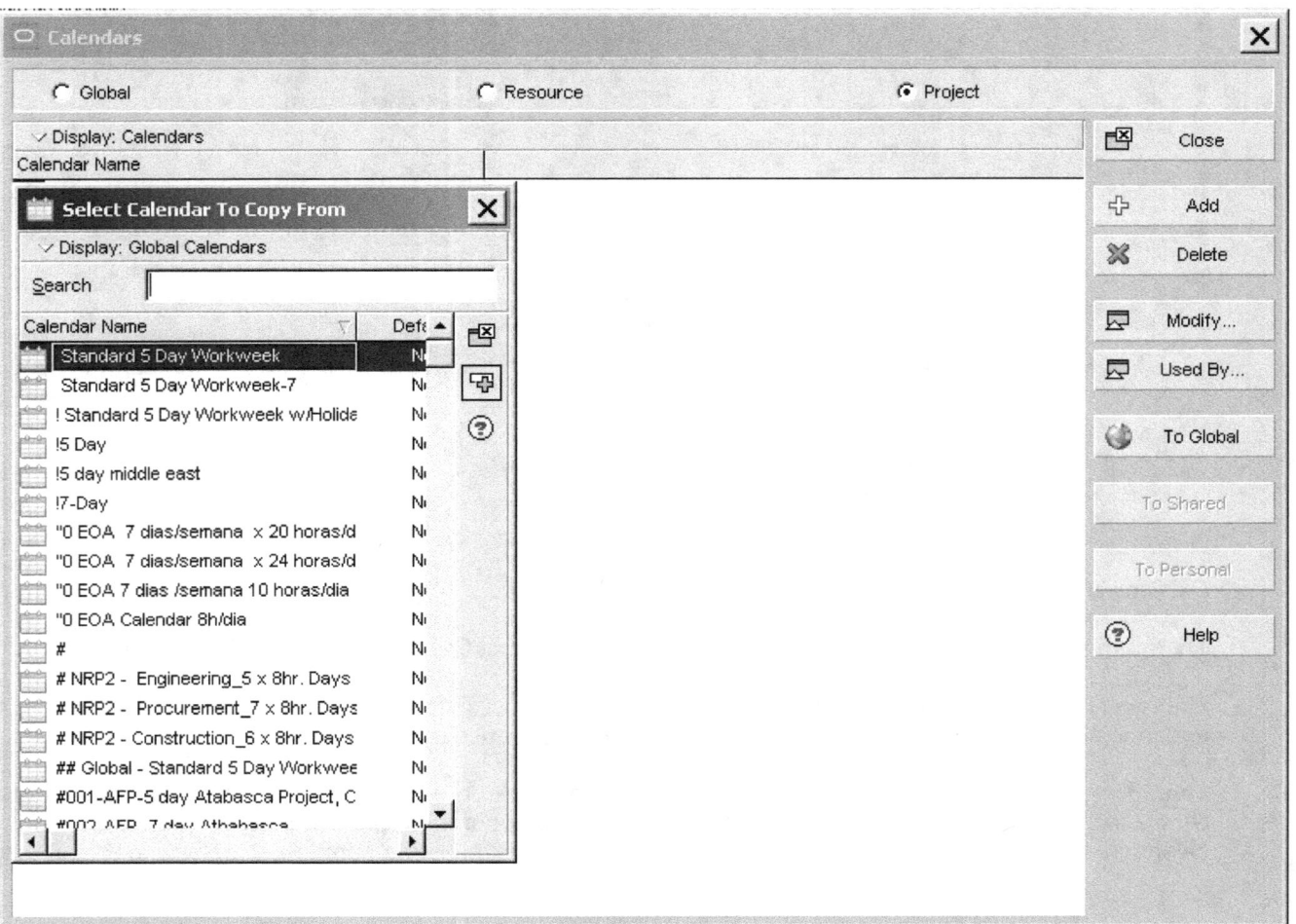

Once your list of project calendars is set up, we need to replace Global calendars our activities are assigned to with the Project calendars we have created.

1. Create/run a Global change for each calendar you want to replace:

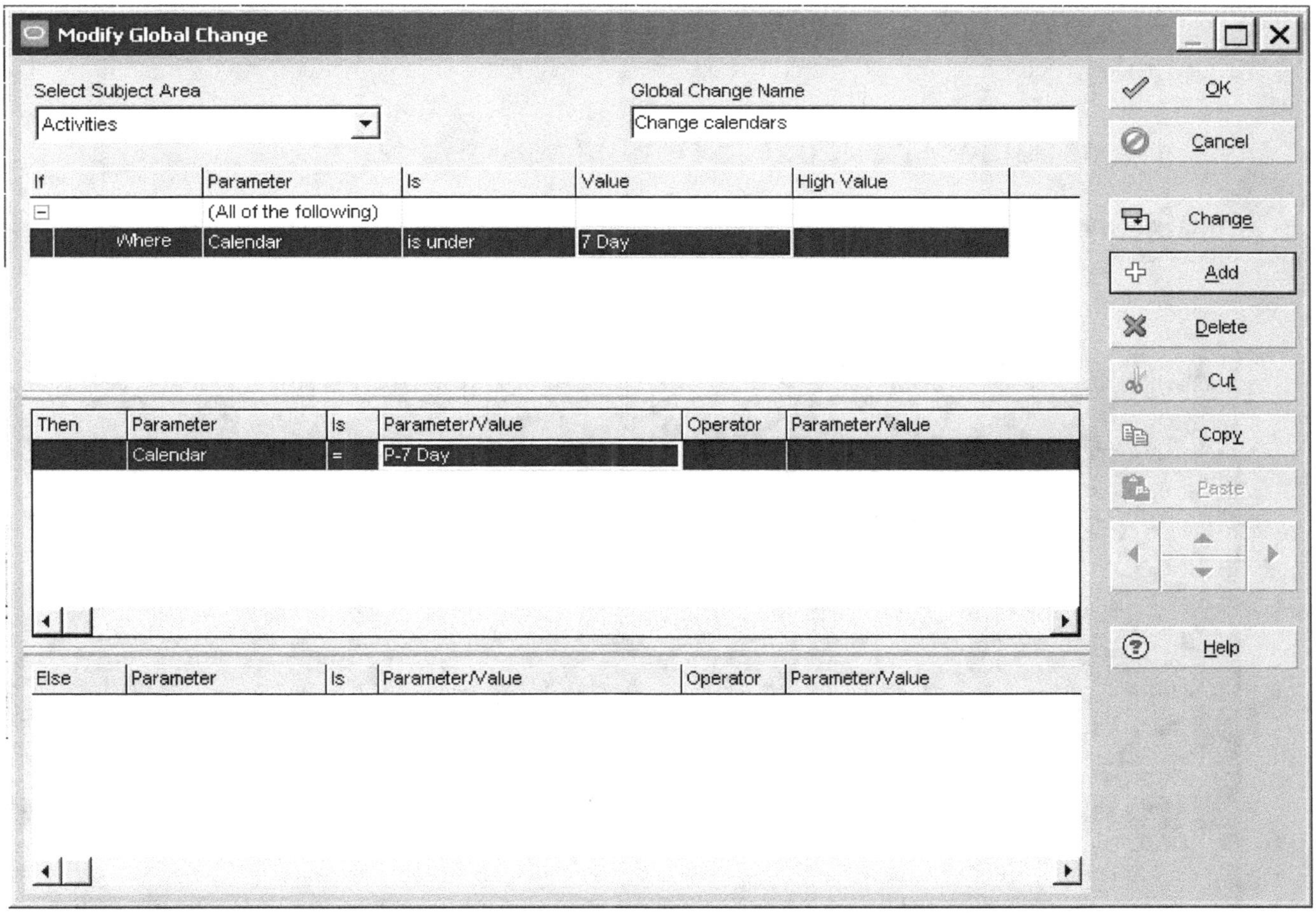

Or

2. Group your schedule by calendar, **disable** Auto-organization as shown below and use Fill Down function in the drop-down menu to replace each calendar:

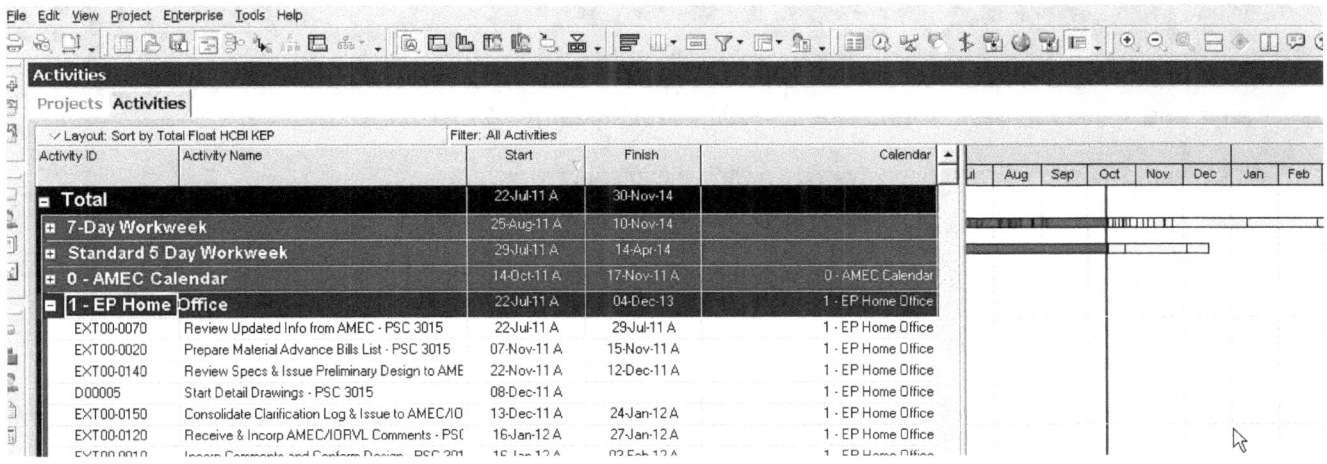

Andrei Sannikov
Tip of the day

02-Nov-13 08:01

## Why float values sometimes seem incorrect?

When we analyze the critical path and sort the schedule by Total Float, sometimes we see something like that on the screen:

| Activity ID | Activity Name | Total Float | Start | Finish | Calendar |
|---|---|---|---|---|---|
| 145d | | 145d | 24-Jan-14 | 27-Jan-14 | KEP - 7 Day x 10hr/d |
| 146d | | 146d | 11-May-14 | 07-Jul-14 | KEP - 7 Day x 10hr/d |
| 146d | | 146d | 09-Dec-13 | 09-Jan-14 | KEP - 7 Day x 10hr/d |
| 146d | | 146d | 07-Dec-13 | 20-Jan-14 | KEP - 7 Day x 10hr/d |
| 183d | | 183d | 20-Apr-14 | 02-May-14 | 7-Day Workweek |
| 147d | | 147d | 26-Jun-13 A | 05-Mar-14 | KEP - 7 Day x 10hr/d |
| 184d | | 184d | 21-Apr-14 | 30-May-14 | 7-Day Workweek |
| 148d | | 148d | 30-May-14 | 05-Jul-14 | KEP - 7 Day x 10hr/d |
| 148d | | 148d | 31-Jan-14 | 04-Mar-14 | KEP - 7 Day x 10hr/d |
| 186d | | 186d | 19-Jul-12 A | 18-Nov-13 | 7-Day Workweek |
| 150d | | 150d | 13-Oct-13 | 29-Jan-14 | |
| EXT01950 | Install HVAC & Dampers E-House #4 -BLD-1314 | 150d | 13-Oct-13 | 06-Nov-13 | KEP - 7 Day x 10hr/d |
| CM150-0320 | EXT-Nuclear Level Profilers-Vndr Final Document | 187d | 05-Nov-13 | 17-Nov-13 | 7-Day Workweek |
| EXT02190 | Install HVAC Ducting E-House #4 -BLD-1314 | 150d | 07-Nov-13 | 01-Dec-13 | KEP - 7 Day x 10hr/d |
| EXTC04710 | Install Field run Cable Tray & off Tray Supports (P | 150d | 20-Nov-13 | 09-Jan-14 | KEP - 7 Day x 10hr/d |
| EXTC04720 | Pull Power Cable (PSC) | 150d | 10-Jan-14 | 29-Jan-14 | KEP - 7 Day x 10hr/d |
| 150d | | 150d | 03-Dec-13 | 18-Jan-14 | KEP - 7 Day x 10hr/d |
| 151d | | 151d | 12-Nov-13 | 22-Nov-13 | KEP - 7 Day x 10hr/d |
| 152d | | 152d | 02-Jun-14 | 01-Jul-14 | KEP - 7 Day x 10hr/d |
| 190d | | 190d | 15-Nov-13 | 15-Nov-13 | 7-Day Workweek |
| 152d | | 152d | 29-May-13 A | 28-Nov-13 | KEP - 7 Day x 10hr/d |
| 153d | | 153d | 30-May-14 | 24-Jun-14 | KEP - 7 Day x 10hr/d |

...and wonder - what is wrong with this picture? The layout is sorted by Total Float and yet 183 days is above 147 days and in the 150 days slot we see an activity with 187 days of float?

It all makes a little more sense when we switch this display to hours:

Andrei Sannikov
Tip of the day

| Activity ID | Activity Name | Total Float | Start | Finish | Calendar |
|---|---|---|---|---|---|
| ⊞ 1447h | | 1447h | 24-Jan-14 | 27-Jan-14 | KEP - 7 Day x 10hr/d |
| ⊞ 1457h | | 1457h | 11-May-14 | 07-Jul-14 | KEP - 7 Day x 10hr/d |
| ⊞ 1459h | | 1459h | 09-Dec-13 | 09-Jan-14 | KEP - 7 Day x 10hr/d |
| ⊞ 1465h | | 1465h | 07-Dec-13 | 20-Jan-14 | KEP - 7 Day x 10hr/d |
| ⊞ 1466h | | 1466h | 20-Apr-14 | 02-May-14 | 7-Day Workweek |
| ⊞ 1467h | | 1467h | 26-Jun-13 A | 05-Mar-14 | KEP - 7 Day x 10hr/d |
| ⊞ 1474h | | 1474h | 21-Apr-14 | 30-May-14 | 7-Day Workweek |
| ⊞ 1480h | | 1480h | 30-May-14 | 05-Jul-14 | KEP - 7 Day x 10hr/d |
| ⊞ 1481h | | 1481h | 31-Jan-14 | 04-Mar-14 | KEP - 7 Day x 10hr/d |
| ⊞ 1491h | | 1491h | 19-Jul-12 A | 18-Nov-13 | 7-Day Workweek |
| ⊟ 1497h | | 1497h | 13-Oct-13 | 29-Jan-14 | |
| EXT01950 | Install HVAC & Dampers E-House #4 -BLD-1314 | 1497h | 13-Oct-13 | 06-Nov-13 | KEP - 7 Day x 10hr/d |
| CM150-0320 | EXT-Nuclear Level Profilers-Vndr Final Document | 1497h | 05-Nov-13 | 17-Nov-13 | 7-Day Workweek |
| EXT02190 | Install HVAC Ducting E-House #4 -BLD-1314 | 1497h | 07-Nov-13 | 01-Dec-13 | KEP - 7 Day x 10hr/d |
| EXTC04710 | Install Field run Cable Tray & off Tray Supports (P | 1497h | 20-Nov-13 | 09-Jan-14 | KEP - 7 Day x 10hr/d |
| EXTC04720 | Pull Power Cable (PSC) | 1497h | 10-Jan-14 | 29-Jan-14 | KEP - 7 Day x 10hr/d |
| ⊞ 1499h | | 1499h | 03-Dec-13 | 18-Jan-14 | KEP - 7 Day x 10hr/d |
| ⊞ 1508h | | 1508h | 12-Nov-13 | 22-Nov-13 | KEP - 7 Day x 10hr/d |
| ⊞ 1517h | | 1517h | 02-Jun-14 | 01-Jul-14 | KEP - 7 Day x 10hr/d |
| ⊞ 1521h | | 1521h | 15-Nov-13 | 15-Nov-13 | 7-Day Workweek |
| ⊞ 1523h | | 1523h | 29-May-13 A | 28-Nov-13 | KEP - 7 Day x 10hr/d |
| ⊞ 1529h | | 1529h | 30-May-14 | 24-Jun-14 | KEP - 7 Day x 10hr/d |

By default P6 calculates total float as the difference between early and late finish dates - activity CM150-0320 is on 8-hours calendar (w/o Xmas break) and its float is 187 days, which is the difference between early and late finish dates - 17-Nov-13 and 23-May-14 respectively, this difference is converted into hours based on the calendar this activity is assigned to.

The rest of the activities are on 10-hours calendar with 19 days Xmas break - the difference between early and late finish dates is 169 days less Xmas break = 150 days.

| Activity ID | Activity Name | Total Float | Start | Finish | Late Finish | Calendar |
|---|---|---|---|---|---|---|
| ⊟ 150d | | 150d | 13-Oct-13 | 29-Jan-14 | 28-Jun-14 | |
| EXT01950 | Install HVAC & Dampers E-House #4 -BLD-1314 | 150d | 13-Oct-13 | 06-Nov-13 | 24-Apr-14 | KEP - 7 Day x 10hr/d |
| CM150-0320 | EXT-Nuclear Level Profilers-Vndr Final Document | 187d | 05-Nov-13 | 17-Nov-13 | 23-May-14 | 7-Day Workweek |
| EXT02190 | Install HVAC Ducting E-House #4 -BLD-1314 | 150d | 07-Nov-13 | 01-Dec-13 | 19-May-14 | KEP - 7 Day x 10hr/d |
| EXTC04710 | Install Field run Cable Tray & off Tray Supports (P | 150d | 20-Nov-13 | 09-Jan-14 | 08-Jun-14 | KEP - 7 Day x 10hr/d |
| EXTC04720 | Pull Power Cable (PSC) | 150d | 10-Jan-14 | 29-Jan-14 | 28-Jun-14 | KEP - 7 Day x 10hr/d |

Since the hours are the primary unit of time in P6 sorting and grouping is based on them.

Note that you will have this sorting peculiarity only when you have a combination of different calendars with different workday durations in your schedule. If you do, it might be a good idea to display them in a column so you know where to expect sorting and grouping discrepancies and what is causing them.

Andrei Sannikov
Tip of the day

19-Nov-13 16:04

## Incorrect float calculation on paths with FF relationships

As you probably noticed, P6 calculates late start and late finish dates even on completed and started activities. Calculating late dates on completed activities is probably just a waste of computing power, however, when this is done on activities in progress you might expect a few surprises.

Say, you have a string of activities on the critical path with two or more activities linked with a start-to-start relationship

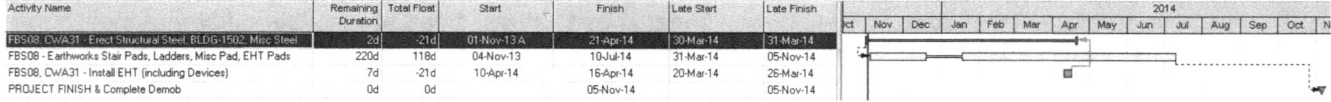

Structural steel activity above is linked to Earthwork with SS relationship and a lag of 3 days; its predecessor is EHT with FF relationship and a lag of 4 days. Project Finish MS is the last milestone in the network and has no successors, Project Must Finish by field is left blank.
Obviously, Project Finish MS has other driving predecessors which I am not showing here for simplicity.

So far so good.

Now, let us assume we did some structural steel work ahead of plan and our structural steel activity will have an actual start. Technically speaking this is not work out of sequence because the schedule logic still determines its finish date (FF to EHT).

Since we started Structural Steel several months earlier than planned this would allow Earthwork to start much earlier as well because of the SS relationship and one would expect some significant improvement in the schedule criticality on this path but remember - I promised you a surprise:

Earthworks gained 118 days of float, structural steel that is not driving anything and EHT (driving its completion date) now have 21 days of negative float. What sense does it make?!

Ladies and gentlemen, welcome to P6.

Here is how it works:

Earlier start of earthworks resulted in some improvement of the project finish date, which now moved from Nov 28 to Nov 5, since the project does not have a must finish by date the total float on this MS will be set to 0 as this is the last activity in the network. On this basis P6 recalculates the late start for the earthworks and it is now 23 days earlier than before - because the project finish date moved by 23 days as well. This is perfectly fine and good old P3 would have done the same thing, what is weird is the calculation of the late start date on structural steel - since earthwork needs to start no later than Mar 31 (in order not to impact the project finish date) the late start date on structural steel is set on Mar 30 (should be in fact Mar 28 because of the 3 days lag we have on this SS relationship but what is 2 days between friends?). Late finish date on structural steel is calculated as late start +

activity duration and is now equal to Mar 31. Since Mar 31 is 21 days earlier than the early finish date (Apr 21) P6 calculates 21 days of negative float on this path.

There is really nothing much we can do about it. Oracle is notoriously slow in fixing bugs like this one - they keep adding more bells and whistles to new versions of P6 but real problems like float calculation seem to be very low in their priority list.

The only fix I can suggest is splitting this structural steel activity into two - one will be completed and the other planned in the future. Be aware that this would affect comparison to your baseline(s) and mapping to your progress database if you update progress via Excel export/import. Other changes like assigning a later Project must finish by date would be purely cosmetic - they would allow you to get rid of negative float but its calculation on this path will still be incorrect.

**A follow up note:**

This issue has been addressed in the latest versions of P6 and you will need to consider it only if you still have versions 8.2 or earlier on your machine.

## How to find driving "out-of-sequence" predecessors using the trace logic function

A few days ago, I sent out a tip about predecessors that might be driving your future or current activities through other completed predecessors in retained logic mode. A list of such predecessors might be still useful in cases when you have a limited number of "out-of-sequence" predecessors or when you do a general cleanup of your schedule logic to make sure it reflects the latest changes in the work execution on your project. However, if you just need to identify the driver or drivers pushing start or finish dates on an activity there is a much simpler and faster way to do it:

Highlight the activity driven by some unknown predecessor(s), then go to View > Show on bottom > Trace logic

For better visibility you can maximize the bottom section. The activity you are analyzing will appear with a blue frame around it:

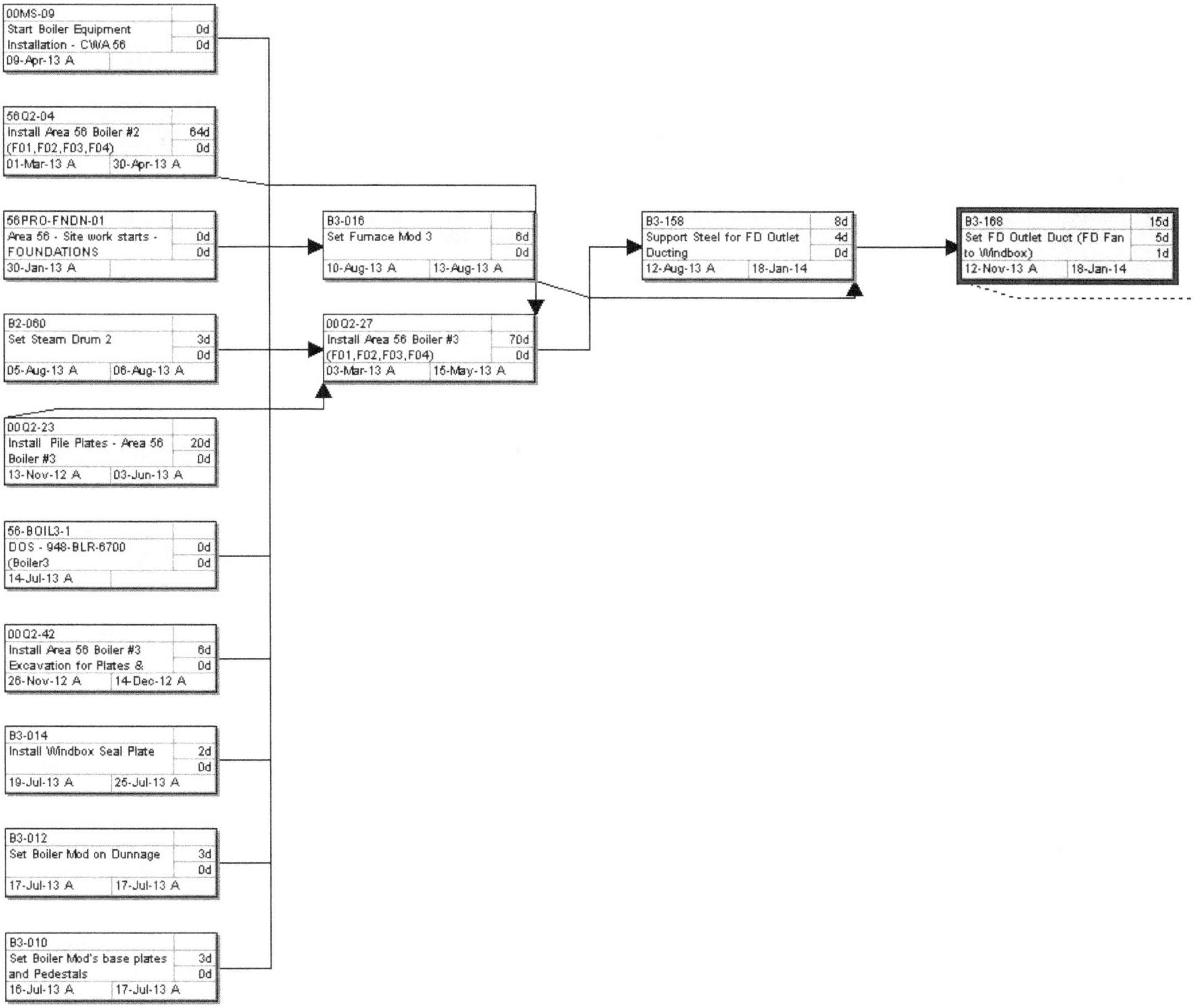

The driver should appear as an activity box surrounded by a red frame, If you don't see anything like that on your screen, right-click on this trace logic layout and go to Trace logic options in the displayed context menu:

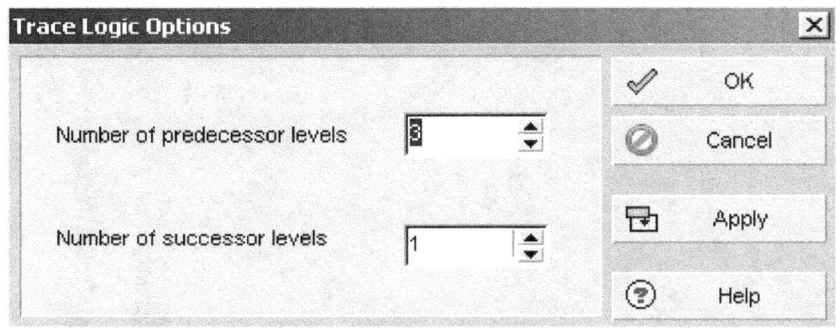

Continue increasing the number of predecessor levels until the driving activity appears on your screen:

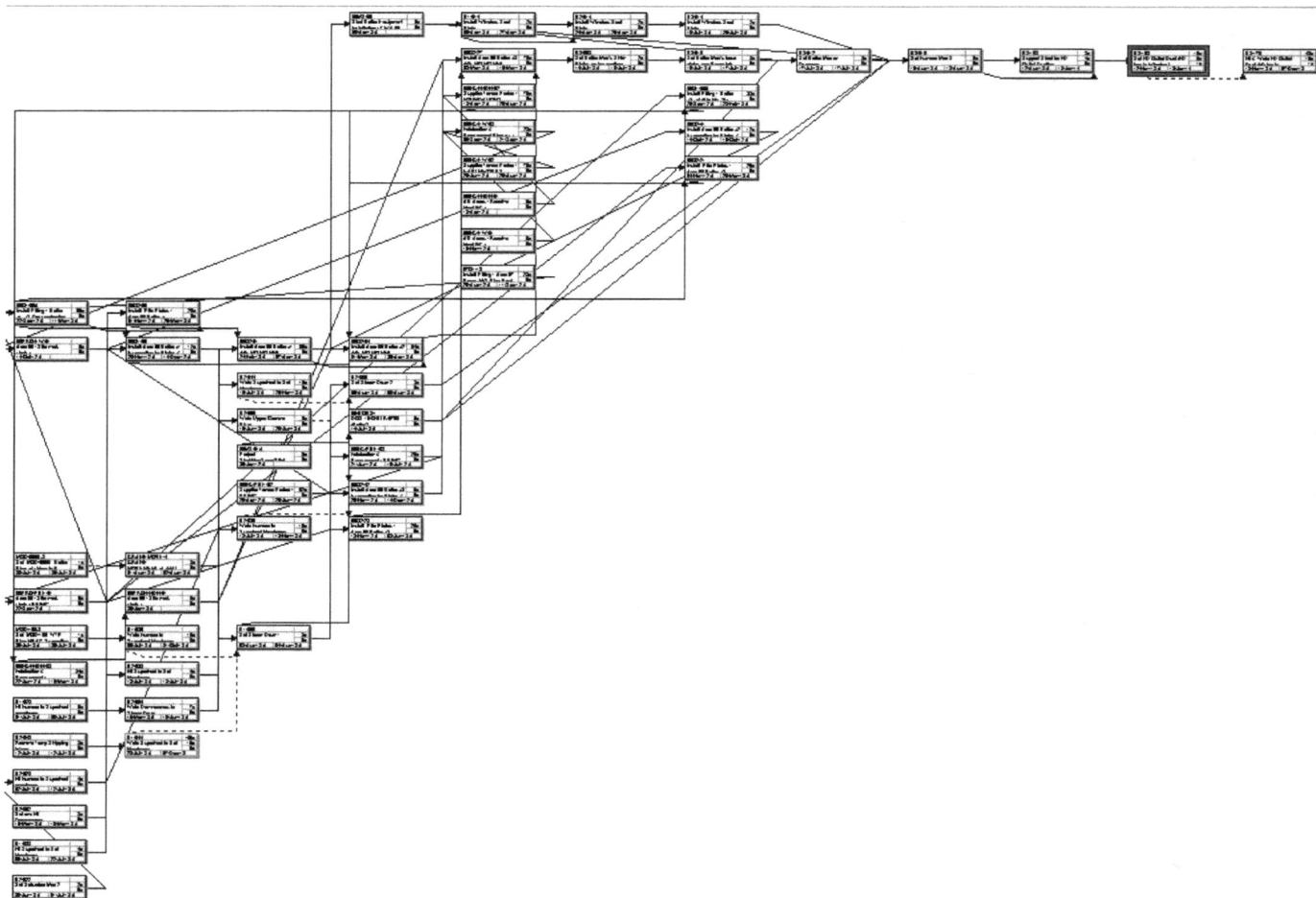

If you have multiple levels of predecessors, dates and other details will be hardly visible on the screen but when you click on the activity with the red frame around it (which is the driver) you can then open it in the bar chart (Gantt chart) layout and adjust the dates or logic as required.

20-Feb-14 11:12

# How to filter in out-of-sequence activities

Imagine you have a very large network (that you might have inherited from someone) and you decide to clean up the logic and find all the activities that might be driven through predecessors completed out of sequence, if you ever tried to do it you will agree that it is like looking for the proverbial needle in a haystack. Here is what you can do to simplify this task:

1. Make a copy of the schedule you intend to clean up.

2. In the **copy** hit F9, go to Options and choose Progress override

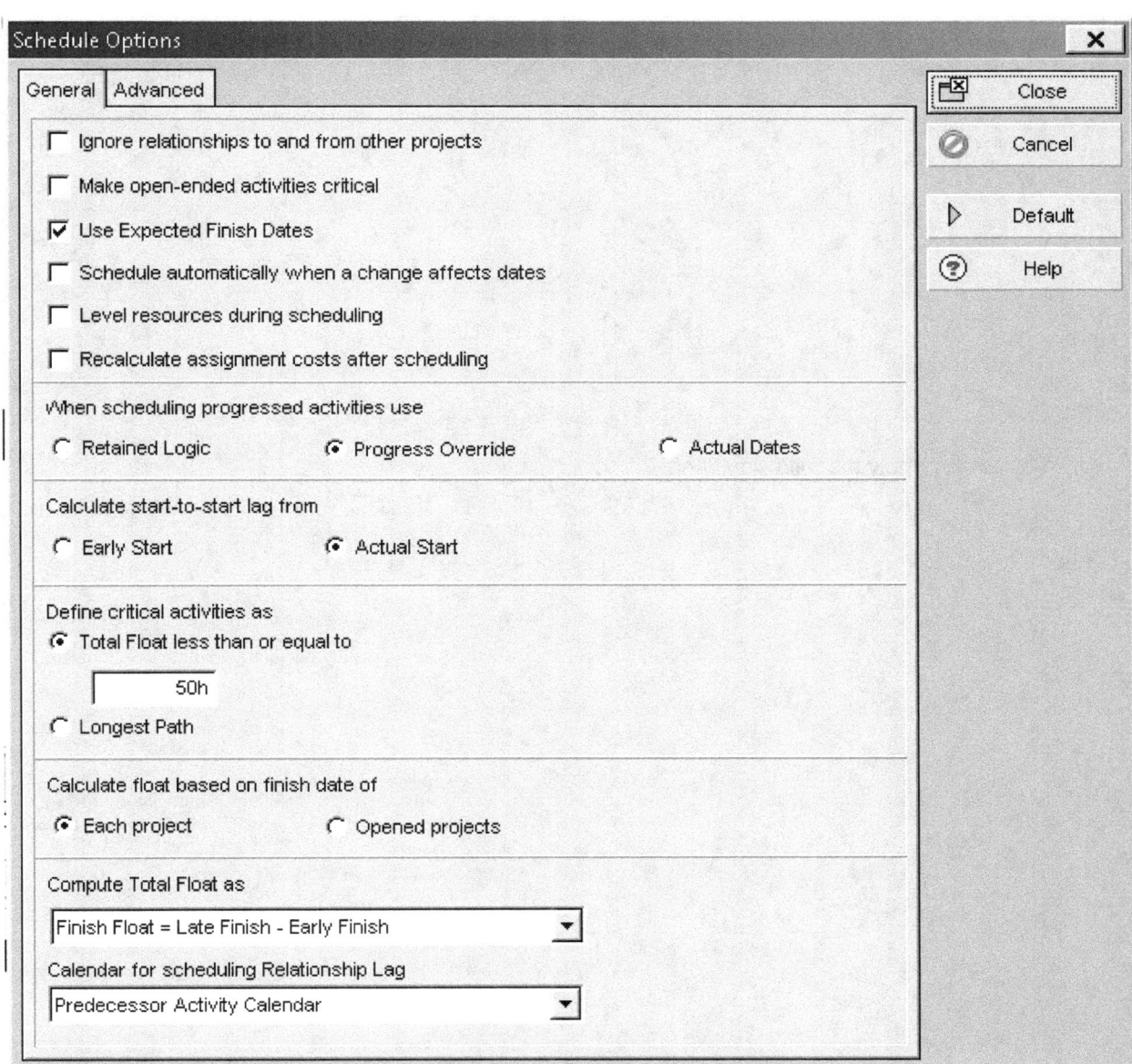

3. Schedule this copy of your project and close it.//
4. Open your original schedule and assign the copy you have just scheduled as the Project Baseline.
5. Display the following columns:

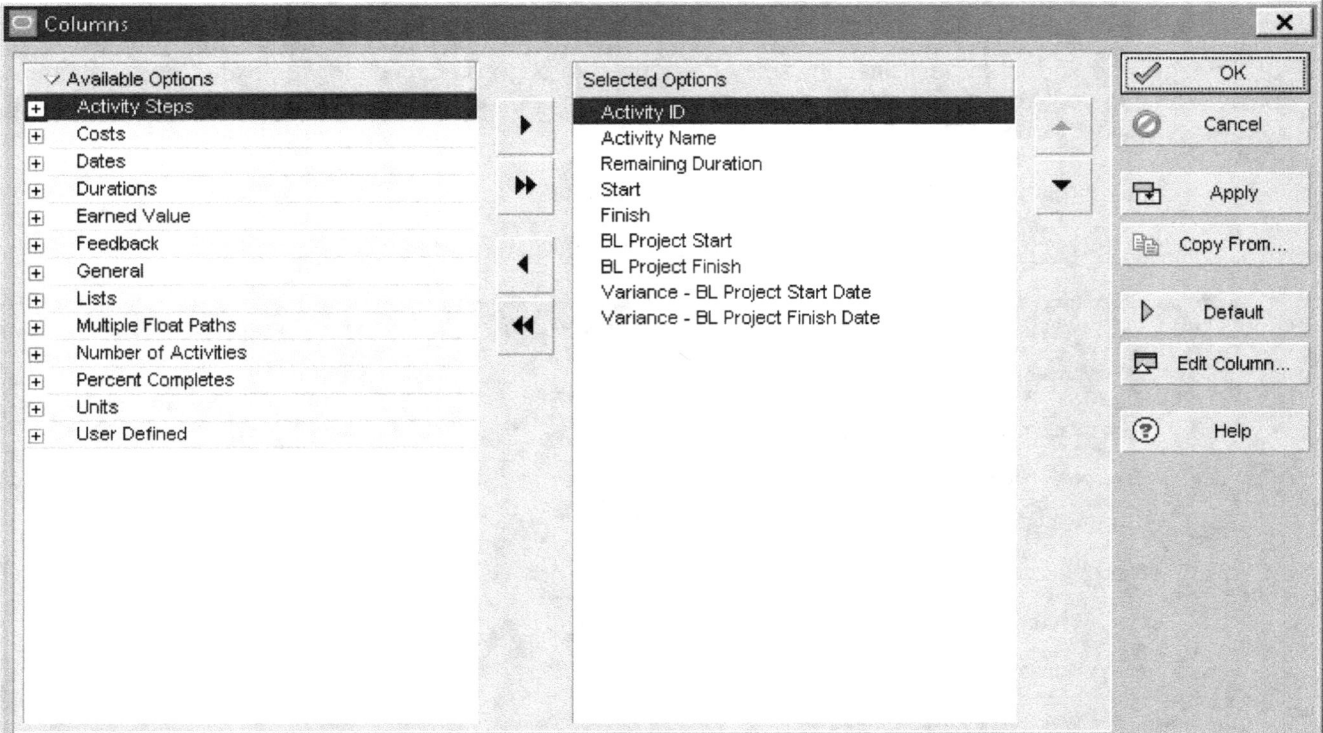

6. Set up and apply the following filter:

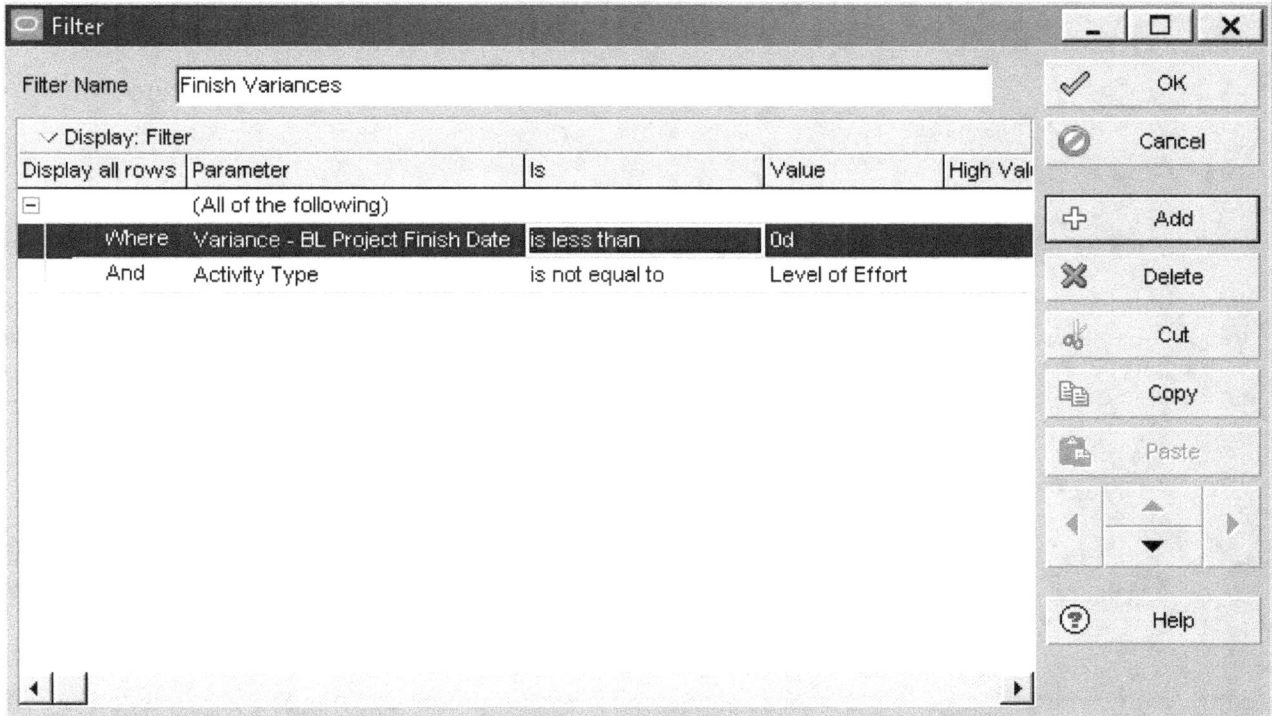

The resulting layout will include activities with finish dates driven through predecessors completed out of sequence.

Setup a similar filter for start variances and repeat this procedure.

Refer to another tip in this book called "How to find all out-of-sequence relationships in a large network" to identify out of sequence activities and adjust their logic and dates.

Andrei Sannikov
Tip of the day

08-Jun-14 12:04

## How to change man-power loading on a portion of activity duration

When we work with task dependent activities sometimes, we need to increase or decrease our manpower loading during an activity duration to show that, say, you have 10 ironworkers for the first week and then 5 of them move to a different task. There might be another situation where you want to show that one resource will work for the first couple of days and then a different resource will show up.

1. In project view go to the Resources tab and make sure the box "Resources can be assigned to the same activity more than once" is checked

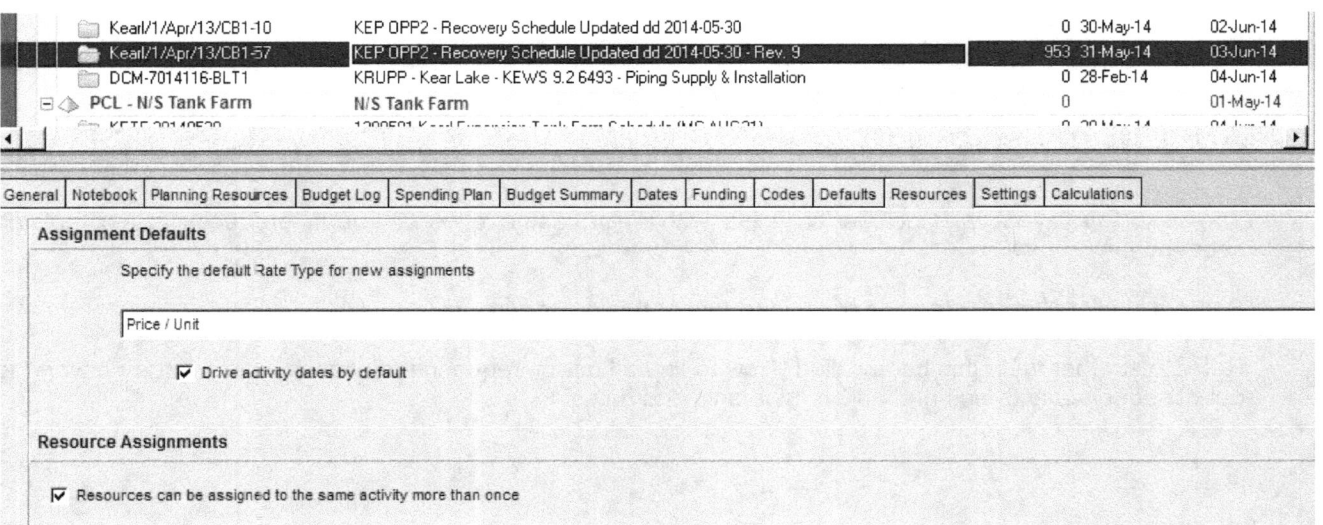

2. Go to the activity on which you want to "split" resources and right-click in the bottom view under the Resources tab to add Remaining duration, Start and Finish columns

3. Say you have a 45 days HVAC activity, which you want to start with 4 HVAC technicians who will work for 30 days and 2 technicians will finish it. Add your HVAC labor resource twice and adjust start/finish dates and/or durations as follows:

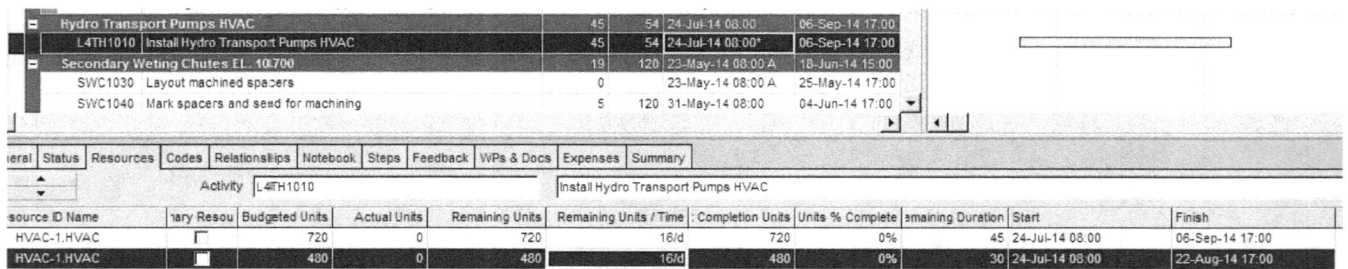

When you go to the resource assignment view, you will see the following labor hours distribution for this task based on 8-hours calendar:

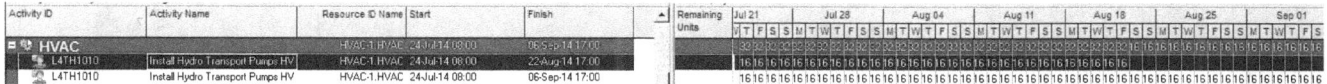

Note that when you change your activity duration or start date, dates on your resources will be also adjusted, make sure you check start and finish dates on such "split" resources when you do your updates to avoid surprises.

09-Jul-14 07:30

## How to merge multiple projects and how to maintain inter-project links after export/import

When we work on EPC projects with multiple contractors, we often need to merge their schedules into one integrated project with numerous links between contractor projects, which can be very time-consuming if we must reinstate these links each time when we get their schedule updates. Let us see if we can simplify/automate this process to some extent:

1. After receiving all the updates from different contractors import them into P6 as separate projects and open the ones you want to link.

2. Set up a separate project with interface milestones only (so-called Bridge File), each of which will have a predecessor and a successor in 2 different projects you intend to link - in this case your interfaces will be visible to everyone and not buried somewhere in P6 logic.

3. Export each project and the Bridge file and send it back to your contractors for updating. When they display activity relationships in their files, they will be able to see their external interfaces as successors or predecessors to their activities.

Say, a week later you receive updates from all your contractors and since these updates obviously would not have any links to the other schedules in your integrated file one might think that you would have to reinstate all these links. Here is what you can do to avoid going through this painful process again:

1. After all the inter-project links have been established in Step 2 above (i.e. prior to merging them), make a copy of all the linked sub-projects by exporting all of them into one xer file or copying them into a separate node.

2. Now we want to import each contractor update and preserve the links to the rest of your sub-projects.

3. Say, you have an update/xer file from contractor X. Open its project in your database, then go to Import > Update Existing Project

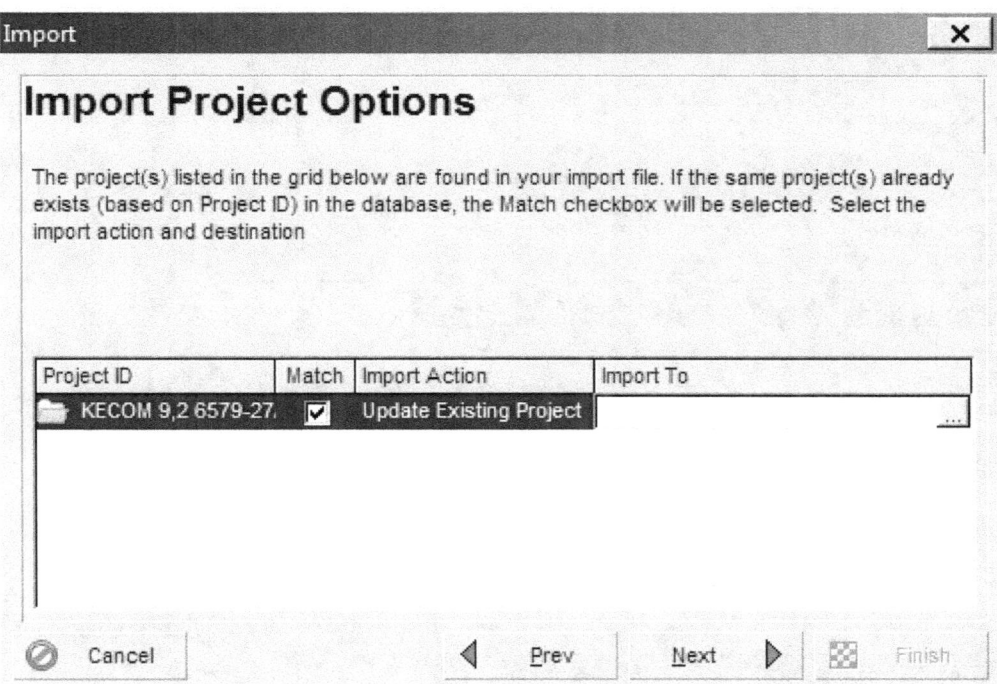

4. Import to the project we have opened:

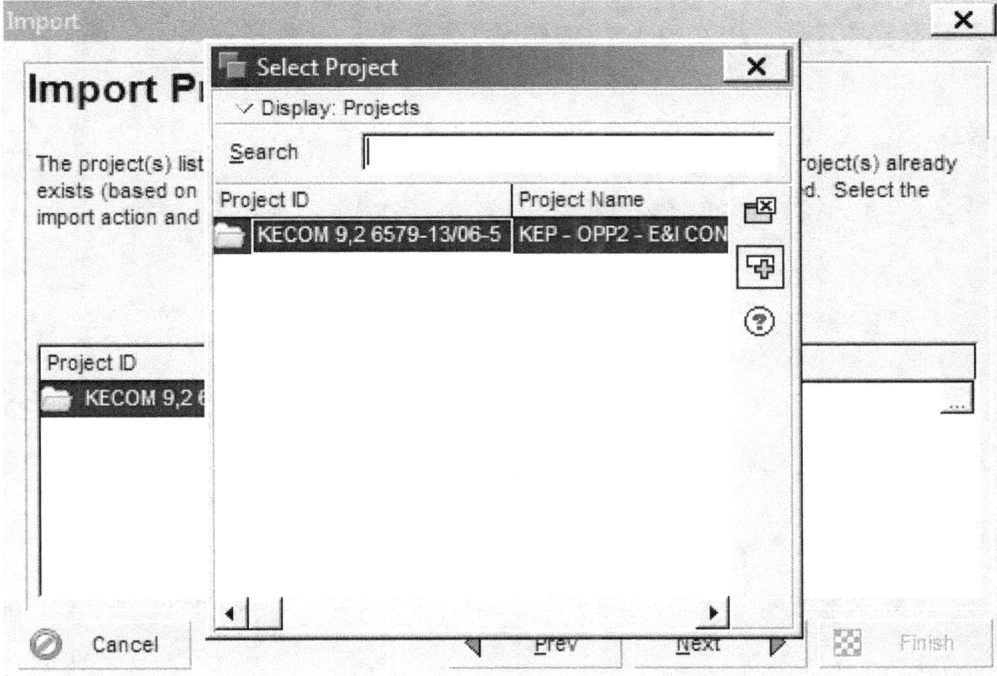

5. In the import template dialogue choose a project update template or create a new one with the following options:

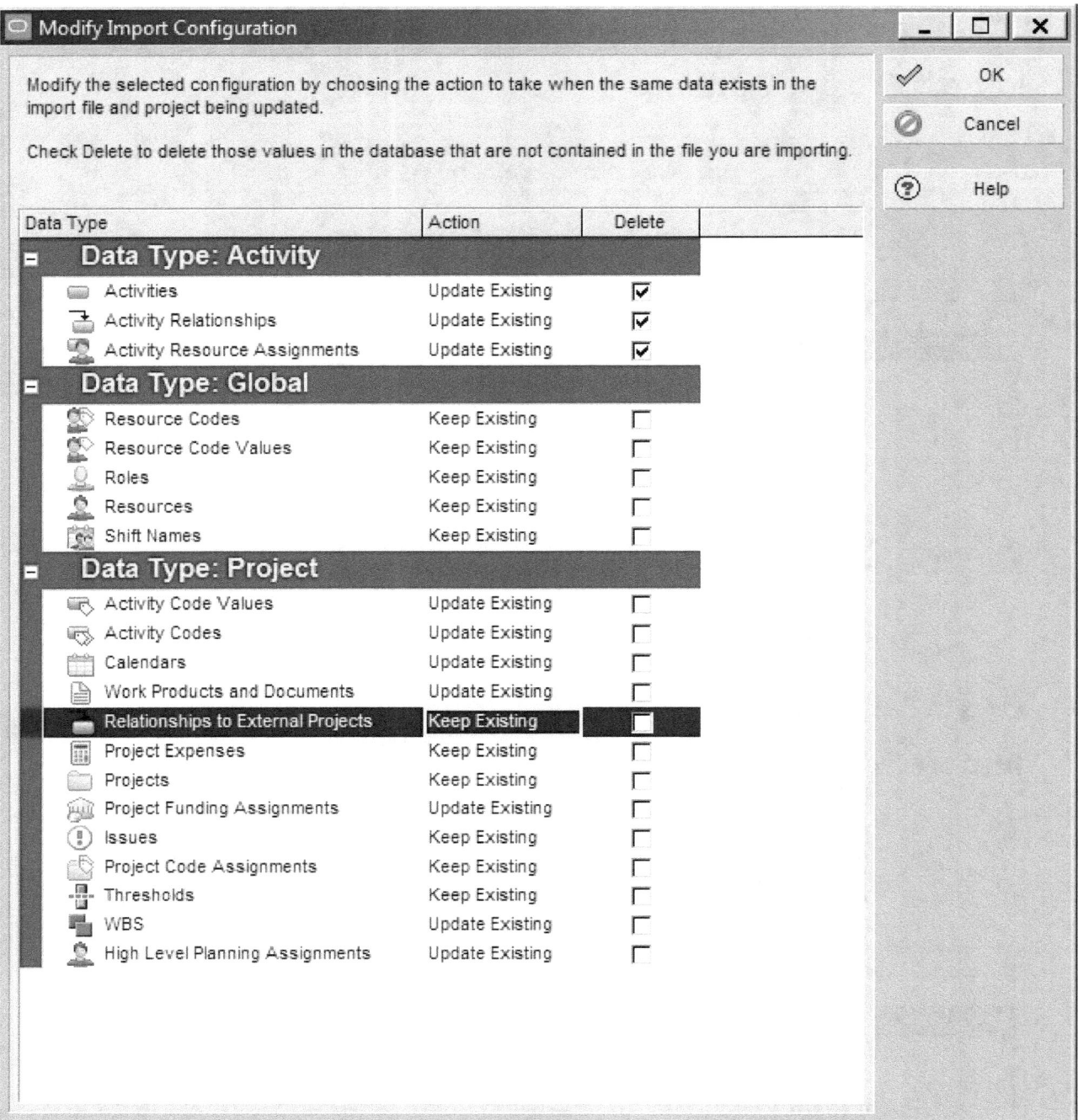

6. Repeat this process for each contractor's schedule, open all the schedules together, press F9 and reschedule them. Now you should have an update of your integrated schedule with all inter-project links preserved.

Note: If you prefer to merge all the sub-projects into one file, follow the steps below:

- Make sure all activity codes and calendars are global.

- Create a new "empty shell" project, set its start date before the earliest data date of your sub-projects, open this empty shell project and the sub-projects at the same time and go to WBS view

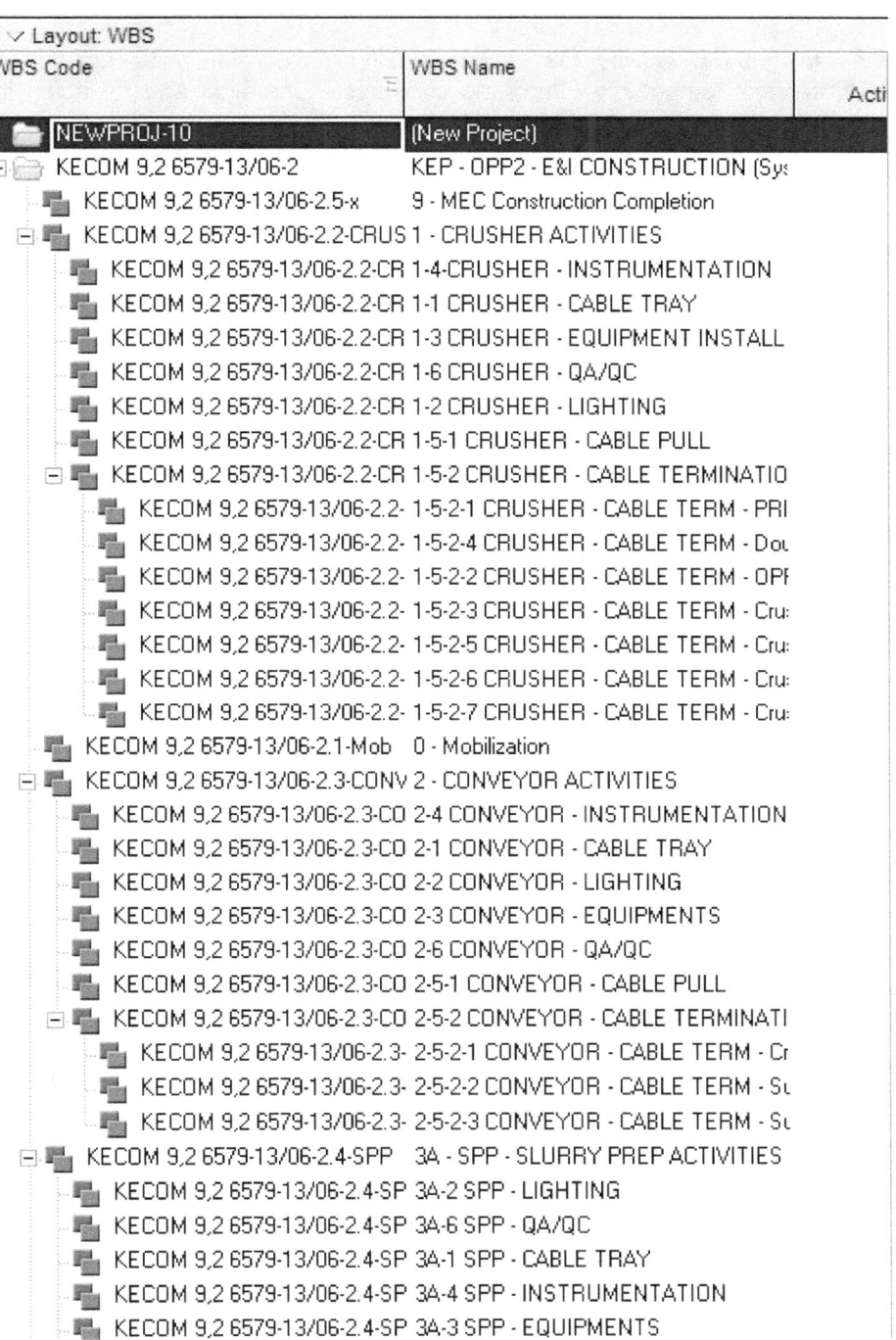

- Highlight all the sub-projects with the mouse and the shift key, then copy - paste them into the new empty shell project we have just created.

Notes:

- The copy – paste function will initiate an activity ID renumbering dialogue, where you will be prompted to renumber all activities that are being copied by either changing the prefix or using an incremental value.

- If you need to preserve the original activity ID's, consider using the cut and paste function instead or changing the activity ID's prefix temporarily during the copy-paste operation and replacing it with the original one afterwards with the Activity ID renumbering tool.

    o P6 will not let you use the cut and paste function for an entire project; however, you can select all WBS levels under the Project name and cut and paste them into a new project.

    o To make sure all WBS levels are properly displayed under the Project name, click on the WBS Code heading until the WBS Tree view appears on the screen:

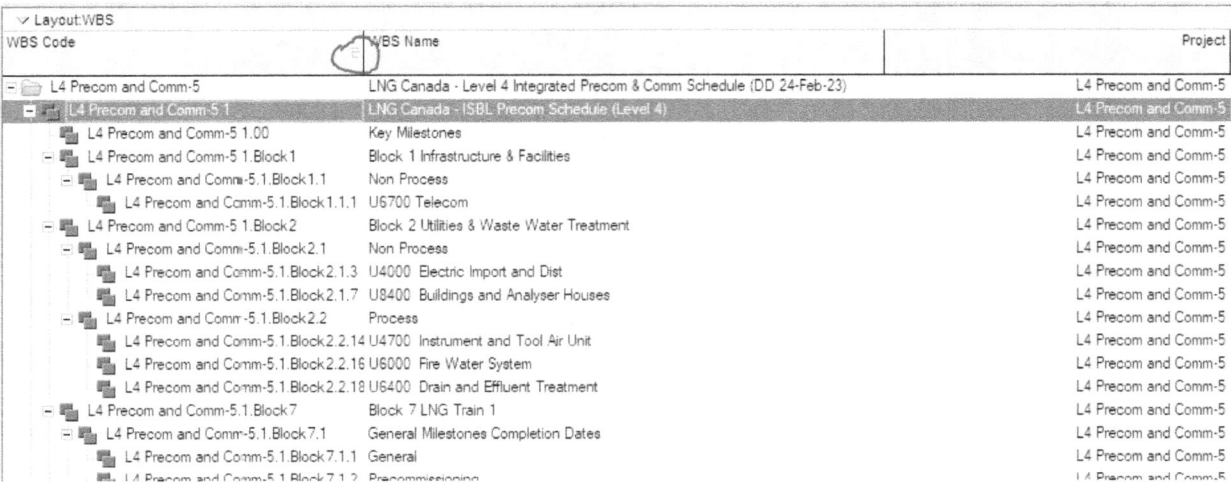

- Projects merging and splitting actions often overwrite project WBS codes. If you intend to preserve the original WBS structures, export all activities with their original WBS codes for future import.

    o Make sure you delete Activity Status column prior to importing to avoid changes in schedule dates, especially when you decide to reinstate your original WBS structure sometime after you split or merged your projects.

- If you don't use detailed WBS in your projects and they are entirely based on activity codes, you can merge multiple projects using a simplified method:

1. Open all projects you intend to merge, go to Group and Sort by and apply the following settings:

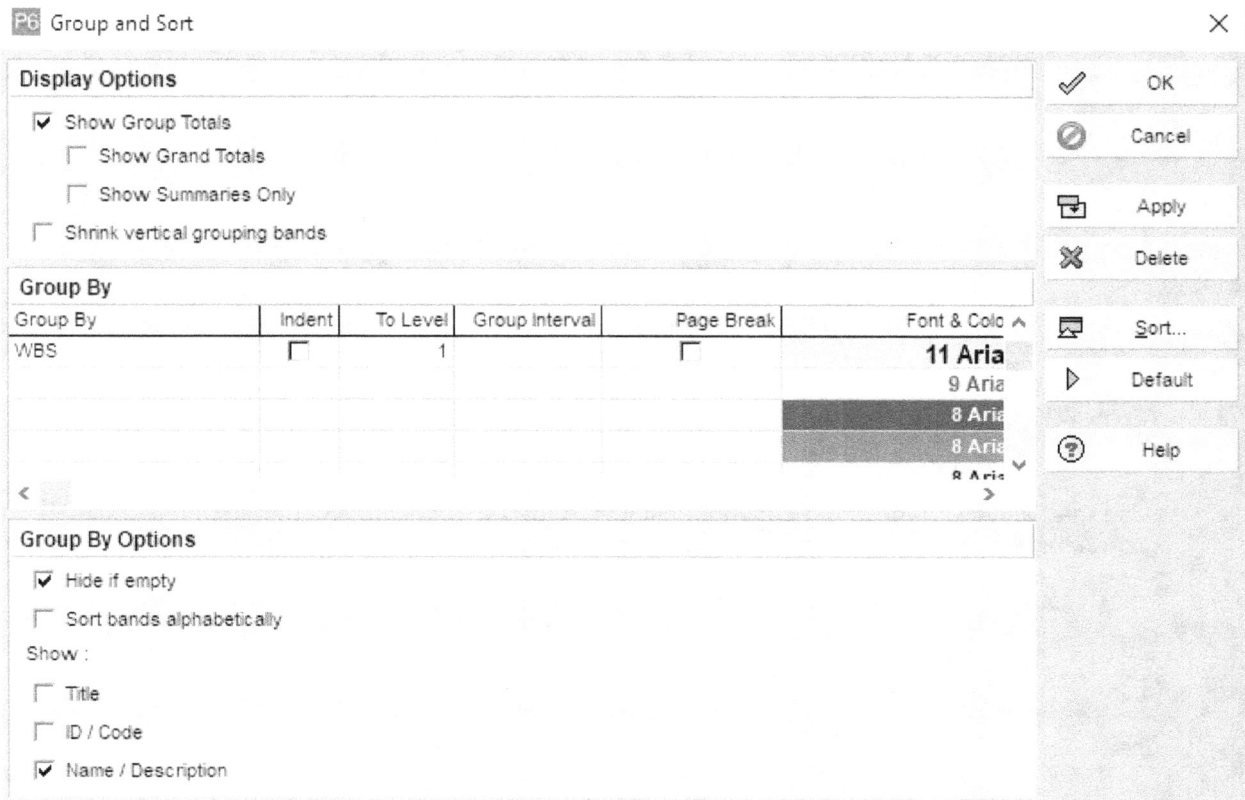

2. Go to WBS view, collapse all projects to WBS Level 1:

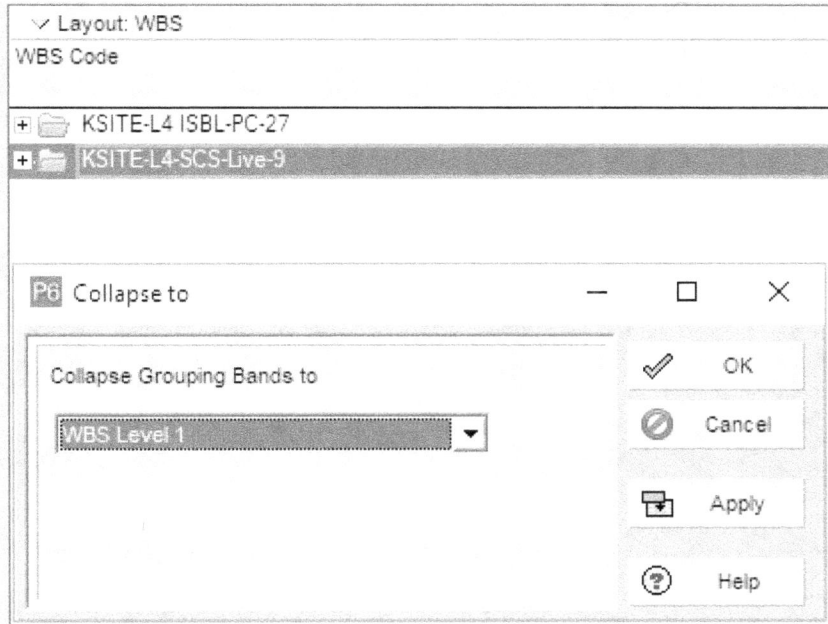

And arrange them using arrow buttons on the right making sure that your target project other projects will be copied to is at the top of the list.

3. Go back to the Activities view and add the WBS column.

Andrei Sannikov
Tip of the day

| Activity ID | Activity Name | Remaining Duration | Start | Finish | WBS | Project ID |
|---|---|---|---|---|---|---|
| **LNG Canada - ISBL Level 4 Systems Completion Schedule - live** | | 55 | 01-Oct-23 A | 04-Apr-24 | | |
| SC-1-42-A7-CW30-PNT | 1-42-A7-CW30 - Pipe Painting Touch-ups | 27 | 01-Nov-23 A | 07-Mar-24 | KSITE-L4-SCS-Live-9 | KSITE-L4-SCS-Live-9 |
| SC-1-42-A7-CW30-EHT | 1-42-A7-CW30 - Pipe EHT Tracer Installation | 34 | 23-Nov-23 A | 14-Mar-24 | KSITE-L4-SCS-Live-9 | KSITE-L4-SCS-Live-9 |
| SC-1-42-A7-CW30-PT | 1-42-A7-CW30 - Pipe Testing & Reinstatement | 0 | 20-Nov-23 A | 08-Feb-24 A | KSITE-L4-SCS-Live-9 | KSITE-L4-SCS-Live-9 |
| SC-1-42-A7-CW30-PI | 1-42-A7-CW30 - Pipe Installation | 5 | 01-Oct-23 A | 14-Feb-24 | KSITE-L4-SCS-Live-9 | KSITE-L4-SCS-Live-9 |
| SC-1-42-A7-CW30-M | 1-42-A7-CW30 - Mechanical Installation | 0 | 05-Feb-24 A | 09-Feb-24 A | KSITE-L4-SCS-Live-9 | KSITE-L4-SCS-Live-9 |
| SC-1-42-A7-CW30-IP | 1-42-A7-CW30 - Pipe Insulation | 55 | 10-Feb-24 | 04-Apr-24 | KSITE-L4-SCS-Live-9 | KSITE-L4-SCS-Live-9 |
| SC-1-42-A7-CW30-IT | 1-42-A7-CW30 - Instrumentation Installation | 0 | 20-Nov-23 A | 23-Nov-23 A | KSITE-L4-SCS-Live-9 | KSITE-L4-SCS-Live-9 |
| SC-1-42-A7-CW30-ET | 1-42-A7-CW30 - Electrical Installation | 15 | 04-Feb-24 A | 24-Feb-24 | KSITE-L4-SCS-Live-9 | KSITE-L4-SCS-Live-9 |
| **LNG Canada - ISBL Precom Schedule** | | 45 | 22-Feb-24 | 06-Apr-24 | | |
| 1-42-A7-CW30-0200 | Unit 1U4200, System 1-42-A7-CW30 Piping Equipment | 1 | 24-Feb-24 | 24-Feb-24 | KSITE-L4 ISBL-PC-27 | KSITE-L4 ISBL-PC-27 |
| 1-42-A7-CW30-5000 | Unit 1U4200, System 1-42-A7-CW30 Mechanically Complete (MC) | 0 | | 06-Apr-24 | KSITE-L4 ISBL-PC-27 | KSITE-L4 ISBL-PC-27 |
| 1-42-A7-CW30-0093 | Unit 1U4200, System 1-42-A7-CW30 Piping Support: Line Hydroblasting Re- | 2 | 01-Apr-24 | 02-Apr-24 | KSITE-L4 ISBL-PC-27 | KSITE-L4 ISBL-PC-27 |
| 1-42-A7-CW30-0092 | Unit 1U4200, System 1-42-A7-CW30 Piping Support: Line Hydroblasting Circ | 10 | 22-Mar-24 | 31-Mar-24 | KSITE-L4 ISBL-PC-27 | KSITE-L4 ISBL-PC-27 |
| 1-42-A7-CW30-0500 | Unit 1U4200, System 1-42-A7-CW30 Buildings/HVAC | 2 | 18-Mar-24 | 19-Mar-24 | KSITE-L4 ISBL-PC-27 | KSITE-L4 ISBL-PC-27 |
| 1-42-A7-CW30-0091 | Unit 1U4200, System 1-42-A7-CW30 Piping Support: Line Hydroblasting Prej | 2 | 20-Mar-24 | 21-Mar-24 | KSITE-L4 ISBL-PC-27 | KSITE-L4 ISBL-PC-27 |
| 1-42-A7-CW30-0120 | Unit 1U4200, System 1-42-A7-CW30 Mechanical | 2 | 18-Mar-24 | 19-Mar-24 | KSITE-L4 ISBL-PC-27 | KSITE-L4 ISBL-PC-27 |
| 1-42-A7-CW30-0700 | Unit 1U4200, System 1-42-A7-CW30 Piping Support: Line Flush/Blow - by K | 2 | 22-Feb-24 | 23-Feb-24 | KSITE-L4 ISBL-PC-27 | KSITE-L4 ISBL-PC-27 |
| 1-42-A7-CW30-0100 | Unit 1U4200, System 1-42-A7-CW30 Instrumentation | 9 | 09-Mar-24 | 17-Mar-24 | KSITE-L4 ISBL-PC-27 | KSITE-L4 ISBL-PC-27 |
| 1-42-A7-CW30-0300 | Unit 1U4200, System 1-42-A7-CW30 Electrical | 2 | 07-Mar-24 | 08-Mar-24 | KSITE-L4 ISBL-PC-27 | KSITE-L4 ISBL-PC-27 |
| 1-42-A7-CW30-0000 | Unit 1U4200, System 1-42-A7-CW30 Final Walk Down | 15 | 23-Mar-24 | 06-Apr-24 | KSITE-L4 ISBL-PC-27 | KSITE-L4 ISBL-PC-27 |

4. Use the Fill Down function to copy the last line in the WBS column in your first project all the way down. You will see that all your opened projects will merge into one.

| Activity ID | Activity Name | Remaining Duration | Start | Finish | WBS | Project ID |
|---|---|---|---|---|---|---|
| **LNG Canada - ISBL Level 4 Systems Completion Schedule - live** | | 45 | 01-Oct-23 A | 12-Apr-24 | | |
| SC-1-42-A7-CW30-PNT | 1-42-A7-CW30 - Pipe Painting Touch-ups | 27 | 01-Nov-23 A | 07-Mar-24 | KSITE-L4-SCS-Live-9 | KSITE-L4-SCS-Live-9 |
| SC-1-42-A7-CW30-EHT | 1-42-A7-CW30 - Pipe EHT Tracer Installation | 34 | 23-Nov-23 A | 14-Mar-24 | KSITE-L4-SCS-Live-9 | KSITE-L4-SCS-Live-9 |
| SC-1-42-A7-CW30-PT | 1-42-A7-CW30 - Pipe Testing & Reinstatement | 0 | 20-Nov-23 A | 08-Feb-24 A | KSITE-L4-SCS-Live-9 | KSITE-L4-SCS-Live-9 |
| SC-1-42-A7-CW30-PI | 1-42-A7-CW30 - Pipe Installation | 5 | 01-Oct-23 A | 14-Feb-24 | KSITE-L4-SCS-Live-9 | KSITE-L4-SCS-Live-9 |
| SC-1-42-A7-CW30-M | 1-42-A7-CW30 - Mechanical Installation | 0 | 05-Feb-24 A | 09-Feb-24 A | KSITE-L4-SCS-Live-9 | KSITE-L4-SCS-Live-9 |
| SC-1-42-A7-CW30-IP | 1-42-A7-CW30 - Pipe Insulation | 55 | 10-Feb-24 | 04-Apr-24 | KSITE-L4-SCS-Live-9 | KSITE-L4-SCS-Live-9 |
| SC-1-42-A7-CW30-IT | 1-42-A7-CW30 - Instrumentation Installation | 0 | 20-Nov-23 A | 23-Nov-23 A | KSITE-L4-SCS-Live-9 | KSITE-L4-SCS-Live-9 |
| SC-1-42-A7-CW30-ET | 1-42-A7-CW30 - Electrical Installation | 15 | 04-Feb-24 A | 24-Feb-24 | KSITE-L4-SCS-Live-9 | KSITE-L4-SCS-Live-9 |
| 1-42-A7-CW30-0200 | Unit 1U4200, System 1-42-A7-CW30 Piping Equipment | 1 | 26-Feb-24 | 26-Feb-24 | KSITE-L4-SCS-Live-9 | KSITE-L4-SCS-Live-9 |
| 1-42-A7-CW30-5000 | Unit 1U4200, System 1-42-A7-CW30 Mechanically Complete (MC) | 0 | | 08-Apr-24 | KSITE-L4-SCS-Live-9 | KSITE-L4-SCS-Live-9 |
| 1-42-A7-CW30-0093 | Unit 1U4200, System 1-42-A7-CW30 Piping Support: Line Hydroblasting Re- | 2 | 01-Apr-24 | 02-Apr-24 | KSITE-L4-SCS-Live-9 | KSITE-L4-SCS-Live-9 |
| 1-42-A7-CW30-0092 | Unit 1U4200, System 1-42-A7-CW30 Piping Support: Line Hydroblasting Circ | 10 | 22-Mar-24 | 04-Apr-24 | KSITE-L4-SCS-Live-9 | KSITE-L4-SCS-Live-9 |
| 1-42-A7-CW30-0500 | Unit 1U4200, System 1-42-A7-CW30 Buildings/HVAC | 2 | 18-Mar-24 | 19-Mar-24 | KSITE-L4-SCS-Live-9 | KSITE-L4-SCS-Live-9 |
| 1-42-A7-CW30-0091 | Unit 1U4200, System 1-42-A7-CW30 Piping Support: Line Hydroblasting Prej | 2 | 20-Mar-24 | 21-Mar-24 | KSITE-L4-SCS-Live-9 | KSITE-L4-SCS-Live-9 |
| 1-42-A7-CW30-0120 | Unit 1U4200, System 1-42-A7-CW30 Mechanical | 2 | 18-Mar-24 | 19-Mar-24 | KSITE-L4-SCS-Live-9 | KSITE-L4-SCS-Live-9 |
| 1-42-A7-CW30-0700 | Unit 1U4200, System 1-42-A7-CW30 Piping Support: Line Flush/Blow - by K | 2 | 22-Feb-24 | 23-Feb-24 | KSITE-L4-SCS-Live-9 | KSITE-L4-SCS-Live-9 |
| 1-42-A7-CW30-0100 | Unit 1U4200, System 1-42-A7-CW30 Instrumentation | 9 | 11-Mar-24 | 21-Mar-24 | KSITE-L4-SCS-Live-9 | KSITE-L4-SCS-Live-9 |
| 1-42-A7-CW30-0300 | Unit 1U4200, System 1-42-A7-CW30 Electrical | 2 | 07-Mar-24 | 08-Mar-24 | KSITE-L4-SCS-Live-9 | KSITE-L4-SCS-Live-9 |
| 1-42-A7-CW30-0000 | Unit 1U4200, System 1-42-A7-CW30 Final Walk Down | 15 | 25-Mar-24 | 12-Apr-24 | KSITE-L4-SCS-Live-9 | KSITE-L4-SCS-Live-9 |

## How to import actuals into your schedule

When we work on large projects and several planners provide input for the same master schedule, our biggest challenge is often to incorporate all the updates especially when all the planners do not have access to the same P6 server and we have to rely on imports and exports. Sometime ago I sent out a tip explaining how to incorporate/import sub-projects into your master file with inter-project links and all the changes your contractors might have made during their schedule update. Even if you have this process in place, you might still want to import actuals or revised budgets into your schedule (and then revise the logic or dates if required) and sometimes these progress updates could be coming from people without P6 access - like foremen or superintendents. Here is what you can do:

1. Say, you have received an update for an area, which is a part of your integrated/master plan.
2. Import this file into P6, open it and go to Export > Excel > Resource assignments

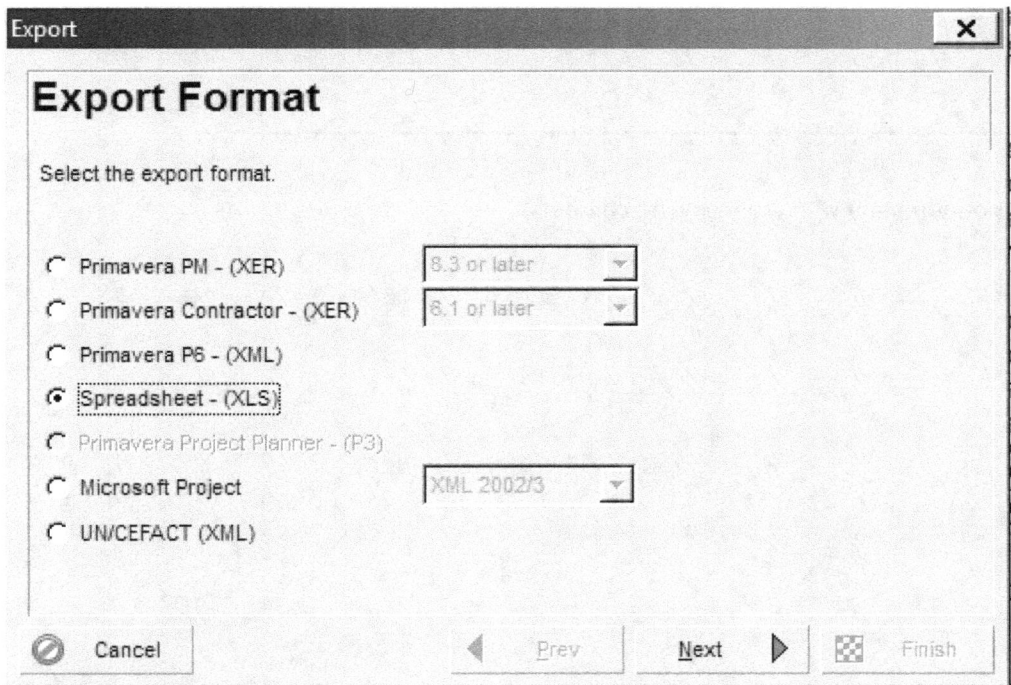

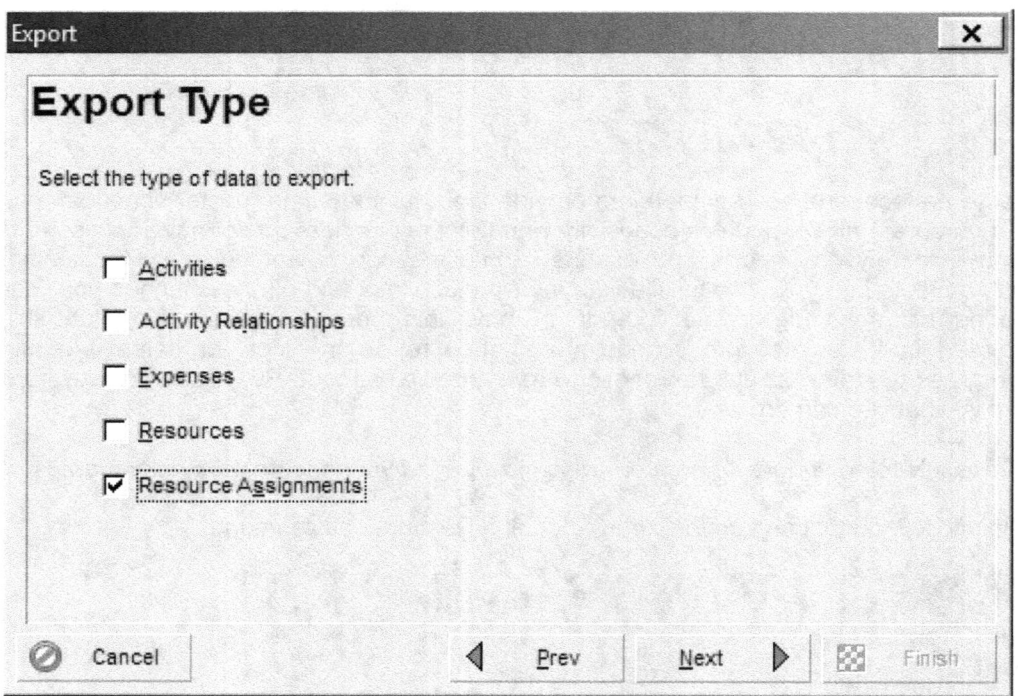

3. Create an export template with the following columns:

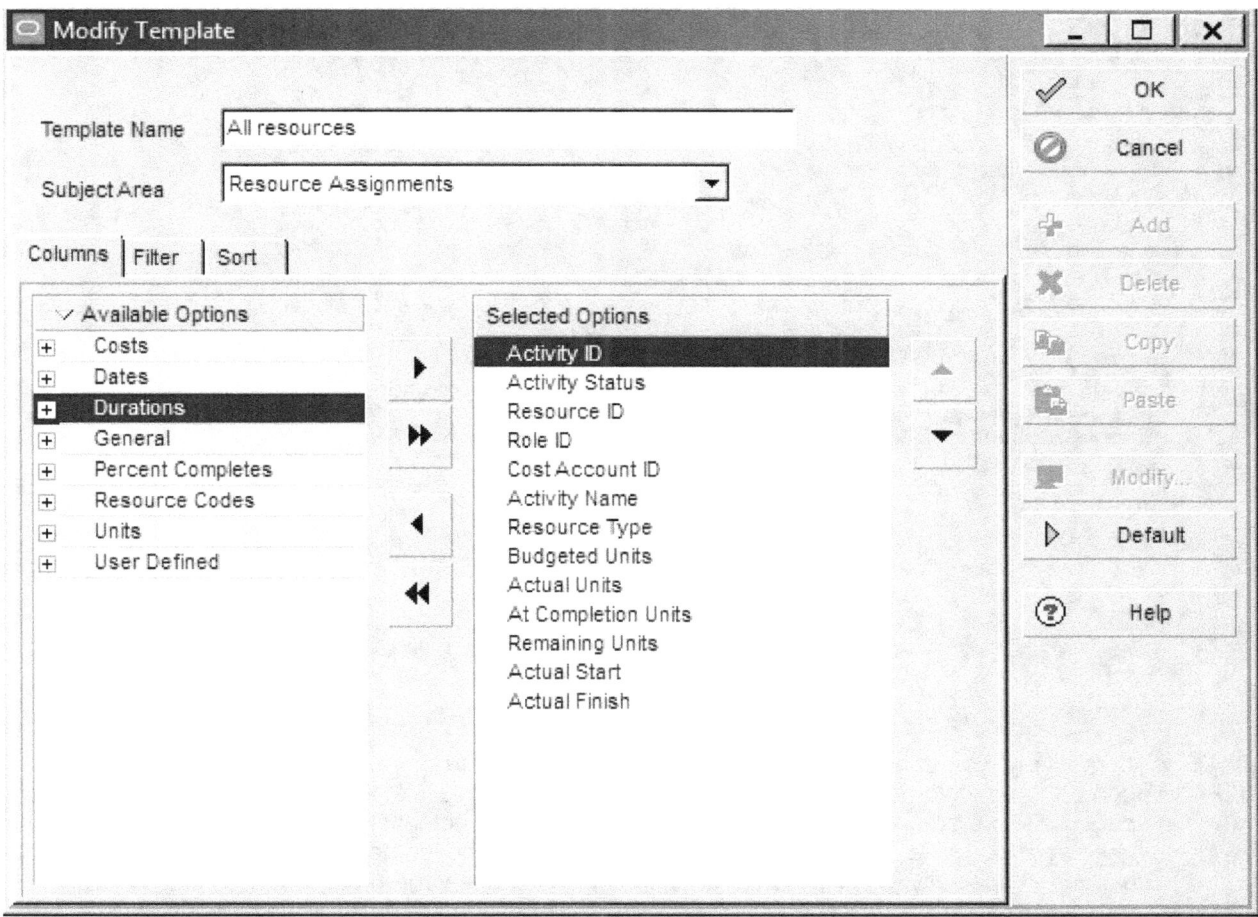

You can set up a filter if you want to exclude specific resources from your export.

4. Once the export is complete, close the project and open your master project. Go to Import > Excel > Resource Assignments. Locate the file we have just created from the Select File to Import dialogue, click Next then Finish, sit back, and relax (optional).

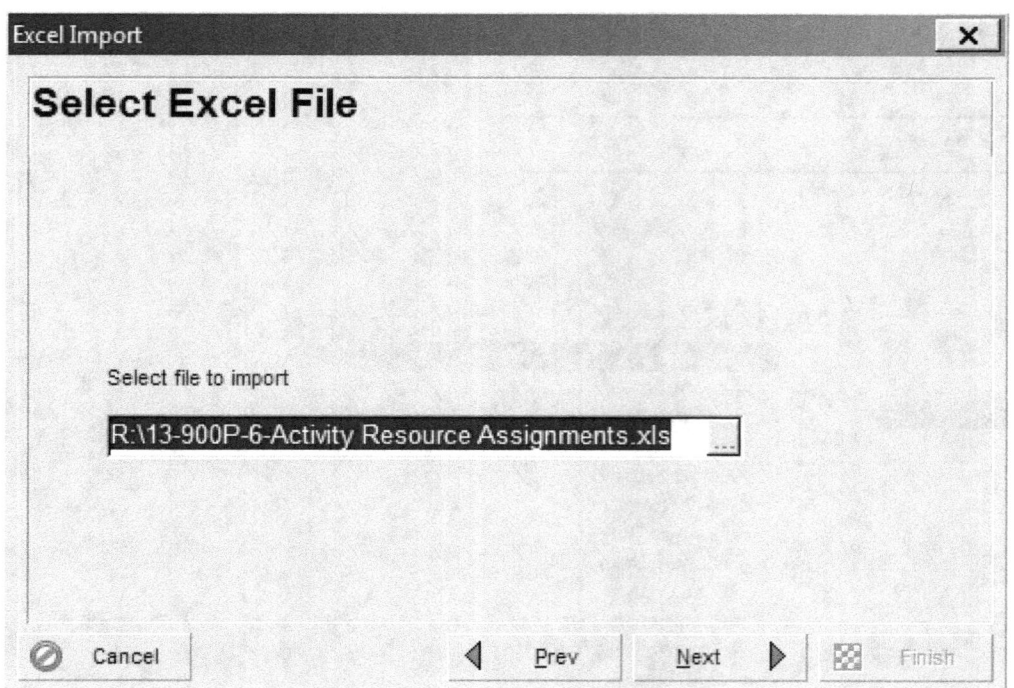

5. Alternatively, you can export a Resource assignment file from your master file, select activities you want updated (and delete the rest of the rows) and send this file to your superintendent or foreman for updating. Make sure you tell them to update Actual units, actual start and/or finish only or At completion if they need to revise their budget; remaining units will be computed automatically after import. Other changes - especially to column headers might compromise your future import.

| act_qty | total_qty | remain_qty | act_start_date | act_end_date |
|---|---|---|---|---|
| Actual Units(h) | At Completion Units(h) | Remaining Early Units(h) | Actual Start | Actual Finish |

Note that if you have multiple resources on an activity, its finish date will be actualized only after you input finish dates on all the resources associated with this activity in the Resource assignment file in Excel.

## How to group activities by start or finish dates

When we produce schedules for specific time periods like 30 or 90-days look-ahead, sometimes it makes sense to group activities by start or finish week, month, date or whatever so that activities planned to start (or finish), say, in November (or on each date or during each week) are grouped together followed by a similar grouping for December etc. We can of course create a series of layouts for each time period and name them accordingly but as the dates move on you would need to change these filters and rename the layouts, which can be very time-consuming especially if you maintain multiple schedules. Here is a much faster way to do it:

1. Open your project(s) and apply your 3-weeks or 90-days filter as required.

2. Go to Group and Sort, choose Start or Finish in the drop down menu on the first line:

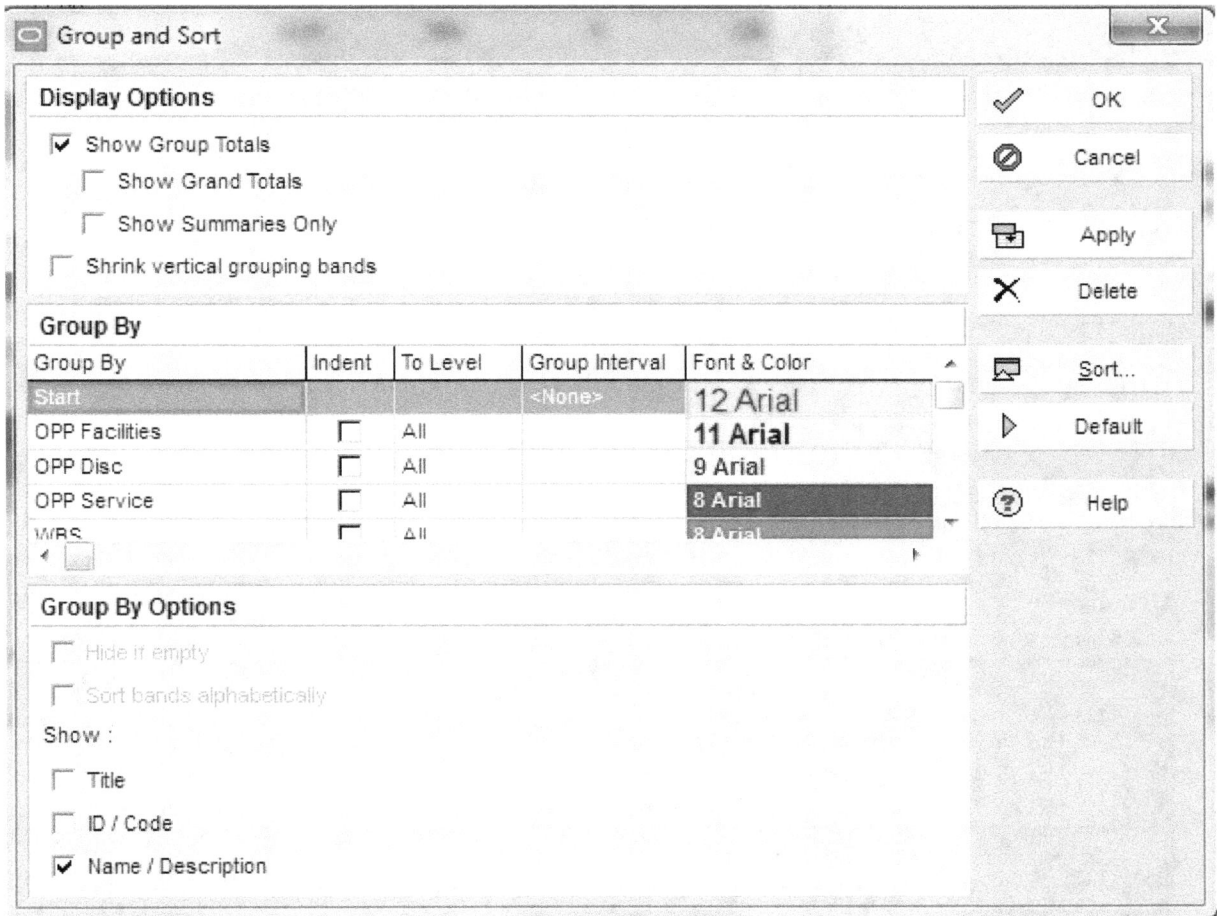

3. Click under Group Interval and choose the required grouping level from the drop-down menu.

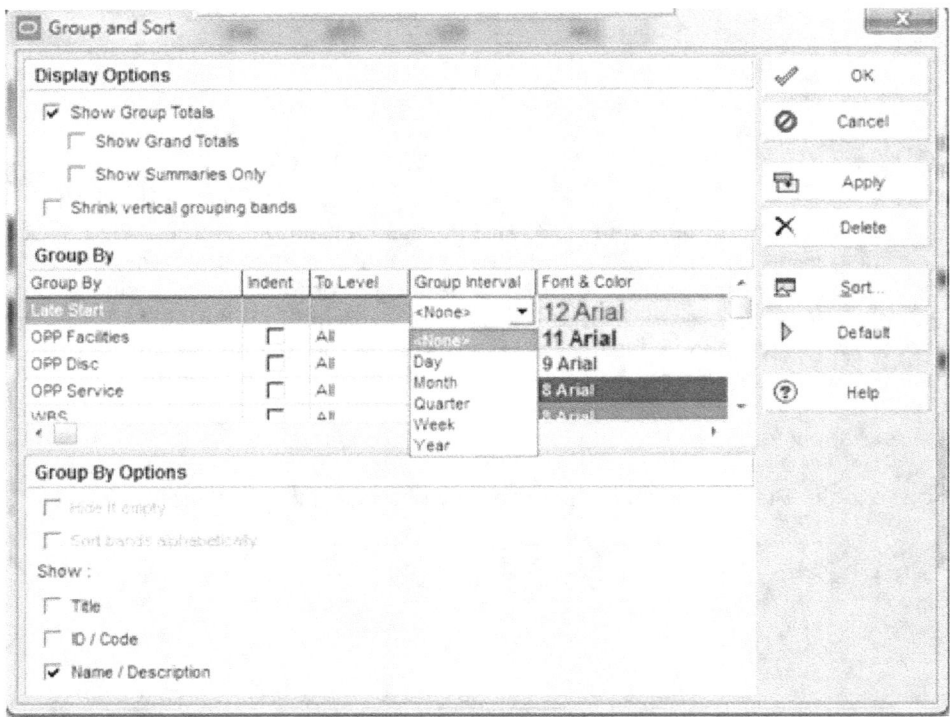

The resulting layout (for start > month) is shown below.

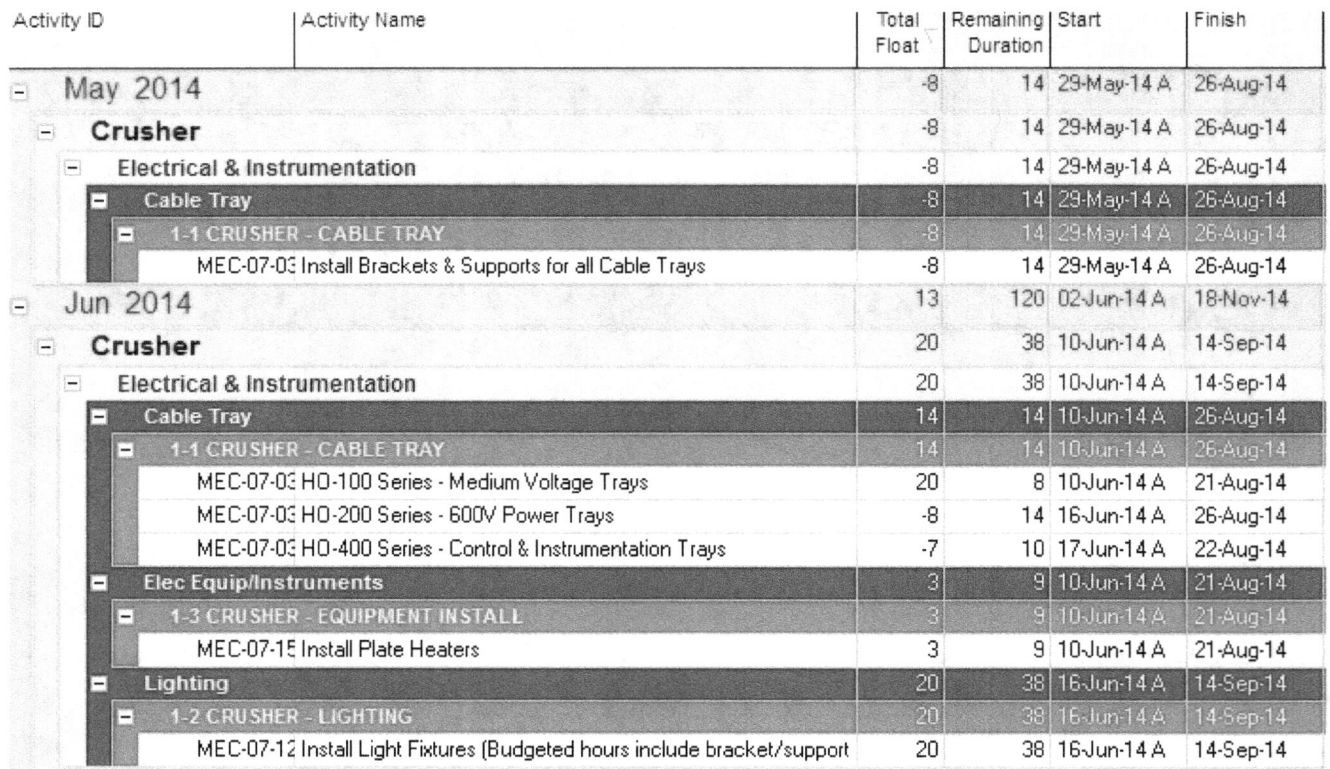

Alternatively, you can group activities by their finish month, week or date.

29-Sep-14 10:31

# How to display material quantities in a column

When we have material quantities (loaded as material resources) in our schedules, sometimes it is really helpful to display them in a column, say, next to the budget labor hours, especially when you do a schedule review and keep getting questions on quantities associated with each activity. P6 shows material resources only in resource assignment view and activity details window at the bottom of the activities view, which is not always practical. There is a reason behind it: as opposed to labor or non-labor (equipment) resources material resources do not have a common denominator (hours) and cannot be summed up in a column, which is how labor and non-labor units are handled/displayed in P6. Let us see if we can trick the system to make it work.

1. Go to your resource dictionary, highlight each material resource you want to show in a column and set the Price / Unit value under the Price & Unit tab to 1.

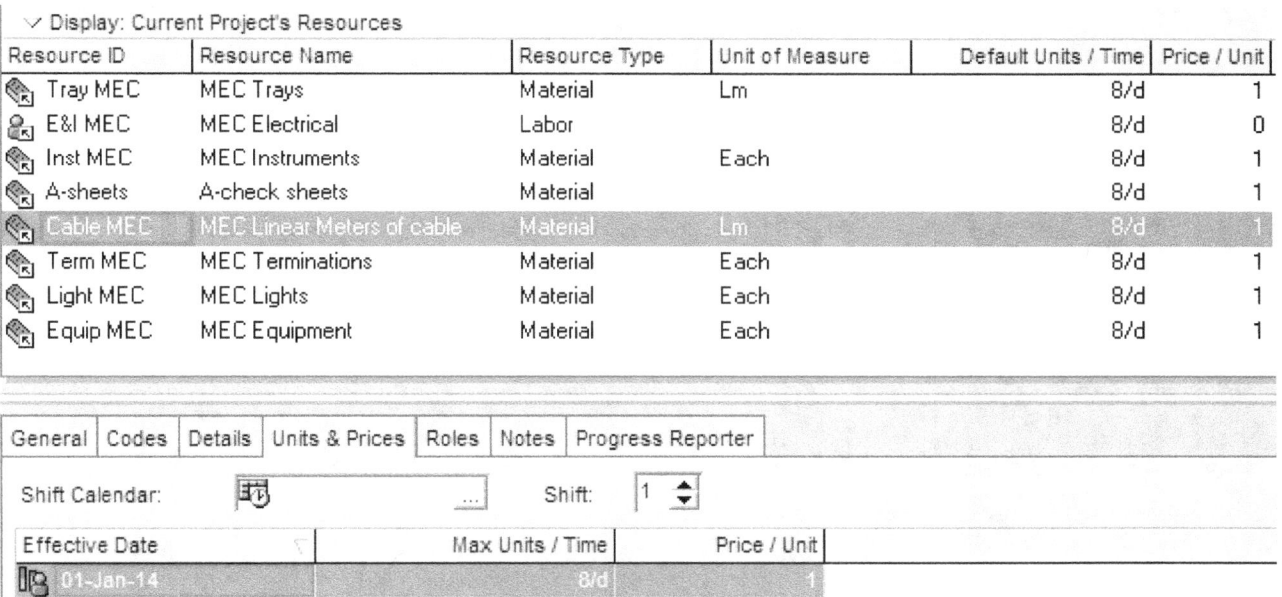

2. Set Price / Unit value for the material resources you do not want to display to 0. The system will prompt you to go to Tools and run Recalculate assignment costs:

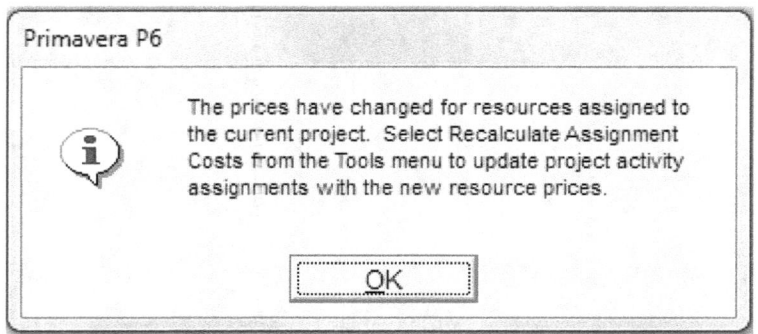

Click OK and follow this advice. When you change your quantities in the future, P6 will automatically recalculate the quantities you display in a column.

3. Go to User Preferences > Currency options and uncheck "Show currency symbol"

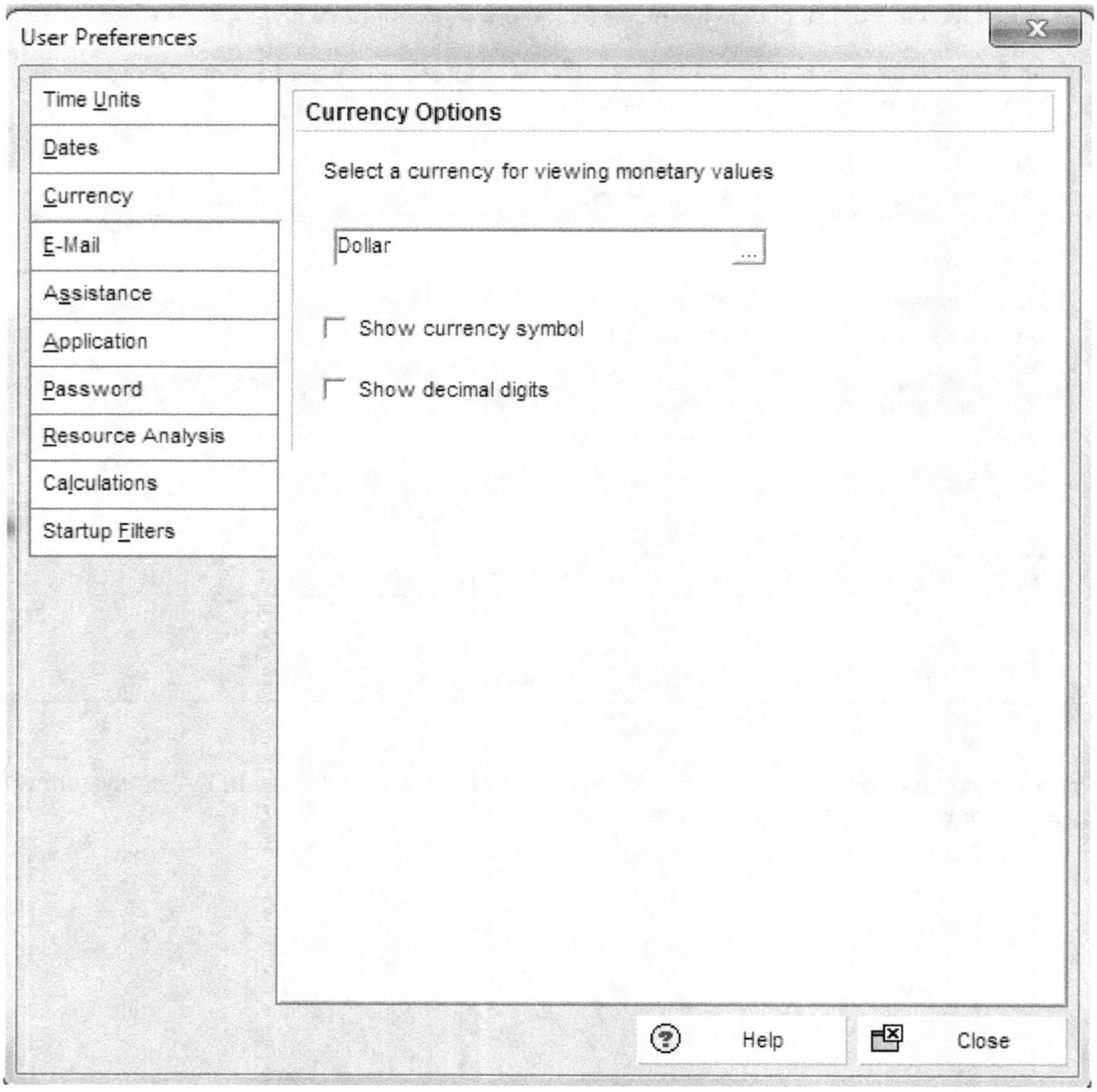

4. Go back to your activities view > columns and add "At Completion Material Cost", rename it to something like "Quantities" to avoid confusion:

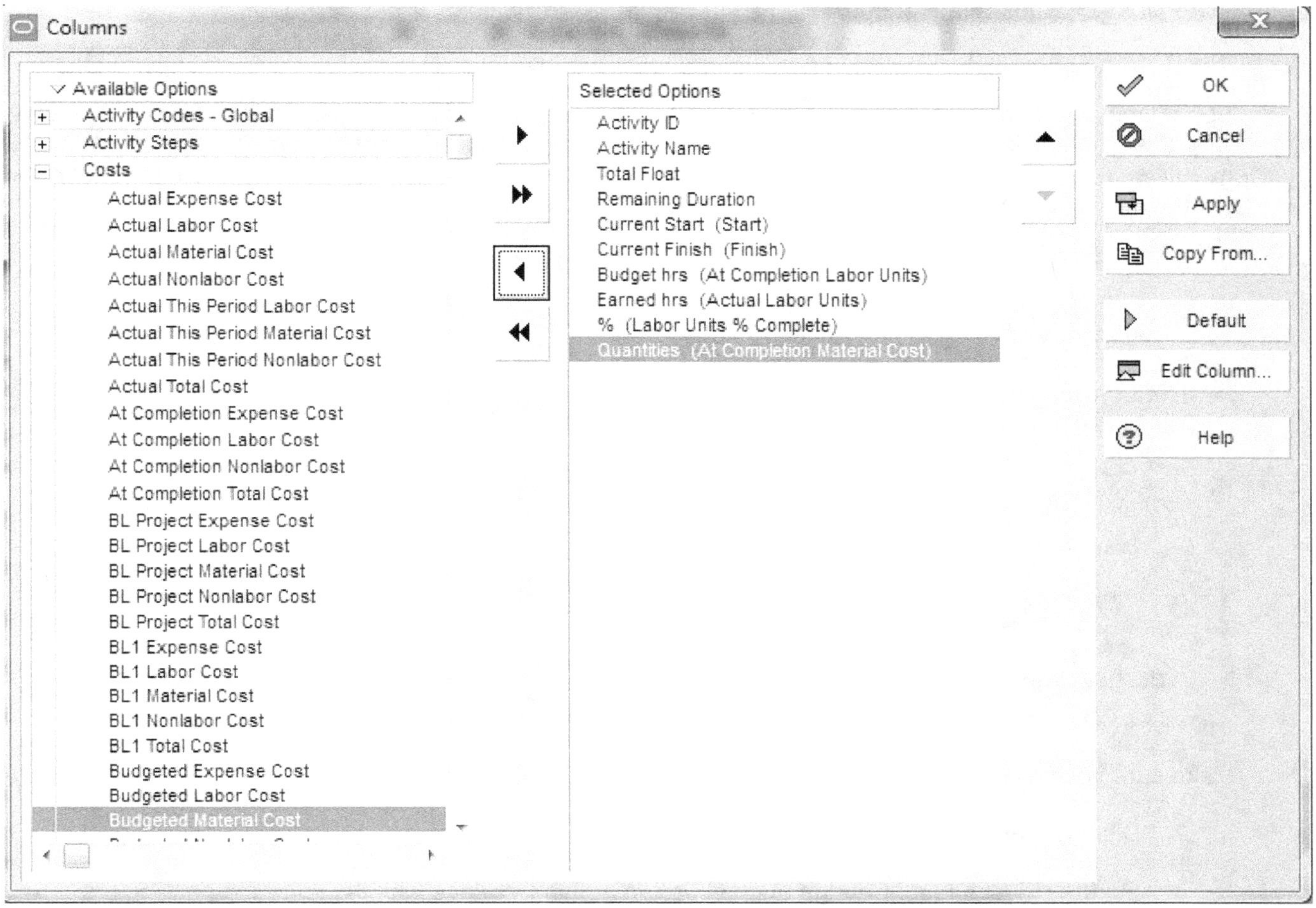

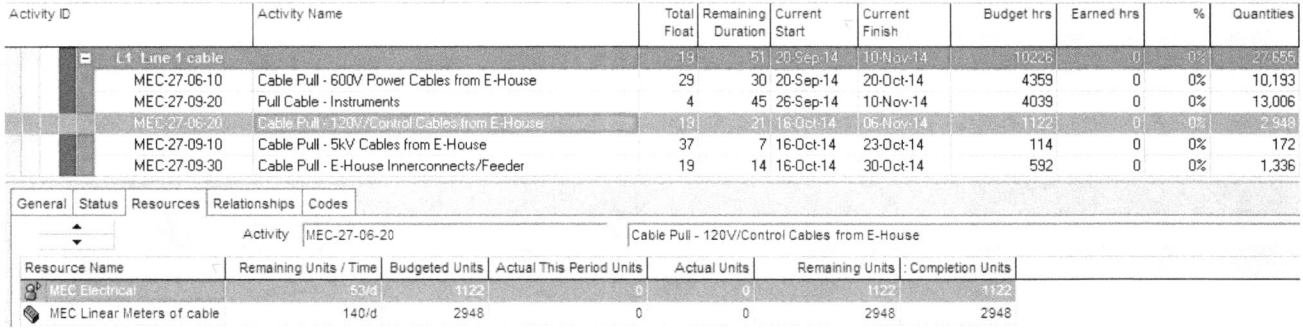

Now you will have a layout similar to the one below:

Notes:
- If you use P6 to track cost of materials you will obviously need to reset their price / unit values back to their actual unit prices once this layout is generated.
- If you group different materials in the same layout you will obviously need to remove subtotals from the columns where these materials are shown, the tip overleaf explains how this can be done.

# How to remove subtotals from columns with user defined fields

05-Nov-14 14:39

Part 1

Some time ago, I sent out a tip explaining how material quantities can be displayed in a column. The only problem with this method is that when you use subtotals in your layouts P6 would sum up all your different material quantities (add, say, linear meters of cable and terminations) and the resulting numbers could be very misleading. Let us see if we can find a workaround for this issue as well.

1. Go to Enterprise > User Defined Fields and set up the following fields for quantities:

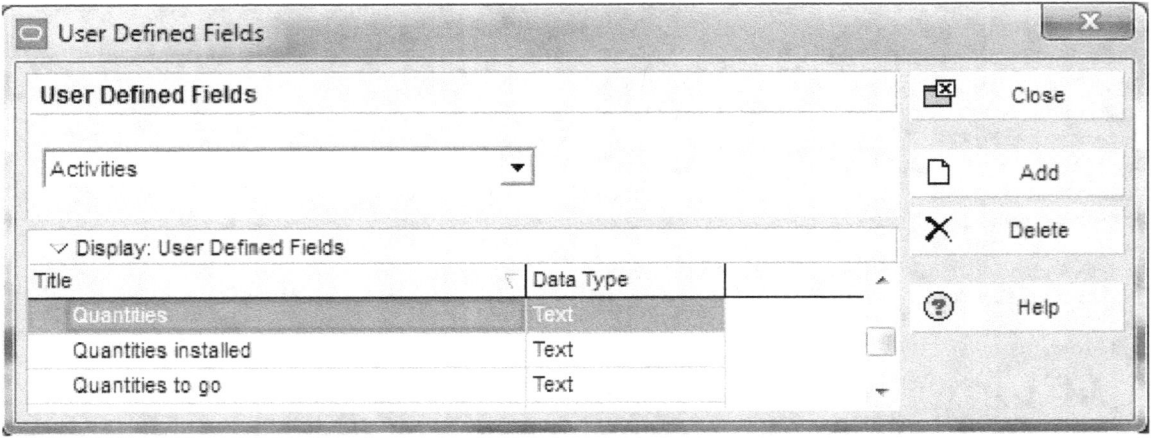

Make sure you set up the Data Type as Text

2. Display these fields as columns in your layout.

3. Go to Tools > Global Change and set up/run a global change with the following parameters:

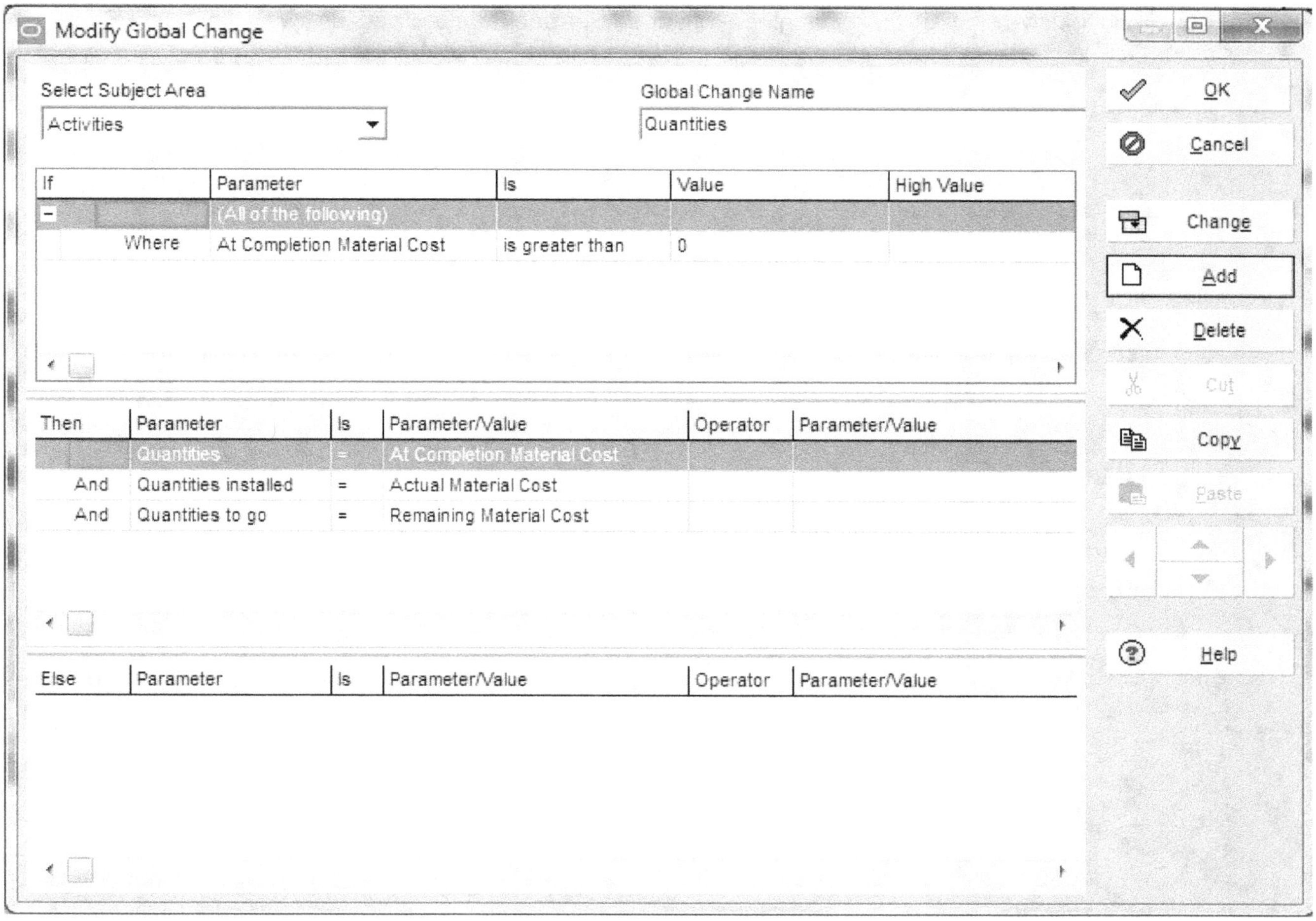

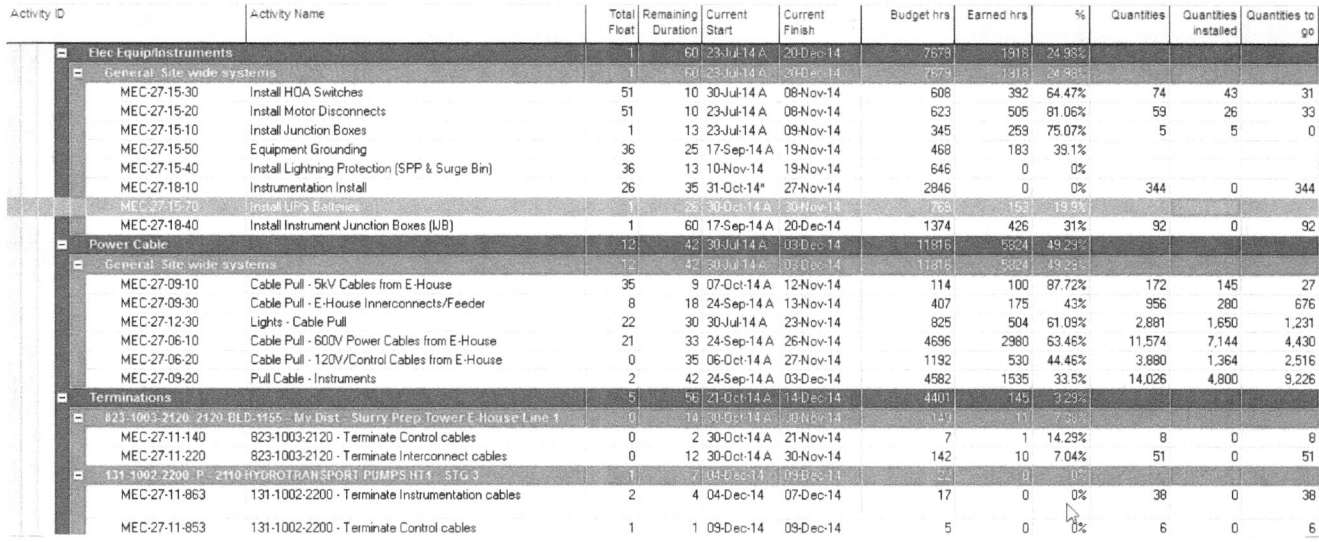

4. Since P6 cannot summarize text fields, the resulting layout will look like the one below:

| Activity ID | Activity Name | Total Float | Remaining Duration | Current Start | Current Finish | Budget hrs | Earned hrs | % | Quantities | Quantities installed | Quantities to go |
|---|---|---|---|---|---|---|---|---|---|---|---|
| Elec Equip/Instruments | | 1 | 60 | 23-Jul-14 A | 20-Dec-14 | 7679 | 1918 | 24.98% | | | |
| General Site wide systems | | 1 | 60 | 23-Jul-14 A | 20-Dec-14 | 7679 | 1918 | 24.98% | | | |
| MEC-27-15-30 | Install HOA Switches | 51 | 10 | 30-Jul-14 A | 08-Nov-14 | 608 | 392 | 64.47% | 74 | 43 | 31 |
| MEC-27-15-20 | Install Motor Disconnects | 51 | 10 | 23-Jul-14 A | 08-Nov-14 | 623 | 505 | 81.06% | 59 | 26 | 33 |
| MEC-27-15-10 | Install Junction Boxes | 1 | 13 | 23-Jul-14 A | 09-Nov-14 | 345 | 259 | 75.07% | 5 | 5 | 0 |
| MEC-27-15-50 | Equipment Grounding | 36 | 25 | 17-Sep-14 A | 19-Nov-14 | 468 | 183 | 39.1% | | | |
| MEC-27-15-40 | Install Lightning Protection (SPP & Surge Bin) | 36 | 13 | 10-Nov-14 | 19-Nov-14 | 646 | 0 | 0% | | | |
| MEC-27-18-10 | Instrumentation Install | 26 | 35 | 31-Oct-14* | 27-Nov-14 | 2846 | 0 | 0% | 344 | 0 | 344 |
| MEC-27-15-70 | Install UPS Batteries | 1 | 26 | 30-Oct-14 A | 30-Nov-14 | 769 | 153 | 19.9% | | | |
| MEC-27-18-40 | Install Instrument Junction Boxes (IJB) | 1 | 60 | 17-Sep-14 A | 20-Dec-14 | 1374 | 426 | 31% | 92 | 0 | 92 |
| Power Cable | | 12 | 42 | 30-Jul-14 A | 03-Dec-14 | 11816 | 5824 | 49.29% | | | |
| General Site wide systems | | 12 | 42 | 30-Jul-14 A | 03-Dec-14 | 11816 | 5824 | 49.29% | | | |
| MEC-27-09-10 | Cable Pull - 5kV Cables from E-House | 35 | 9 | 07-Oct-14 A | 12-Nov-14 | 114 | 100 | 87.72% | 172 | 145 | 27 |
| MEC-27-09-30 | Cable Pull - E-House Innerconnects/Feeder | 8 | 18 | 24-Sep-14 A | 13-Nov-14 | 407 | 175 | 43% | 956 | 280 | 676 |
| MEC-27-12-30 | Lights - Cable Pull | 22 | 30 | 30-Jul-14 A | 23-Nov-14 | 825 | 504 | 61.09% | 2,881 | 1,650 | 1,231 |
| MEC-27-06-10 | Cable Pull - 600V Power Cables from E-House | 21 | 33 | 24-Sep-14 A | 26-Nov-14 | 4696 | 2980 | 63.46% | 11,574 | 7,144 | 4,430 |
| MEC-27-06-20 | Cable Pull - 120V/Control Cables from E-House | 0 | 35 | 06-Oct-14 A | 27-Nov-14 | 1192 | 530 | 44.46% | 3,880 | 1,364 | 2,516 |
| MEC-27-09-20 | Pull Cable - Instruments | 2 | 42 | 24-Sep-14 A | 03-Dec-14 | 4582 | 1535 | 33.5% | 14,026 | 4,800 | 9,226 |
| Terminations | | 5 | 56 | 21-Oct-14 A | 14-Dec-14 | 4401 | 145 | 3.29% | | | |
| 823-1003-2120 2120-BLD-1155 - Mv Dist - Slurry Prep Tower E-House Line 1 | | 0 | 14 | 30-Oct-14 A | 30-Nov-14 | 149 | 11 | 7.38% | | | |
| MEC-27-11-140 | 823-1003-2120 - Terminate Control cables | 0 | 2 | 30-Oct-14 A | 21-Nov-14 | 7 | 1 | 14.29% | 8 | 0 | 8 |
| MEC-27-11-220 | 823-1003-2120 - Terminate Interconnect cables | 0 | 12 | 30-Oct-14 A | 30-Nov-14 | 142 | 10 | 7.04% | 51 | 0 | 51 |
| 131-1002-2200 P - 2110 HYDROTRANSPORT PUMPS HT1 - STG 3 | | 1 | 7 | 04-Dec-14 | 09-Dec-14 | 22 | 0 | 0% | | | |
| MEC-27-11-863 | 131-1002-2200 - Terminate Instrumentation cables | 2 | 4 | 04-Dec-14 | 07-Dec-14 | 17 | 0 | 0% | 38 | 0 | 38 |
| MEC-27-11-853 | 131-1002-2200 - Terminate Control cables | 1 | 1 | 09-Dec-14 | 09-Dec-14 | 5 | 0 | 0% | 6 | 0 | 6 |

You will obviously need to rerun this global change after each update because user fields in P6 are not updated automatically.

06-Nov-14 15:27

Part 2

User defined fields are often used in P6 to perform calculations that are not available in the standard selection of columns. For instance, you can show your average crew size on activities of your choice by dividing remaining labor units by remaining durations and, if necessary, by overall or task specific productivity factor. All you need to do is to create a user defined field and a global change to run the required calculations like in the example below:

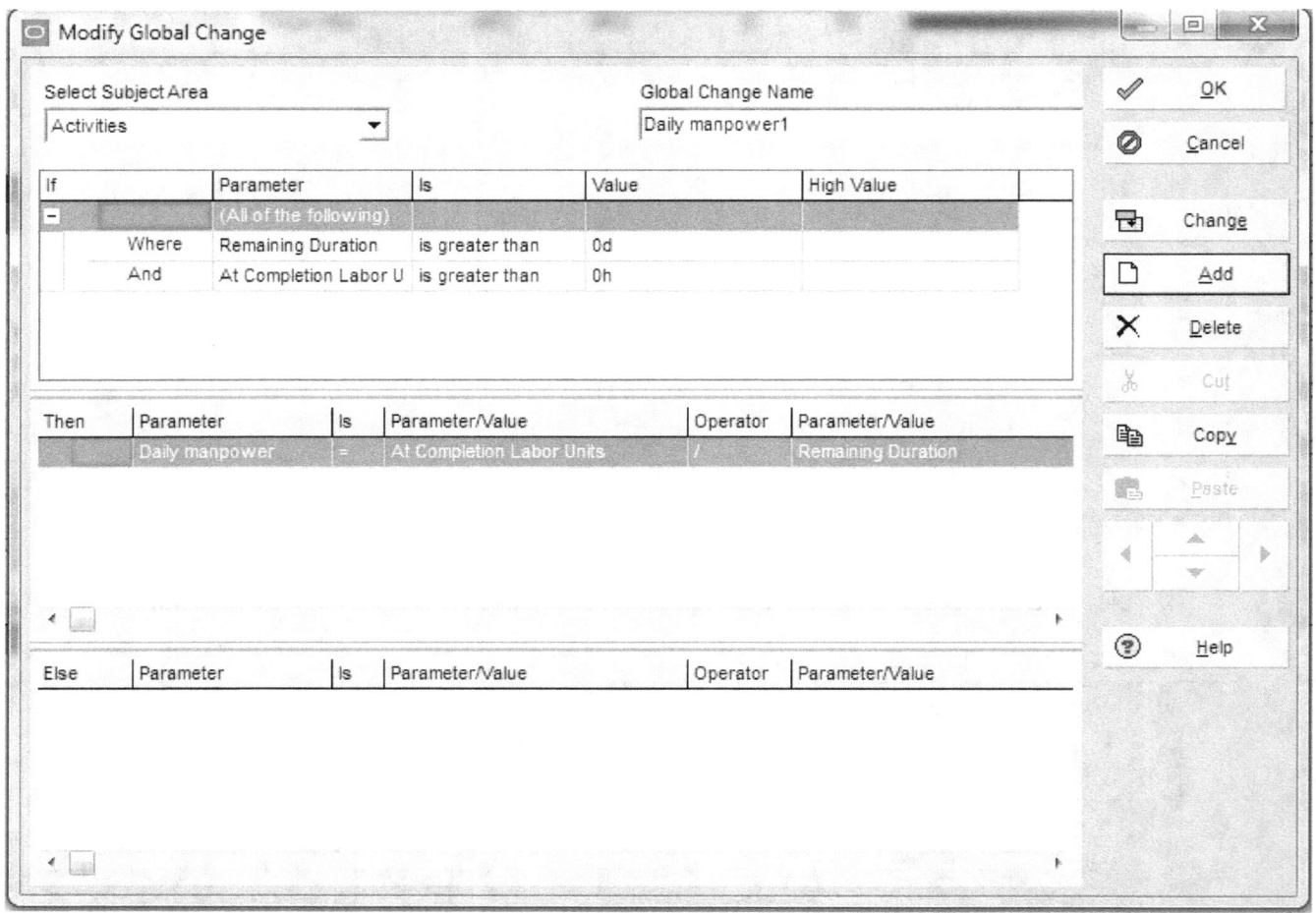

For any calculations to work this user field needs to be either a number or an integer and if you use grand total/subtotals in your layout, P6 adds up all the values found in these user fields and the resulting subtotals will be completely meaningless and even misleading like in the example below:

| Activity Name | Total Float | Remaining Duration | Current Start | Current Finish | Budget hrs | Earned hrs | Remaining hrs | Daily manpower |
|---|---|---|---|---|---|---|---|---|
| -2205 HYDROTRANSPORT PUMPS HT2 - STG 1 & 2 | 57 | 40 | 14-Dec-14 | 03-Feb-15 | 538 | 0 | 538 | 9 |
| 131-1005-2200 - Terminate Control cables | 71 | 2 | 14-Dec-14 | 17-Dec-14 | 13 | 0 | 13 | 1 |
| 131-1005-2200 - Terminate Interconnect cables | 76 | 2 | 05-Jan-15 | 08-Jan-15 | 24 | 0 | 24 | 2 |
| 131-1005-2200 - Terminate 600V cables | 39 | 8 | 05-Jan-15 | 14-Jan-15 | 260 | 0 | 260 | 4 |
| 131-1005-2200 - Terminate Instrumentation cables | 57 | 20 | 18-Jan-15 | 03-Feb-15 | 241 | 0 | 241 | 2 |

Here is what you can do to maintain your subtotals for dates, hours, % complete etc. and remove them for user defined fields.

Go to Enterprise > User defined fields and set up another user field, make sure you define its type as text:

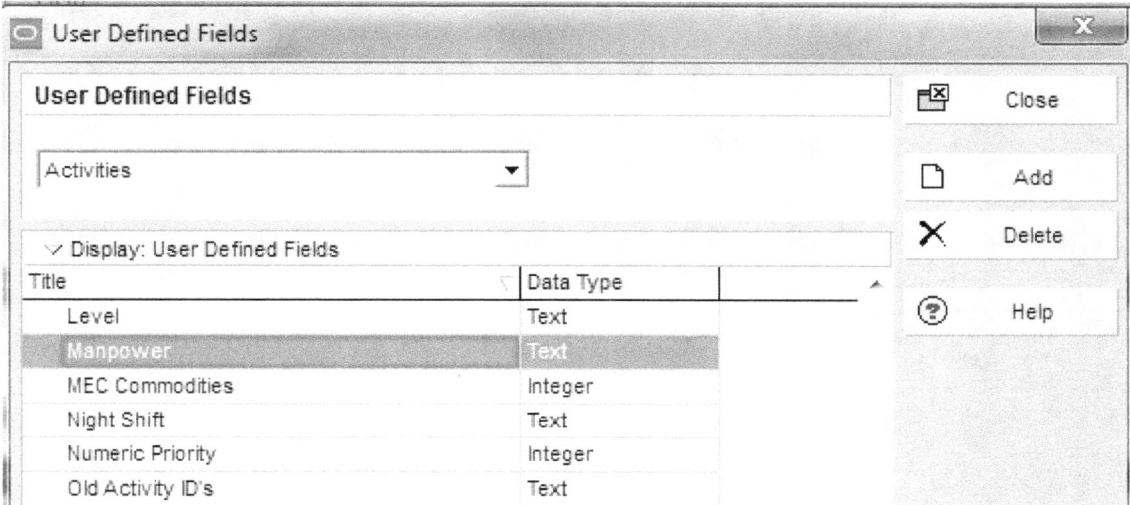

Set up/run another global change like the one below to transfer the data from a numeric calculated field to the text field we have just set up:

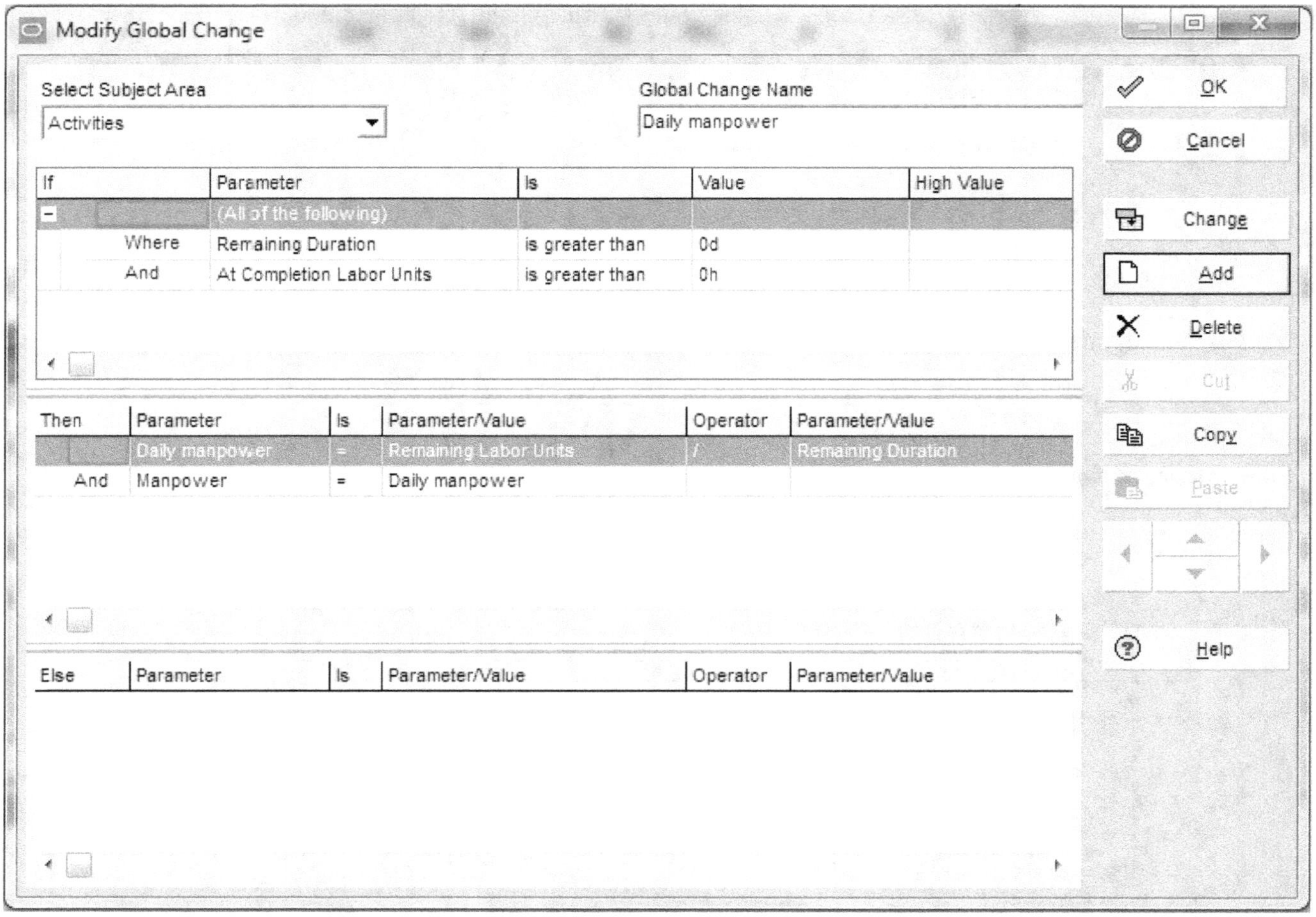

Andrei Sannikov
Tip of the day

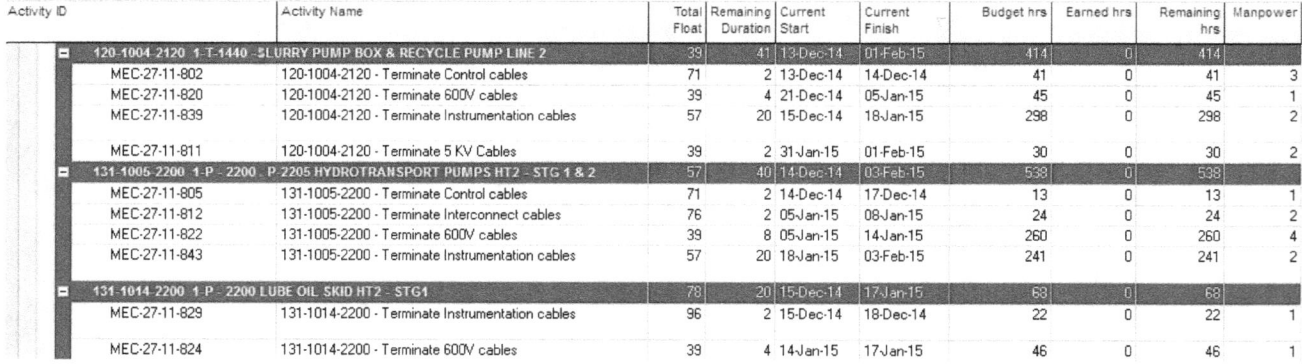

When you display this text field in a column the resulting layout will look like the one below:

# How to add code values to activity names

Fragnets (small typical schedules with a standard set of activities and logic) are very useful for preparation of large schedules - you set up a group of typical activities in, say, a system completions schedule, link them, load them with required resources and copy/paste this group as many times as necessary. The only problem is that you will end up with a large number of activities with identical names and when you show them outside of their normal WBS or coding structure this might be very confusing. Consider the following:

1. When you set up your coding structure make sure your code values are as descriptive as possible e.g. Use full (sub)system numbers, commonly used acronyms for construction areas, disciplines etc.

2. Say, we set up a large E&I or system completion schedule and want to see subsystem numbers in front of each activity name.

    - set up your fragnet, copy/paste it as needed and code the newly pasted activities to each subsystem - the easiest way to do is to display the required codes in columns and use the Fill Down function

3. Go to Tools > Global Change and set up a global change similar to the one below:

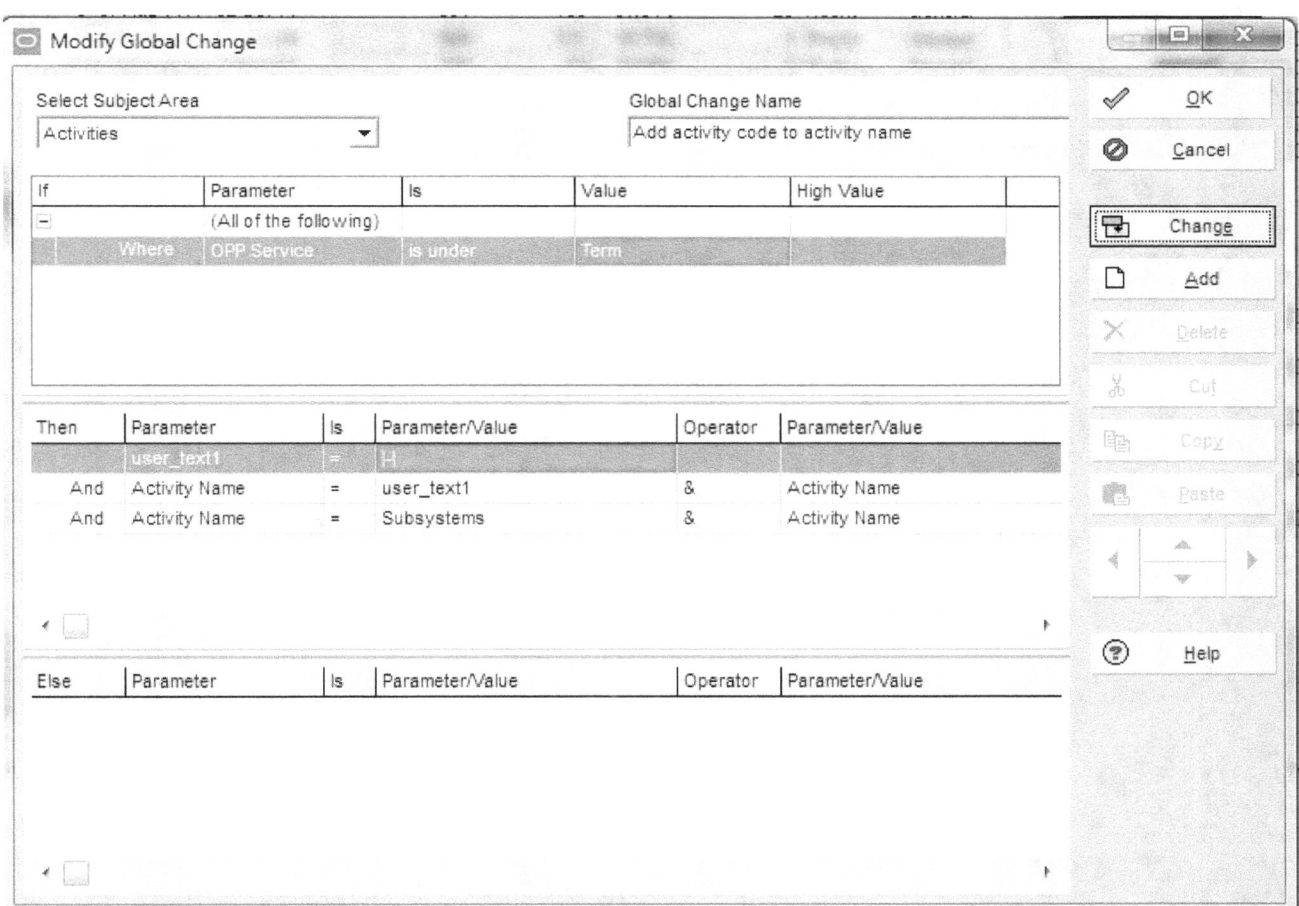

Note: you will need a text user field to make sure your activity code is separated from the activity name by a dash or your symbol of choice. Unfortunately, you cannot have a dash and a space on each side of it in a user field -

spaces in user text fields are accepted only when you have more than one character, say, 2 dashes can be separated by a space; if you do need a space use a symbol that you don't normally have in your schedule before and after the dash character like "|" in the example above and replace it with spaces using the Replace function (Ctrl + R) after running the global change.

The end result will look like shown below:

| Terminations | |
|---|---|
| **823-1003-2120  2120-BLD-1155 - Mv Dist - Slurry Prep Tower E-House Line 1** | |
| MEC-27-12-6430 | 823-1003-2120 - Terminate Control cables |
| MEC-27-12-6830 | 823-1003-2120 - Terminate Interconnect cables |
| **822-1010-2120  2120-BLD-1155 - LV. Dist - Slurry Prep Tower E-House Line 1** | |
| MEC-27-12-13830 | 822-1010-2120 - Terminate Instrumentation cables |
| MEC-27-12-13930 | 822-1010-2120 - Terminate 600V cables |
| MEC-27-12-14130 | 822-1010-2120 - Terminate lighting cables |
| MEC-27-12-13630 | 822-1010-2120 - Terminate Control cables |
| MEC-27-12-14030 | 822-1010-2120 - Terminate Interconnect cables |
| **825-1003-2120  2120-BLD-1155 - UPS - Slurry Prep Tower E-House Line 1** | |
| MEC-27-12-7630 | 825-1003-2120 - Terminate lighting cables |
| MEC-27-12-7330 | 825-1003-2120 - Terminate Instrumentation cables |
| MEC-27-12-7130 | 825-1003-2120 - Terminate Control cables |
| MEC-27-12-7530 | 825-1003-2120 - Terminate Interconnect cables |
| MEC-27-12-7430 | 825-1003-2120 - Terminate 600V cables |
| **738-1003-2120  2120-BKD-1155 - PCS - Slurry Prep Tower E-House Line 1** | |
| MEC-27-12-13130 | 738-1003-2120 - Terminate Instrumentation cables |
| MEC-27-12-13230 | 738-1003-2120 - Terminate Control cables |
| **733-1003-2120  2120-BLD-1155 - PSD/ESD- Slurry Prep Tower E-House Line 1** | |
| MEC-27-12-5530 | 733-1003-2120 - Terminate lighting cables |
| MEC-27-12-5030 | 733-1003-2120 - Terminate Control cables |
| MEC-27-12-5230 | 733-1003-2120 - Terminate Instrumentation cables |

# How to display and correct activities with necks

When you update schedules with multiple actual start dates, I am sure you have seen activity bars, which go all the way to the data date on the left and then restart sometime in the future. If you enable the Activity non-work interval option in the bar necking settings, graphically you will see a thin bar that would start at the data date and extend until the activity restart date. There are three main reasons for necking or apparent non-work interval on an activity:

a) an activity in progress has been suspended in the activity status window.

b) an activity has a predecessor with an FF relationship and the remaining duration of this predecessor (+ any applicable lag) is longer than the remaining duration of this activity.

c) an activity started out of sequence - say, it has a predecessor with a FS relationship, which is not complete, but this activity has already started.

Cases B and C have an adverse impact on our logic, labor distribution and completion forecast, and it might be a good idea to filter in such activities and check/revise their logic and/or remaining durations.

1. Set up the following filter to display all necked activities:

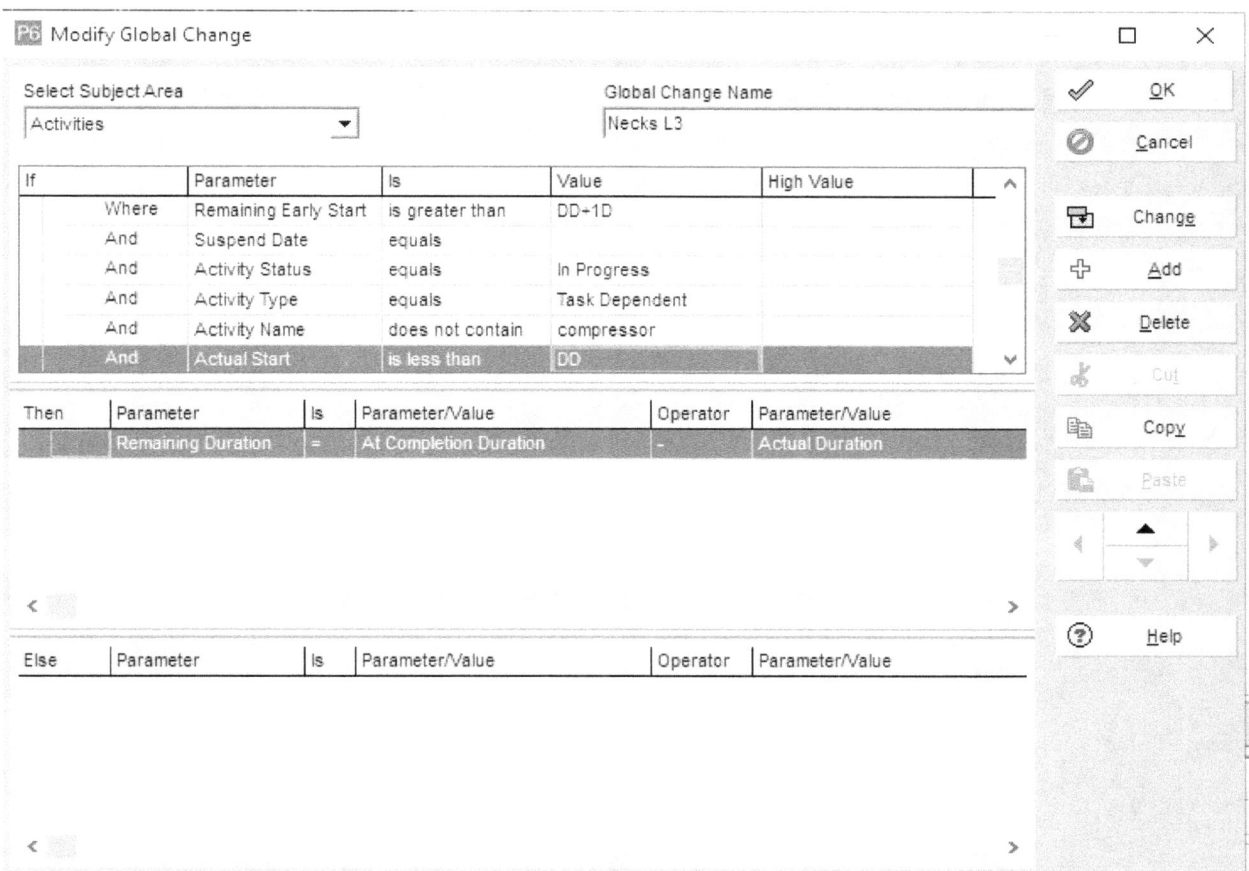

Notes:

- If you need to filter in only activities with necks larger than a certain number of days, change the parameter in the Value column on the first line to DD+XD, where X is the length of the neck in days.

- We have filtered out activities with Actual start date after the Data Date because such activities will also have Remaining Early Start date greater than the Data Date and have "In progress" status but cannot have any necking – Actual start dates after the Data Date are usually caused by progress imports from a progress tracking system, see Chapter "How to link your schedule to a progress tracking system" in this book.

- Remaining Early start is the date when the work can resume after the Data Date. On activities without a neck this date is equal to the Data Date, on necked activities this date represents work restart after the neck.

2. Check your schedule for out-of-sequence logic – see my tip "How to find all out-of-sequence relationships in a large network."

3. Once your out-of-sequence logic has been cleared, you might want to address the necks caused by FF relationships described in item C above. You can look at each of them individually after running the above filter again or close the non-work gaps automatically using a Global change. If you choose to run a Global change to get rid of the necks selected based on your criteria, do the following:

a) Add/assign a copy of your current project as a baseline.

b) Display the following columns: "BL Project Finish" and "Variance - BL Project Finish Date".

    a. Go to Tools > Global Change and set up the following global change:

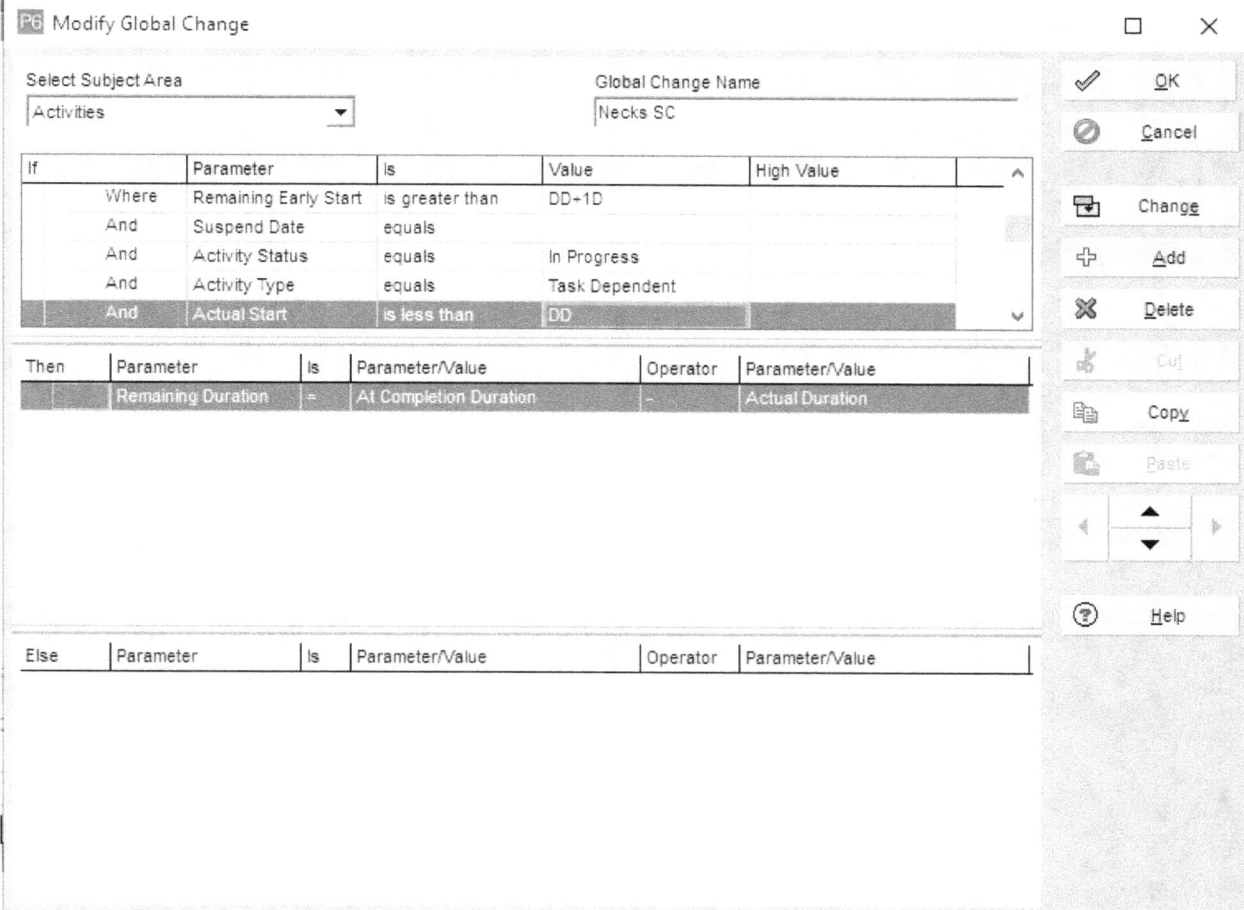

Notes:

- You can add other selection criteria in the upper portion of the Global Change window to include/exclude activities like you do in a normal task filter.

- This Global Change will only close the gaps caused by FF relationships as described in section B above. If your necks are caused by out-of-sequence logic, it will simply increase the remaining durations.

c) Run the global change, calculate (F9) your schedule, and apply the filter below:

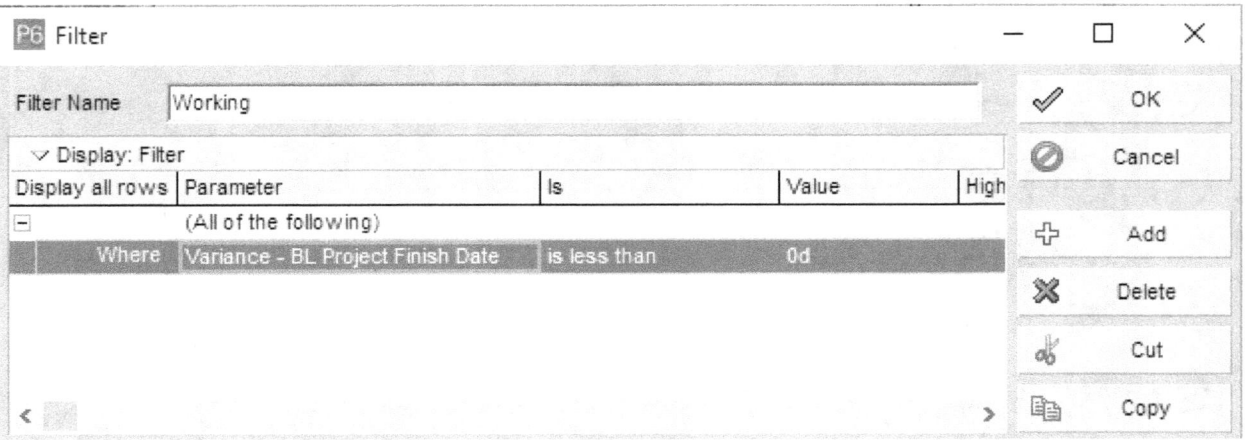

d) Check the filtered in activities and make the necessary corrections. Most probably variances on them will be caused by out-of-sequence logic that you have missed.

Andrei Sannikov
Tip of the day

23-Nov-14 12:00

## How to split a schedule into separate projects

When we work with large projects sometimes, it is a good idea to segregate a portion of it into a separate file and establish inter-project links between this new project and our main schedule so we can issue it to someone who has no access to our P6 server (e.g. a contractor). We can then incorporate their updates using the method described in my tip called "How to merge multiple projects and how to maintain inter-project links after export/import".

1. Organize the schedule you intend to split by WBS and make sure all activities you intend to place into a new project are located in the same WBS level. You can display WBS in a column to quickly change WBS on a particular activity or a group of activities using Fill Down function - you should disable automatic reorganization first for that (User preferences > Applications> uncheck "Reorganize automatically").

2. Make sure all project calendars are changed to Global, project activity codes (as opposed to Global) will not move to the new project - if you need them, either change them to global as well or import them via Excel later.

3. Make two copies of the schedule you are about to split. One copy will be used as a backup in case something goes wrong.

4. Open one of the copies and delete all the activities - it might be a good idea to change the name of this empty project to avoid confusion, I normally add the word "Shell" at the end of the project name.

5. Go to WBS view and delete all WBS levels below the first level representing the project.

6. Hold Ctrl key and select the project we are splitting and the empty shell project with your mouse to open them at the same time.

7. Go to WBS view and select the WBS level(s) containing activities you want to segregate into a separate project:

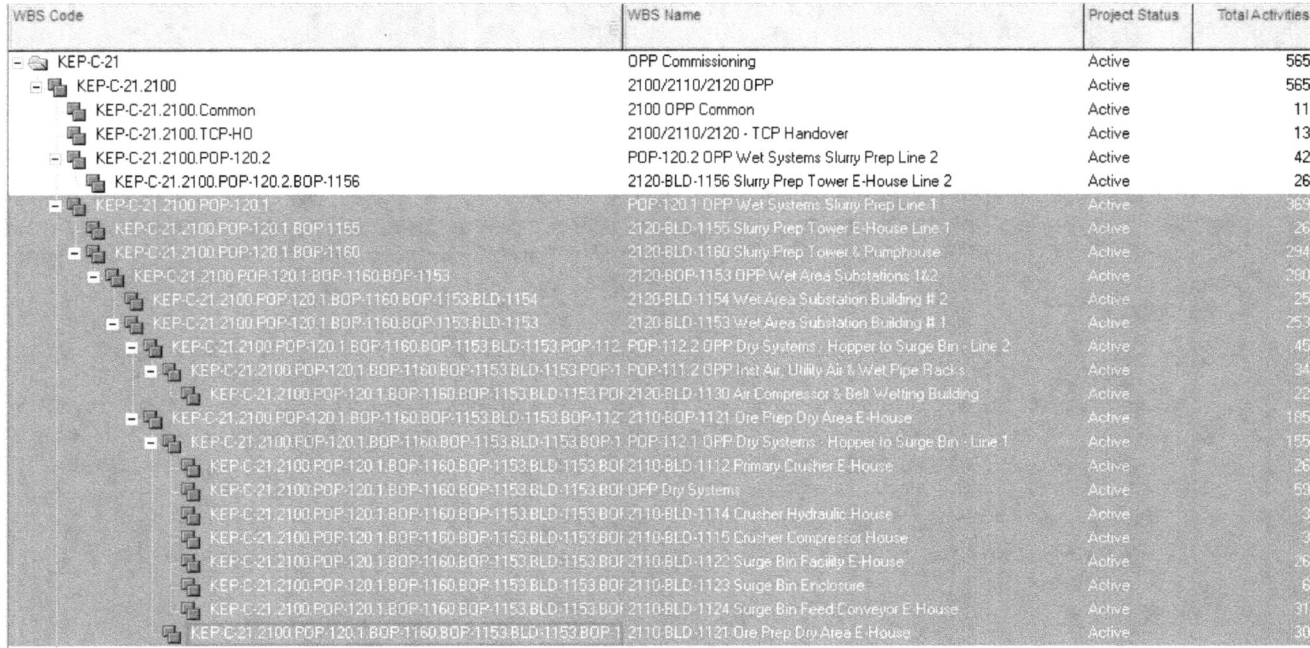

Right click > Cut

8) Go to your empty target project:

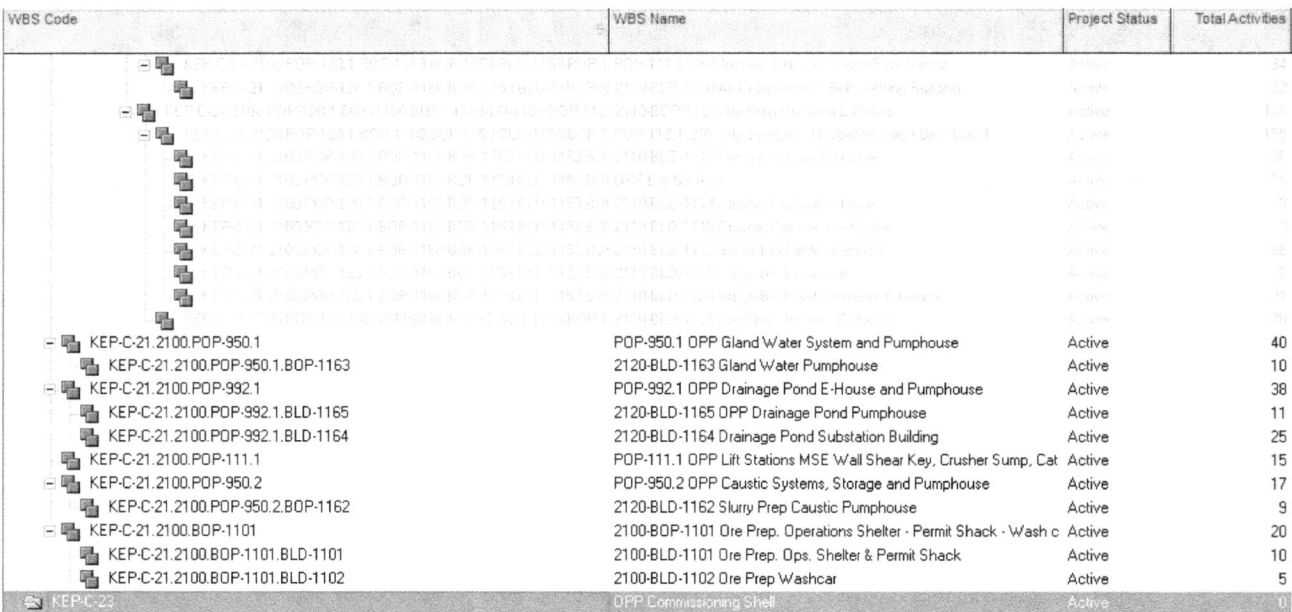

Right click > paste:

| WBS Code | WBS Name | Project Status | Total Activities |
|---|---|---|---|
| KEP-C-21.2100.POP-992.1.BLD-1164 | 2120-BLD-1164 Drainage Pond Substation Building | Active | 25 |
| KEP-C-21.2100.POP-111.1 | POP-111.1 OPP Lift Stations MSE Wall Shear Key, Crusher Sump, Cat | Active | 15 |
| KEP-C-21.2100.POP-950.2 | POP-950.2 OPP Caustic Systems, Storage and Pumphouse | Active | 17 |
| KEP-C-21.2100.POP-950.2.BOP-1162 | 2120-BLD-1162 Slurry Prep Caustic Pumphouse | Active | 9 |
| KEP-C-21.2100.BOP-1101 | 2100-BOP-1101 Ore Prep. Operations Shelter - Permit Shack - Wash c | Active | 20 |
| KEP-C-21.2100.BOP-1101.BLD-1101 | 2100-BLD-1101 Ore Prep. Ops. Shelter & Permit Shack | Active | 10 |
| KEP-C-21.2100.BOP-1101.BLD-1102 | 2100-BLD-1102 Ore Prep Washcar | Active | 5 |
| KEP-C-23 | OPP Commissioning Shell | Active | 369 |
| KEP-C-23.POP-120.1 | POP-120.1 OPP Wet Systems Slurry Prep Line 1 | Active | 369 |
| KEP-C-23.POP-120.1.BOP-1155 | 2120-BLD-1155 Slurry Prep Tower E-House Line 1 | Active | 26 |
| KEP-C-23.POP-120.1.BOP-1160 | 2120-BLD-1160 Slurry Prep Tower & Pumphouse | Active | 294 |
| KEP-C-23.POP-120.1.BOP-1160.BOP-1153 | 2120-BOP-1153 OPP Wet Area Substations 1&2 | Active | 280 |
| KEP-C-23.POP-120.1.BOP-1160.BOP-1153.BLD-1154 | 2120-BLD-1154 Wet Area Substation Building # 2 | Active | 25 |
| KEP-C-23.POP-120.1.BOP-1160.BOP-1153.BLD-1153 | 2120-BLD-1153 Wet Area Substation Building # 1 | Active | 253 |
| KEP-C-23.POP-120.1.BOP-1160.BOP-1153.BLD-1153.POP-112.2 | POP-112.2 OPP Dry Systems - Hopper to Surge Bin - Line 2 | Active | 45 |
| KEP-C-23.POP-120.1.BOP-1160.BOP-1153.BLD-1153.POP-112.2.POF | POP-111.2 OPP Inst Air, Utility Air & Wet Pipe Racks | Active | 34 |
| KEP-C-23.POP-120.1.BOP-1160.BOP-1153.BLD-1153.POP-112.2.F | 2120-BLD-1130 Air Compressor & Belt Wetting Building | Active | 22 |
| KEP-C-23.POP-120.1.BOP-1160.BOP-1153.BLD-1153.BOP-1121 | 2110-BOP-1121 Ore Prep Dry Area E-House | Active | 185 |
| KEP-C-23.POP-120.1.BOP-1160.BOP-1153.BLD-1153.BOP-1121.POF | POP-112.1 OPP Dry Systems - Hopper to Surge Bin - Line 1 | Active | 155 |
| KEP-C-23.POP-120.1.BOP-1160.BOP-1153.BLD-1153.BOP-1121.P | 2110-BLD-1112 Primary Crusher E-House | Active | 26 |
| KEP-C-23.POP-120.1.BOP-1160.BOP-1153.BLD-1153.BOP-1121.P | OPP Dry Systems | Active | 59 |
| KEP-C-23.POP-120.1.BOP-1160.BOP-1153.BLD-1153.BOP-1121.P | 2110-BLD-1114 Crusher Hydraulic House | Active | 3 |
| KEP-C-23.POP-120.1.BOP-1160.BOP-1153.BLD-1153.BOP-1121.P | 2110-BLD-1115 Crusher Compressor House | Active | 3 |
| KEP-C-23.POP-120.1.BOP-1160.BOP-1153.BLD-1153.BOP-1121.P | 2110-BLD-1122 Surge Bin Facility E-House | Active | 26 |
| KEP-C-23.POP-120.1.BOP-1160.BOP-1153.BLD-1153.BOP-1121.P | 2110-BLD-1123 Surge Bin Enclosure | Active | 6 |
| KEP-C-23.POP-120.1.BOP-1160.BOP-1153.BLD-1153.BOP-1121.P | 2110-BLD-1124 Surge Bin Feed Conveyor E-House | Active | 31 |
| KEP-C-23.POP-120.1.BOP-1160.BOP-1153.BLD-1153.BOP-1121.BLD | 2110-BLD-1121 Ore Prep Dry Area E-House | Active | 30 |

Now we have 2 projects linked between each other, if we open both at the same time, we can still sort/filter them using the global codes we had in the original project prior to splitting; we can check one of them out and issue to a third party for updating etc.

Note: if you make a mistake by placing an activity in the wrong project, open both of them at the same time, organize by project and WBS and cut/paste the activities you want to move between projects in the activity view. Alternatively, you can display WBS in a column (with both project open), click on WBS name and change it to WBS of the project where you want to move this activity in the Select WBS dialogue box:

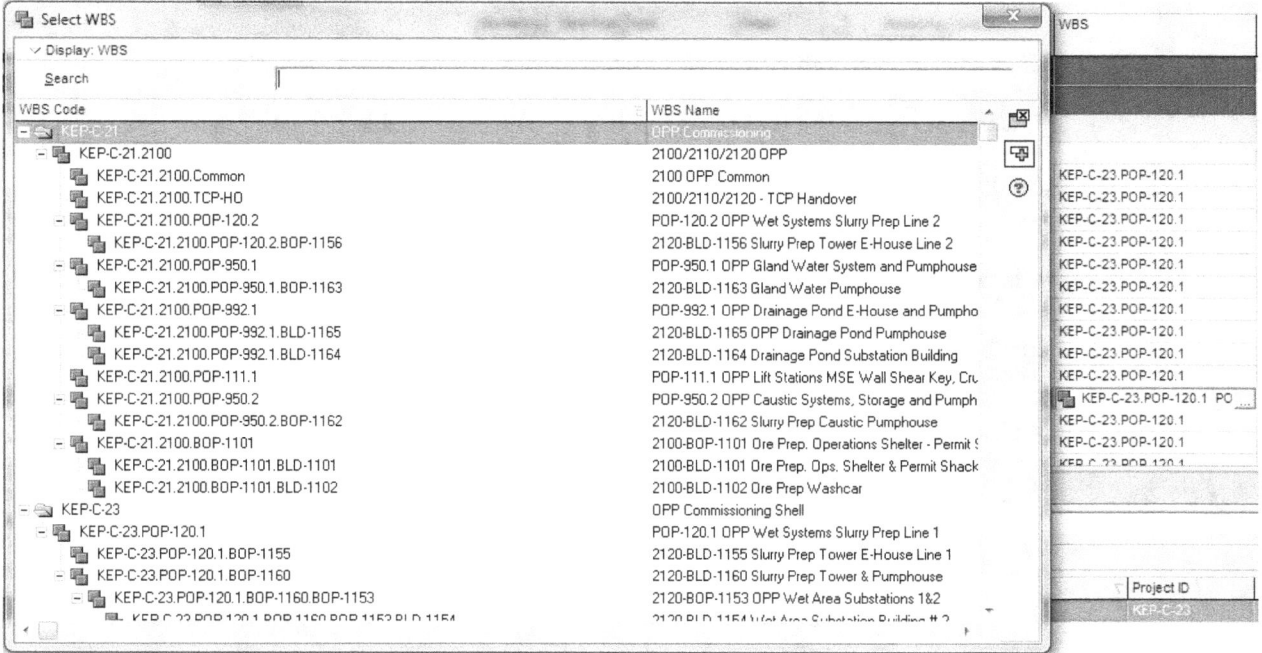

If your schedule is based on codes and all activities are under the same WBS level or if it is not important to maintain existing WBS levels in the project activities will be moved to, there is a much simpler way to move some of the activities into a separate project and preserve the links between the new and existing projects.

1) Create a new project. If your project uses EPS codes, do it in the same node or in a node these EPS codes apply to.

2) Hold Ctrl and select the new project and the one you intend to split.

3) Open both projects.

4) Filter in activities you intend to move or organize your schedule in such a way that all of them are grouped together.

5) Add the WBS column. If your layout is organized by WBS, click on the Disable Auto-Reorganization button or press Shift + F12

6) Click on the WBS cell on the first activity – this will open the Display WBS dialogue:

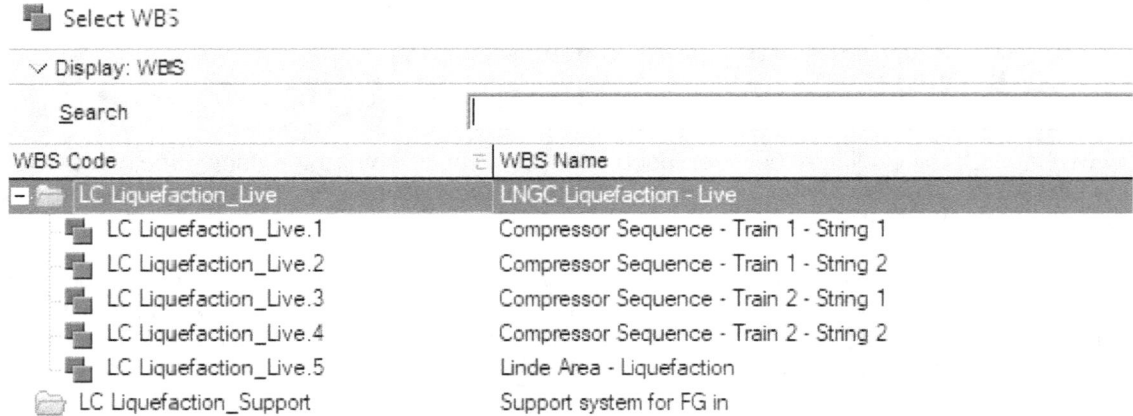

The project at the bottom of the above list is the one we will be moving activities to.

7) Highlight it with your mouse and click on the Select button or double click on it.

8) Use the Fill down function in the WBS column to assign all activities you intend to move to this new WBS/Project.

Note: When projects are split, all Project Activity codes assignments that you had in the "mother" project will be lost in the new project. To reinstate them follow instructions in my tip "How to reinstate deleted activities from a baseline" later in this book.

22-Apr-15 09:55

# How to generate schedule scenarios without using reflections

When we work with different schedule scenarios the most common method is to create reflections of your master file, modify these reflections and then merge all or some of the changes with the master project to produce a new baseline or forecast. This works when your master file is not changed or updated while you are working on the reflection(s), however, if it is not the case and someone else is updating progress or changing dates in the master project you might lose these changes when you merge your reflection into the master. There are other complications like changes to the logic - if you delete logical links in the reflection project, they are not deleted automatically during the merging process, you will need to go to your master file and delete them manually; you either merge all changes or select each activity you want to merge and if changes are numerous you will have a lot of clicking to do; if changes to the logic conflict with what you had in your master file you will probably end up with loops etc. etc. I think you get it - this method is far from being perfect. Let us look at possible alternatives.

1. Make a copy of your master file and start modifying it as required to produce your re-forecast, scenario or whatever.

2. If your master file needs to be updated at the same time, try to limit these changes to progress, durations and actualizing start/finish dates without changing the logic and try to keep track of updated activities in a user or a code field. If you want P6 to keep track of these changes, run a global change to make all planned start and finish dates equal to start and finish respectively, save a copy of your master file as a user baseline and filter in all the changes using variance filters - unfortunately there is no built-in variance filter to compare actuals - you will need to display baseline actual labor units in a column, dump your schedule into Excel, add a formula to calculate/filter all the activities where actuals are higher than in the baseline, export your activities into Excel using an export layout with a user field (integer) column displayed and then populate this column with actuals variances using a lookup function. The resulting file can be imported back into P6 and you will be able to filter in all the activities that have been progressed in the master project after you copied it.

3. Once the update of your master file is complete, you might want to transfer these changes to the project you have been working on to produce a new scenario or re-forecast. This can be done using one of the two methods below:

A) Update baseline.

1. When you are ready to transfer progress data from your master file make a copy of your scenario project and assign it as a baseline to your master project. Keep the original file as a backup in case something goes wrong.

2. Go to Project > Maintain Baseline. Highlight the project we have just assigned and click on Update.

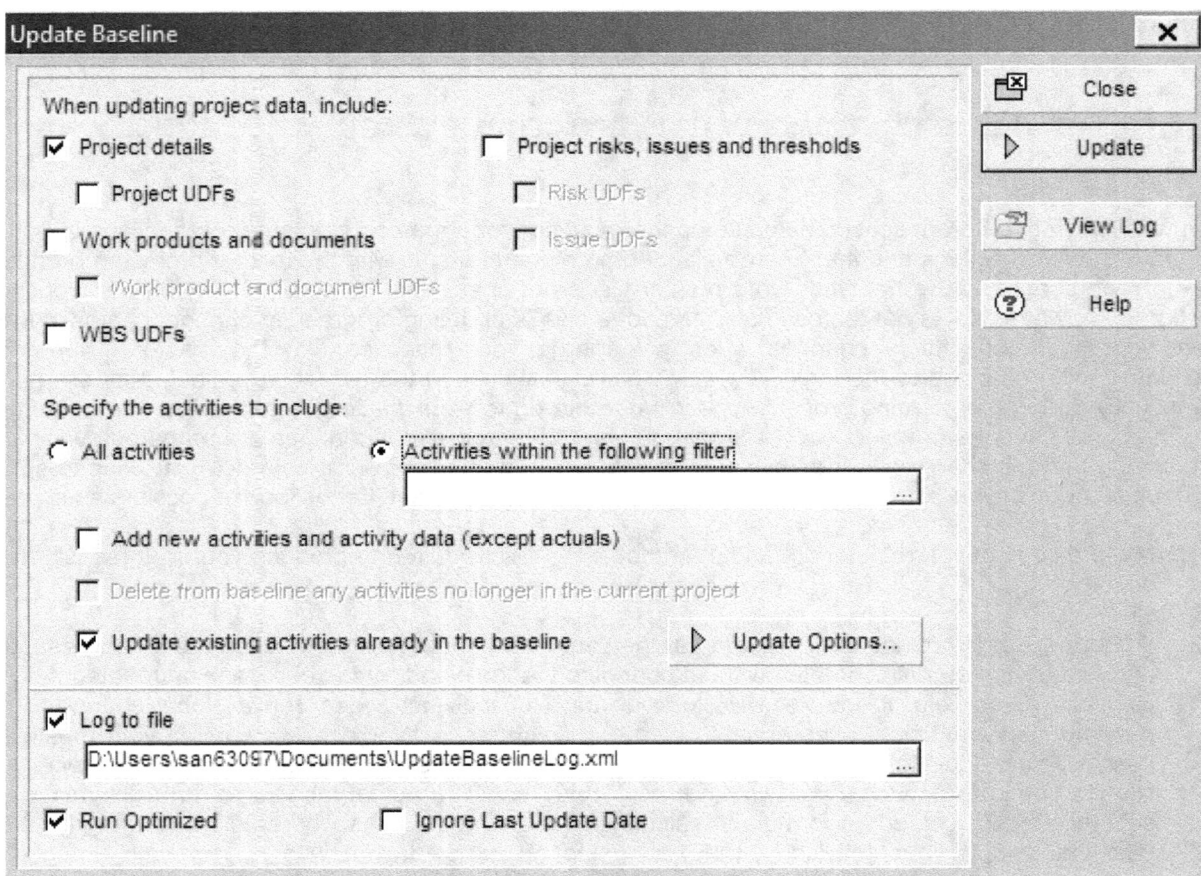

If you have created a filter for progressed activities in step 2 above, click Activities within the following filter and select the filter you need. If not, keep the default setting - All activities

3. Click on Update Options.

Update options would depend on the type of changes you have made to your master i.e. progress only or also changes in duration, logic, constraints etc.

As a minimum, you should use the following options:

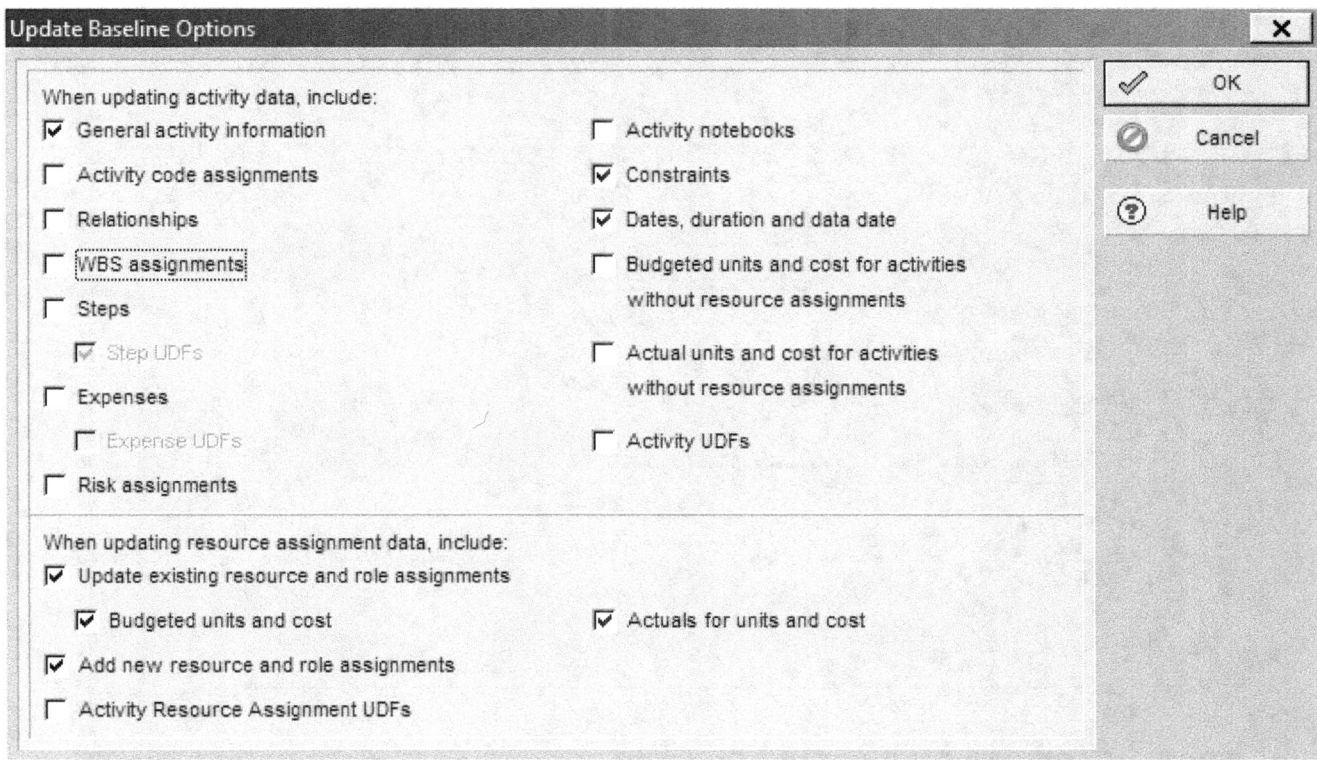

If your update does not return any error messages, restore this updated baseline and continue using it for developing your scenario or re-forecast.

B) Export - import

1. Open your master file and go to Export > Excel > Resource assignments

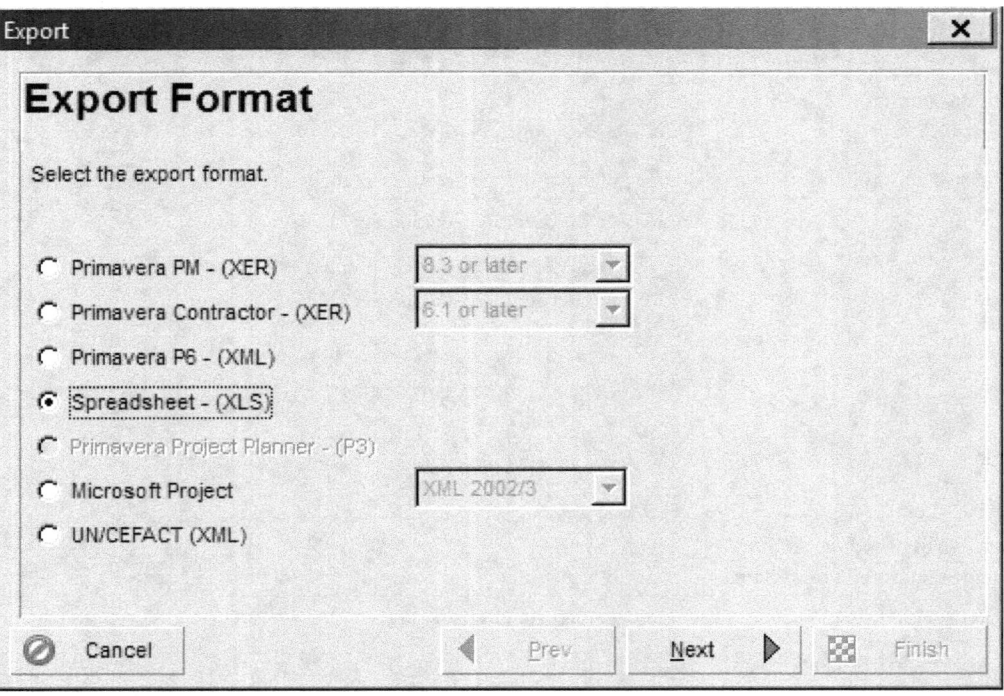

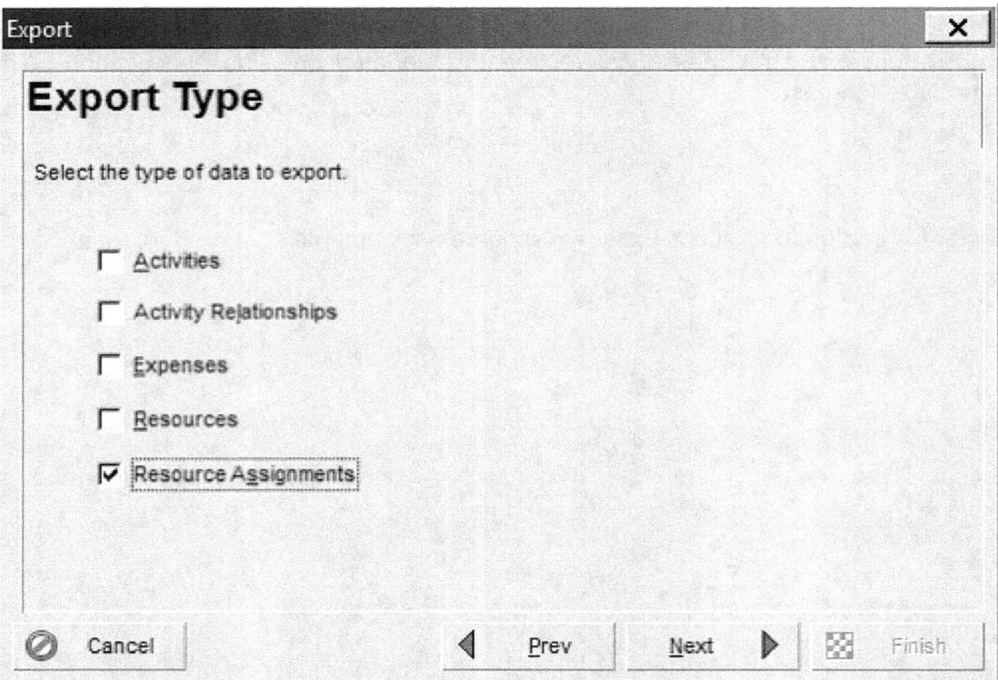

2. Create an export template with the following columns:

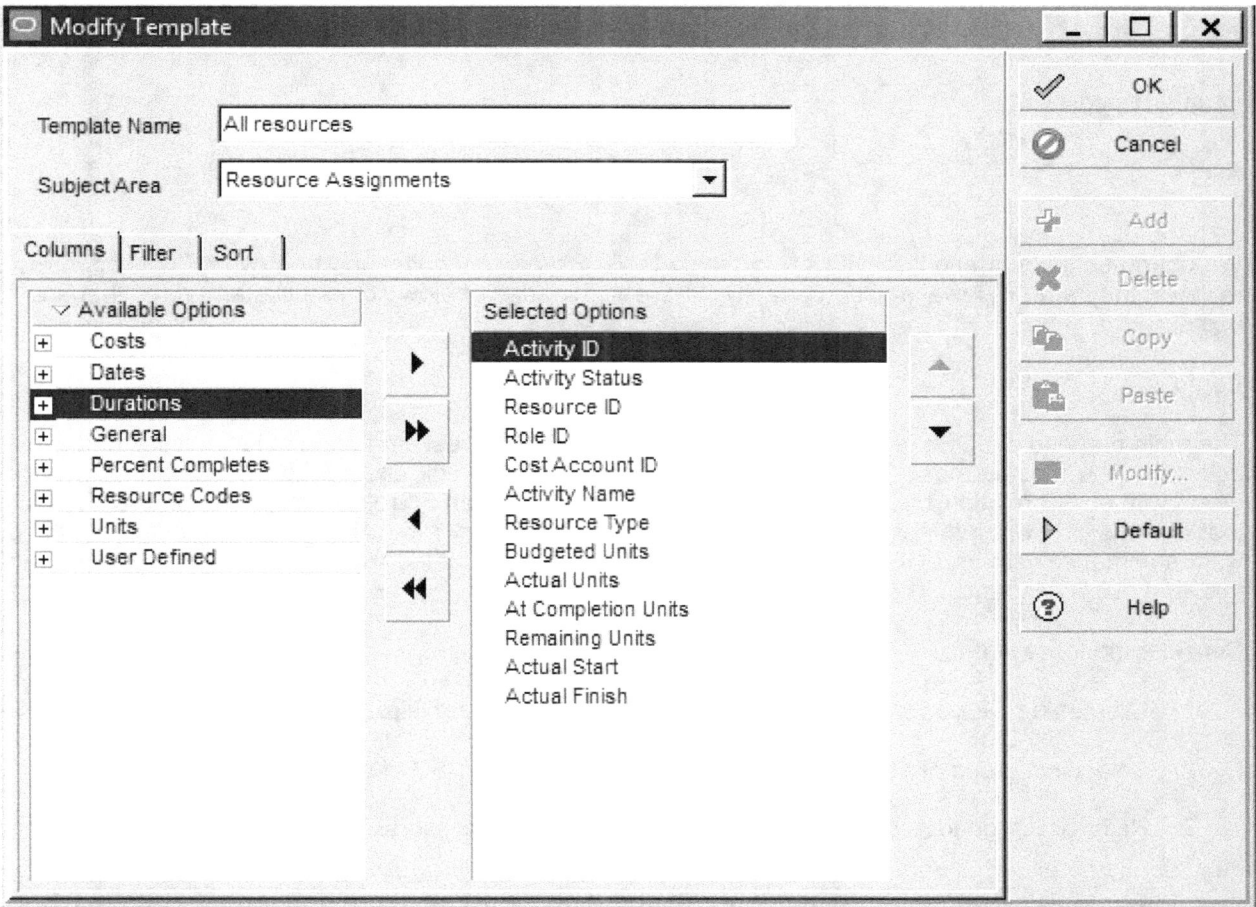

You can set up a filter if you want to exclude specific resources from your export.

3. Once the export is complete, close the project and open your scenario/re-forecast project. Go to Import > Excel > Resource Assignments. Locate the file we have just created from the Select File to Import dialogue, click Next then Finish.

Note that this import would include progress/budget data only. A different export/import will be required to update constrained dates or durations if such changes have been made to your master project.

Andrei Sannikov
Tip of the day

# Level of efforts – tricks and rules

14-May-15 10:41

Part 1

We often use level of effort activities to produce Level 2 type schedules and from what I noticed in my schedule reviews, they are not always used correctly. I have summarized below some tricks and rules that you might find useful:

**Logic**

The main purpose of LOE's is to show at a summary level the earliest start and the latest finish dates in a group of activities. The most common mistake many planners make is to link an LOE to the earliest start activity in this group with an SS relationship and to the latest finish activity with an FF relationship. The problem with this logic is that it works only when things go exactly as planned, which is very rarely the case. If an activity in the group you want summarize with an LOE starts earlier than the one you assumed would the first your LOE will not capture this start out of sequence. The same goes for finish dates.

Consider the following:

1. Create an LOE you want to use to summarize a group of activities, copy or write down its ID.

2. Select this group of activities with the mouse (holding Cntrl or Shift key)

3. Right click > go to Assign (in the drop down menu) > Successors...

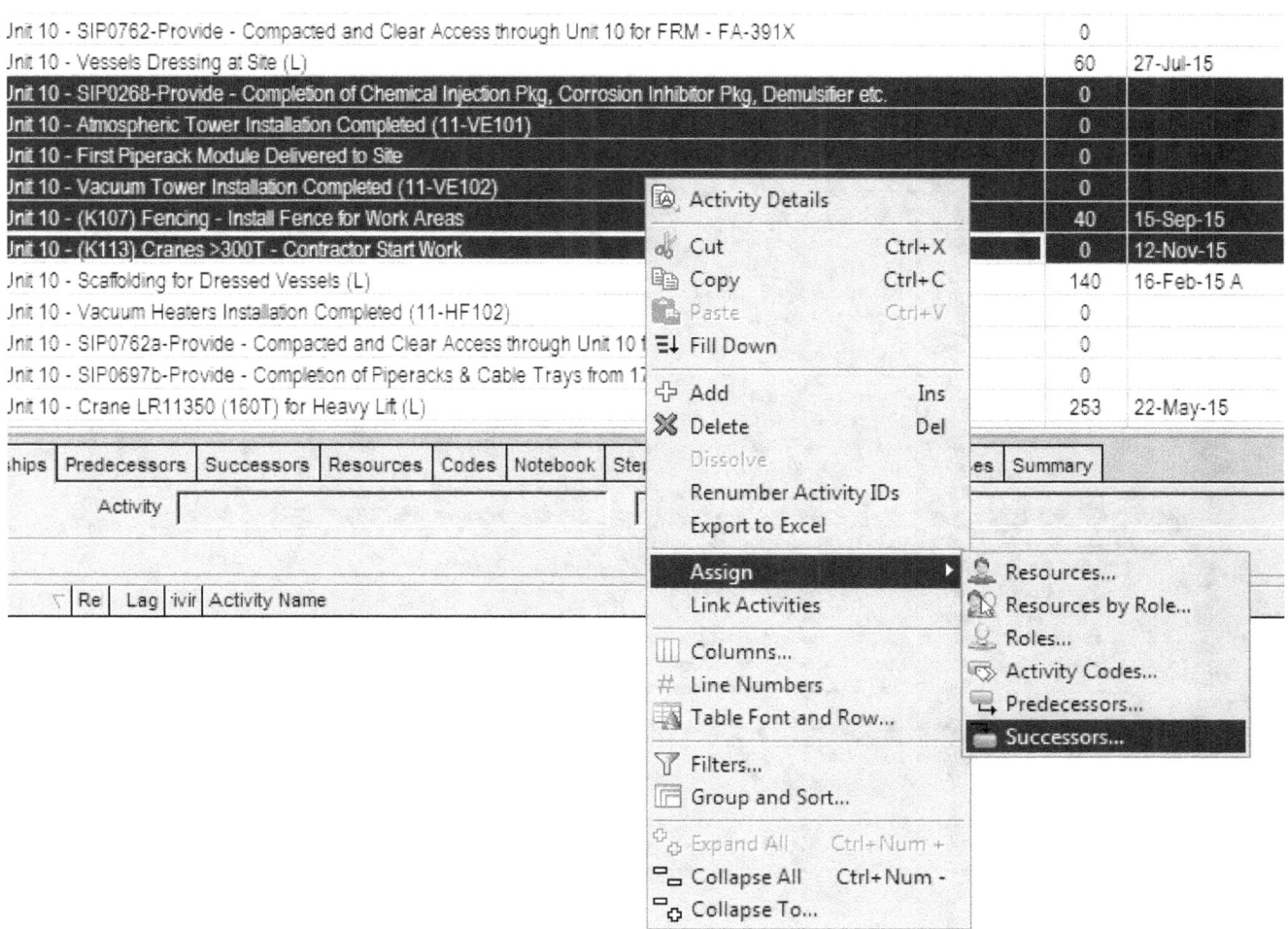

4. Find the LOE you have created in the Assign successors window:

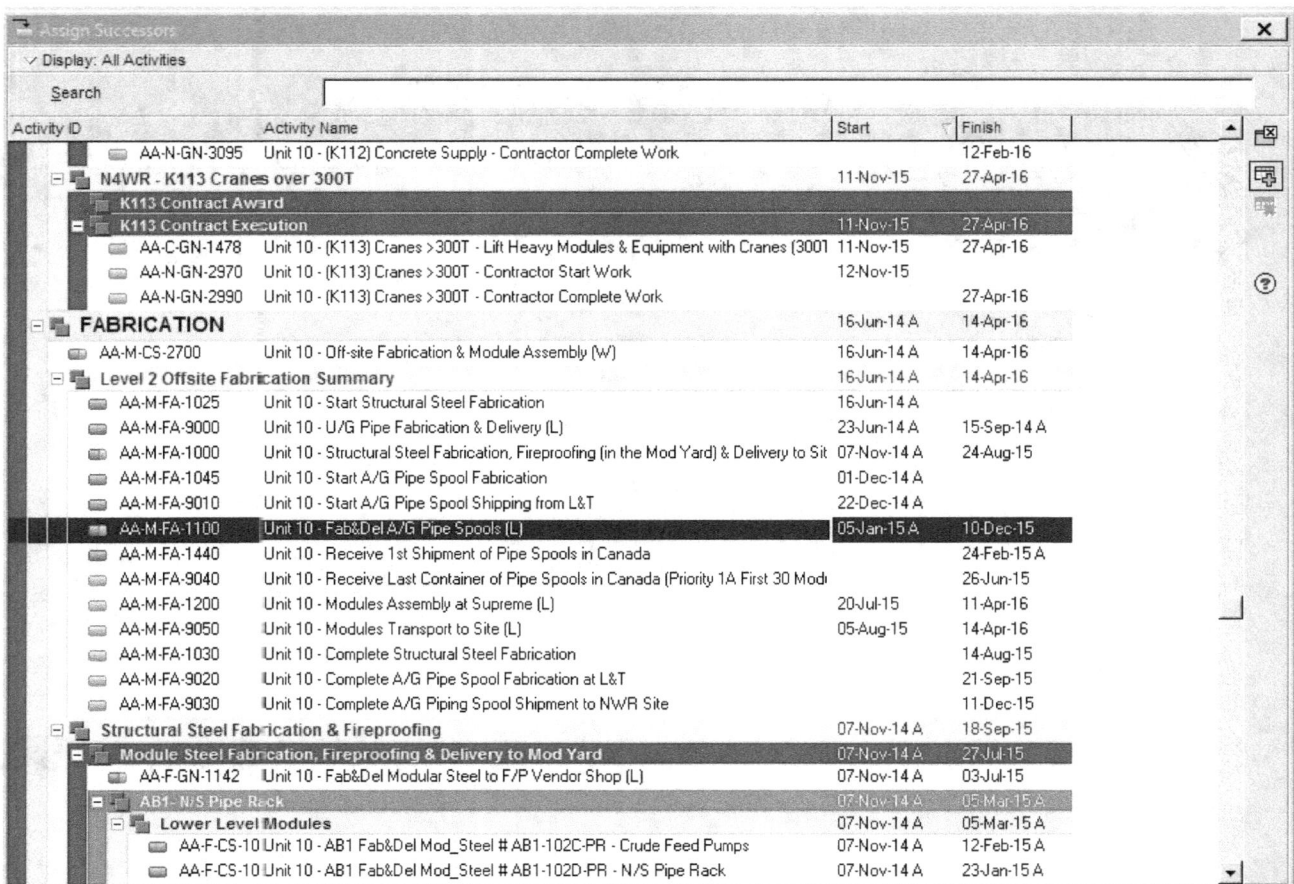

... and click on the Assign icon (green cross) <u>three</u> times.

5. This will assign each activity in the group you want to summarize with your LOE as a predecessor with SS, FF, and FS relationships.

6. Go to your LOE, display relationships in the bottom view, sort by Relationship type and delete all FS relationships.

7. When you hit F9, your LOE will always have the earliest start and the latest finish date in the selected group of activities. You don't need any successors:

Andrei Sannikov
Tip of the day

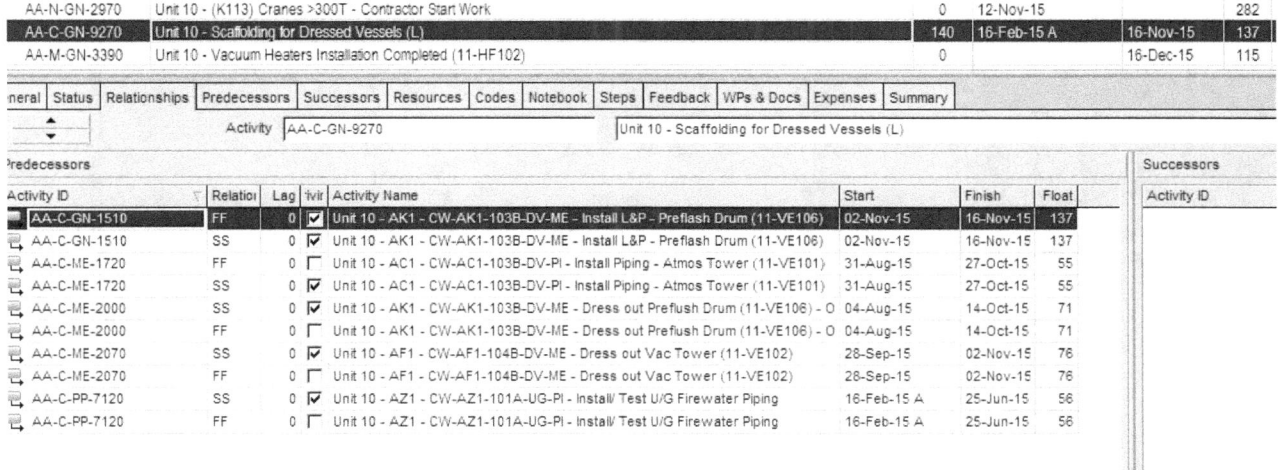

**Float**

1. Your schedule float is typically based on the finish float and the float displayed on your LOE will correspond to the float of its predecessor activity that finishes last. See example above.

2. You might see a minor difference if your LOE and the activity "driving" its finish date are on different calendars. If this float figure is important for your L2 (or whatever) make sure the LOE is on the same calendar as its drivers

3. Try to avoid linking one LOE to another as it impacts float calculation on the successor LOE and the resulting numbers would be impossible to explain.

**Resources**

LOE can be loaded with all types of resources, however, it is not recommended to do so for two reasons:

1. As start and finish dates in the group of activities you summarize with an LOE change your resources will be spread throughout their entire duration (including periods of inactivity), which will result in unrealistic resource profiles.

2. For some strange reason P6 sets late start dates on LOE equal to the earliest actual start of its predecessor (or to the next working day in the calendar if the predecessor actual start falls in a non-working period) and if you need to plot a mean-value/mid-point curve from a schedule with multiple resource-loaded LOE's in progress you will see that it simply does not work because your LOE in progress with positive floats will have remaining late units in the past - something you would normally see on tasks with negative floats. See example below:

Andrei Sannikov
Tip of the day

24-May-15 11:32

Part 2

Some time ago I sent out a tip about level of effort activities (LOE) and one of the topics was about resources on LOE's in general and their strange behavior on LOE's in progress in particular. My advise was to avoid loading resources on this type of activities and one of the reason was resource distribution on the late curve. In most cases, these late units start from the actual start, which means that if you want to plot a mean value/mid-point curve you will need to exclude LOE's from your data dump and then add them manually etc.

However, sometimes it is not practical to remove resources (labor hours) from LOE's you already have in your schedule and re-distribute them among tasks and you face a difficult question - how to produce a mid-point curve for your upcoming re-forecast or re-baseline and keep your resource-loaded LOE's in progress in your data dump.

Here is a solution.

1. If you must have resources on LOE's try to keep the number of such activities to a reasonable minimum. Before proceeding have another look at your LOE's and decide if it is not better to add, say, a scaffolding resource to each vessel instead of having one scaffolding LOE stretching through the entire length of the project etc.

2. Create a layout containing only resource loaded LOE's in progress.

3. Go to the bottom view/resources tab. Right-click > Customize Resource Columns > Add "Drive Activity Dates".

4. Now you will see a check box in this column:

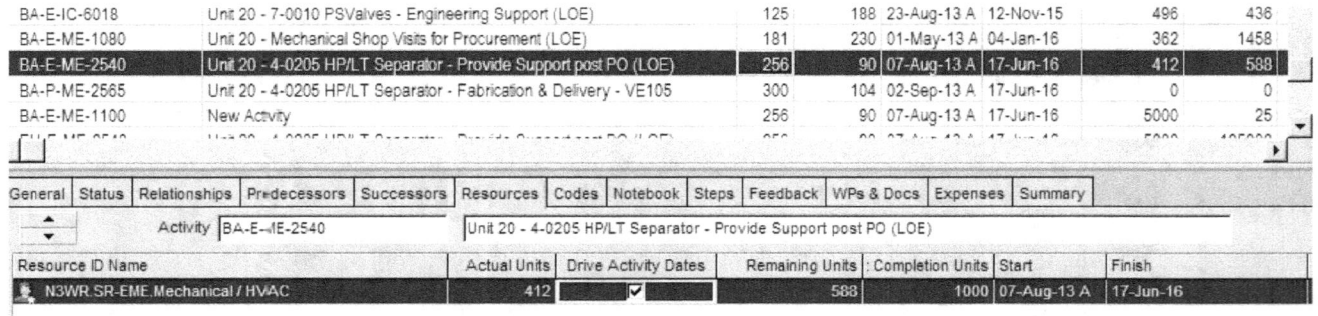

When this box is checked on LOE's, which is the default setting when you add a new resource, resource availability dates are aligned with the activity dates but the time distribution of late units is not done correctly - even if you have positive float on such an LOE (90 days) in the example above - you will see late units in the past, something you would normally expect when you have negative float:

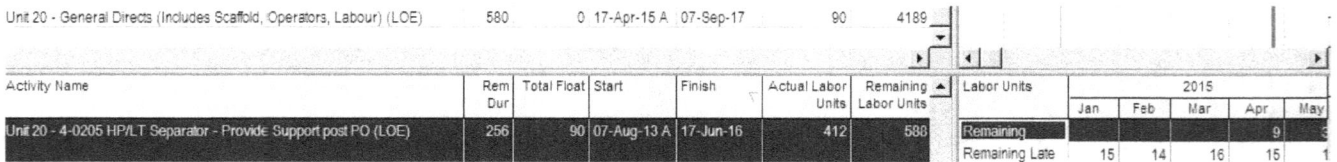

5. Uncheck this box and hit F9 again:

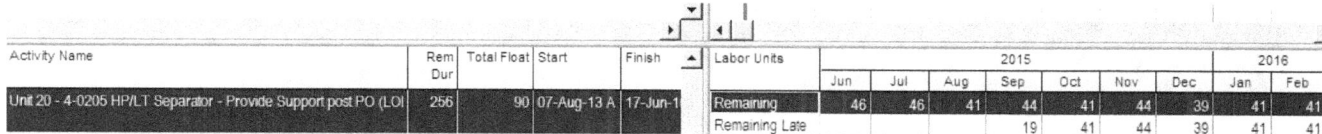

See the difference?

6. Once you have unchecked the Drive Activity Dates boxes on all LOE's in progress, hit F9 again, display the bottom view/resource tab and make sure resource start and finish dates are aligned with the activity dates. If not, correct resource dates manually and reschedule (F9) the project.

7. When you are done with your data dump you should probably return all the check boxes on LOE's to their original setting (checked) to make sure your regular resource profiles (which are based on remaining early units) are plotted correctly and repeat the drill explained above when the time is right for yet another re-forecast.

## How to make massive changes in logical sequence

18-May-15 14:38

Part 1

Those of you who worked with detailed L4 type schedules, I am sure, will agree that massive sequence changes is a planner's nightmare. Say, you have 200-300 modules linked between each other because this logic represents their planned installation sequence - like everything in your schedule (and in real life for that matter) this planned sequence will probably not stand the test of time and you will have to redo it over and over again, you will need to unlink and re-link all the impacted activities and will probably make a few mistakes in the process. Let us see if we can make this exercise a little less painful.

1. As a starting point, you will obviously need your revised sequence in a spreadsheet with new sequence numbers in a column against each activity.

2. Set up a filter in P6 to select activities that you want to re-sequence. In order the method described below to work properly you need to make sure these activities are easily identifiable by their activity names i.e. They need to have clear description of the work, phase and place like "Set module" + "Area" + "Contractor" etc. so you can clearly see what this activity is about in its description without checking WBS or codes. If your schedule has only generic activity names like "pull cables" or "electrical work" you should consider running global changes described in my earlier tips to add, say, area codes as a prefix to your activity names. If you use smart activity ID's containing all necessary information it might work as well but it is better to add all necessary details to the activity names to be on the safe side.

**Note: Make a backup copy of your schedule before you proceed in case something goes wrong during import.**

3. In P6 go to File > Export > Spreadsheet (XLS) > Activities > Create the following export template:

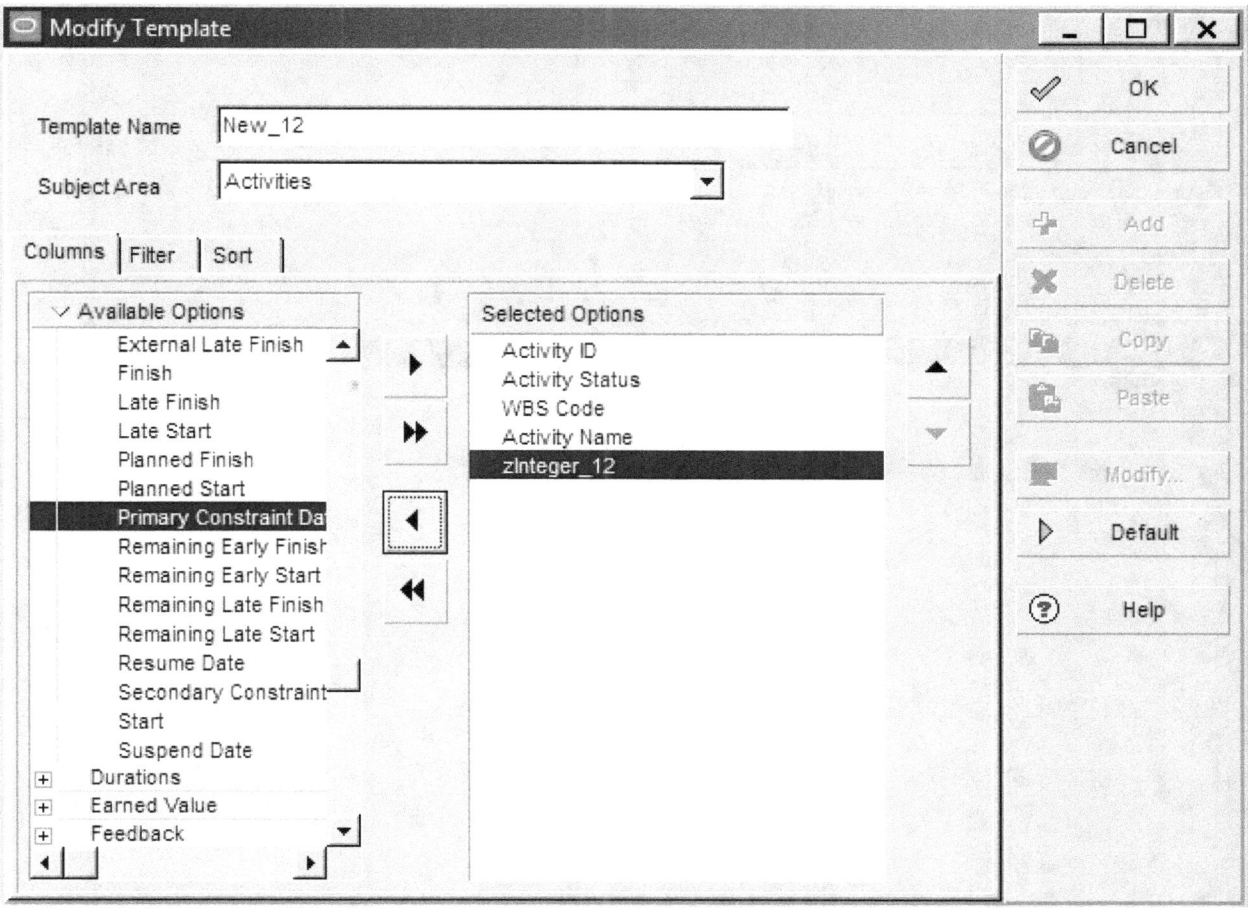

The last field is a user defined integer, you can create your own and call it "Revised sequence" if you have the necessary rights in your system.

Go to filter tab and apply the filter you created in Step 2 above.

4. In the resulting export spreadsheet use a lookup formula to populate the user defined integer field shown above with your new sequence numbers.

In the example below, I used MID function to extract module numbers from activity descriptions and then VLOOKUP to pull revised setting sequence from another table:

| task_code | status_code | wbs_id | task_name | | | | user_field_2241 | delete_record_flag |
|---|---|---|---|---|---|---|---|---|
| Activity ID | Activity Status | WBS Code | Activity Name | | | Mod ## | zInteger_12 | Delete This Row |
| BA-C-ME-2200 | Not Started | N4WR20.P-12.OS.BG1.1 | Unit 20 - CWP-BG1-102-B-EQ - Set Module | BG1-102 | B-EQ | BG1-102B-EQ | 152 | |
| BA-C-ME-3804 | Not Started | N4WR20.P-12.OS.BG1.1 | Unit 20 - CWP-BG1-102-C-EQ - Set Module | BG1-102 | C-EQ | BG1-102C-EQ | 153 | |
| BA-C-ME-3808 | Not Started | N4WR20.P-12.OS.BG1.1 | Unit 20 - CWP-BG1-103-B-EQ - Set Module | BG1-103 | B-EQ | BG1-103B-EQ | 151 | |
| BA-C-ME-4430 | Not Started | N4WR20.P-12.OS.BJ1.6 | Unit 20 - CWP-BJ1-120-B-SA - Set Module | BJ1-120 | B-SA | BJ1-120B-SA | 78 | |
| BA-C-ME-3311 | Not Started | N4WR20.P-12.OS.BJ1.6 | Unit 20 - CWP-BJ1-114-B-PR - Set Module | BJ1-114 | B-PR | BJ1-114B-PR | 80 | |
| BA-C-ME-4419 | Not Started | N4WR20.P-12.OS.BJ1.6 | Unit 20 - CWP-BJ1-119-C-PR - Set Module | BJ1-119 | C-PR | BJ1-119C-PR | 75 | |
| BA-C-ME-4423 | Not Started | N4WR20.P-12.OS.BJ1.6 | Unit 20 - CWP-BJ1-119-D-PR - Set Module | BJ1-119 | D-PR | BJ1-119D-PR | 76 | |

5. Save this spreadsheet, convert formulas into values and import it back into P6.

6. Go to back to File > Export > Spreadsheet (XLS) > Activity relationships > Create the following export template:

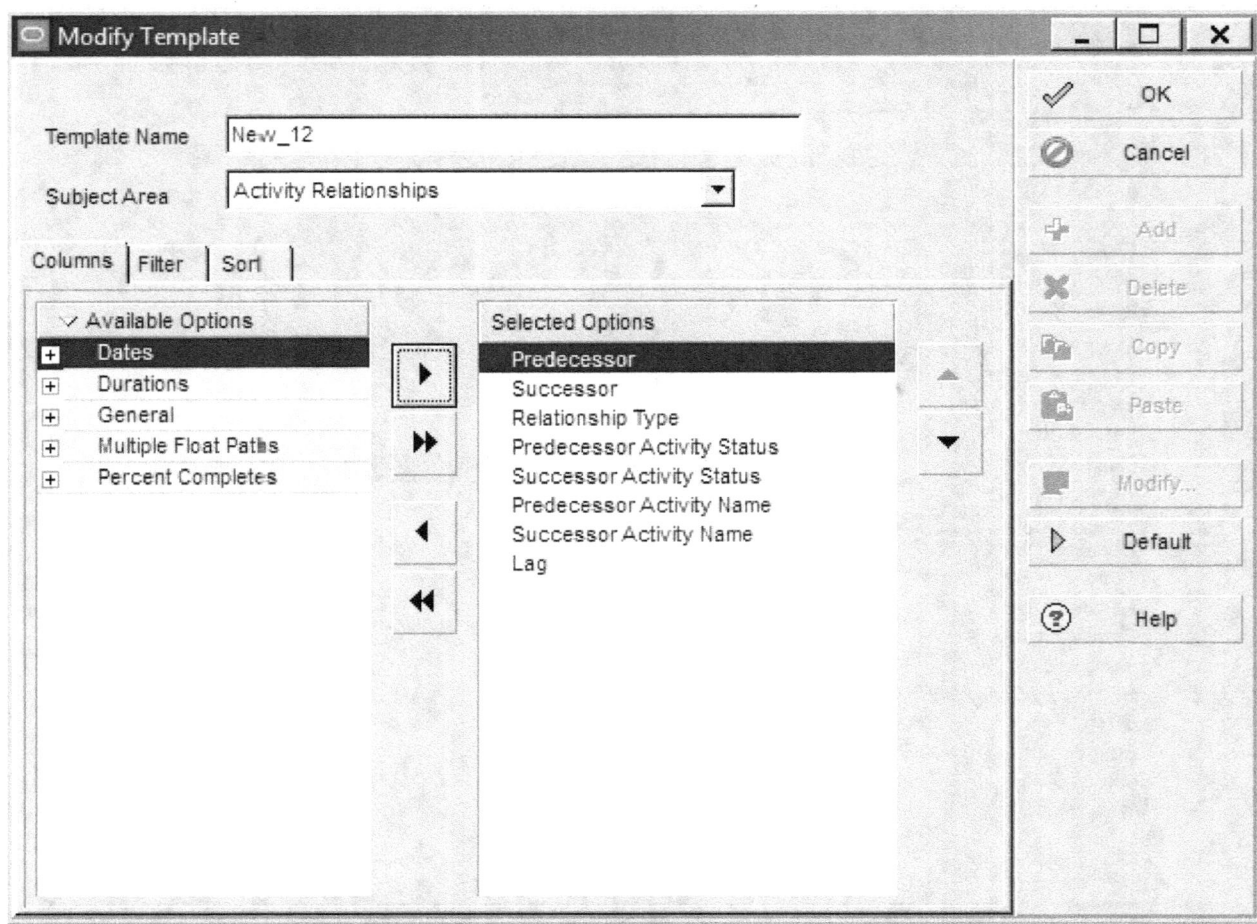

7. In the resulting spreadsheet use text filters in the Predecessor Activity Name and Successor Activity Name columns to display activities with relationships that you want to change - e.g. All module setting in a particular area or by a particular crew or contractor - this is where your well-defined activity descriptions come into play. In order to change the planned sequence we need to delete these relationships and replace them with news ones reflecting the new sequence. To delete put letter D in the Delete This Row column:

| pred_task_id | task_id | pred_type | predtask_task_name | task_task_name | lag_hr_cnt | delete_record_flag |
|---|---|---|---|---|---|---|
| Predecessor | Successor | Relationship Type | (*)Predecessor Activity Name | (*)Successor Activity Name | Lag(d) | Delete This Row |
| BA-C-ME-3428 | BA-C-ME-4403 | FS | Unit 20 - CWP-BH1-107-B-EQ - Set Module | Unit 20 - CWP-BJ1-102-G-SA - Set Module | 0 | D |
| BA-C-ME-3712 | BA-C-ME-3748 | FS | Unit 20 - CWP-BE1-105-D-EQ - Set Module | Unit 20 - CWP-BE1-110-B-EQ - Set Module | 0 | D |
| BA-C-ME-3941 | BA-C-ME-3432 | FS | Unit 20 - CWP-BE1-112-F-PR - Set Module | Unit 20 - CWP-BH1-107-C-EQ - Set Module | 0 | D |
| BA-C-ME-2050 | BA-C-ME-3760 | FS | Unit 20 - CWP-BE1-105-B-EQ - Set Module | Unit 20 - CWP-BE1-112-B-PR - Set Module | 0 | D |

Delete all rows other than those in which you put D in the Step above. Save the file and import it back into P6.

8. Go to Activity view; apply the filter set up in Step 2 above, display the user defined integer field (zinteger_12 in our example). Go to Group and Sort and remove all sorting:

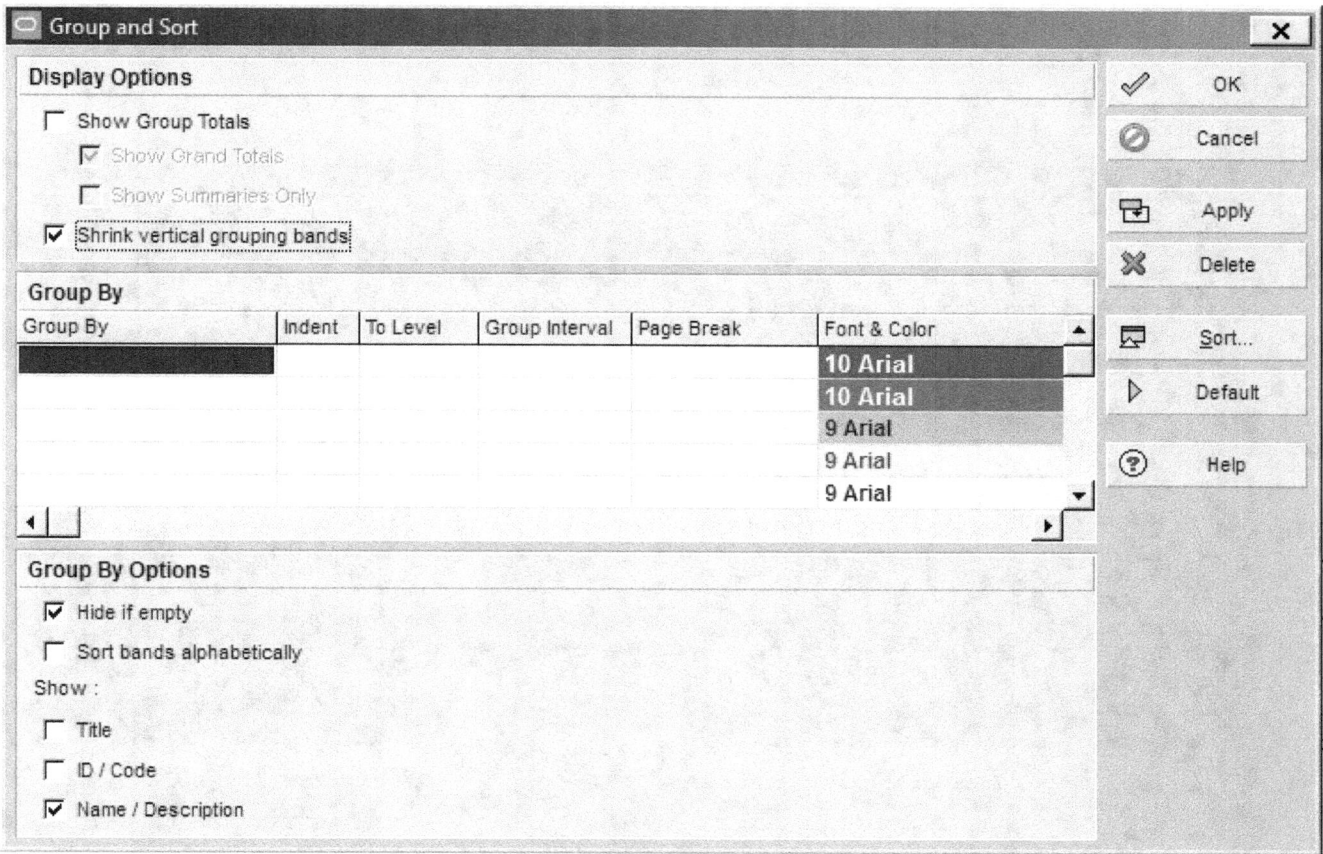

9. Click on the user integer column one time to sort the values in it in ascending order (smallest to largest). Select all activities in this view, right click and select Link Activities in the drop-down menu.

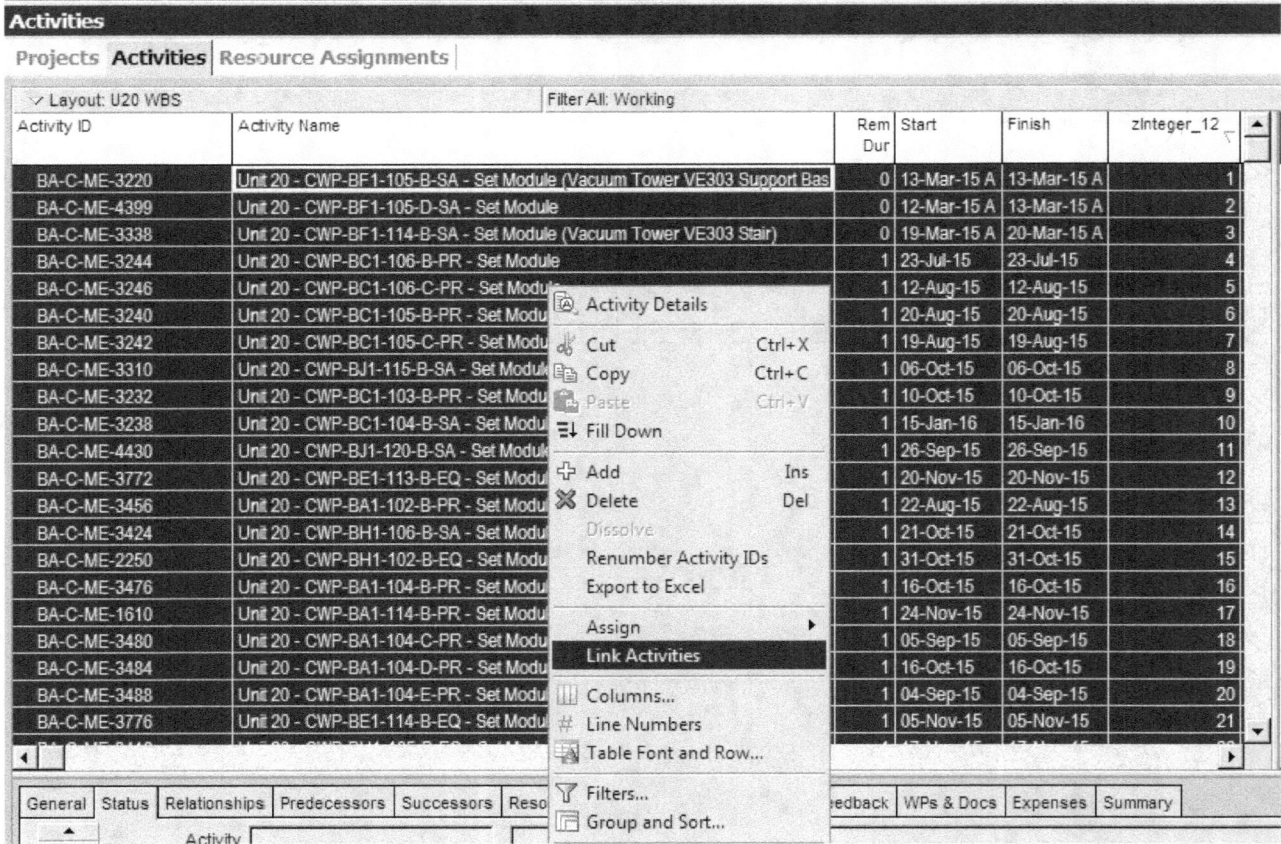

Part 2

A couple of years ago I sent out a tip explaining how to change the installation sequence of, say, modules via export/import. This method works when each installation activity is represented by a single task but sometimes you might have multiple activities for, say, several pipe-cleaning subsystems, which you need to arrange in a new order:

| Activity ID | Activity Name | Remaining Duration | MHRS | Start | Finish |
|---|---|---|---|---|---|
| ⊟ Spread 1 | | 214 | 7535 | 05-Jun-17 | 21-Sep-17 |
| ⊟ 12-INA-01 - Instrument Air | | 20 | 660 | 05-Jun-17 | 14-Jun-17 |
| ⊟ Pre-com Piping | | 20 | 660 | 05-Jun-17 | 14-Jun-17 |
| PC-12-INA-01-CFTT-1 | 12-INA-01 - TTCCC (construction to precom) | 0 | 0 | 05-Jun-17 | |
| PC-12-INA-01-CFS-01 | 12-INA-01 - Setup | 4 | 440 | 05-Jun-17 | 07-Jun-17 |
| PC-12-INA-01-CFC-01 | 12-INA-01 - Cleaning | 15 | 220 | 07-Jun-17 | 14-Jun-17 |
| PC-12-INA-01-CFT-02 | 12-INA-01 - Cleaning complete | 0 | 0 | | 14-Jun-17 |
| ⊟ 12-NIT-01 - Nitrogen | | 20 | 660 | 15-Jun-17 | 24-Jun-17 |
| ⊟ Pre-com Piping | | 20 | 660 | 15-Jun-17 | 24-Jun-17 |
| PC-12-NIT-01-CFTT-1 | 12-NIT-01 - TTCCC (construction to precom) | 0 | 0 | 15-Jun-17 | |
| PC-12-NIT-01-CFS-01 | 12-NIT-01 - Setup | 4 | 440 | 15-Jun-17 | 17-Jun-17 |
| PC-12-NIT-01-CFC-01 | 12-NIT-01 - Cleaning | 15 | 220 | 17-Jun-17 | 24-Jun-17 |
| PC-12-NIT-01-CFT-02 | 12-NIT-01 - Cleaning complete | 0 | 0 | | 24-Jun-17 |
| ⊟ 12-OMS-01 - Oil Mist System | | 32 | 990 | 28-Jul-17 | 12-Aug-17 |
| ⊟ Pre-com Piping | | 32 | 990 | 28-Jul-17 | 12-Aug-17 |
| PC-12-OMS-01-CFTT-1 | 12-OMS-01 - TTCCC (construction to precom) | 0 | 0 | 28-Jul-17 | |
| PC-12-OMS-01-CFS-01 | 12-OMS-01 - Setup | 5 | 550 | 28-Jul-17 | 30-Jul-17 |
| PC-12-OMS-01-CFC-01 | 12-OMS-01 - Cleaning | 26 | 440 | 31-Jul-17 | 12-Aug-17 |
| PC-12-OMS-01-CFT-02 | 12-OMS-01 - Cleaning complete | 0 | 0 | | 12-Aug-17 |
| ⊟ 12-FUG-01 - Fuel Gas | | 9 | 660 | 21-Jul-17 | 25-Jul-17 |
| ⊟ Pre-com Piping | | 9 | 660 | 21-Jul-17 | 25-Jul-17 |
| PC-12-FUG-01-CFTT-1 | 12-FUG-01 - TTCCC (construction to precom) | 0 | 0 | 21-Jul-17 | |
| PC-12-FUG-01-CFS-01 | 12-FUG-01 - Setup | 4 | 440 | 21-Jul-17 | 22-Jul-17 |
| PC-12-FUG-01-CFC-01 | 12-FUG-01 - Cleaning | 5 | 220 | 23-Jul-17 | 25-Jul-17 |
| PC-12-FUG-01-CFT-02 | 12-FUG-01 - Cleaning complete | 0 | 0 | | 25-Jul-17 |

If you have a few dozen subsystems with constantly changing sequence, manual update of this logic will represent a significant challenge.

Before you proceed, you will obviously need to have your revised sequence in a spreadsheet, also make sure each set of activities has a start and finish milestone like in the example above.

1. Go to File > Export > Spreadsheet (XLS) > Activities and create a template similar to the one below:

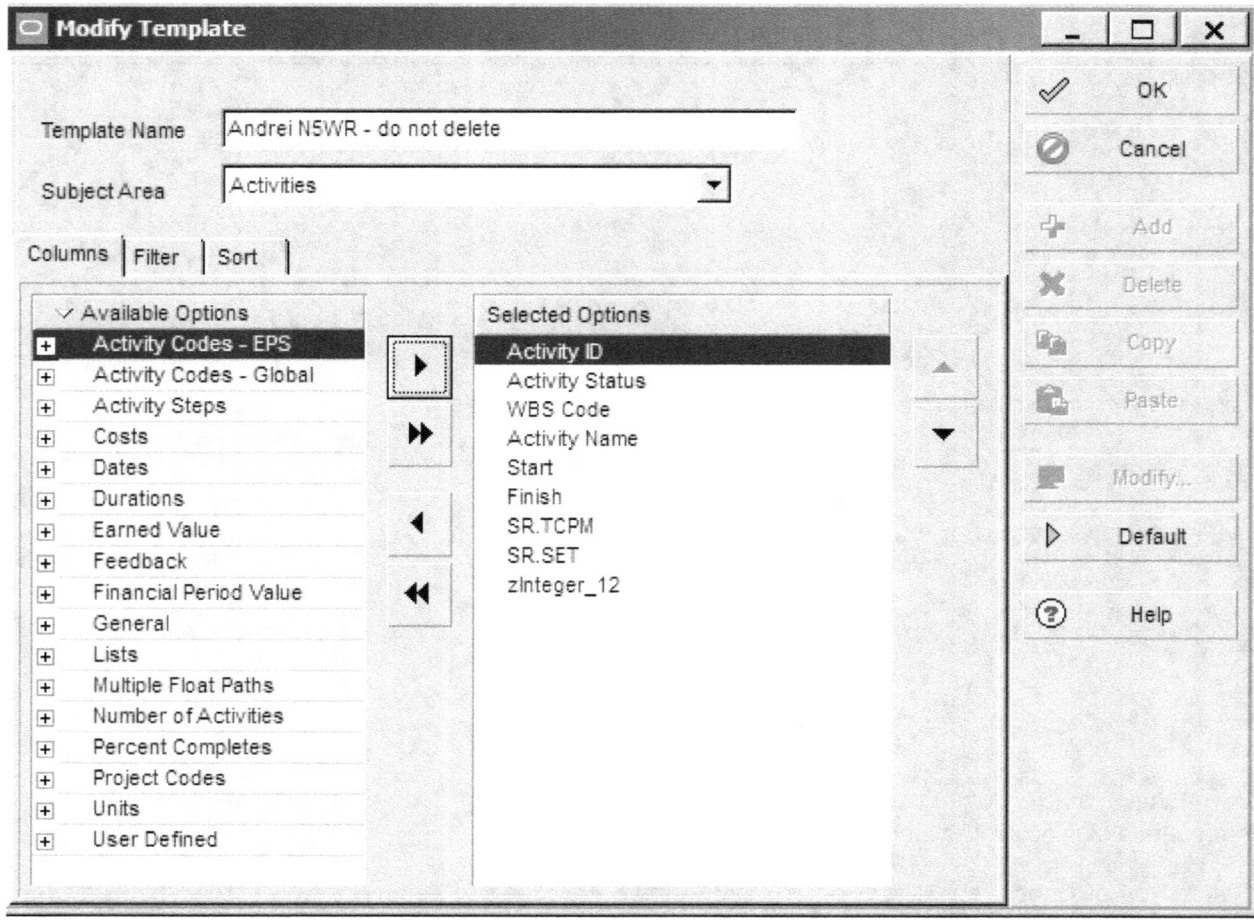

Note that SR.TCPM in my example is a subsystem code (like 12-INA-01) and SR.SET is a crew code (or "spread" in pipeline jargon). Zinteger_12 is a user defined Integer field.

2. In the resulting spreadsheet filter in only subsystem start and finish milestones and delete the rest of the lines:

Andrei Sannikov
Tip of the day

| task_code / Activity ID | status_code / Activity Stat | wbs_id / WBS Code | task_name / Activity Name | actv_code_srtcpm_176465_id / SR.TCPM | actv_code_srset_176465_id / SR.SET | user_field_2241 / zInteger_12 | delete_record_flag / Delete This Row |
|---|---|---|---|---|---|---|---|
| PC-12-MVG-01-CFT-02 | Not Started | N5WRPC-2017_0602 | 12-MVG-01 - Cleaning complete | 12-MVG-01 | S1 | 30 | |
| PC-12-INA-01-CFTT-1 | Not Started | N5WRPC-2017_0602 | 12-INA-01 - TTCCC (construction to precom) | 12-INA-01 | S1 | 1 | |
| PC-12-TWT-01-CFTT-1 | Not Started | N5WRPC-2017_0602 | 12-TWT-01 - TTCCC (construction to precom) | 12-TWT-01 | S1 | 41 | |
| PC-12-HOS-01-CFTT-1 | Not Started | N5WRPC-2017_0602 | 12-HOS-01 - TTCCC (construction to precom) | 12-HOS-01 | S2 | 20 | |
| PC-12-DTH-01-CFTT-1 | Not Started | N5WRPC-2017_0602 | 12-DTH-01 - TTCCC (construction to precom) | 12-DTH-01 | S2 | 37 | |
| PC-12-SOS-06-CFTT-1 | Not Started | N5WRPC-2017_0602 | 12-SOS-06 - TTCCC (construction to precom) | 12-SOS-06 | S1 | 95 | |
| PC-12-CSO-01-CFTT-1 | Not Started | N5WRPC-2017_0602 | 12-CSO-01 - TTCCC (construction to precom) | 12-CSO-01 | S2 | 15 | |
| PC-12-SOS-03-CFTT-1 | Not Started | N5WRPC-2017_0602 | 12-SOS-03 - TTCCC (construction to precom) | 12-SOS-03 | S2 | 89 | |
| PC-12-SOS-04-CFT-02 | Not Started | N5WRPC-2017_0602 | 12-SOS-04 - Cleaning complete | 12-SOS-04 | S1 | 90 | |
| PC-12-LOS-09-CFT-02 | Not Started | N5WRPC-2017_0602 | 12-LOS-09 - Cleaning complete | 12-LOS-09 | S2 | 91 | |
| PC-12-LOS-02-CFTT-1 | Not Started | N5WRPC-2017_0602 | 12-LOS-02 - TTCCC (construction to precom) | 12-LOS-02 | S1 | 47 | |
| PC-12-SOS-05-CFT-02 | Not Started | N5WRPC-2017_0602 | 12-SOS-05 - Cleaning complete | 12-SOS-05 | S1 | 94 | |
| PC-12-SOS-01-CFT-02 | Not Started | N5WRPC-2017_0602 | 12-SOS-01 - Cleaning complete | 12-SOS-01 | S2 | 124 | |
| PC-12-VWO-01-CFT-02 | Not Started | N5WRPC-2017_0602 | 12-VWO-01 - Cleaning complete | 12-VWO-01 | S2 | 18 | |
| PC-12-VTO-01-CFT-02 | Not Started | N5WRPC-2017_0602 | 12-VTO-01 - Cleaning complete | 12-VTO-01 | S2 | 19 | |
| PC-12-LOS-06-CFTT-1 | Not Started | N5WRPC-2017_0602 | 12-LOS-06 - TTCCC (construction to precom) | 12-LOS-06 | S1 | 86 | |
| PC-12-SRF-01-CFTT-1 | Not Started | N5WRPC-2017_0602 | 12-SRF-01 - TTCCC (construction to precom) | 12-SRF-01 | S2 | 9 | |
| PC-12-MVG-01-CFTT-1 | Not Started | N5WRPC-2017_0602 | 12-MVG-01 - TTCCC (construction to precom) | 12-MVG-01 | S1 | 30 | |
| PC-12-SRO-01-CFT-02 | Not Started | N5WRPC-2017_0602 | 12-SRO-01 - Cleaning complete | 12-SRO-01 | S1 | 3 | |
| PC-12-CSO-01-CFT-02 | Not Started | N5WRPC-2017_0602 | 12-CSO-01 - Cleaning complete | 12-CSO-01 | S2 | 15 | |
| PC-12-INA-01-CFT-02 | Not Started | N5WRPC-2017_0602 | 12-INA-01 - Cleaning complete | 12-INA-01 | S1 | 1 | |
| PC-12-LOS-10-CFTT-1 | Not Started | N5WRPC-2017_0602 | 12-LOS-10 - TTCCC (construction to precom) | 12-LOS-10 | S2 | 92 | |
| PC-12-LOS-02-CFT-02 | Not Started | N5WRPC-2017_0602 | 12-LOS-02 - Cleaning complete | 12-LOS-02 | S1 | 47 | |
| PC-12-ATO-01-CFT-02 | Not Started | N5WRPC-2017_0602 | 12-ATO-01 - Cleaning complete | 12-ATO-01 | S1 | 5 | |
| PC-12-ADS-01-CFT-02 | Not Started | N5WRPC-2017_0602 | 12-ADS-01 - Cleaning complete | 12-ADS-01 | S1 | 26 | |
| PC-12-FUG-01-CFT-02 | Not Started | N5WRPC-2017_0602 | 12-FUG-01 - Cleaning complete | 12-FUG-01 | S1 | 6 | |
| PC-12-NAG-01-CFT-02 | Not Started | N5WRPC-2017_0602 | 12-NAG-01 - Cleaning complete | 12-NAG-01 | S1 | 4 | |
| PC-12-SRO-01-CFTT-1 | Not Started | N5WRPC-2017_0602 | 12-SRO-01 - TTCCC (construction to precom) | 12-SRO-01 | S1 | 3 | |
| PC-12-SRF-01-CFT-02 | Not Started | N5WRPC-2017_0602 | 12-SRF-01 - Cleaning complete | 12-SRF-01 | S2 | 9 | |
| PC-12-LOS-04-CFT-02 | Not Started | N5WRPC-2017_0602 | 12-LOS-04 - Cleaning complete | 12-LOS-04 | S1 | 84 | |
| PC-12-LOS-04-CFTT-1 | Not Started | N5WRPC-2017_0602 | 12-LOS-04 - TTCCC (construction to precom) | 12-LOS-04 | S1 | 84 | |
| PC-12-NIT-01-CFT-02 | Not Started | N5WRPC-2017_0602 | 12-NIT-01 - Cleaning complete | 12-NIT-01 | S1 | 2 | |
| PC-12-OMS-01-CFT-02 | Not Started | N5WRPC-2017_0602 | 12-OMS-01 - Cleaning complete | 12-OMS-01 | S1 | 13 | |
| PC-12-TWT-01-CFT-02 | Not Started | N5WRPC-2017_0602 | 12-TWT-01 - Cleaning complete | 12-TWT-01 | S1 | 41 | |
| PC-12-HOS-01-CFT-02 | Not Started | N5WRPC-2017_0602 | 12-HOS-01 - Cleaning complete | 12-HOS-01 | S2 | 20 | |

3. Use Vlookup or another Excel function to populate column zinteger_12 (your UDF integer column might obviously have a different name in your system) with the new sequence.

4. Save and import this spreadsheet back into your schedule.

5. Go back to File > Export > Spreadsheet (XLS) > Activity relationships and create the following template.

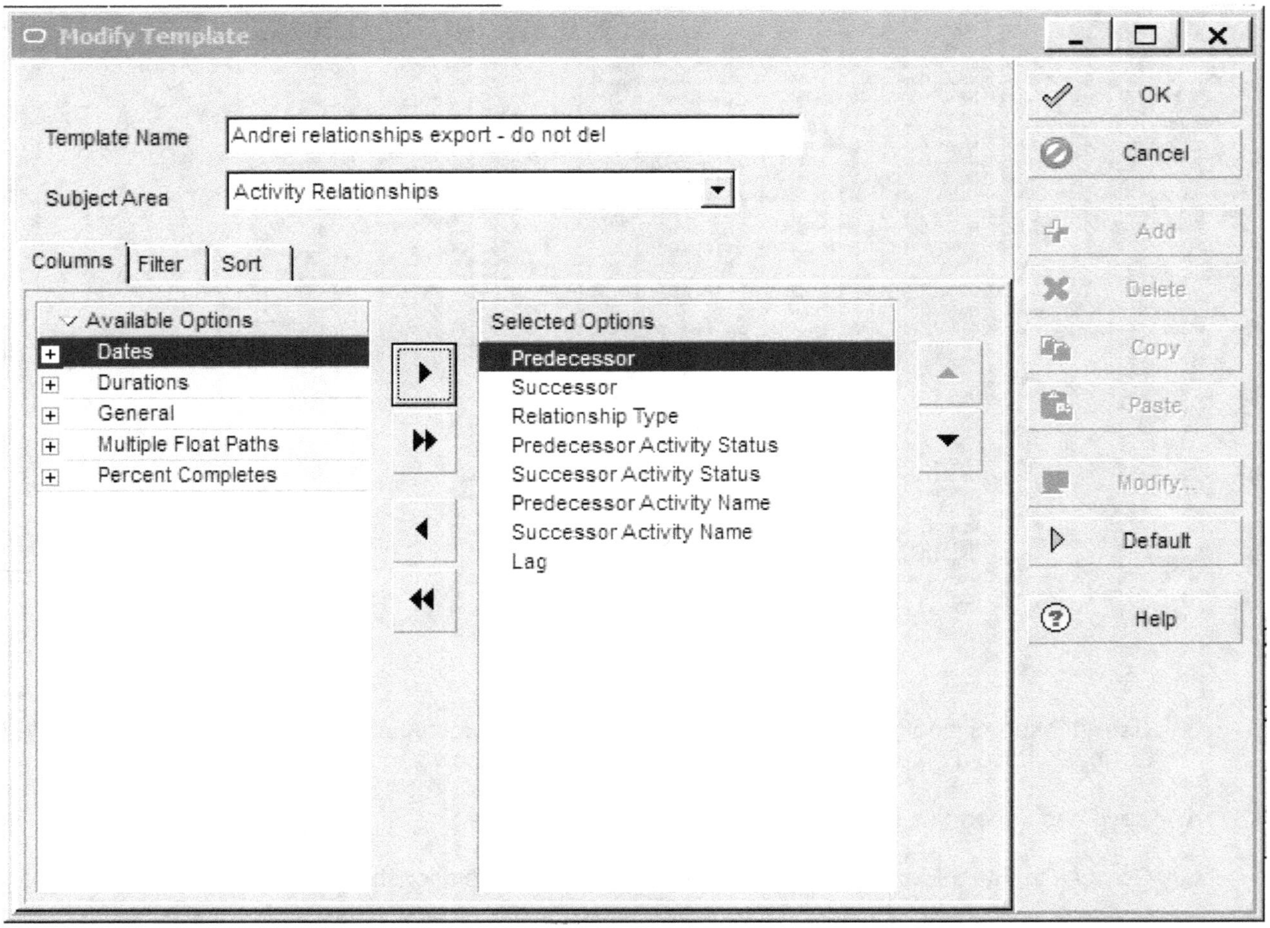

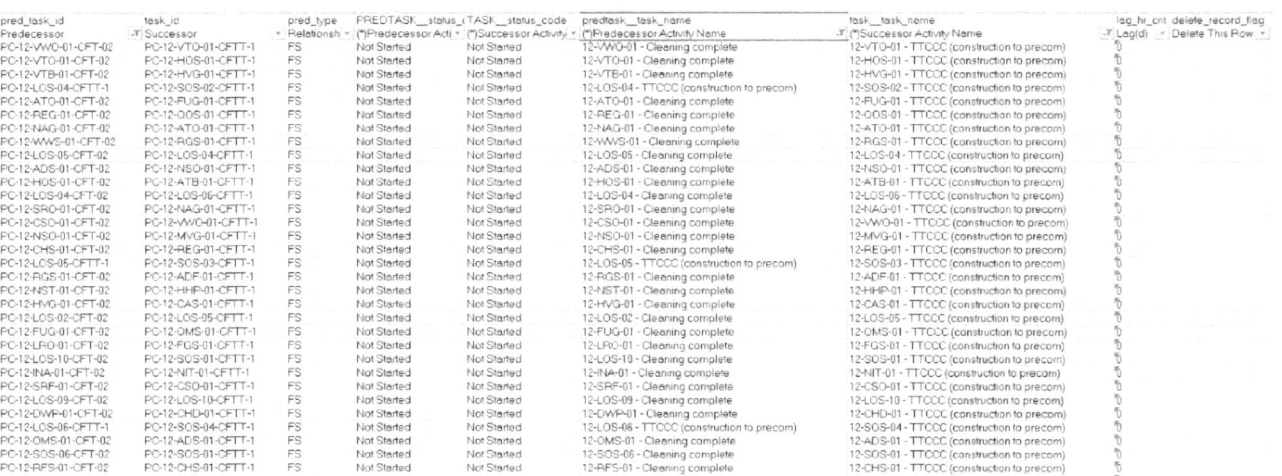

6. In the resulting spreadsheet filter in only subsystem start and finish milestones and delete the rest of the lines:

| pred_task_id<br>Predecessor | task_id<br>Successor | pred_type<br>Relationsh | PREDTASK__status_(<br>(*)Predecessor Acti | TASK__status_code<br>(*)Successor Activity | predtask__task_name<br>(*)Predecessor Activity Name | task__task_name<br>(*)Successor Activity Name | lag_hr_cnt<br>Lag(d) | delete_record_flag<br>Delete This Row |
|---|---|---|---|---|---|---|---|---|
| PC-12-VWO-01-CFT-02 | PC-12-VTO-01-CFTT-1 | FS | Not Started | Not Started | 12-VWO-01 - Cleaning complete | 12-VTO-01 - TTCCC (construction to precom) | 0 | |
| PC-12-VTO-01-CFT-02 | PC-12-HOS-01-CFTT-1 | FS | Not Started | Not Started | 12-VTO-01 - Cleaning complete | 12-HOS-01 - TTCCC (construction to precom) | 0 | |
| PC-12-VTB-01-CFT-02 | PC-12-HVG-01-CFTT-1 | FS | Not Started | Not Started | 12-VTB-01 - Cleaning complete | 12-HVG-01 - TTCCC (construction to precom) | 0 | |
| PC-12-LOS-04-CFTT-1 | PC-12-SOS-02-CFTT-1 | FS | Not Started | Not Started | 12-LOS-04 - TTCCC (construction to precom) | 12-SOS-02 - TTCCC (construction to precom) | 0 | |
| PC-12-ATO-01-CFT-02 | PC-12-FUG-01-CFTT-1 | FS | Not Started | Not Started | 12-ATO-01 - Cleaning complete | 12-FUG-01 - TTCCC (construction to precom) | 0 | |
| PC-12-REG-01-CFT-02 | PC-12-QOS-01-CFTT-1 | FS | Not Started | Not Started | 12-REG-01 - Cleaning complete | 12-QOS-01 - TTCCC (construction to precom) | 0 | |
| PC-12-NAG-01-CFT-02 | PC-12-ATO-01-CFTT-1 | FS | Not Started | Not Started | 12-NAG-01 - Cleaning complete | 12-ATO-01 - TTCCC (construction to precom) | 0 | |
| PC-12-WWS-01-CFT-02 | PC-12-RGS-01-CFTT-1 | FS | Not Started | Not Started | 12-WWS-01 - Cleaning complete | 12-RGS-01 - TTCCC (construction to precom) | 0 | |
| PC-12-LOS-05-CFT-02 | PC-12-LOS-04-CFTT-1 | FS | Not Started | Not Started | 12-LOS-05 - Cleaning complete | 12-LOS-04 - TTCCC (construction to precom) | 0 | |
| PC-12-ADS-01-CFT-02 | PC-12-NSO-01-CFTT-1 | FS | Not Started | Not Started | 12-ADS-01 - Cleaning complete | 12-NSO-01 - TTCCC (construction to precom) | 0 | |
| PC-12-HOS-01-CFT-02 | PC-12-ATB-01-CFTT-1 | FS | Not Started | Not Started | 12-HOS-01 - Cleaning complete | 12-ATB-01 - TTCCC (construction to precom) | 0 | |
| PC-12-LOS-04-CFT-02 | PC-12-LOS-06-CFTT-1 | FS | Not Started | Not Started | 12-LOS-04 - Cleaning complete | 12-LOS-06 - TTCCC (construction to precom) | 0 | |
| PC-12-SRO-01-CFT-02 | PC-12-NAG-01-CFTT-1 | FS | Not Started | Not Started | 12-SRO-01 - Cleaning complete | 12-NAG-01 - TTCCC (construction to precom) | 0 | |
| PC-12-CSO-01-CFT-02 | PC-12-VWO-01-CFTT-1 | FS | Not Started | Not Started | 12-CSO-01 - Cleaning complete | 12-VWO-01 - TTCCC (construction to precom) | 0 | |
| PC-12-NSO-01-CFT-02 | PC-12-MVG-01-CFTT-1 | FS | Not Started | Not Started | 12-NSO-01 - Cleaning complete | 12-MVG-01 - TTCCC (construction to precom) | 0 | |
| PC-12-CHS-01-CFT-02 | PC-12-REG-01-CFTT-1 | FS | Not Started | Not Started | 12-CHS-01 - Cleaning complete | 12-REG-01 - TTCCC (construction to precom) | 0 | |
| PC-12-LOS-05-CFTT-1 | PC-12-SOS-03-CFTT-1 | FS | Not Started | Not Started | 12-LOS-05 - TTCCC (construction to precom) | 12-SOS-03 - TTCCC (construction to precom) | 0 | |
| PC-12-RGS-01-CFT-02 | PC-12-ADF-01-CFTT-1 | FS | Not Started | Not Started | 12-RGS-01 - Cleaning complete | 12-ADF-01 - TTCCC (construction to precom) | 0 | |
| PC-12-NST-01-CFT-02 | PC-12-HHP-01-CFTT-1 | FS | Not Started | Not Started | 12-NST-01 - Cleaning complete | 12-HHP-01 - TTCCC (construction to precom) | 0 | |
| PC-12-HVG-01-CFT-02 | PC-12-CAS-01-CFTT-1 | FS | Not Started | Not Started | 12-HVG-01 - Cleaning complete | 12-CAS-01 - TTCCC (construction to precom) | 0 | |
| PC-12-LOS-02-CFT-02 | PC-12-LOS-05-CFTT-1 | FS | Not Started | Not Started | 12-LOS-02 - Cleaning complete | 12-LOS-05 - TTCCC (construction to precom) | 0 | |
| PC-12-FUG-01-CFT-02 | PC-12-OMS-01-CFTT-1 | FS | Not Started | Not Started | 12-FUG-01 - Cleaning complete | 12-OMS-01 - TTCCC (construction to precom) | 0 | |
| PC-12-LRO-01-CFT-02 | PC-12-FGS-01-CFTT-1 | FS | Not Started | Not Started | 12-LRO-01 - Cleaning complete | 12-FGS-01 - TTCCC (construction to precom) | 0 | |
| PC-12-LOS-10-CFT-02 | PC-12-SOS-01-CFTT-1 | FS | Not Started | Not Started | 12-LOS-10 - Cleaning complete | 12-SOS-01 - TTCCC (construction to precom) | 0 | |
| PC-12-INA-01-CFT-02 | PC-12-NIT-01-CFTT-1 | FS | Not Started | Not Started | 12-INA-01 - Cleaning complete | 12-NIT-01 - TTCCC (construction to precom) | 0 | |
| PC-12-SRF-01-CFT-02 | PC-12-CSO-01-CFTT-1 | FS | Not Started | Not Started | 12-SRF-01 - Cleaning complete | 12-CSO-01 - TTCCC (construction to precom) | 0 | |
| PC-12-LOS-09-CFT-02 | PC-12-LOS-10-CFTT-1 | FS | Not Started | Not Started | 12-LOS-09 - Cleaning complete | 12-LOS-10 - TTCCC (construction to precom) | 0 | |
| PC-12-DWP-01-CFT-02 | PC-12-CHD-01-CFTT-1 | FS | Not Started | Not Started | 12-DWP-01 - Cleaning complete | 12-CHD-01 - TTCCC (construction to precom) | 0 | |
| PC-12-LOS-06-CFTT-1 | PC-12-SOS-04-CFTT-1 | FS | Not Started | Not Started | 12-LOS-06 - TTCCC (construction to precom) | 12-SOS-04 - TTCCC (construction to precom) | 0 | |
| PC-12-OMS-01-CFT-02 | PC-12-ADS-01-CFTT-1 | FS | Not Started | Not Started | 12-OMS-01 - Cleaning complete | 12-ADS-01 - TTCCC (construction to precom) | 0 | |
| PC-12-SOS-06-CFT-02 | PC-12-SOS-01-CFTT-1 | FS | Not Started | Not Started | 12-SOS-06 - Cleaning complete | 12-SOS-01 - TTCCC (construction to precom) | 0 | |
| PC-12-RFS-01-CFT-02 | PC-12-CHS-01-CFTT-1 | FS | Not Started | Not Started | 12-RFS-01 - Cleaning complete | 12-CHS-01 - TTCCC (construction to precom) | 0 | |

Andrei Sannikov
Tip of the day

Note that you need to apply this filter to both Successor and Predecessor Activity Name columns:

7. Add letter "D" (for delete) to all lines in the far-right column.

8. Save and import this spreadsheet back into your schedule.

   a. Now we have removed all relationships between different subsystems and brought in our revised sequence in a UDF field.

9. Create a layout similar to the one below in your schedule:

| Activity ID | Activity Name | Start | Finish | SR.SET | SR.TCPM | :Integer_12 |
|---|---|---|---|---|---|---|
| PC-12-INA-01-CFTT-1 | 12-INA-01 - TTCCC (construction to precom) | 05-Jun-17 |  | S1 | 12-INA-01 | 1 |
| PC-12-INA-01-CFT-02 | 12-INA-01 - Cleaning complete |  | 14-Jun-17 | S1 | 12-INA-01 | 1 |
| PC-12-NIT-01-CFTT-1 | 12-NIT-01 - TTCCC (construction to precom) | 15-Jun-17 |  | S1 | 12-NIT-01 | 2 |
| PC-12-NIT-01-CFT-02 | 12-NIT-01 - Cleaning complete |  | 24-Jun-17 | S1 | 12-NIT-01 | 2 |
| PC-12-SRO-01-CFTT-1 | 12-SRO-01 - TTCCC (construction to precom) | 25-Jun-17 |  | S1 | 12-SRO-01 | 3 |
| PC-12-SRO-01-CFT-02 | 12-SRO-01 - Cleaning complete |  | 05-Jul-17 | S1 | 12-SRO-01 | 3 |
| PC-12-NAG-01-CFTT-1 | 12-NAG-01 - TTCCC (construction to precom) | 05-Jul-17 |  | S1 | 12-NAG-01 | 4 |
| PC-12-NAG-01-CFT-02 | 12-NAG-01 - Cleaning complete |  | 10-Jul-17 | S1 | 12-NAG-01 | 4 |
| PC-12-ATO-01-CFTT-1 | 12-ATO-01 - TTCCC (construction to precom) | 10-Jul-17 |  | S1 | 12-ATO-01 | 5 |
| PC-12-ATO-01-CFT-02 | 12-ATO-01 - Cleaning complete |  | 16-Jul-17 | S1 | 12-ATO-01 | 5 |
| PC-12-FUG-01-CFTT-1 | 12-FUG-01 - TTCCC (construction to precom) | 21-Jul-17 |  | S1 | 12-FUG-01 | 6 |
| PC-12-FUG-01-CFT-02 | 12-FUG-01 - Cleaning complete |  | 25-Jul-17 | S1 | 12-FUG-01 | 6 |
| PC-12-OMS-01-CFTT-1 | 12-OMS-01 - TTCCC (construction to precom) | 28-Jul-17 |  | S1 | 12-OMS-01 | 13 |
| PC-12-OMS-01-CFT-02 | 12-OMS-01 - Cleaning complete |  | 12-Aug-17 | S1 | 12-OMS-01 | 13 |
| PC-12-ADS-01-CFTT-1 | 12-ADS-01 - TTCCC (construction to precom) | 25-Aug-17 |  | S1 | 12-ADS-01 | 26 |
| PC-12-ADS-01-CFT-02 | 12-ADS-01 - Cleaning complete |  | 12-Sep-17 | S1 | 12-ADS-01 | 26 |
| PC-12-NSO-01-CFTT-1 | 12-NSO-01 - TTCCC (construction to precom) | 12-Sep-17 |  | S1 | 12-NSO-01 | 28 |
| PC-12-NSO-01-CFT-02 | 12-NSO-01 - Cleaning complete |  | 14-Sep-17 | S1 | 12-NSO-01 | 28 |
| PC-12-MVG-01-CFTT-1 | 12-MVG-01 - TTCCC (construction to precom) | 15-Sep-17 |  | S1 | 12-MVG-01 | 30 |
| PC-12-MVG-01-CFT-02 | 12-MVG-01 - Cleaning complete |  | 21-Sep-17 | S1 | 12-MVG-01 | 30 |
| PC-12-SRF-01-CFTT-1 | 12-SRF-01 - TTCCC (construction to precom) | 14-Jul-17 |  | S2 | 12-SRF-01 | 9 |

Note: Your filter must include ONLY start and finish milestones for each subsystem.

10. Go to Group and Sort, click on Sort and add the followings sorting to your layout:

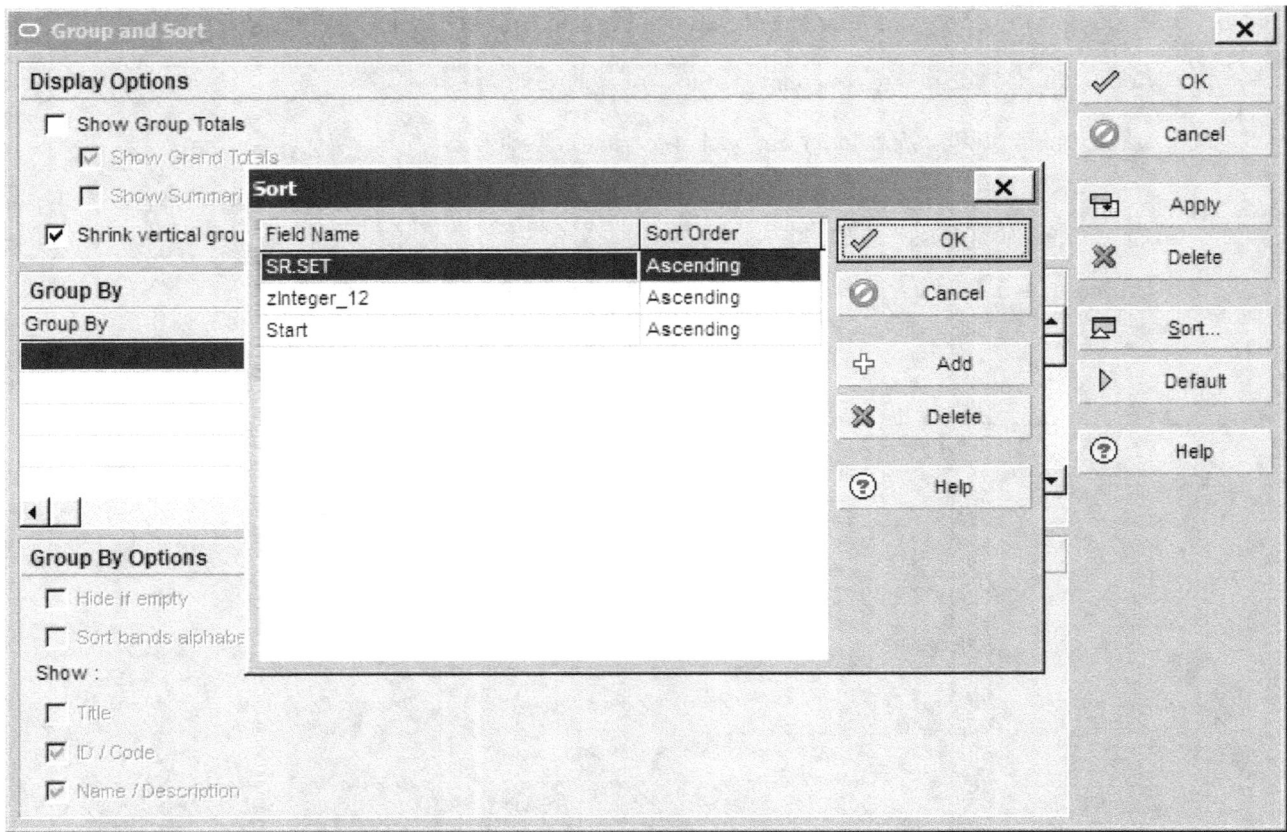

11. Now your subsystem milestones will be arranged in the new order for each crew, but the new logic is not in yet.

12. Select each crew milestones with your mouse, right-click > link activities.

13. Repeat this step for each crew.

Andrei Sannikov
Tip of the day

22-Jul-15 10:46

## How and when to use resource leveling function

I am sure all of us tried to use the resource leveling function in P6 and after getting rather weird results most people finally give up using it - if you enable the option "preserve early and late dates" you cannot see any noticeable leveling on your resource histogram, if you disable it P6 randomly distributes activities over time adding a few months to your project completion date.

There is one instance, however, in which resource leveling actually works. In construction we often deal with limited resources, on linear activities we can easily forecast completion dates or durations resulting from lack of resources by simply dividing estimated labor hours by available manpower - 1000 hrs / (20 men/day x 10) = 5 days. However, if you have a network with rather complicated logic, your limited resource is required only on certain activities and you know that its availability will change over time this calculation might be rather complex. If all we are trying to do is estimate the impact of limited resource availability on the project completion date (rather than building a workable schedule) resource leveling function could be a very useful tool.

Consider the following:

1. Go to your resource dictionary and set up daily availability or production limits:

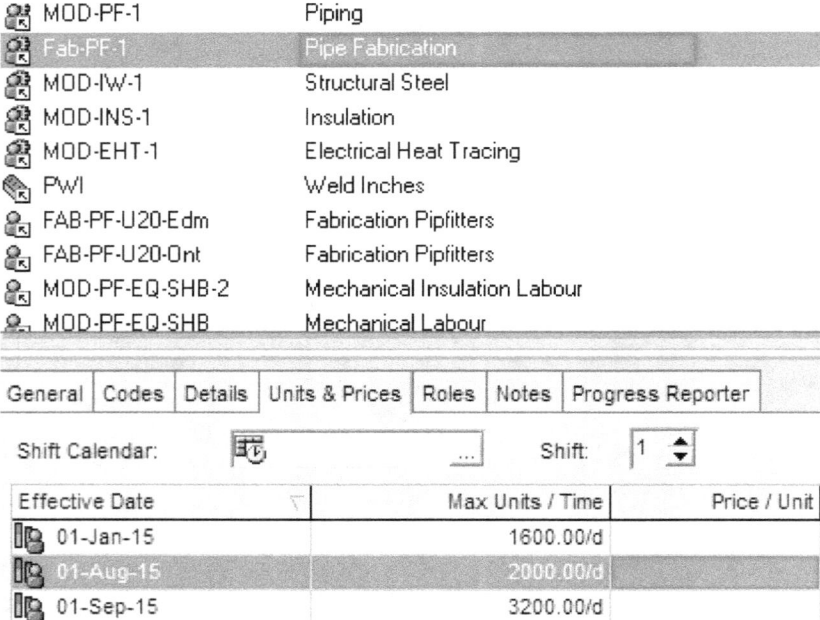

Note: if you have limited resource availability in a specific area (like a fab shop), you need to create a separate resource just for this area rather than loading the impacted activities with generic resources like welders or pipefitters.

2. Go to activity view. You will be prompted to recalculate assignment costs:

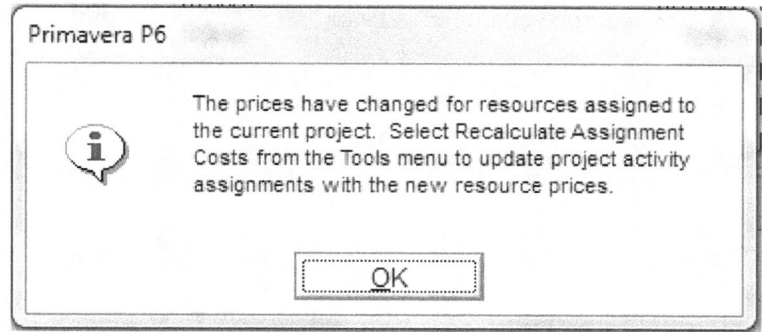

Go to Tools menu and choose Recalculate Assignment Costs, this is a onetime operation that you will not need to repeat if you don't change resource availability limits again.

3. Go to Tools > Level Resources and use the settings shown below:

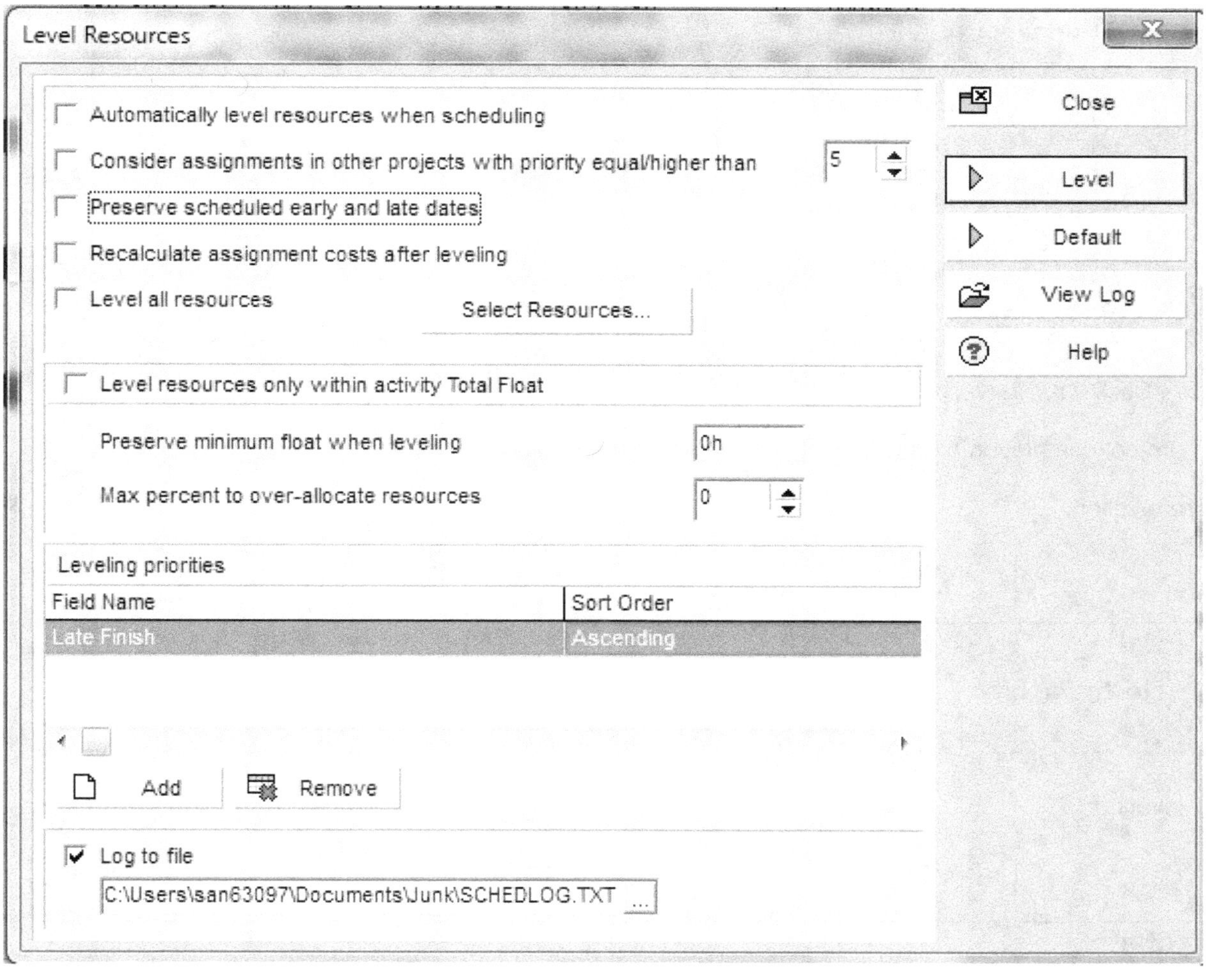

Note: I have chosen Late Finish in the leveling priorities field to make sure leveling is done based on criticality, if you have different needs, you can choose other options (like area or others codes set up in your system) in the drop-down list.

4. Click on Select resources... and check the resource you intend to level:

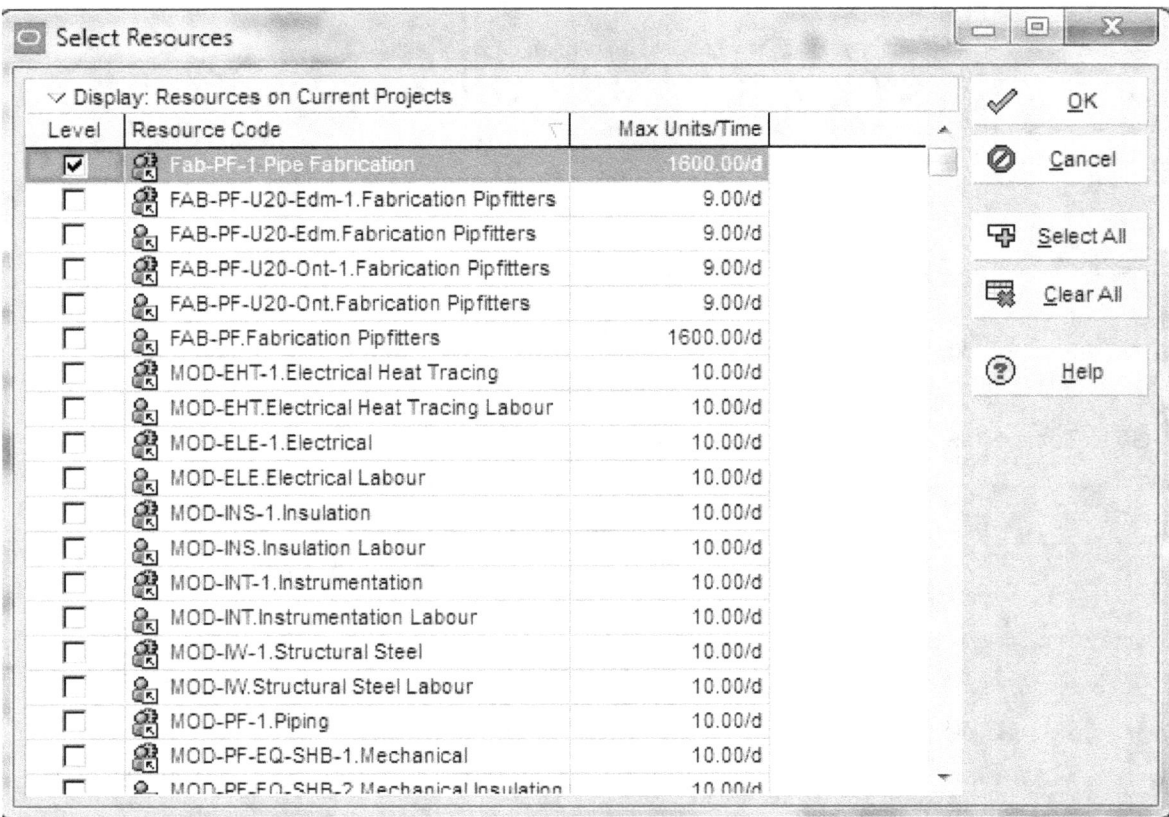

5. Click OK > Level

Your project completion date is likely to change, in our example:

Before leveling:

| Activity ID | Activity Name | Remaining Duration | Start | Finish | Late Finish |
|---|---|---|---|---|---|
| Total | | 119 | 05-Jan-15 A | 24-Dec-15 | 13-Jan-16 |
| North Facility | | 117 | 17-Feb-15 A | 22-Dec-15 | 13-Jan-16 |
| South Facility | | 119 | 05-Jan-15 A | 24-Dec-15 | 08-Jan-16 |

After leveling:

| Activity ID | Activity Name | Remaining Duration | Start | Finish | Late Finish |
|---|---|---|---|---|---|
| Total | | 128 | 05-Jan-15 A | 14-Jan-16 | 13-Jan-16 |
| North Facility | | 128 | 17-Feb-15 A | 14-Jan-16 | 13-Jan-16 |
| South Facility | | 119 | 05-Jan-15 A | 24-Dec-15 | 08-Jan-16 |

When you display your resource histogram you will see that resource limits we have set in Step 1 above have been essentially preserved (there might be some exceptions since it is not a very exact science):

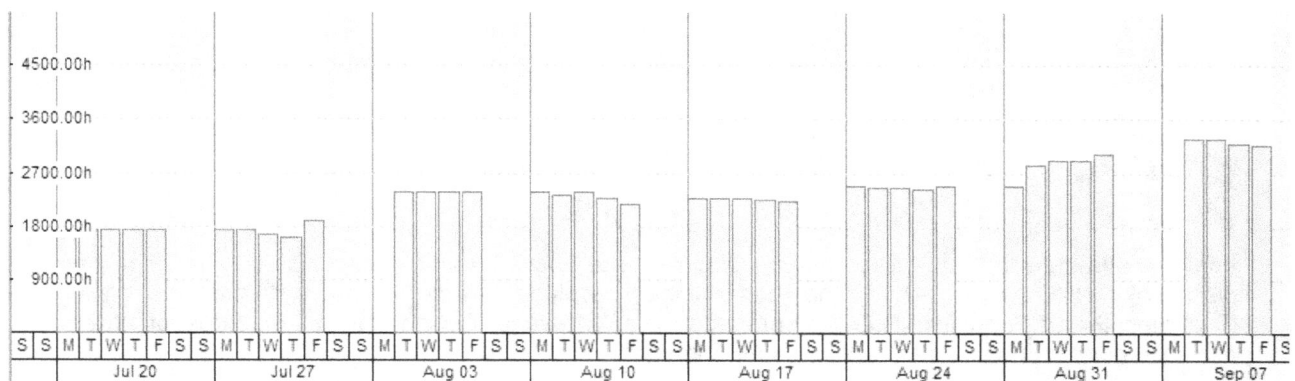

6. Now you can see the impact of the resource availability limits we have set on the project completion date. Hit F9 to recalculate your project and undo all the changes.

24-Jul-15 12:10

# How to find all out-of-sequence relationships in a large network

I think we all agree that out-of-sequence logic in a large network can represent a real challenge - you can spend hours looking for an old activity that has not been statused as completed and continue driving your dates sometimes through multiple levels of predecessors. I have proposed several methods of how to locate this proverbial needle in a haystack in my earlier tips - here is a new one:

1. Go to File > Export > Excel > Activity relationships > Select your project for export.

2. In the Template window set up an export template with the following fields:

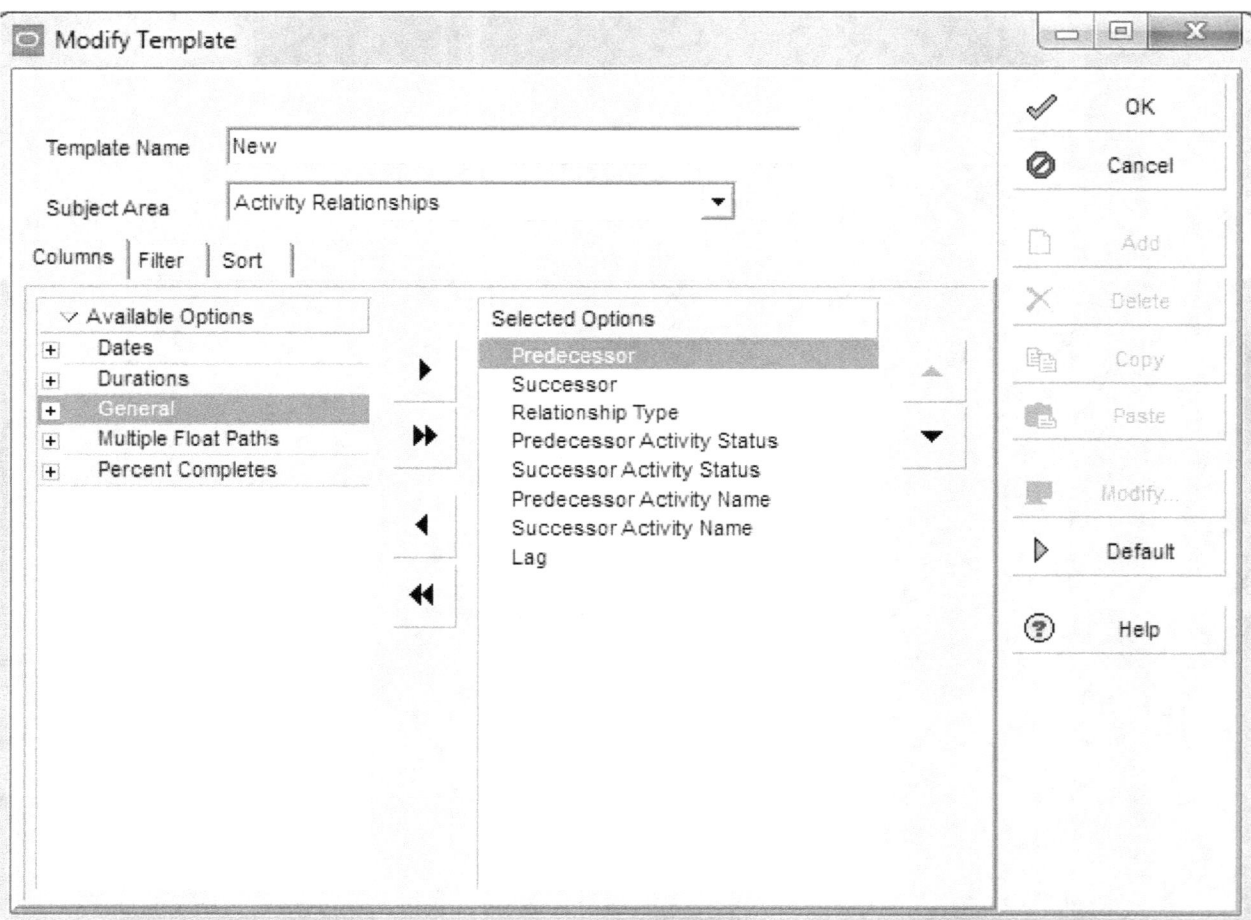

3. Export your project.

4. Open the file you have exported and apply filters to all columns

5. Filter in FS and FF relationships in Relationship type column; Completed in the Successor status column and In progress/Not Started in the Predecessor status column:

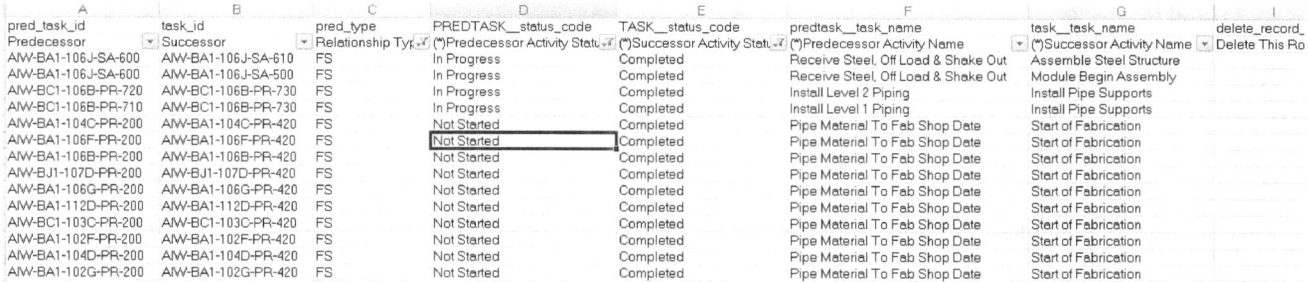

6) The resulting list will include all the bad guys and now you have 2 options - you can either delete such relationships if they are no longer relevant by adding letter D to the last column and importing it back into P6:

Or you can run an Excel activity export with a user field that you can populate in Excel using Vlookups from the filtered list we have created in step 5 above, import it back into P6 and then filter in these out-of-sequence predecessors using this user field. Then you will decide if you want to actualize them or change their successor relationships or whatever.

Notes:

- In some cases, out of sequence logic can be caused by SS or SF relationships as well - to isolate those you can run another set of filters in step 5 above:

    o For SS - select SS in Relationship type, Completed or In Progress in Successor Activity Status and Not Started in the Predecessor Activity Status column.

    o For SF relationships you will need - SF in Relationship type, Completed in Successor Activity Status and Not Started or In Progress in the Predecessor Activity Status column.

- Obviously, all Level of effort activities will be included in the SS and FF filters above, although, they cannot cause any out-of-sequence issues. It might be a good idea to always add "LOE" to their description so you can filter them out in the exported spreadsheet.

Andrei Sannikov
Tip of the day

31-Jul-15 15:39

## Quick fix for late finish dates on completed activities

I think we all noticed that when you actualize an activity or a milestone P6 recalculates its late finish date and these late dates sometimes don't make much sense - you have a finish on or before (or late finish) constraint on a Milestone set for, say, March 2015, all activities driving this milestone are critical so you show negative float but the minute you actualize these activities your late finish dates change to the last date you have in your project:

| Activity ID | Activity Name | Remaining Duration | Start | Finish | Late Finish |
|---|---|---|---|---|---|
| Total | | 184 | 05-Jan-15 A | 22-Apr-16 | 22-Aug-16 |
| Mod seq: 1 | | 0 | 28-Jan-15 A | 11-Mar-15 A | 22-Aug-16 |
| BF1-105B-SA | | 0 | 28-Jan-15 A | 11-Mar-15 A | 22-Aug-16 |
| | Module Assembly Activities Milestone | 0 | 28-Jan-15 A | 28-Jan-15 A | 22-Aug-16 |
| | Structural Steel | 0 | 28-Jan-15 A | 11-Mar-15 A | 22-Aug-16 |
| | Ready For Shipment | 0 | 10-Mar-15 A | 11-Mar-15 A | 22-Aug-16 |
| | Module Final Walkdown | 0 | 10-Mar-15 A | 11-Mar-15 A | 22-Aug-16 |
| | Ready for Shipping | 0 | | 11-Mar-15 A | 22-Aug-16 |

The problem is that when an activity is actualized P6 calculates its late date based on the late finish of its next incomplete successor, in our example the only logical successor of this module is the overall project completion, P6 ignores the late finish constraint (finish on or before) we had on this finish milestone prior to actualizing it and "assumes" we could have finished on Aug 22, 2016 without impacting anything, which is the true meaning of Late Finish.

Planners familiar with this odd logic in P6 simply ignore late dates on completed activities, however, when you present your schedule to the upper management you will undoubtedly get questions about these strange looking late dates especially if you display float bars, which will be crossing your entire page on most of your completed activities and you can either entertain your audience with an exciting discussion about mysterious ways P6 calculations work (which most people would not understand anyway) or you can use a simple trick to manually reset these late finish dates to match your actual finish dates or whatever you want. This is how this trick works:

Create a "dummy" milestone that you should probably hide in your standard layouts/filters and assign a finish on or before constraint to it with a date corresponding to the late finish date you want to display on a particular (completed) milestone, let's say March 16, 2015 for our example above, link it as a successor to this milestone and hit F9:

| Activity ID | Activity Name | Remaining Duration | Start | Finish | Late Finish |
|---|---|---|---|---|---|
| Total | | 184 | 05-Jan-15 A | 22-Apr-16 | 29-Mar-16 |
| Mod seq: 1 | | 0 | 28-Jan-15 A | 11-Mar-15 A | 16-Mar-15 |
| BF1-105B-SA | | 0 | 28-Jan-15 A | 11-Mar-15 A | 16-Mar-15 |
| | Module Assembly Activities Milestone | 0 | 28-Jan-15 A | 28-Jan-15 A | 16-Mar-15 |
| | Structural Steel | 0 | 28-Jan-15 A | 11-Mar-15 A | 16-Mar-15 |
| | Ready For Shipment | 0 | 10-Mar-15 A | 11-Mar-15 A | 16-Mar-15 |
| | Module Fina Walkdown | 0 | 10-Mar-15 A | 11-Mar-15 A | 16-Mar-15 |
| | Ready for Shipping | 0 | | 11-Mar-15 A | 16-Mar-15 |

See the difference?

Andrei Sannikov
Tip of the day

24-Aug-15 14:41

# Time saving schedule updating techniques

A) When we update our schedules probably the most time-consuming activity is actualizing start and finish dates on completed activities and aligning actual units with at completion values especially when we have multiple resources assigned to the same activity. This process can be automated to some extent if you enable the option "Recalculate Actual Units and Cost when duration % complete changes", however, the down side of it would be recalculation of your actual/earned units each time you adjust remaining duration on activities in progress - something you don't want to do when your progress is based on earned value. Consider the following:

1. Before moving the data date filter in activities completed between two updates. Adjust start and finish dates on each activity you are about to actualize to make sure they match actual start and finish.

2. Display Activity Status and Unit % complete in columns:

| Activity Name | Remaining Duration | Start | Finish | Activity Status | Units % Complete | Actual Labor Units | Remaining Labor Units |
|---|---|---|---|---|---|---|---|
| Electrical | 13 | 14-Sep-15 | 30-Sep-15 | | 0% | 0.00 | 1067.00 |
| Install Electrical Supports | 4 | 14-Sep-15 | 17-Sep-15 | Not Started | 0% | 0.00 | 220.00 |
| Install Electrical Cable Trays | 4 | 18-Sep-15 | 23-Sep-15 | Not Started | 0% | 0.00 | 220.00 |
| Install Grounding | 4 | 24-Sep-15 | 29-Sep-15 | Not Started | 0% | 0.00 | 594.00 |
| Prep To Ship | 1 | 30-Sep-15 | 30-Sep-15 | Not Started | 0% | 0.00 | 33.00 |

3. Change Activity Status to In Progress on the first row and use the Fill Down function to copy it down.

4. Change Units % complete to 100% on the first row and use the Fill Down function to copy it down.

| Activity Name | Remaining Duration | Start | Finish | Activity Status | Units % Complete | Actual Labor Units | Remaining Labor Units |
|---|---|---|---|---|---|---|---|
| Electrical | 13 | 14-Sep-15 A | 30-Sep-15 | | 100% | 1067.00 | 0.00 |
| Install Electrical Supports | 4 | 14-Sep-15 A | 17-Sep-15 | In Progress | 100% | 220.00 | 0.00 |
| Install Electrical Cable Trays | 4 | 18-Sep-15 A | 23-Sep-15 | In Progress | 100% | 220.00 | 0.00 |
| Install Grounding | 4 | 24-Sep-15 A | 29-Sep-15 | In Progress | 100% | 594.00 | 0.00 |
| Prep To Ship | 1 | 30-Sep-15 A | 30-Sep-15 | In Progress | 100% | 33.00 | 0.00 |

5. Go back to Activity Status column, change the status to Completed on the first row and use the Fill Down function to copy it down.

| Activity Name | Remaining Duration | Start | Finish | Activity Status | Units % Complete | Actual Labor Units | Remaining Labor Units |
|---|---|---|---|---|---|---|---|
| Electrical | 0 | 14-Sep-15 A | 30-Sep-15 A | | 100% | 1067.00 | 0.00 |
| Install Electrical Supports | 0 | 14-Sep-15 A | 17-Sep-15 A | Completed | 100% | 220.00 | 0.00 |
| Install Electrical Cable Trays | 0 | 18-Sep-15 A | 23-Sep-15 A | Completed | 100% | 220.00 | 0.00 |
| Install Grounding | 0 | 24-Sep-15 A | 29-Sep-15 A | Completed | 100% | 594.00 | 0.00 |
| Prep To Ship | 0 | 30-Sep-15 A | 30-Sep-15 A | Completed | 100% | 33.00 | 0.00 |

Now you can move the data date.

Note: if you skip step 3 above and change the Status to Completed right away you won't be able to modify Units % complete in this column and copy it down, you will have to do it manually on each resource assigned to each activity. However, if your activities are not resource-loaded Step 3 is obviously not required.

B) When you update a large network with a lot of high-level activities in progress one of time-consuming tasks is "pulling back" all the dates that shifted after you advance the data date. If you want to keep all or some of the dates planned after the new data date the same as in your previous update, consider the following:

1. Before moving the data date save a copy of your project as a baseline.

2. Go to Tools > Global Change and set up the following Global Change:

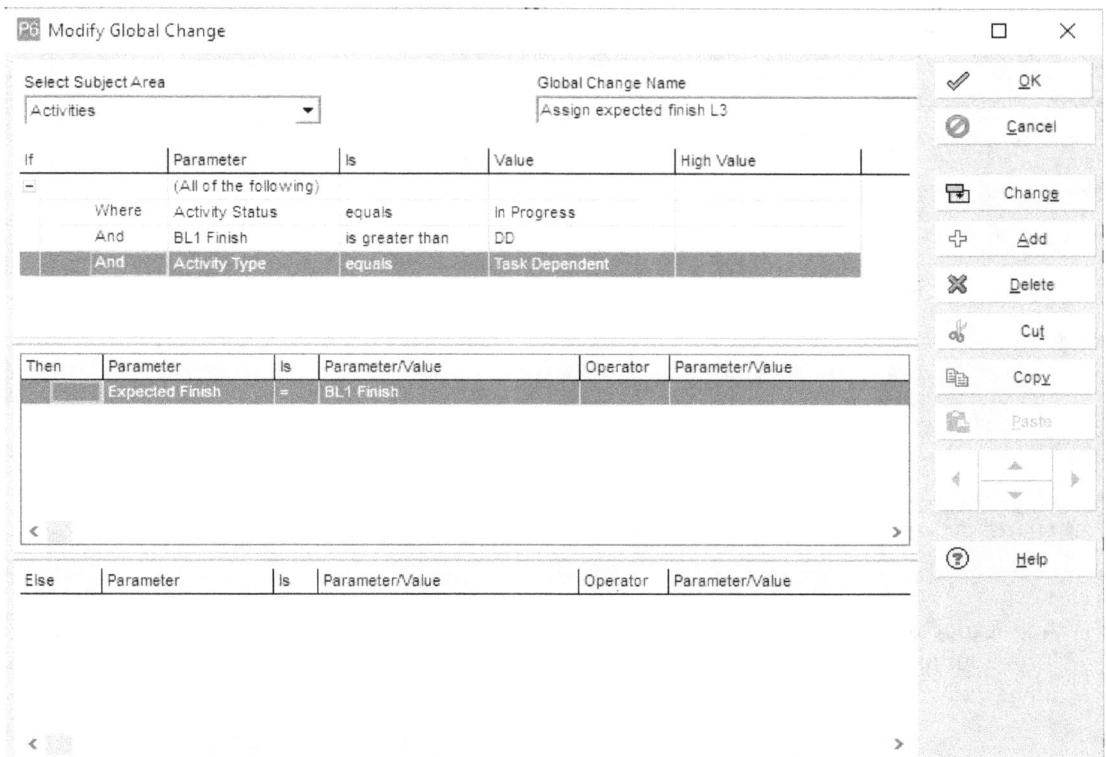

Add other conditions in the top section to include or exclude activities from this change.

3. After running this change, schedule (F9) your project – make sure the Use Expected Finish option is checked:

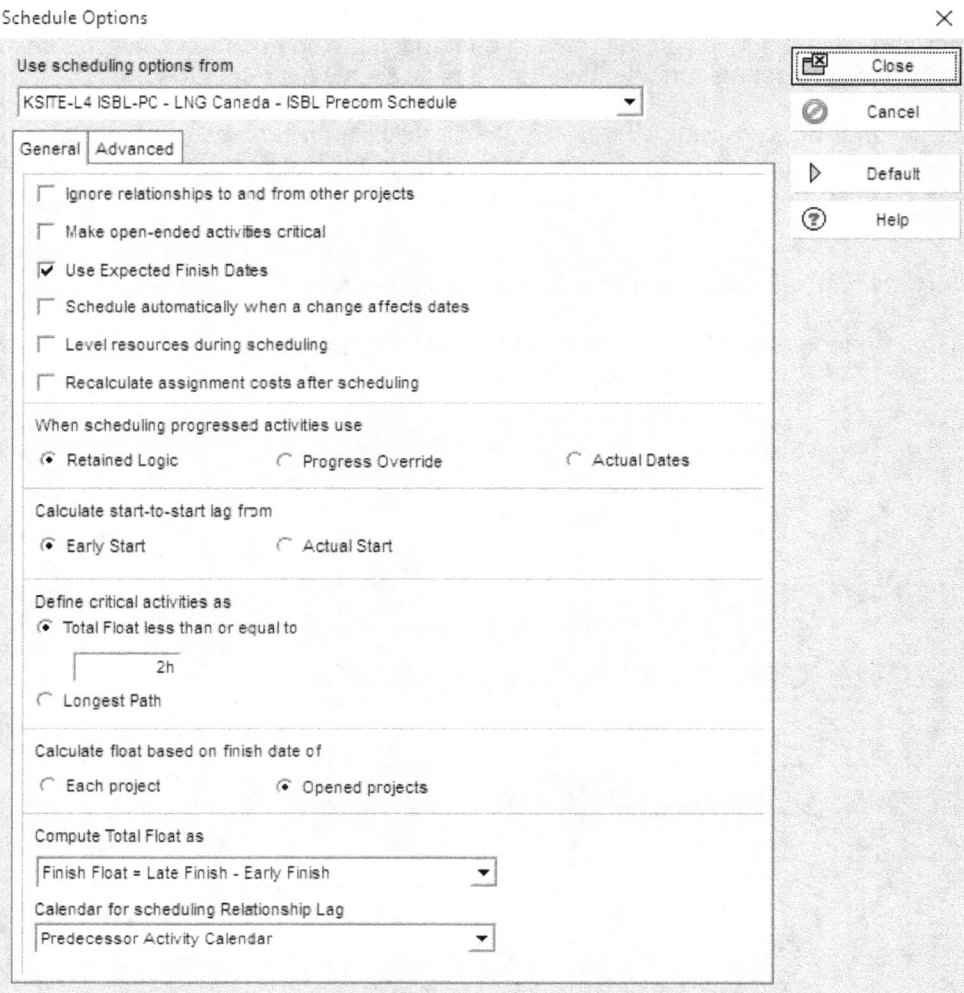

4. Add Expected Finish column to your layout and use Fill Down function to remove Expected Finish dates from your project as their use is not recommended in most cases.

## How to check the impact of different predecessors on completion milestones

When we make significant changes to the logic or simply when we have multiple predecessors on particular activities or milestones sometimes it is useful to know what our dates would be if a particular predecessor is excluded. Say, your system completion milestones are linked to different construction activities in your schedule and you want to know what would happen to each milestone date if you turn your systems over without finishing final grading in each area. You can, of course, make a copy of your schedule, unlink all your turnover milestones from final grading and produce a scenario. But if you have lots of system turnover milestones this exercise might be very labor intensive, especially if you have to do it on a regular basis with different changes to the logic. Let us see if there is an easier way.

With your schedule open go to Reports > New Report > Activities

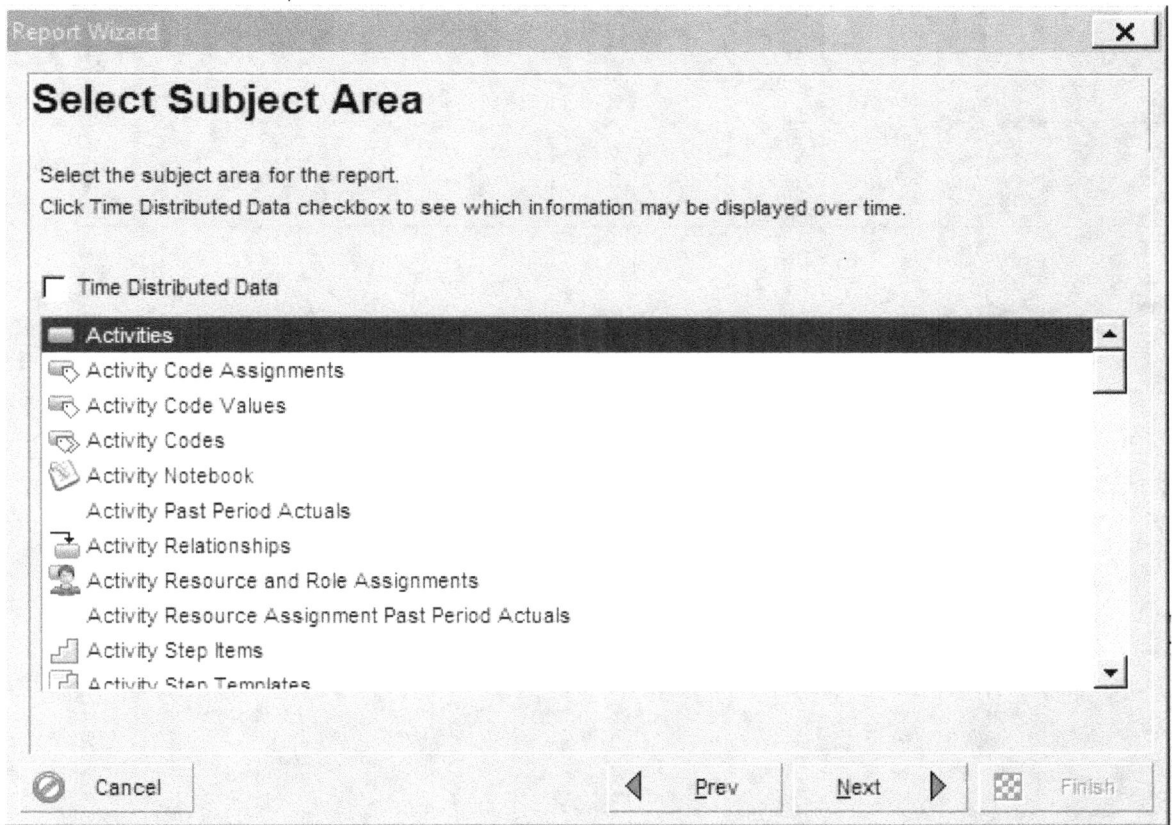

Choose Predecessors in the next window and move it to the Selected Subject areas

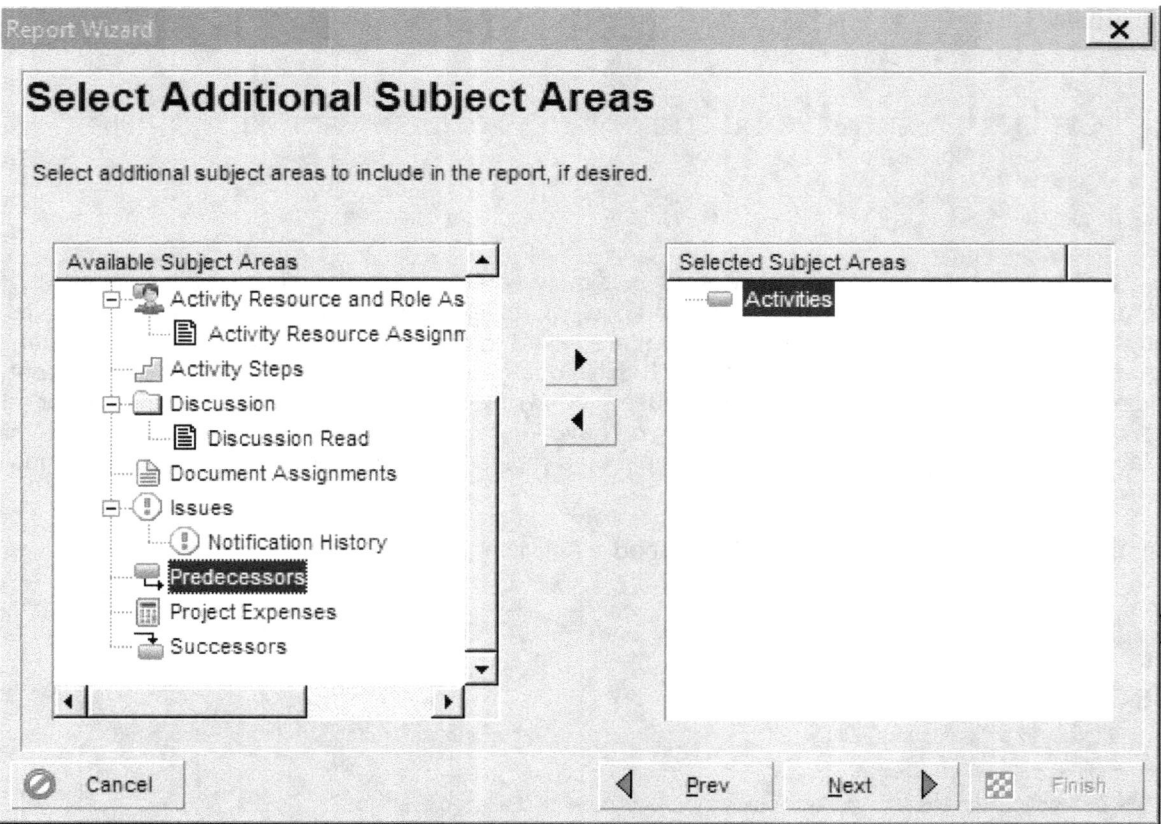

Click Next

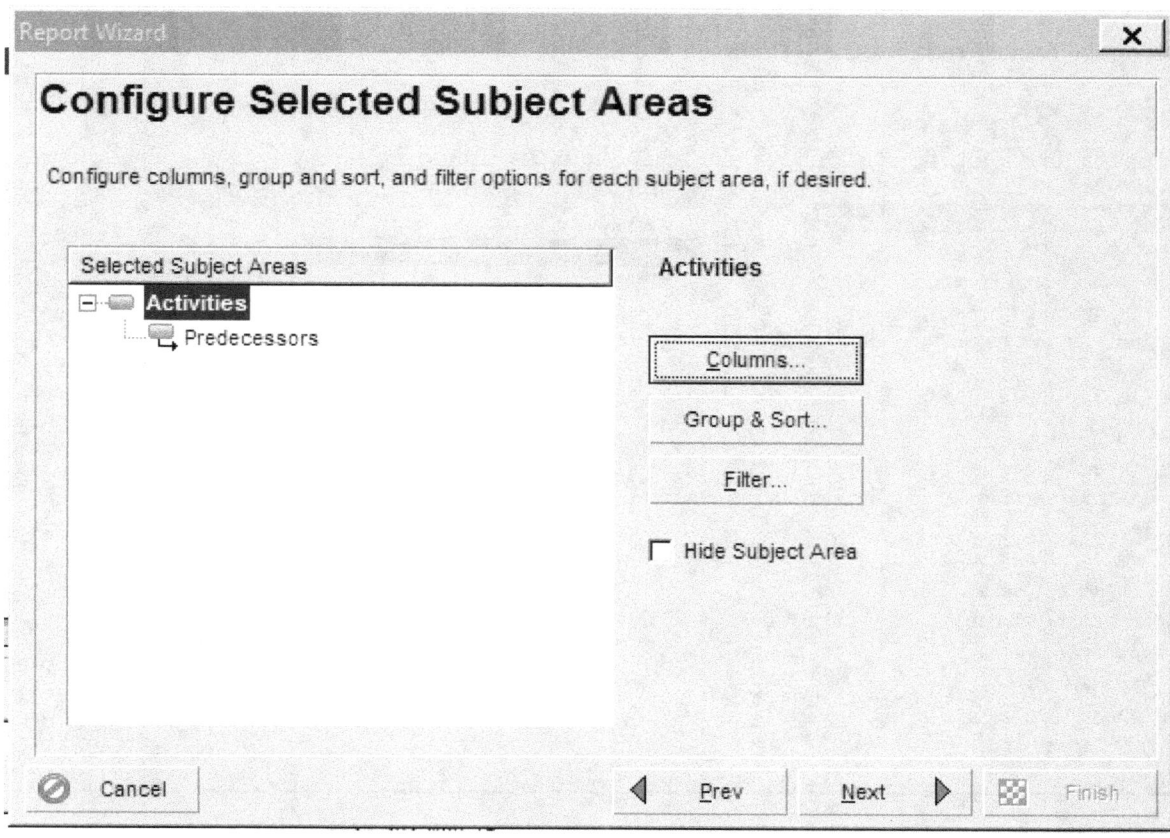

In the configuration window highlight Activities and click on columns, you probably need Activity ID, name and finish date + some other columns depending on your project setup:

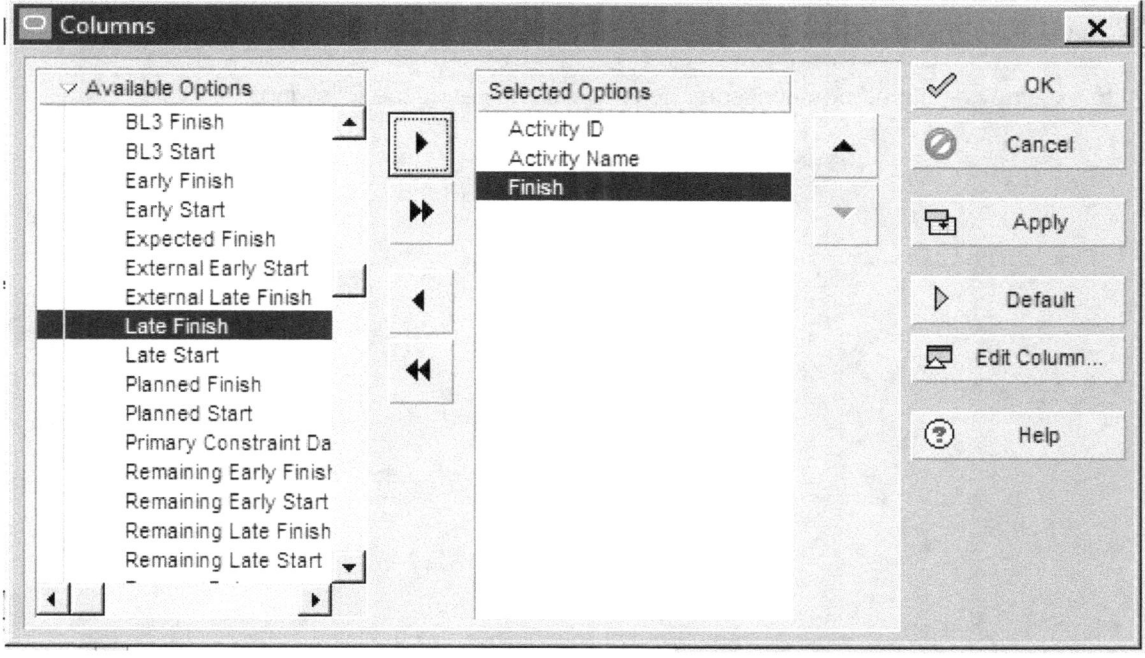

Click OK to return to the configuration window and set up your filter to display, say, system turnover MS.

Click OK again, select Predecessors > Columns and add the following:

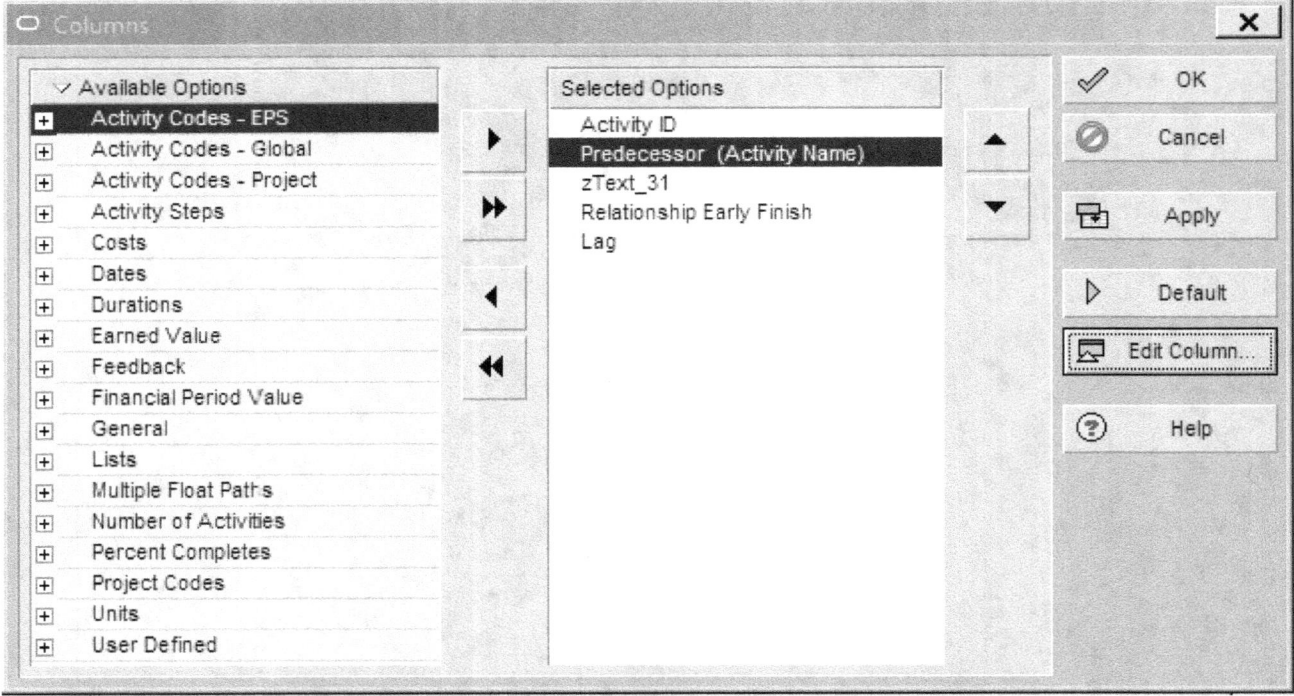

Notes:
You need a blank column (if you have the rights to create user defined fields in your system) or an empty text column from user defined fields to make sure activity finish dates and relationship finish dates are displayed in 2 separate columns.

I have changed Activity Name field to "Predecessor" for clarity

If you want to exclude completed predecessors, go to filters and set up the following:

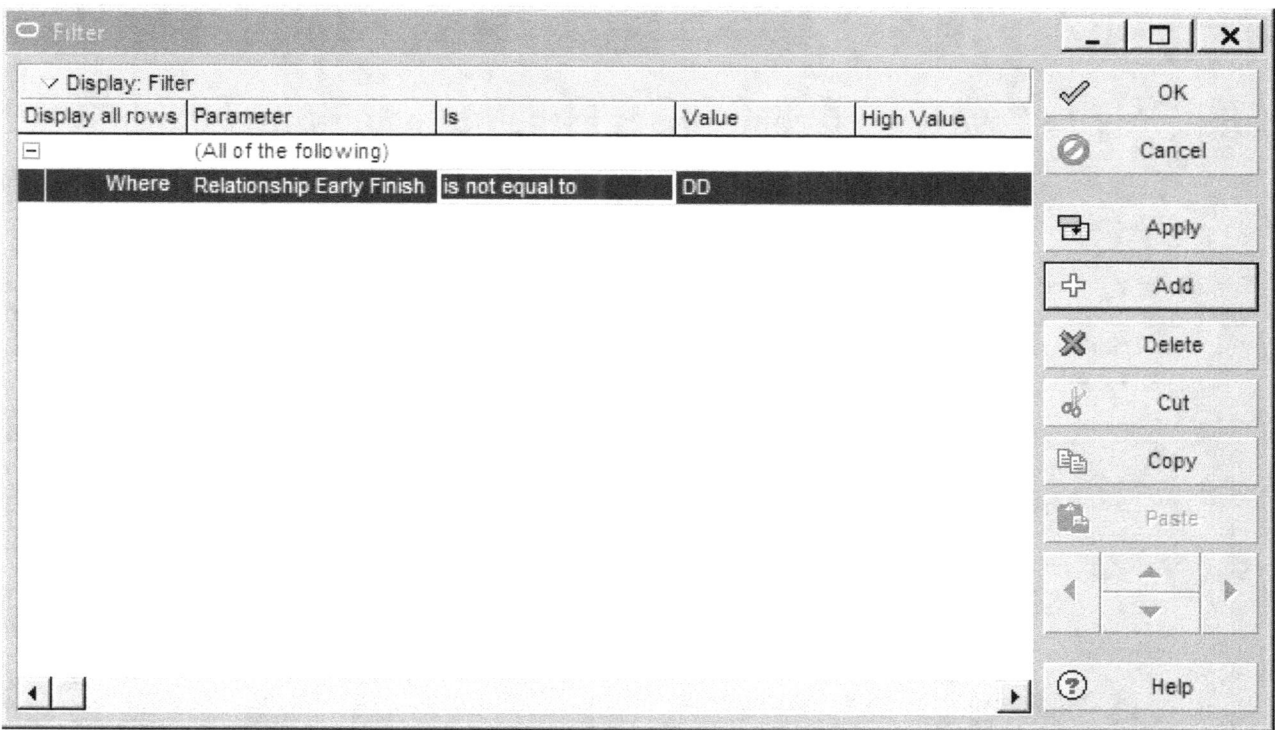

Run your report and in the resulting spreadsheet you will see something similar to the one below:

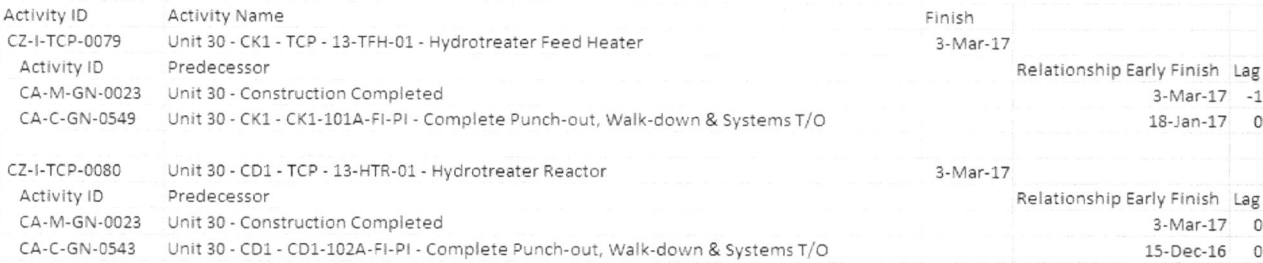

Now you can see what the date on which turnover MS would be if the driving predecessor is excluded or when you have a long list you can delete some of the predecessors and use the MAX function to figure out what would be your forecast date in this case or whatever.

## How to find all external relationships in your schedule

Inter-projects relationships can be a very useful tool when two or more projects are maintained by different planners in the same system and the links between these projects are real - like module assembly and module installation schedules. Very often, however, planners link, say, engineering and procurement schedules, one schedule does not get updated and if you inherit such a schedule from someone else you will have hard time understanding what is driving some of your dates and impacting your float. You can of course choose to ignore inter-project relationships in the scheduling options:

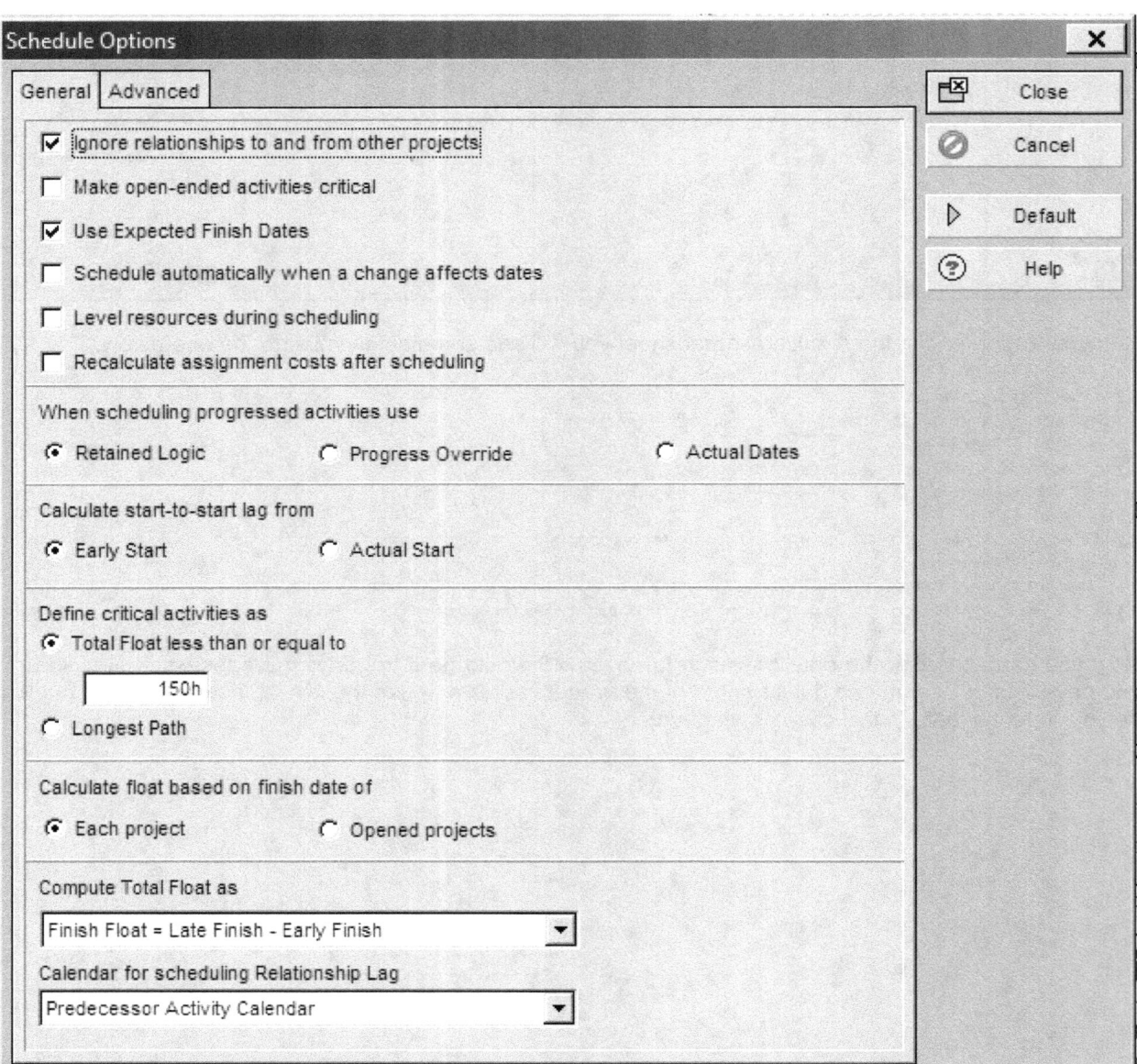

...but your project might be linked to several other projects and some of these links could be valid. First, we need to understand which projects our schedule is linked to and then decide if we want to keep, modify or remove these relationships.

Unfortunately, when you export your relationships from only one project P6 does not include any inter-project links in the export file and we need to find a different way to identify these external links.

Go to Reports > New > Activity Relationships

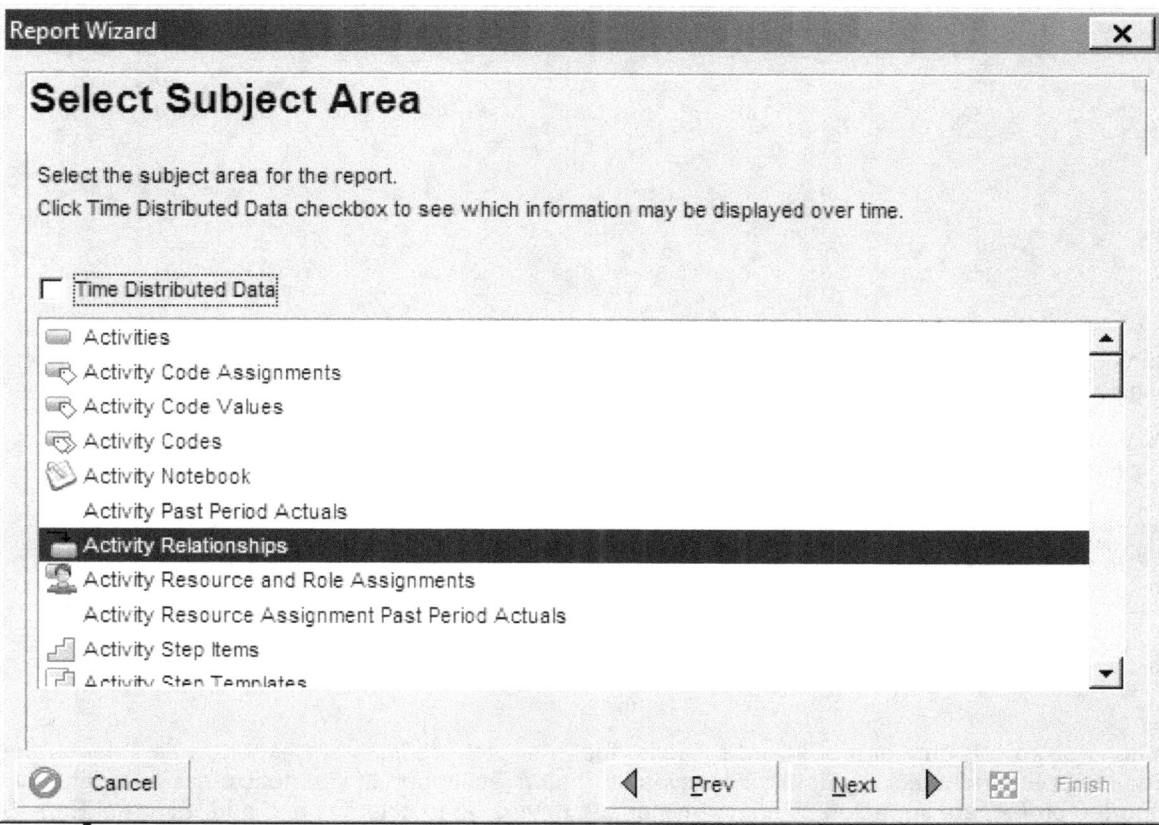

Click Next and set up a report with the following columns:

Andrei Sannikov
Tip of the day

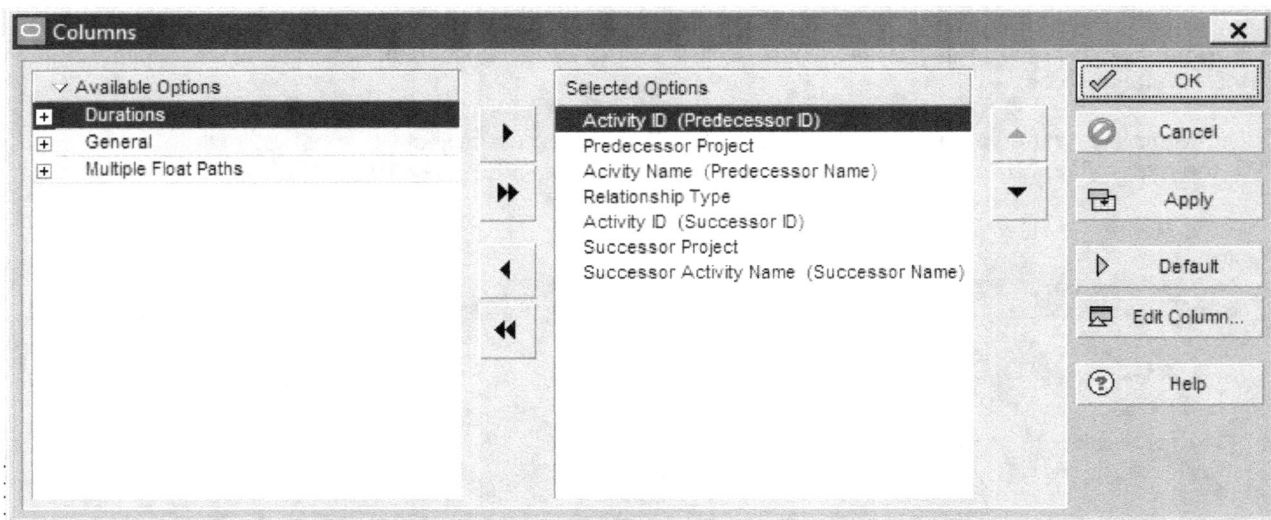

After running the report you will have a spreadsheet in which you can easily filter in all activities with inter-project relationships that you can then find in your schedule and adjust as necessary:

| Inter-project Relationship Report | | | | | | |
|---|---|---|---|---|---|---|
| Activity ID | Predecessor Pro | Acivity Name | Relationship Type | Activity ID | Successor Project | Successor Activity Name |
| BA-C-PP-4538 | N4WR20.P | Unit 20 - BA1-102B-PR-PI - Module Interconnect Wel | SS | BA-C-L4-PP-1060 | N4WR20.P-L4 | EWP - Starting Milestone - BA1-102-PR-PI |
| BA-C-PP-1400 | N4WR20.P | Unit 20 - BA1-102A-FI-PI - Install Shipped Loose Pipir | SS | BA-C-L4-PP-1040 | N4WR20.P-L4 | EWP - Starting Milestone - BA1-102A-FI-PI |
| BA-C-PP-4538 | N4WR20.P | Unit 20 - BA1-102B-PR-PI - Module Interconnect Wel | FF | BA-C-L4-PP-1070 | N4WR20.P-L4 | EWP - Finishing Milestone - BA1-102-PR-PI |
| BA-C-PP-1400 | N4WR20.P | Unit 20 - BA1-102A-FI-PI - Install Shipped Loose Pipir | FF | BA-C-L4-PP-1050 | N4WR20.P-L4 | EWP - Finishing Milestone - BA1-102A-FI-PI |
| BA-C-PP-4120 | N4WR20.P | Unit 20 - BA1-104A-FI-PI - Install Shipped Loose Pipir | SS | BA-C-L4-PP-10738 | N4WR20.P-L4 | EWP - Starting Milestone - BA1-104A-FI-PI |
| BA-C-PP-4120 | N4WR20.P | Unit 20 - BA1-104A-FI-PI - Install Shipped Loose Pipir | FF | BA-C-L4-PP-10728 | N4WR20.P-L4 | EWP - Finishing Milestone - BA1-104A-FI-PI |
| BA-C-PP-4568 | N4WR20.P | Unit 20 - BA1-104B-PR-PI - Module Interconnect Wel | SS | BA-C-L4-PP-10858 | N4WR20.P-L4 | EWP - Starting Milestone - BA1-104-PR-PI |
| BA-C-PP-4568 | N4WR20.P | Unit 20 - BA1-104B-PR-PI - Module Interconnect Wel | FF | BA-C-L4-PP-10848 | N4WR20.P-L4 | EWP - Finishing Milestone - BA1-104-PR-PI |
| BA-C-PP-4124 | N4WR20.P | Unit 20 - BA1-106A-FI-PI - Install Shipped Loose Pipir | SS | BA-C-L4-PP-10758 | N4WR20.P-L4 | EWP - Starting Milestone - BA1-106A-FI-PI |
| BA-C-PP-4124 | N4WR20.P | Unit 20 - BA1-106A-FI-PI - Install Shipped Loose Pipir | FF | BA-C-L4-PP-10748 | N4WR20.P-L4 | EWP - Finishing Milestone - BA1-106A-FI-PI |

Note: When you export only one of linked projects, the inter-projects links are exported as external constraints, which do not appear in the activity details window after the project import. If you notice that your dates and/or float in an imported project are impacted by some mysterious drivers go to columns and add "External Early Start" and "External Late Finish"

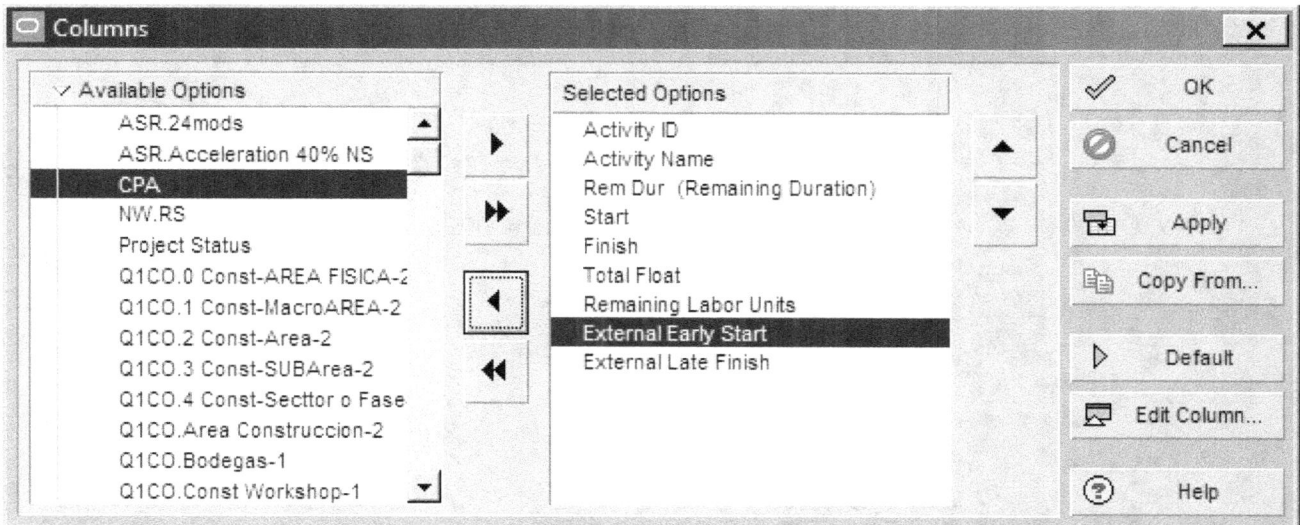

Plus a filter to display activities with external constraints:

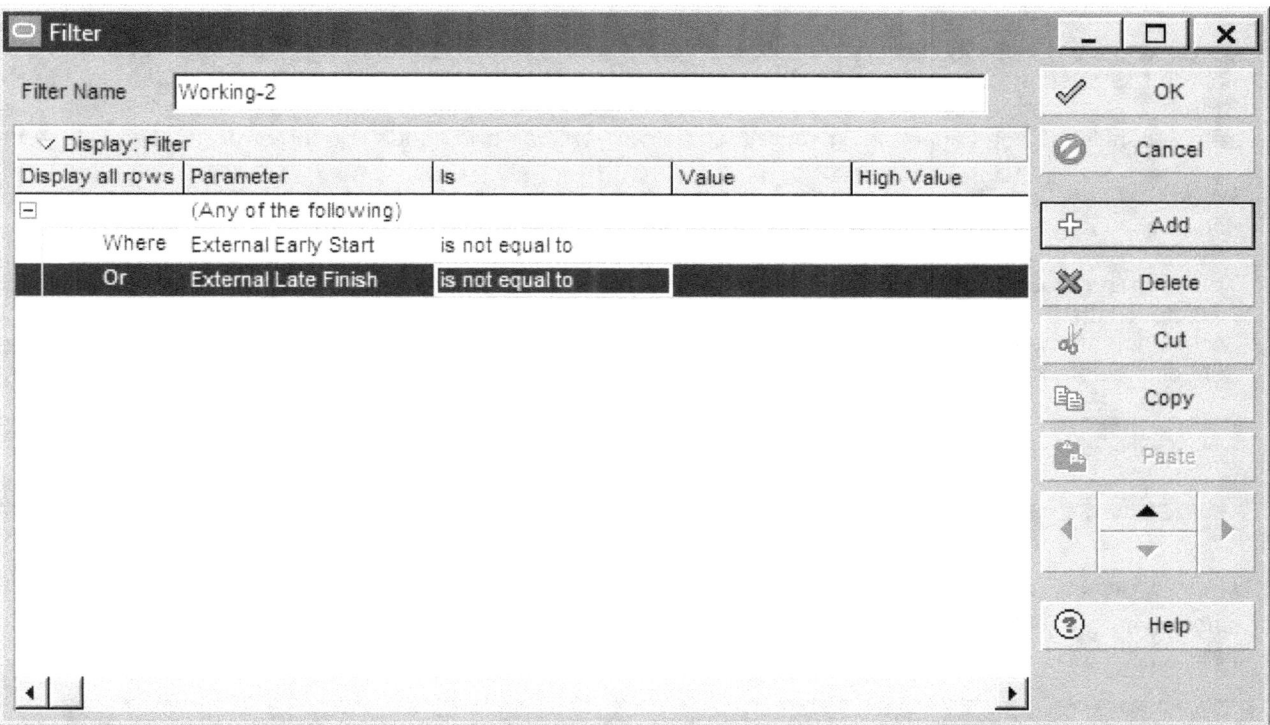

... and remove them from these columns if necessary.

Andrei Sannikov
Tip of the day

09-Feb-16 10:59

## What to do if P6 does not let you use the actual finish date of your choice

When we actualize activity finish dates we often see this very annoying pop-up:

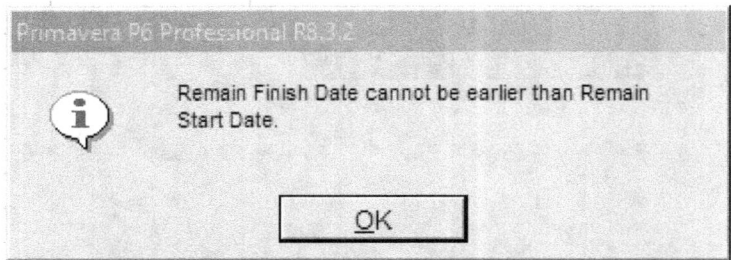

This happens when we change the date in the Finish box before we change the activity status to Completed by checking the Finished box in the activity status window.

Remaining Start is the earliest possible date the remaining work for the activity is scheduled to begin. Before the activity is started, the Remaining Start is the same as the Start date. Once the activity has started, the Remaining Start is equal to the Data Date, therefore, when you change the finish date to a date earlier than the data date P6 sees a conflict as you cannot finish something before you start and sends you the error message shown above.

When you check the Finished box the activity status changes to completed, the Remaining Start becomes blank and now you can adjust the actual finish date to any date that is later than the actual start date.

This morning, however, we came across a very strange situation - we actualized an activity but could not change its actual finish date from Feb 26 to any other date, it seemed locked for some reason. It is a rather rare occurrence and when it happens the place to look at is not the schedule logic or settings - go to the resources tab, right click and add finish and actual finish columns.

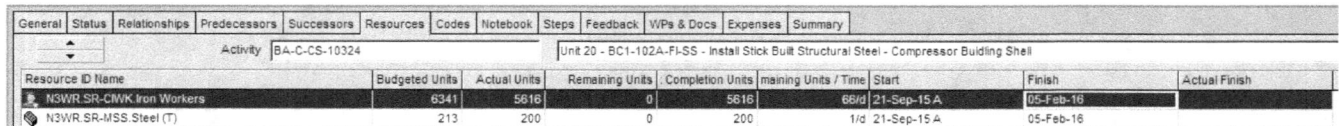

In this particular instance the actual finish date on the primary resource got "stuck" after it was set at Feb 26 and since in our project settings resource dates drive activity dates by default we could not change the activity finish date.

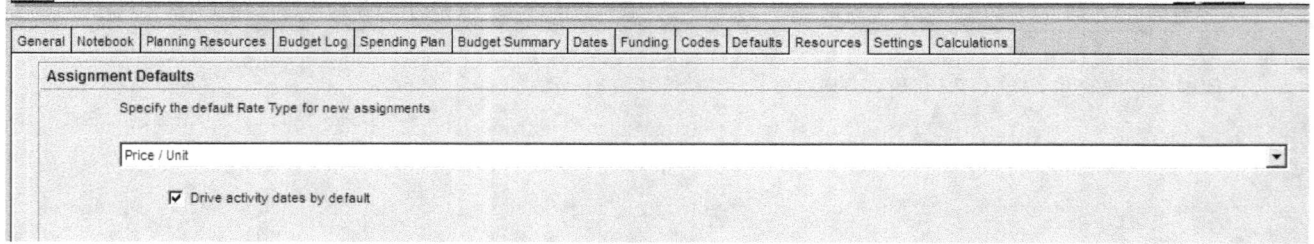

Andrei Sannikov
Tip of the day

If you see something similar in your schedule, go to the activity resources tab and adjust the resource actual finish date to match the actual finish date you need to set on your activity, this will unlock the actual finish date and everything will be back to normal.

Andrei Sannikov
Tip of the day

22-Feb-16 14:17

## How to plot a rolling forecast curve straight from P6

Sometimes we need to produce a quick "rolling forecast" curve straight from P6 without dumping the data into Excel first - you can even save this curve as a layout so it is readily available after each schedule update.

The problem is that when you simply choose actual and remaining early labor in the Activity Usage profile options:

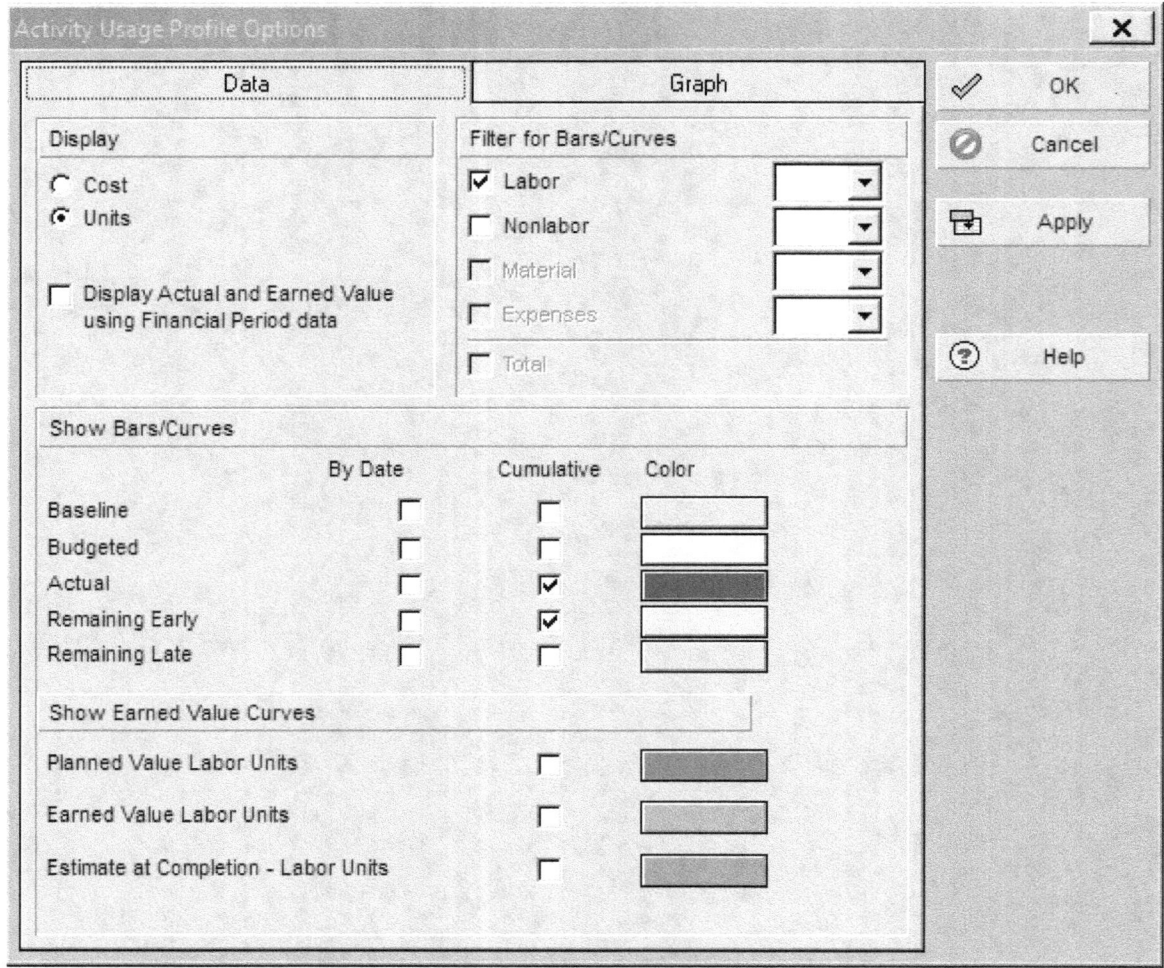

your remaining curve will not start at the end of the actual curve and will look like this:

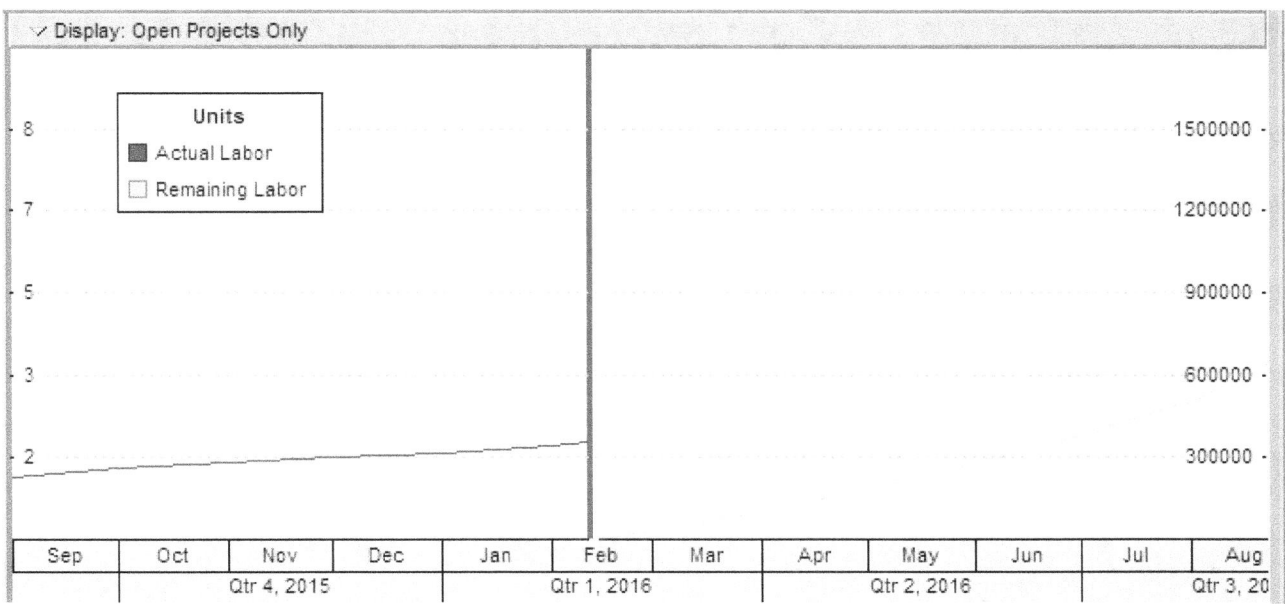

This can be easily fixed by choosing Actual Labor and Estimate at Completion - Labor units like shown below:

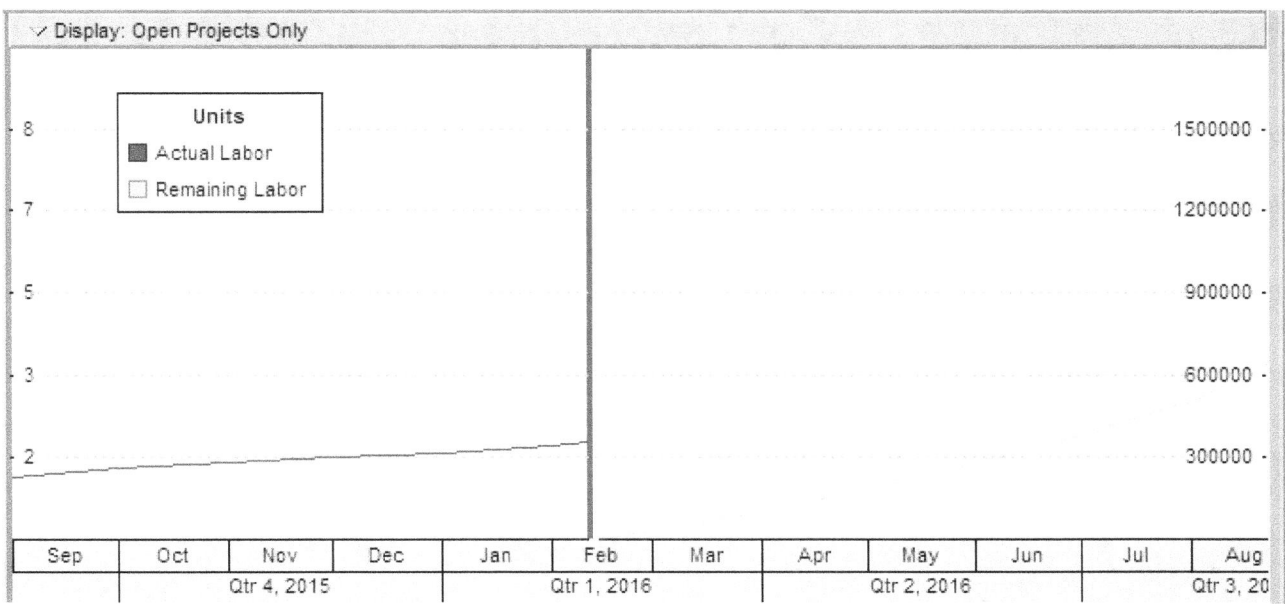

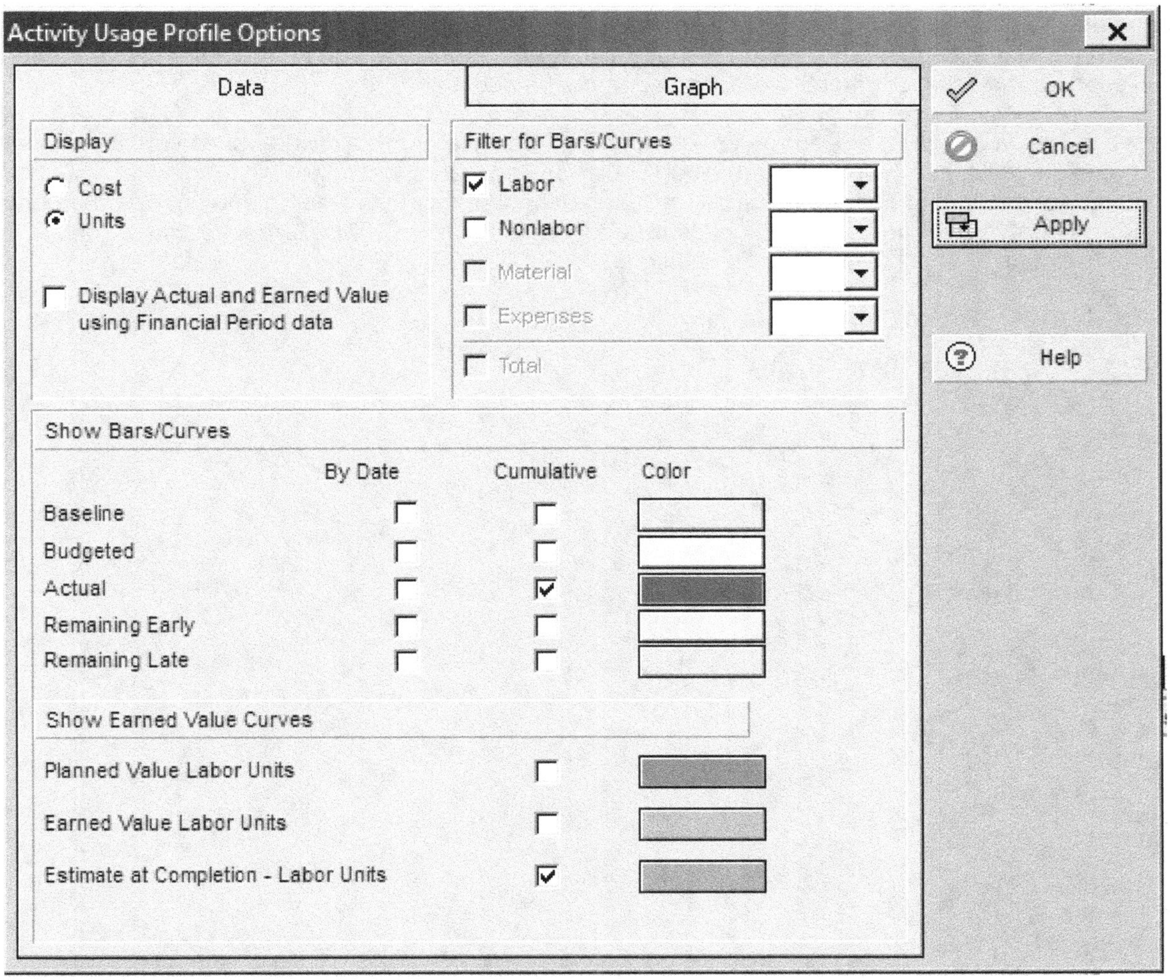

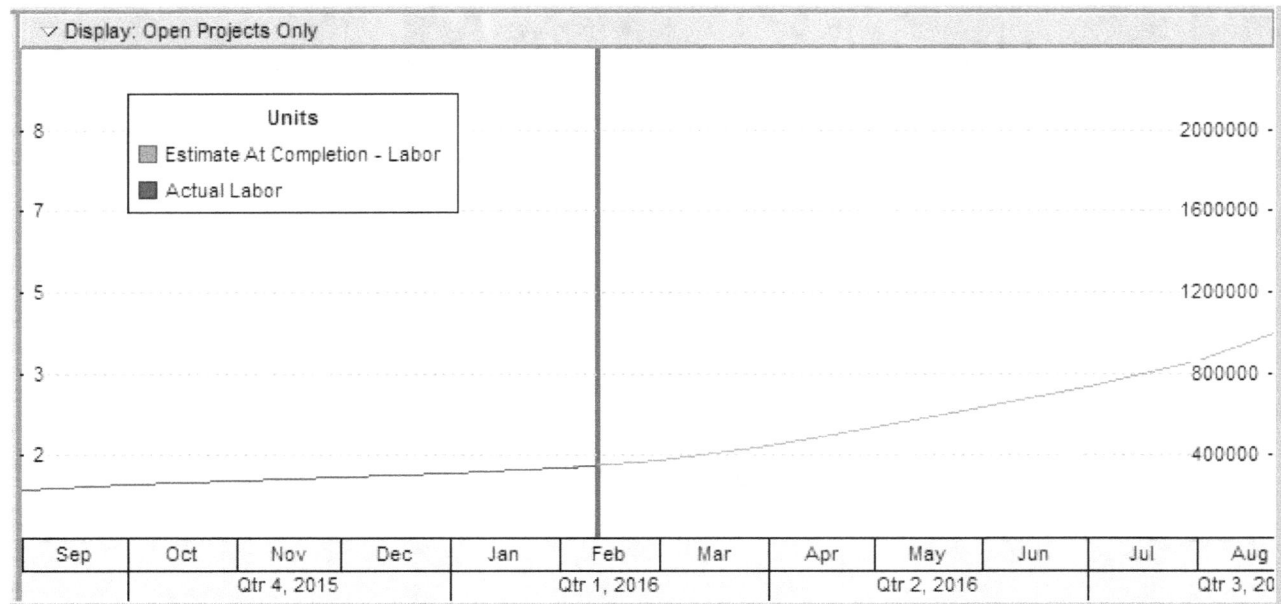

However, with this curve you can run into a different problem: your at completion labor units at the point corresponding to the project completion sometimes could be different from the figure (At Completion Labor Units) that you carry in your schedule. The reason is that Estimate at completion can be the same as your budget hours (At Completion Labor Units) or different - depending upon the settings.

In P6 you can use your actual or anticipated Productivity Factor (PF) to calculate your total labor hours you will need to complete a task. If you see that labor hours on the curve are different from what you have in the schedule, first go to columns and add Estimate at Completion - Labor Units column and check if the bottom line is different from what you see in the At Completion Labor Units column. If it is, it means that someone has been playing with Estimate to Complete calculation settings.

Go to WBS view and click on Earned Value tab:

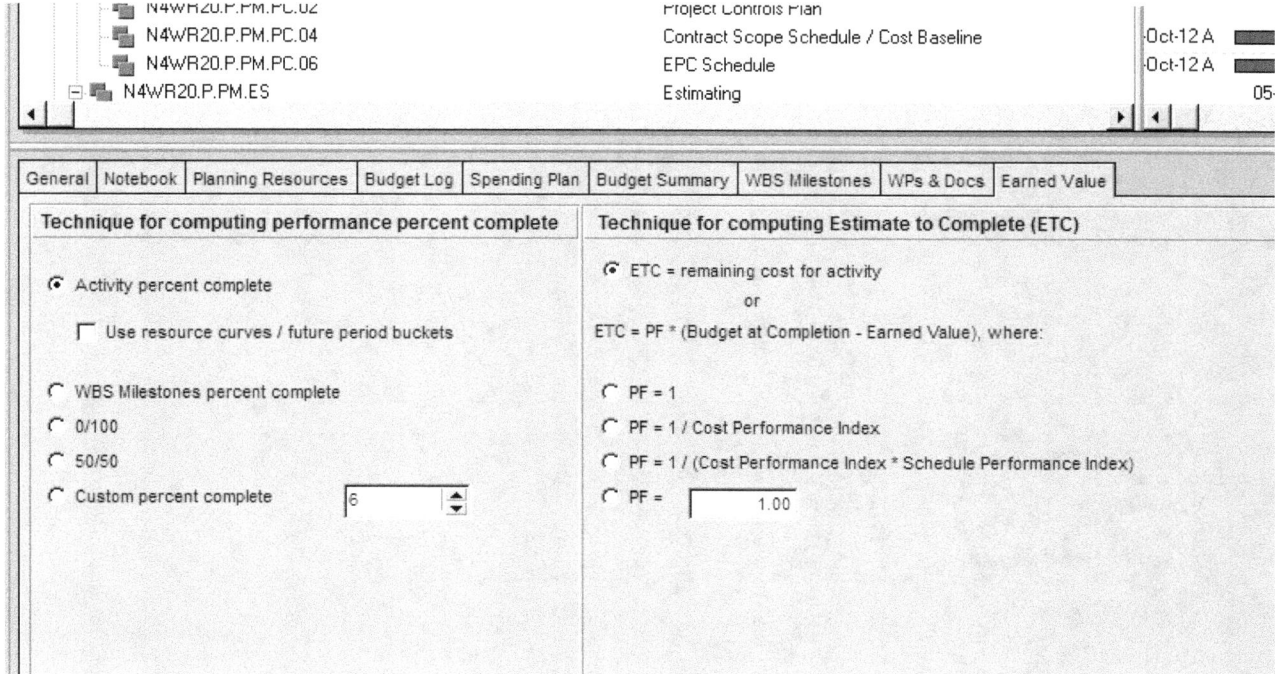

This setting can be different at each WBS level and you can either change it for a particular WBS or the entire project, in which case your built-in curve for Estimate at Completion will always match your At completion labor units. To change it for the entire project Go to the top WBS level and set ETC = Remaining cost for activity.

You will be asked if you want to apply this setting to the entire project:

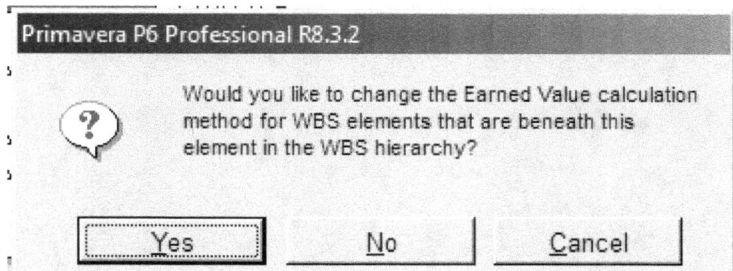

Click on Yes. Now you can save your Activity Usage Profile curve as a layout for future use.

Note that although you select All activities in the Activity Usage Profile options:

The curve will pull labor hours only from activities included in the current filter.

# How to add mid-point target dates to your schedule

We all know that we can assign a baseline schedule with a few clicks and P6, in theory, will show if a particular activity is ahead or behind what was planned in this baseline. This variance, however, could be very misleading because it is based on comparison of forecast dates in the current schedule vs. baseline dates and we might or might not change our forecast in each update. It would be much more accurate to compare planned progress at activity level vs. actual to see if we are really earning what we said we were going to earn and how far behind or ahead we are. However, the tools available in P6 let you see this comparison based on early dates only whilst planned progress curves on most projects are derived from mid-point dates (or mean values of early and late) so technically speaking you are not really behind until you have eaten up half of total float that was available on a particular activity in your baseline schedule. Let us see if we can make P6 run this calculation for us.

1. Make a copy of your baseline schedule and rename this copy to make sure you do not mix it with your normal project baseline - add "mid-point plan" or something like that to the description.

2. Open this copy, undo all the filters and run the following global changes:

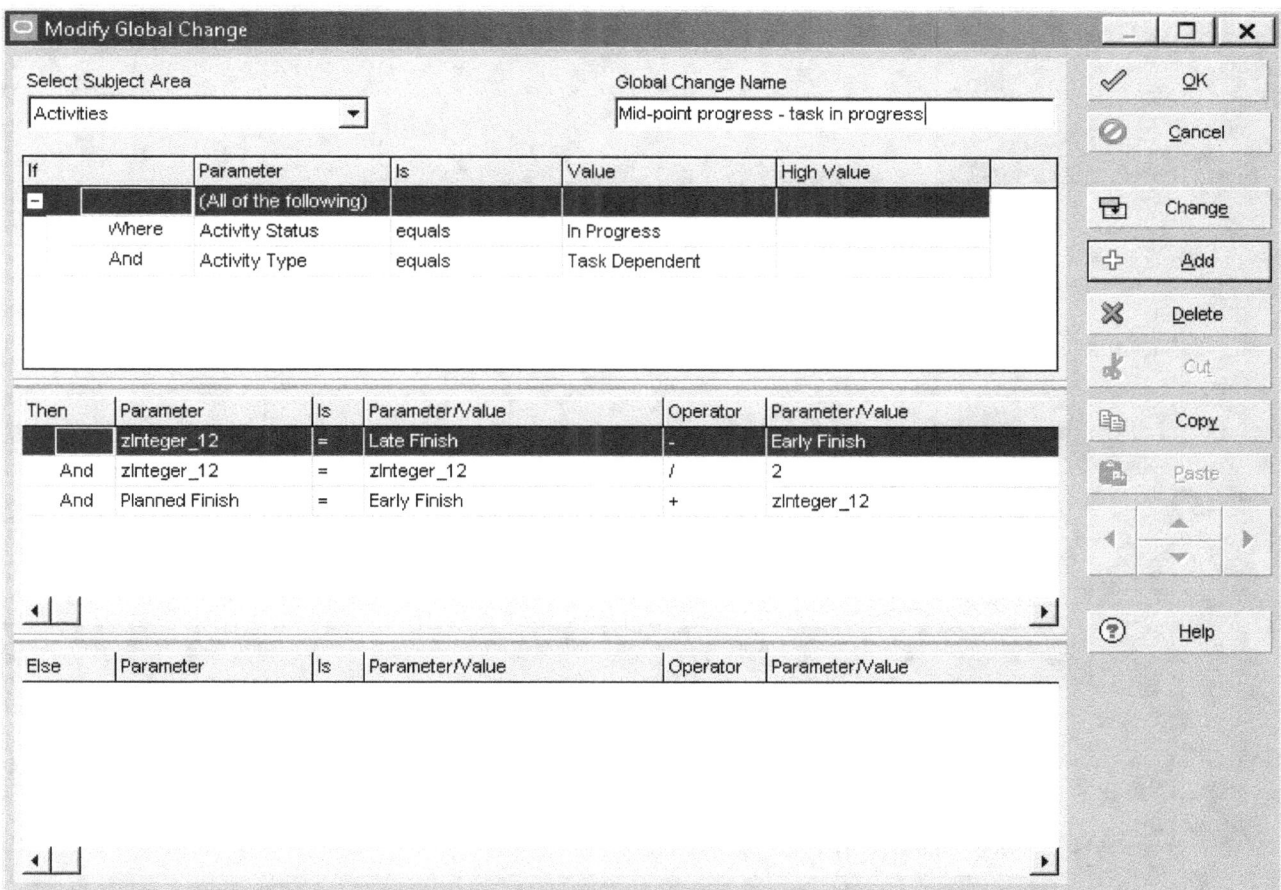

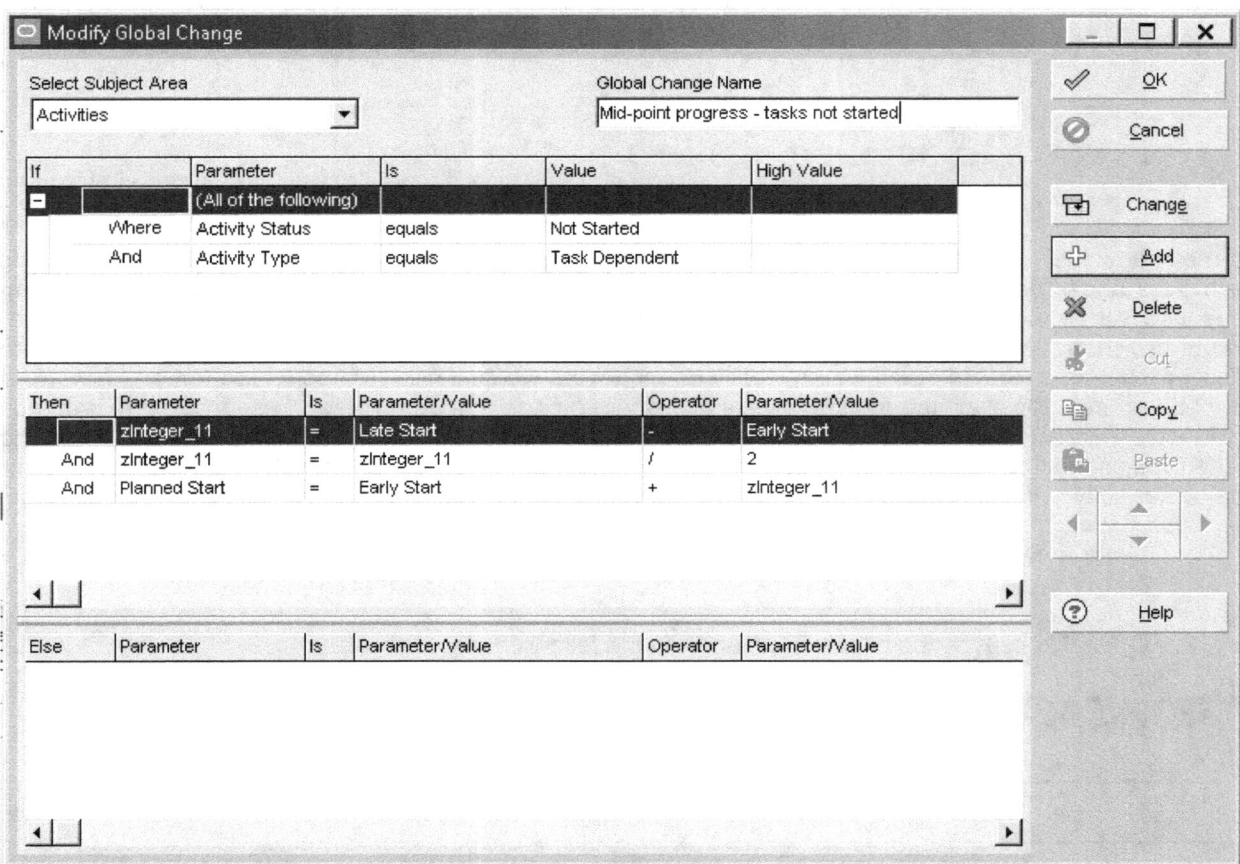

Note: zinteger_11 and zinteger_12 are user fields that we will use for temporary storage of data necessary for the calculation to work

3. Create a layout with the columns below to do some spot checks and make sure both global changes actually worked (with global changes you never know :))

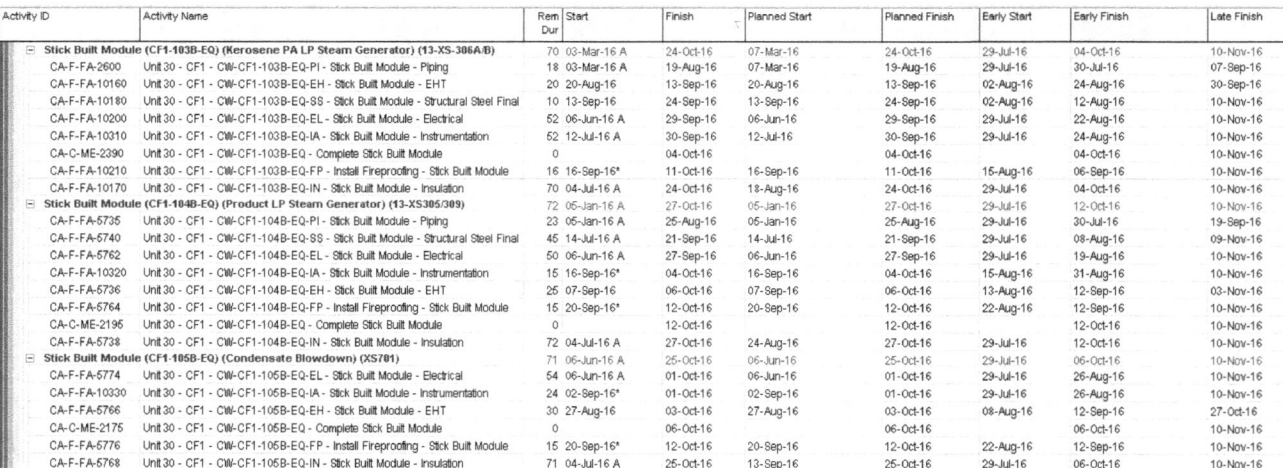

You will notice that your **Activity** Planned Finish dates are now approximately between Early and Late Finish - remember it is not a very exact science because of calendars and holidays but it should be close enough for

Andrei Sannikov
Tip of the day

planned progress purposes. Our global changes should not have impacted any of the milestone dates or schedule logic but it would not hurt to double-check.

4. Go back to your current project and assign the copy we have just created as your **Project baseline**.

5. Go to Columns and add Planned Value Labor Units, it will display labor hours planned to be earned at cutoff (data date) based on mid-point dates.

You can display mid-point dates, finish dates from your original baseline or both - you just need to assign your original baseline as Primary User Baseline (BL1) to have this flexibility. Remember, however, that your labor hours plan at cutoff is always pulled from your **Project Baseline**.

| Activity ID | Activity Name | Rem Dur | Start | Finish | Mid-Point Finish | BL1 Finish | Late Finish | Planned Value Labor Units | Actual Labor Units | At Completion Labor Units |
|---|---|---|---|---|---|---|---|---|---|---|
| CC1- A/G Piping | | 67 | 10-Mar-16 A | 19-Oct-16 | 07-Nov-16 | 19-Oct-16 | 12-Jan-17 | 17783 | 22826 | 40695 |
| Interconnects | | 60 | 31-May-16 A | 08-Oct-16 | 01-Nov-16 | 08-Oct-16 | 12-Jan-17 | 860 | 1288 | 1872 |
| CA-C-PP-4380 | Unit 30 - CC1 - CW-CC1-109D-PR-PI - Complete Module Interconnect Welds (1 | 6 | 27-Jun-16 A | 05-Aug-16 | 01-Oct-16 | 30-Jun-16 | 07-Dec-16 | 2 | 6 | 6 |
| CA-C-PP-2700 | Unit 30 - CC1 - CW-CC1-104B-PR-PI - Complete Module Interconnect Welds (1 | 6 | 15-Jul-16 A | 05-Aug-16 | 01-Oct-16 | 30-Jun-16 | 07-Dec-16 | 8 | 37 | 46 |
| CA-C-PP-4350 | Unit 30 - CC1 - CW-CC1-104C-PR-PI - Complete Module Interconnect Welds (2 | 27 | 11-Jul-16 A | 30-Aug-16 | 31-Oct-16 | 30-Aug-16 | 12-Jan-17 | 3 | 0 | 14 |
| CA-C-PP-4360 | Unit 30 - CC1 - CW-CC1-108D-PR-PI - Complete Module Interconnect Welds (3 | 27 | 11-Jul-16 A | 30-Aug-16 | 31-Oct-16 | 30-Aug-16 | 12-Jan-17 | 3 | 0 | 15 |
| CA-C-PP-4370 | Unit 30 - CC1 - CW-CC1-108E-PR-PI - Complete Module Interconnect Welds (3 | 27 | 12-Jul-16 A | 30-Aug-16 | 31-Oct-16 | 30-Aug-16 | 12-Jan-17 | 9 | 2 | 55 |
| CA-C-PP-2730 | Unit 30 - CC1 - CW-CC1-107C-PR-PI - Complete Module Interconnect Welds (6 | 27 | 06-Jun-16 A | 30-Aug-16 | 31-Oct-16 | 20-Jun-16 | 12-Jan-17 | 64 | 21 | 183 |
| CA-C-PP-2740 | Unit 30 - CC1 - CW-CC1-108B-PR-PI - Complete Module Interconnect Welds (36 | 27 | 31-May-16 A | 30-Aug-16 | 31-Oct-16 | 13-Jun-16 | 12-Jan-17 | 104 | 246 | 281 |
| CA-C-PP-2750 | Unit 30 - CC1 - CW-CC1-109B-PR-PI - Complete Module Interconnect Welds (49 | 27 | 31-May-16 A | 30-Aug-16 | 15-Sep-16 | 13-Jun-16 | 29-Sep-16 | 668 | 976 | 1272 |
| CA-C-PP-2680 | Unit 30 - CC1 - Complete Module Interconnect Welds FI Packages (9 EWPs) | 60 | 05-Jul-16 A | 08-Oct-16 | 01-Nov-16 | 08-Oct-16 | 24-Nov-16 | 0 | 0 | 0 |
| Stick Built | | 67 | 10-Mar-16 A | 19-Oct-16 | 07-Nov-16 | 19-Oct-16 | 24-Nov-16 | 16923 | 21538 | 38823 |
| CA-C-PP-2350 | Unit 30 - CC1 - CW-CC1-109A-FI-PI - Install Stick Built A/G Piping | 18 | 24-May-16 A | 19-Aug-16 | 01-Oct-16 | 18-Jul-16 | 17-Nov-16 | 955 | 583 | 2844 |
| CA-C-PP-1840 | Unit 30 - CC1 - CW-CC1-103A-FI-PI - Install Stick Built A/G Piping (13-VE102) | 18 | 13-Jun-16 A | 19-Aug-16 | 04-Oct-16 | 04-Aug-16 | 24-Nov-16 | 350 | 224 | 907 |
| CA-C-PP-1870 | Unit 30 - CC1 - CW-CC1-106A-FI-PI - Install Stick Built A/G Piping - Exchanger | 18 | 10-Mar-16 A | 19-Aug-16 | 04-Oct-16 | 17-Sep-16 | 24-Nov-16 | 14233 | 17789 | 26581 |
| CA-C-PP-1860 | Unit 30 - CC1 - CW-CC1-105A-FI-PI - Install Stick Built A/G Piping | 20 | 14-Jul-16 A | 22-Aug-16 | 05-Oct-16 | 22-Aug-16 | 24-Nov-16 | 217 | 255 | 1163 |
| CA-C-PP-1890 | Unit 30 - CC1 - CW-CC1-108A-FI-PI - Install Stick Built A/G Piping | 23 | 27-Jun-16 A | 25-Aug-16 | 07-Oct-16 | 02-Sep-16 | 24-Nov-16 | 798 | 2497 | 3794 |
| CA-C-PP-1830 | Unit 30 - CC1 - CW-CC1-102A-FI-PI - Install Stick Built A/G Piping | 25 | 04-Jul-16 A | 27-Aug-16 | 29-Sep-16 | 27-Aug-16 | 02-Nov-16 | 75 | 140 | 257 |
| CA-C-PP-1850 | Unit 30 - CC1 - CW-CC1-104A-FI-PI - Install Stick Built A/G Piping | 25 | 12-Jul-16 A | 27-Aug-16 | 01-Oct-16 | 27-Aug-16 | 09-Nov-16 | 295 | 50 | 1936 |
| CA-C-PP-0570 | Unit 30 - CC1 - CW-CC1-101A-FI-PI - Install Stick Built A/G Piping | 40 | 31-Aug-16 | 19-Oct-16 | 07-Nov-16 | 19-Oct-16 | 24-Nov-16 | 0 | 0 | 1340 |

## How to fix row height in your schedule

I am sure some of you had very frustrating experience with row height setting/optimization function in P6 - you choose Optimize height by row content and for no apparent reason P6 adds empty rows where visually it does not seem to be necessary:

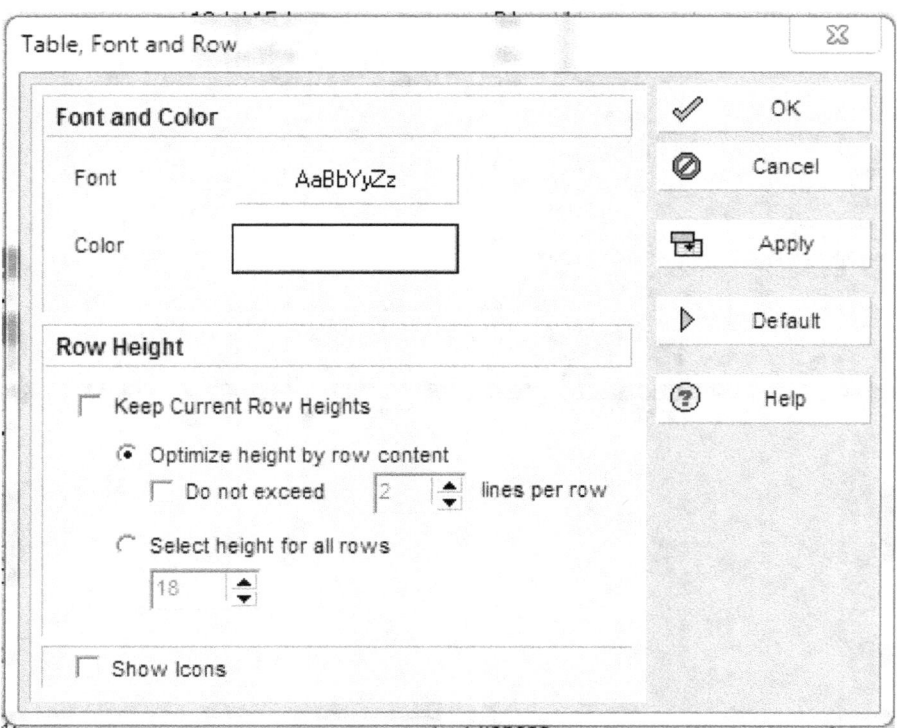

| Activity ID | Activity Name | Original Duration | Remaining Duration | Start | Finish |
|---|---|---|---|---|---|
| **Construction Milestones** | | 650 | 175 | 15-Jul-14 A | 08-Mar-17 |
| AA-M-GN-1115 | Unit 10 - Construction Mobilization | 0 | 0 | 15-Jul-14 A | |
| AA-M-GN-1145 | Unit 10 - Start Module Assembly | 0 | 0 | 27-May-15 A | |
| AA-M-GN-1440 | Unit 10 - First Piperack Module Delivered to Site | 0 | 0 | | 30-Oct-15 A |
| AA-M-GN-1195 | Unit 10 - Set Vacuum Tower (11-VE102) | 0 | 0 | | 09-Jan-16 A |
| AA-M-GN-1205 | Unit 10 - Set Atmospheric Tower (11-VE101) | 0 | 0 | | 13-Jan-16 A |
| AA-M-GN-1170 | Unit 10 - Complete Installation of Desalters (Dress-out) | 0 | 0 | | 26-Feb-16 A |
| AA-M-PR-1110 | Unit 10 - Deliver Last Tagged Equipment to Site | 0 | 0 | | 14-Mar-16 A |
| AA-M-GN-5040 | Unit 10 - Complete Modules Assembly at SMFI | 0 | 0 | | 13-May-16 A |
| AA-M-GN-5050 | Unit 10 - Complete Modules Assembly at WPC | 0 | 0 | | 13-Jun-16 A |
| AA-M-GN-1210 | Unit 10 - Deliver Last Module to Site | 0 | 0 | | 21-Jun-16 |
| AA-M-GN-5010 | Unit 10 - Set Last Module on Site | 0 | 0 | | 30-Jun-16 |
| AA-M-GN-3400 | Unit 10 - Complete Installation of Air Coolers | 0 | 0 | | 14-Jul-16 |
| AA-C-GN-9440 | Unit 10 - Install Last Mechanical Equipment | 0 | 0 | | 18-Jul-16 |
| AA-M-CS-5140 | Unit 10 - Complete Area paving | 0 | 0 | | 11-Aug-16 |
| AA-M-GN-1105 | Unit 10 - Complete Installation of Fired Heaters | 0 | 0 | | 31-Aug-16 |
| AA-M-CS-1190 | Unit 10 - Complete Structural Steel Erection | 0 | 0 | | 15-Sep-16 |
| AA-C-GN-9420 | Unit 10 - Complete All Stick Built Modules at Site | 0 | 0 | | 18-Oct-16 |

The reason is that P6 has something like 16 space characters preceding Activity ID number, you don't see them in the activity details or Activity ID column but they do appear when you copy an activity into a text editor like MS Word.

Activity ID → Activity Name→Original Duration → Remaining Duration→ Start → Finish¶

∙∙∙∙∙∙∙∙∙∙∙∙∙∙AA-E-PR-0150 → Unit 10 - Update & Re-issue System Diagrams IFD→17 → 0 → 04-Mar-13 A→ 26-Mar-13 A¶

These space characters seem to affect the row height optimization function we are trying to use.

Let us see if we can find a work around for that.

1. Open the layout where you want to optimize the height of all rows to fit as much information as possible.

2. Go to Columns and remove Activity ID column from the current view.

3. Go to View > Table, Font and Row. Uncheck Keep Current Row Height, check Optimize height by row content and click OK

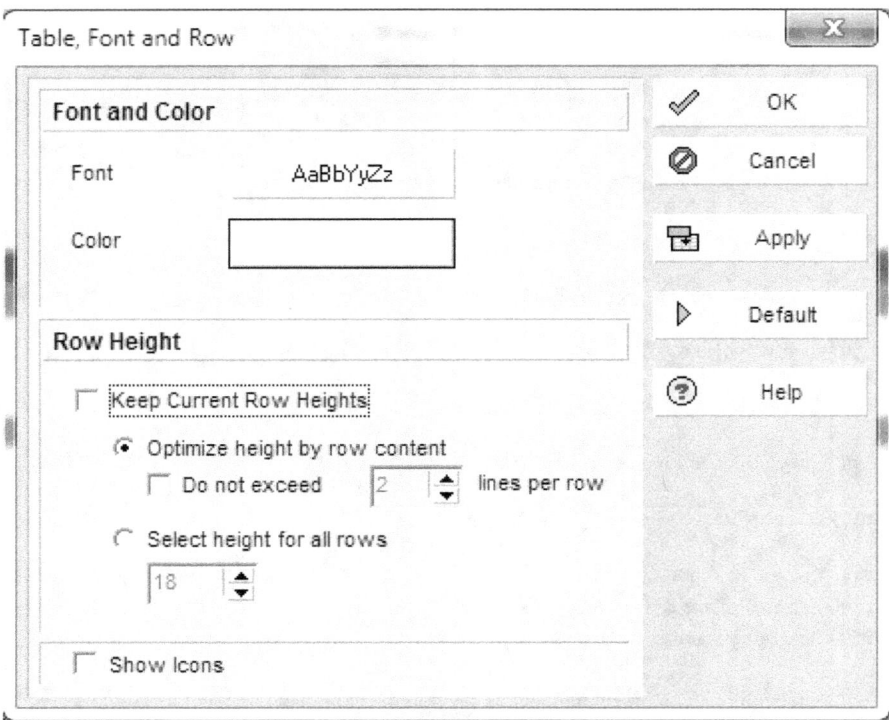

4. With your mouse expand the Activity Name column so that all text fits well in one row - if you do it right you will see that P6 has not added any empty rows although your Activity name column looks too wide:

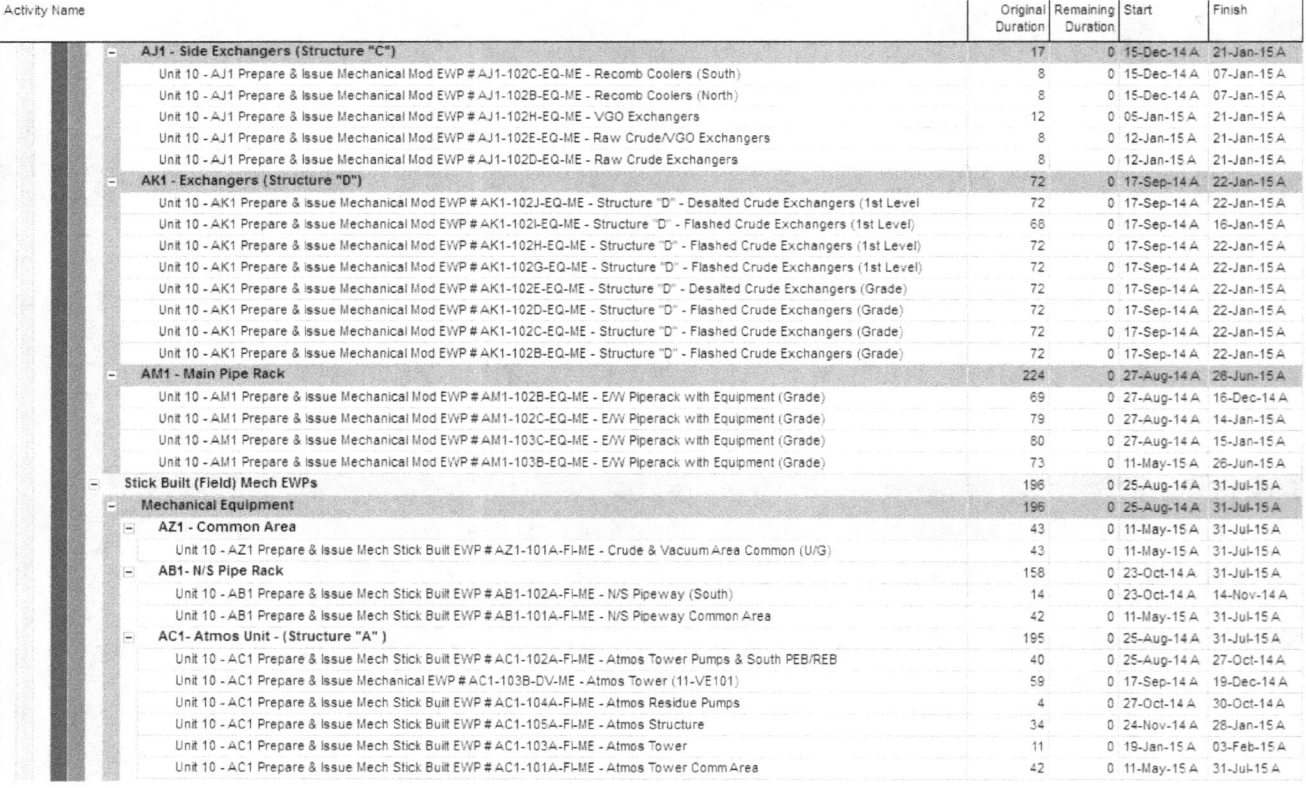

5. Using your mouse again reduce the width of the Activity name column to something that would work best for your paper size. You will notice that text strings will be wrapped but it is not quite like in Excel or Word - some lines might get cut etc. Anyway, after a few attempts you should be able to optimize your row height and fit as much as text as possible:

| Activity Name | Original Duration | Remaining Duration | Start | Finish |
|---|---|---|---|---|
| Equipment Module EWPs | 100 | 0 | 24-Oct-14 A | 20-Apr-15 A |
| Unit 10 - Start Issueing Mechanical E.W.Ps Group 1 | 0 | 0 | | 24-Oct-14 A |
| Unit 10 - Issue Mechanical E.W.Ps Group 2 | 0 | 0 | | 02-Dec-14 A |
| Unit 10 - Issue Mechanical E.W.Ps Group 3 | 0 | 0 | | 12-Jan-15 A |
| Unit 10 - Issue Mechanical E.W.Ps Group 4 | 0 | 0 | | 05-Feb-15 A |
| Unit 10 - Issue Mechanical E.W.Ps Group 5 | 0 | 0 | | 05-Mar-15 A |
| Unit 10 - Issue Mechanical E.W.Ps Group 6 | 0 | 0 | | 20-Apr-15 A |
| AC1- Atmos Unit - (Structure "A") | 133 | 0 | 25-Aug-14 A | 08-Apr-15 A |
| Unit 10 - AC1 Prepare & Issue Mechanical Mod EWP # AC1-104B-EQ-ME - Atmos Residue Pumps | 74 | 0 | 25-Aug-14 A | 19-Dec-14 A |
| Unit 10 - AC1 Prepare & Issue Mechanical Mod EWP # AC1-105C-EQ-ME - Structure "A" (Ground level - East) | 77 | 0 | 25-Aug-14 A | 07-Jan-15 A |
| Unit 10 - AC1 Prepare & Issue Mechanical Mod EWP # AC1-102B-EQ-ME - Atmos Tower Pumps | 10 | 0 | 05-Jan-15 A | 19-Jan-15 A |
| Unit 10 - AC1 Prepare & Issue Mechanical Mod EWP # AC1-105B-EQ-ME - Structure "A" (Ground level - | 10 | 0 | 05-Jan-15 A | 19-Jan-15 A |
| Unit 10 - AC1 Prepare & Issue Mechanical Mod EWP # AC1-105E-EQ-ME - Structure "A" (1st level - East) | 3 | 0 | 19-Jan-15 A | 21-Jan-15 A |
| Unit 10 - AC1 Prepare & Issue Mechanical Mod EWP # AC1-105D-EQ-ME - Structure "A" (1st level - West) | 24 | 0 | 02-Mar-15 A | 08-Apr-15 A |
| AF1 - Vacuum Unit - (Structure "B") | 213 | 0 | 25-Aug-14 A | 30-Jun-15 A |
| Unit 10 - AF1 Prepare & Issue Mechanical Mod EWP # AF1-102B-EQ-ME - Vacuum Tower Pumps | 72 | 0 | 25-Aug-14 A | 17-Dec-14 A |
| Unit 10 - AF1 Prepare & Issue Mechanical Mod EWP # AF1-105E-EQ-ME - Structure "B" (1st level - East) | 64 | 0 | 30-Sep-14 A | 22-Jan-15 A |
| Unit 10 - AF1 Prepare & Issue Mechanical Mod EWP # AF1-105F-EQ-ME - Structure "B" (2nd level - West) | 64 | 0 | 30-Sep-14 A | 22-Jan-15 A |
| Unit 10 - AF1 Prepare & Issue Mechanical Mod EWP # AF1-105B-EQ-ME - Structure "B" (Ground level - West) | 10 | 0 | 05-Jan-15 A | 19-Jan-15 A |
| Unit 10 - AF1 Prepare & Issue Mechanical Mod EWP # AF1-105C-EQ-ME - Structure "B" (Ground level - East) | 10 | 0 | 05-Jan-15 A | 19-Jan-15 A |
| Unit 10 - AF1 Prepare & Issue Mechanical Mod EWP # AF1-103B-EQ-ME - Vacuum Tower Pumps and Filters | 65 | 0 | 12-Jan-15 A | 23-Apr-15 A |
| Unit 10 - AF1 Prepare & Issue Mechanical Mod EWP # AF1-105G-EQ-ME - Structure "B" (2nd level - East) | 56 | 0 | 19-Jan-15 A | 16-Apr-15 A |
| Unit 10 - AF1 Prepare & Issue Mechanical Mod EWP # AF1-105H-EQ-ME - Structure "B" (3rd level - West) | 30 | 0 | 02-Mar-15 A | 16-Apr-15 A |
| Unit 10 - AF1 Prepare & Issue Mechanical Mod EWP # AF1-105I-EQ-ME - Structure "B" (3rd level - East) | 42 | 0 | 02-Mar-15 A | 22-Apr-15 A |

6. Now go to Columns and bring back the activity ID column, adjust its width and the Activity name column width (as it usually changes a little bit after we put Activity ID back in) in the Column setup dialogue:

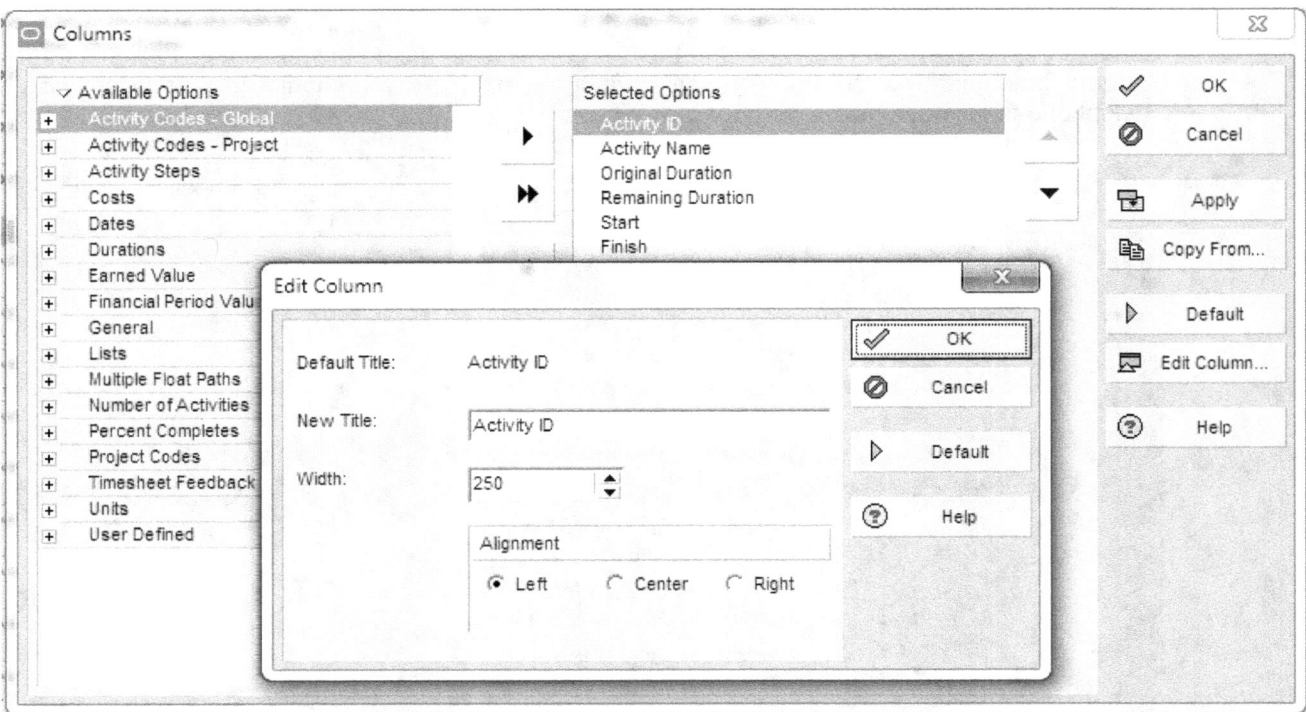

You will see that the layout we have just created still looks the same i.e. P6 has not added any blank rows that we saw in our first attempt:

| Activity ID | Activity Name | Original Duration | Remaining Duration | Start | Finish |
|---|---|---|---|---|---|
| AA-E-ME-2280 | Unit 10 - AF1 Prepare & Issue Mechanical Mod EWP # AF1-105G-EQ-ME - Structure "B" (2nd level - East) | 56 | 0 | 19-Jan-15 A | 16-Apr-15 A |
| AA-E-ME-2270 | Unit 10 - AF1 Prepare & Issue Mechanical Mod EWP # AF1-105H-EQ-ME - Structure "B" (3rd level - West) | 30 | 0 | 02-Mar-15 A | 16-Apr-15 A |
| AA-E-ME-2290 | Unit 10 - AF1 Prepare & Issue Mechanical Mod EWP # AF1-105I-EQ-ME - Structure "B" (3rd level - East) | 42 | 0 | 02-Mar-15 A | 22-Apr-15 A |
| AA-E-ME-2210 | Unit 10 - AF1 Prepare & Issue Mechanical Mod EWP # AF1-105L-EQ-ME - Structure "B" (4th level - West) | 30 | 0 | 02-Mar-15 A | 16-Apr-15 A |
| AA-E-ME-2220 | Unit 10 - AF1 Prepare & Issue Mechanical Mod EWP # AF1-105J-EQ-ME - Structure "B" (4th level - East) | 42 | 0 | 02-Mar-15 A | 22-Apr-15 A |
| AA-E-ME-2230 | Unit 10 - AF1 Prepare & Issue Mechanical Mod EWP # AF1-105K-EQ-ME - Structure "B" (5th level - Ejector Piping) | 30 | 0 | 02-Mar-15 A | 16-Apr-15 A |
| AA-E-ME-2240 | Unit 10 - AF1 Prepare & Issue Mechanical Mod EWP # AF1-105D-EQ-ME - Structure "B" (1st level - West) | 60 | 0 | 11-May-15 A | 30-Jun-15 A |
| **AG1 - Desalters** | | 77 | 0 | 25-Aug-14 A | 07-Jan-15 A |
| AA-E-ME-2090 | Unit 10 - AG1 Prepare & Issue Mechanical Mod EWP # AG1-102B-EQ-ME - Fuel Gas Filters | 77 | 0 | 25-Aug-14 A | 07-Jan-15 A |
| **AH1 - Flares** | | 25 | 0 | 09-Mar-15 A | 15-Apr-15 A |
| AA-E-ME-2510 | Unit 10 - AH1 Prepare & Issue Mechanical Mod EWP # AH1-102B-EQ-ME - HC Drain | 25 | 0 | 09-Mar-15 A | 15-Apr-15 A |
| AA-E-ME-8300 | Unit 10 - AH1 Prepare & Issue Mechanical Mod EWP # AH1-103B-EQ-ME - KO Drum | 21 | 0 | 09-Mar-15 A | 09-Apr-15 A |
| **AJ1 - Side Exchangers (Structure "C")** | | 17 | 0 | 15-Dec-14 A | 21-Jan-15 A |
| AA-E-ME-2320 | Unit 10 - AJ1 Prepare & Issue Mechanical Mod EWP # AJ1-102C-EQ-ME - Recomb Coolers (South) | 8 | 0 | 15-Dec-14 A | 07-Jan-15 A |
| AA-E-ME-2330 | Unit 10 - AJ1 Prepare & Issue Mechanical Mod EWP # AJ1-102B-EQ-ME - Recomb Coolers (North) | 8 | 0 | 15-Dec-14 A | 07-Jan-15 A |
| AA-E-ME-2340 | Unit 10 - AJ1 Prepare & Issue Mechanical Mod EWP # AJ1-102H-EQ-ME - VGO Exchangers | 12 | 0 | 05-Jan-15 A | 21-Jan-15 A |
| AA-E-ME-2300 | Unit 10 - AJ1 Prepare & Issue Mechanical Mod EWP # AJ1-102E-EQ-ME - Raw Crude/VGO Exchangers | 8 | 0 | 12-Jan-15 A | 21-Jan-15 A |
| AA-E-ME-2310 | Unit 10 - AJ1 Prepare & Issue Mechanical Mod EWP # AJ1-102D-EQ-ME - Raw Crude Exchangers | 8 | 0 | 12-Jan-15 A | 21-Jan-15 A |
| **AK1 - Exchangers (Structure "D")** | | 72 | 0 | 17-Sep-14 A | 22-Jan-15 A |
| AA-E-ME-2350 | Unit 10 - AK1 Prepare & Issue Mechanical Mod EWP # AK1-102J-EQ-ME - Structure "D" - Desalted Crude Exchangers (1st Level) | 72 | 0 | 17-Sep-14 A | 22-Jan-15 A |
| AA-E-ME-2360 | Unit 10 - AK1 Prepare & Issue Mechanical Mod EWP # AK1-102I-EQ-ME - Structure "D" - Flashed Crude Exchangers (1st Level) | 68 | 0 | 17-Sep-14 A | 16-Jan-15 A |

**Note**: if you start changing the column width with your mouse now i.e. with Activity ID column displayed blank rows will appear again - you either need to change the column width in the column setup dialogue (text wrapping might not work in this case) or remove the activity ID column from your view first.

Andrei Sannikov
Tip of the day

18-Mar-17 18:15

## What to do with the driving flags on completed activities

I am sure all of you have noticed that in retained logic mode P6 places a driving flag on all completed activities - this would make sense when you have out of sequence logic i.e. a completed activity or milestone is driving its successors because it has predecessors that are not completed. However, even completed milestones that are constrained and have no predecessors would appear as driving in the predecessors details window:

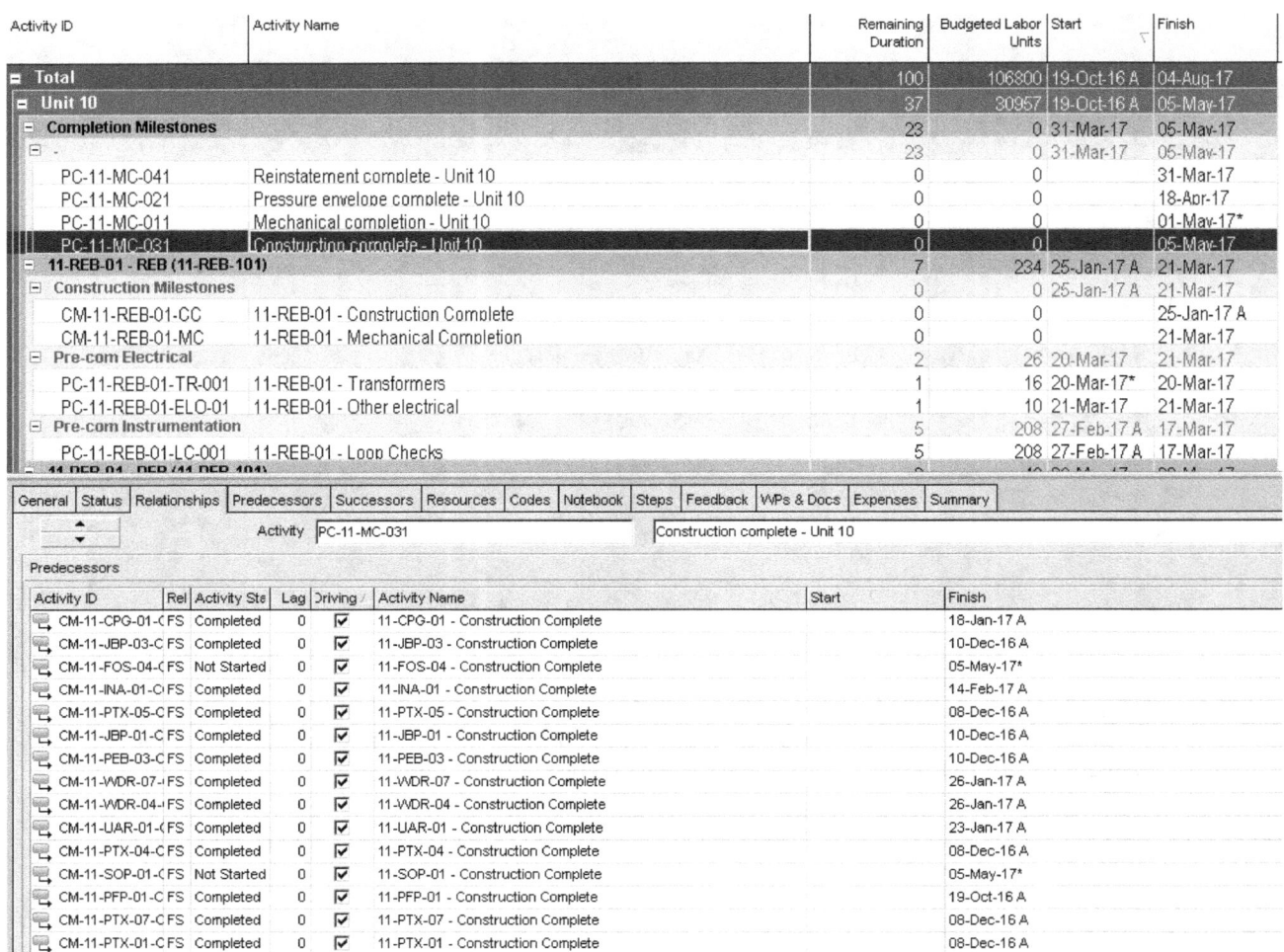

I will never understand how an activity that finished in January can "drive" a completion milestone scheduled for May and driven by a bunch of other real predecessors but P6 algorithms is not something we can control.

Most planners try to overcome this problem by simply adding the activity status column, sorting by activity status and searching for the real drivers among not started or in progress activities as shown in the example below:

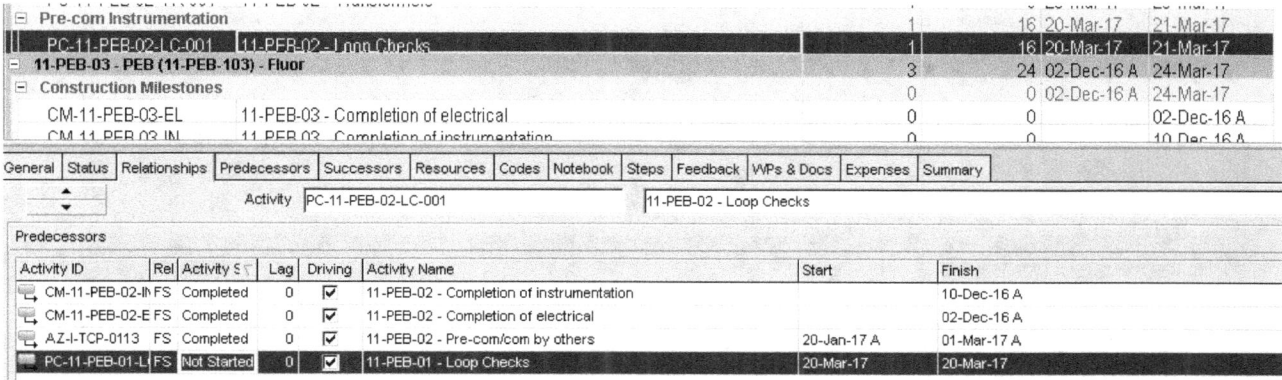

This method works when the activity you are looking at has only a handful of predecessors but imagine you are checking your project MC milestone linked to few hundred activities in a schedule review meeting with your screen displayed through an overhead projector and your project manager wants to know what is driving his MC date. If you sort your predecessors by driving status, you will see tons of "drivers" some of which are completed and some not like shown in the first screenshot above, you will have to look through this list with everybody waiting for answers. This could be a very embarrassing experience. Let us see what we can do to avoid it.

If we are confident that we do not have any out of sequence logic problems in our schedule and our drivers can be only not started and in progress activities there is a way to show them at the top of your "drivers" list.

1. Right click in the predecessor details window and go to Customize Predecessor Columns:

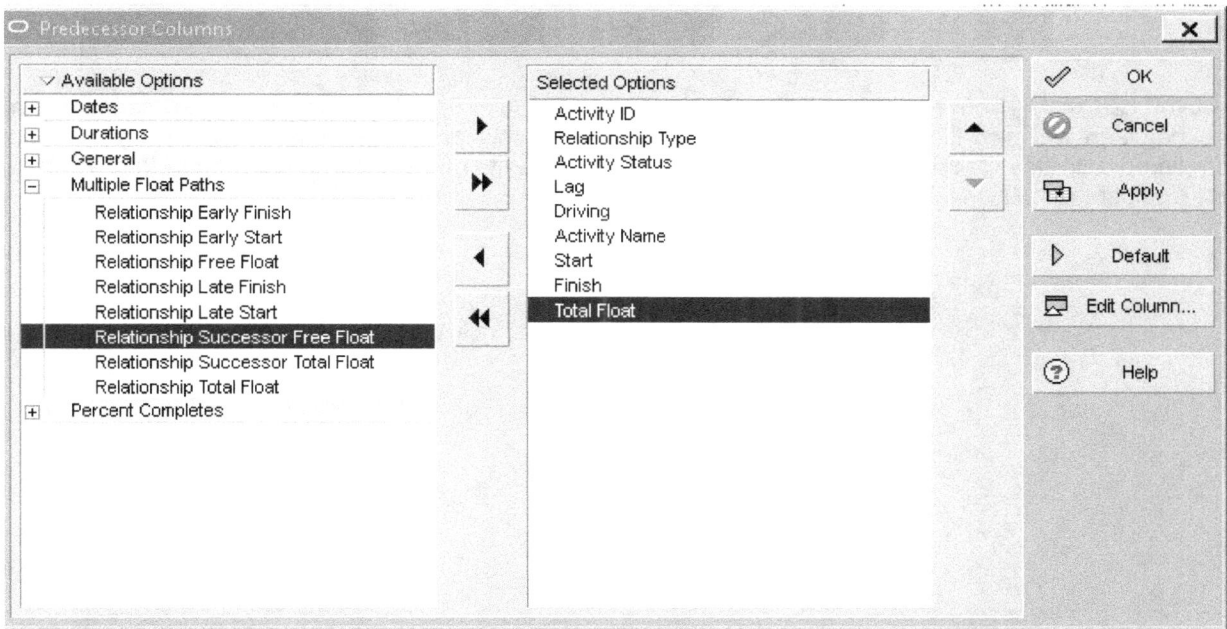

2. Add Relationship Successor Free Float column

3. Go to your milestone with multiple drivers and click on this column in the predecessors details window:

Andrei Sannikov
Tip of the day

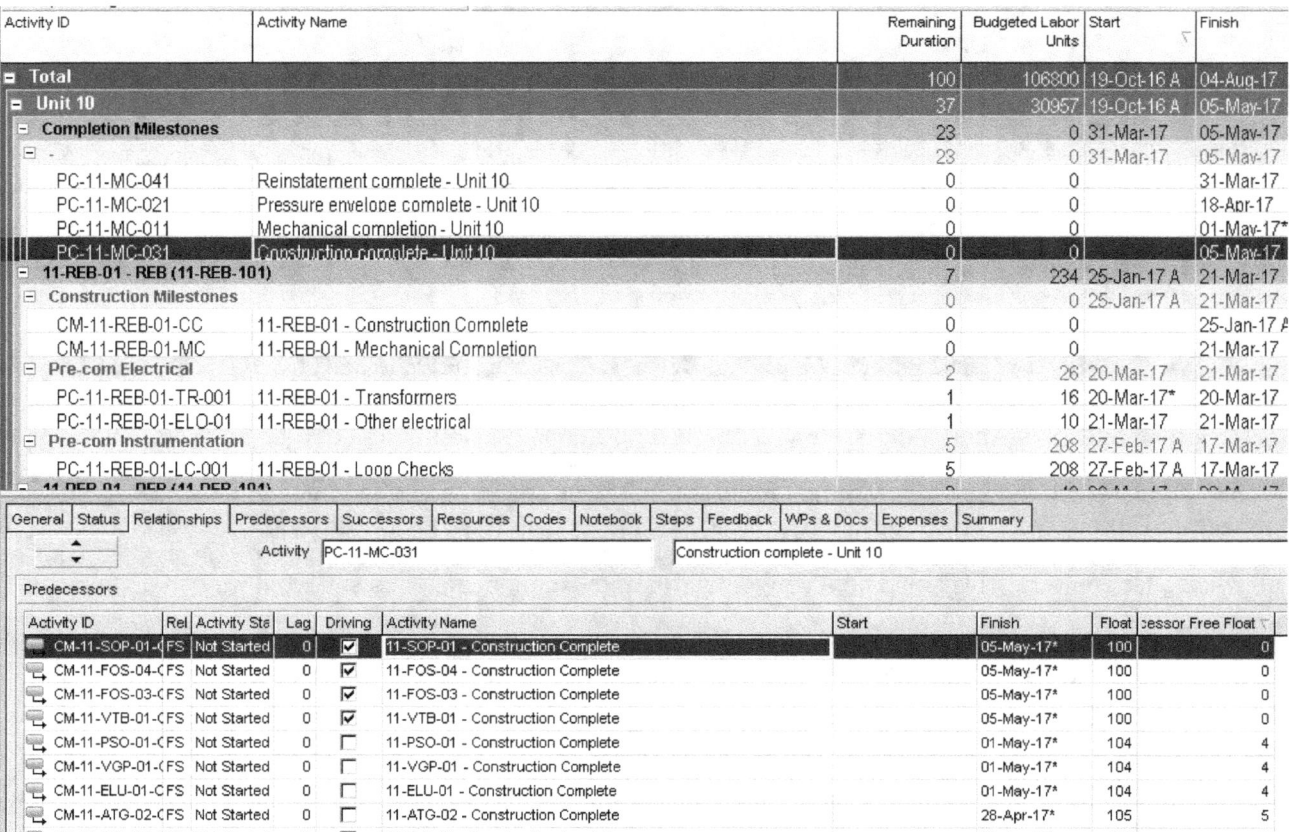

Now you can see all your real drivers at the top of the list because Free Float essentially represents the amount of time between two activities in a relationship and if it is 0 this predecessor is really driving its successor(s). Completed activities for this reason will have significant amounts of free float and although they will have driving flags against them, they will be way down this list:

Andrei Sannikov
Tip of the day

| Activity ID | Activity Name | Remaining Duration | Budgeted Labor Units | Start | Fin |
|---|---|---|---|---|---|
| **Total** | | 100 | 106800 | 19-Oct-16 A | 04 |
| **Unit 10** | | 37 | 30957 | 19-Oct-16 A | 05 |
| **Completion Milestones** | | 23 | 0 | 31-Mar-17 | 05 |
| - | | 23 | 0 | 31-Mar-17 | 05 |
| PC-11-MC-041 | Reinstatement complete - Unit 10 | 0 | 0 | | 31 |
| PC-11-MC-021 | Pressure envelope complete - Unit 10 | 0 | 0 | | 18 |
| PC-11-MC-011 | Mechanical completion - Unit 10 | 0 | 0 | | 01 |
| PC-11-MC-031 | Construction complete - Unit 10 | 0 | 0 | | 05 |
| **11-REB-01 - REB (11-REB-101)** | | 7 | 234 | 25-Jan-17 A | 21 |
| **Construction Milestones** | | 0 | 0 | 25-Jan-17 A | 21 |
| CM-11-REB-01-CC | 11-REB-01 - Construction Complete | 0 | 0 | | 25 |
| CM-11-REB-01-MC | 11-REB-01 - Mechanical Completion | 0 | 0 | | 21 |
| **Pre-com Electrical** | | 2 | 26 | 20-Mar-17 | 21 |
| PC-11-REB-01-TR-001 | 11-REB-01 - Transformers | 1 | 16 | 20-Mar-17* | 20 |
| PC-11-REB-01-ELO-01 | 11-REB-01 - Other electrical | 1 | 10 | 21-Mar-17 | 21 |
| **Pre-com Instrumentation** | | 5 | 208 | 27-Feb-17 A | 17 |
| PC-11-REB-01-LC-001 | 11-REB-01 - Loop Checks | 5 | 208 | 27-Feb-17 A | 17 |

General | Status | Relationships | Predecessors | Successors | Resources | Codes | Notebook | Steps | Feedback | WPs & Docs | Expenses | Summary

Activity: PC-11-MC-031 — Construction complete - Unit 10

**Predecessors**

| Activity ID | Rel | Activity Sta | Lag | Driving | Activity Name | Start | Finish | Float | cessor Free Float |
|---|---|---|---|---|---|---|---|---|---|
| CM-11-PTX-07-C | FS | Completed | 0 | ✓ | 11-PTX-07 - Construction Complete | | 08-Dec-16 A | | 37 |
| CM-11-PFP-01-C | FS | Completed | 0 | ✓ | 11-PFP-01 - Construction Complete | | 19-Oct-16 A | | 37 |
| CM-11-PTX-04-C | FS | Completed | 0 | ✓ | 11-PTX-04 - Construction Complete | | 08-Dec-16 A | | 37 |
| CM-11-UAR-01-( | FS | Completed | 0 | ✓ | 11-UAR-01 - Construction Complete | | 23-Jan-17 A | | 37 |
| CM-11-WDR-04- | FS | Completed | 0 | ✓ | 11-WDR-04 - Construction Complete | | 26-Jan-17 A | | 37 |
| CM-11-WDR-07- | FS | Completed | 0 | ✓ | 11-WDR-07 - Construction Complete | | 26-Jan-17 A | | 37 |
| CM-11-PEB-03-C | FS | Completed | 0 | ✓ | 11-PEB-03 - Construction Complete | | 10-Dec-16 A | | 37 |
| CM-11-JBP-01-C | FS | Completed | 0 | ✓ | 11-JBP-01 - Construction Complete | | 10-Dec-16 A | | 37 |
| CM-11-PTX-05-C | FS | Completed | 0 | ✓ | 11-PTX-05 - Construction Complete | | 08-Dec-16 A | | 37 |
| CM-11-INA-01-C | FS | Completed | 0 | ✓ | 11-INA-01 - Construction Complete | | 14-Feb-17 A | | 37 |

Andrei Sannikov
Tip of the day

10-Jul-17 12:13

## How to check your schedule for driving external relationships

On very large projects with a lot of moving parts sometimes it is necessary to link multiple projects so the impact of any delays in, say, engineering can be quickly seen on construction and commissioning. That's the theory. In practice engineering updates are often neglected and nobody even touches commissioning schedules until it is time to start commissioning or do another re-baseline. When you start seeing something strange happening to your dates, it might be a good idea to check all your inter-project links... However, if you have a few hundred you might want to start with the driving ones. Of course, you can run a successor-predecessor report and display the "Driving" column but as we all know P6 adds a driving flag to all completed relationships in the retained logic mode and if your project has a lot of actuals this column/filter would not do you any good.

Consider the following:

1. Go to Reports > Add New > Activity Relationships

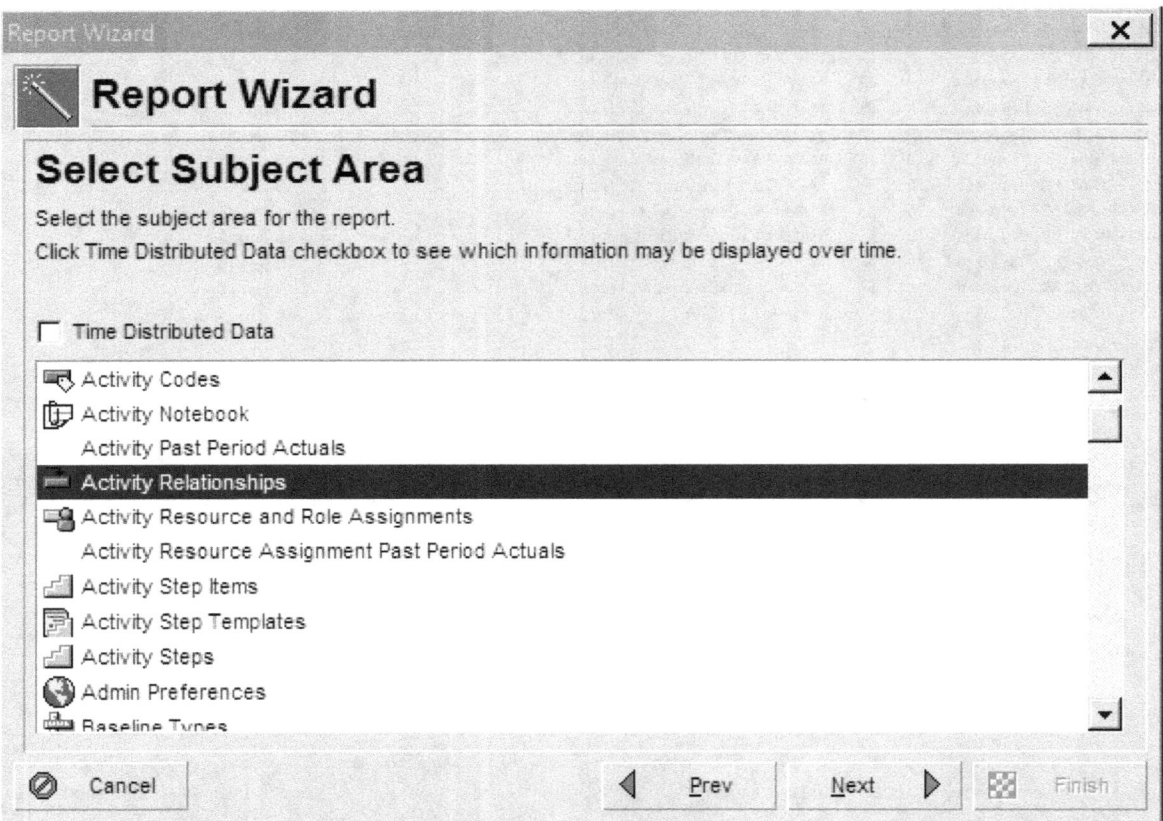

2. Click Next and add the following columns (I have renamed some of them to save space):

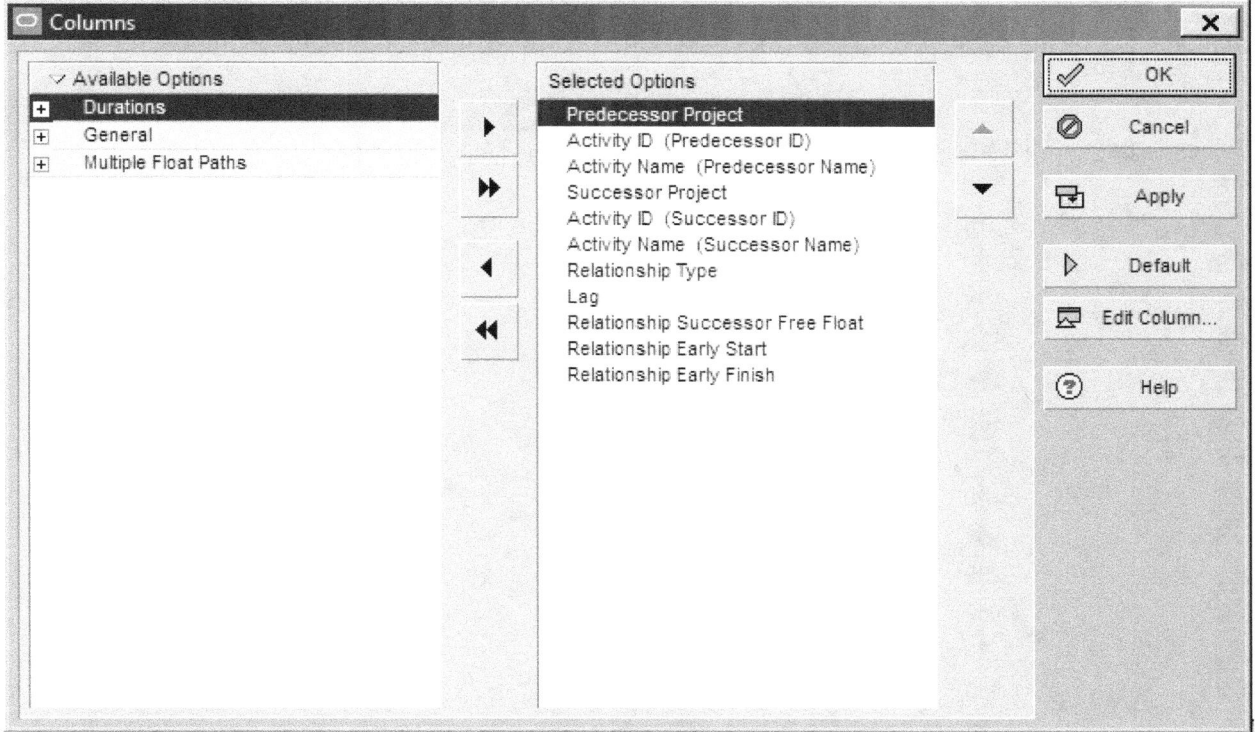

3. Click OK, open Filter and make sure no filters are applied to your report. I prefer to remove all sorting as well since it is better done in Excel after export.

4. Click Next and run your report in ASCII format:

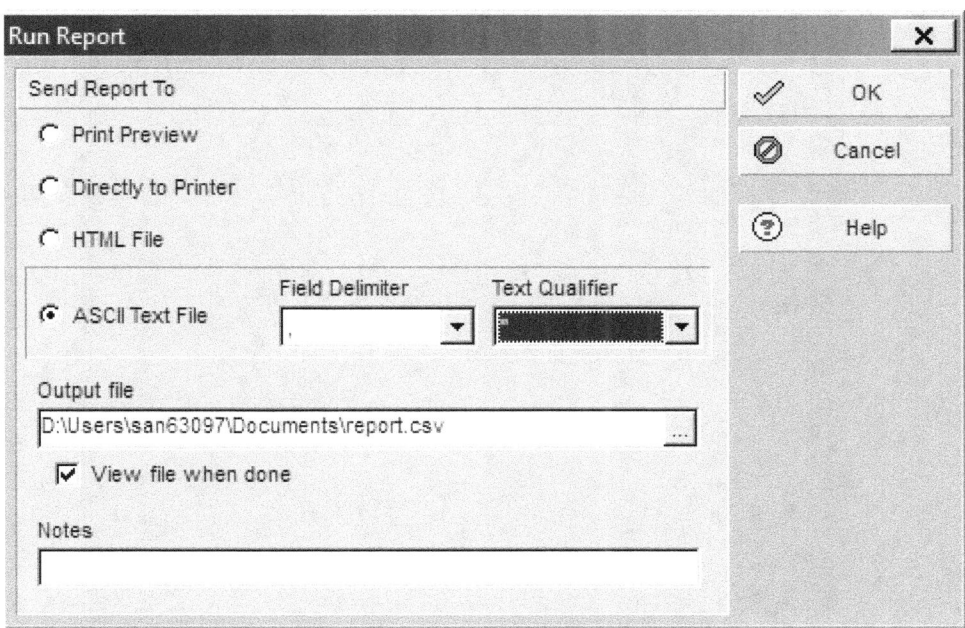

5. In the resulting spreadsheet select your project in the filter applied to Successor project column and then uncheck your project in the filter applied to Predecessor project column.

Now your filter contains only external predecessors. To display the driving ones - go to Relationship Early Finish and uncheck all the dates prior to your data date or use the date filters for the same purpose

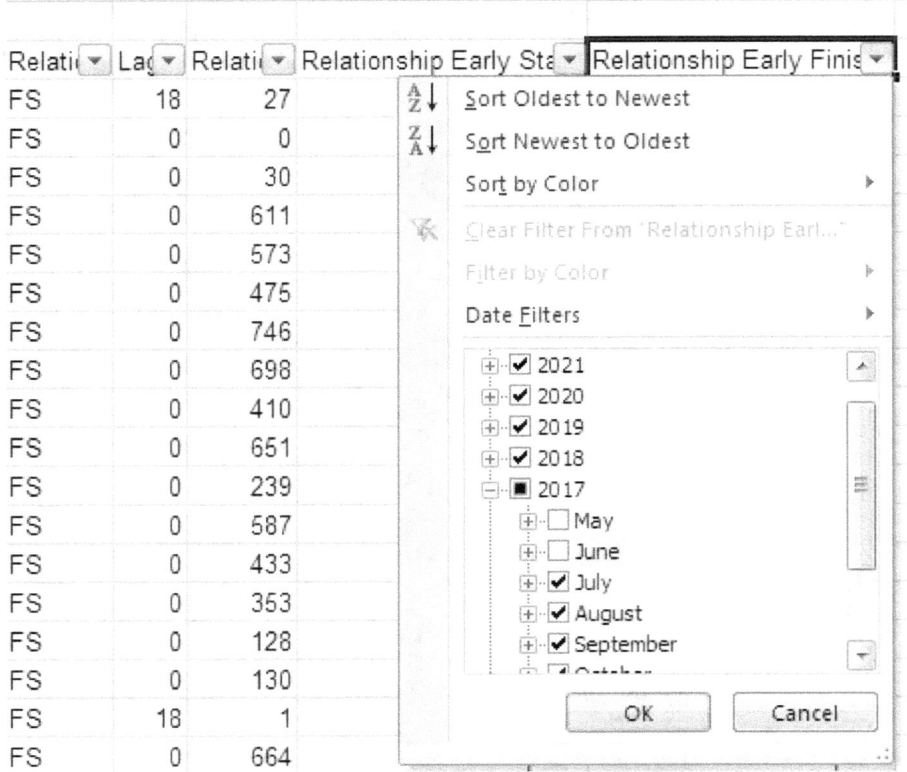

6. Go to Relationship Successor Free Float and select 0 only.

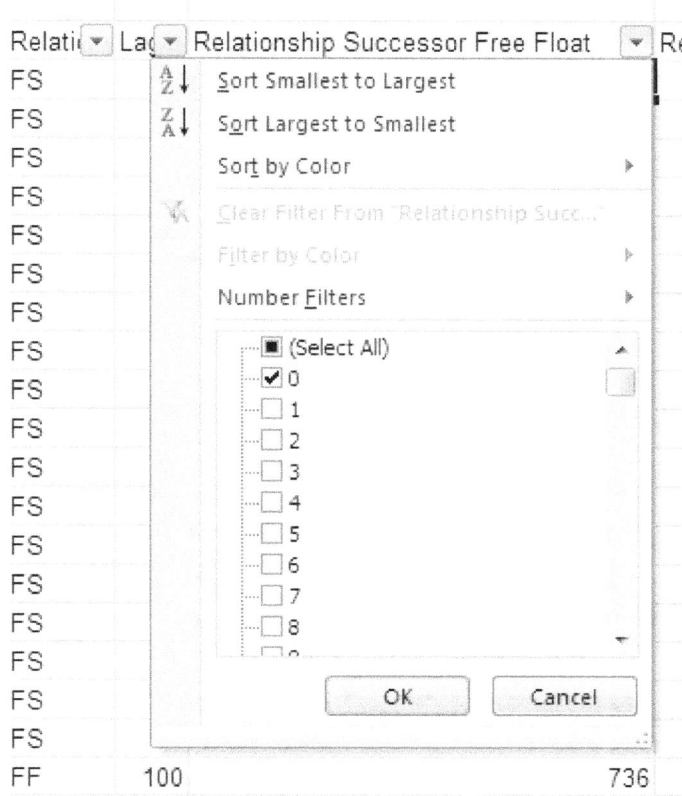

Now your filter will contain only driving external predecessors because Successor Free float is essentially the number of days between start and finish in a relationship and if it is equal to 0 the relationship is most probably driving. Happy cleaning!

# How to replace existing resources with new ones on activities with actuals

When we make major changes to our schedules sometimes it is necessary to replace existing resources with new ones, which in theory can be done with a global change, however, if resources you are trying to replace have actuals you will see the following error message when you try to run your global change:

Error: Cannot change resource because the previous resource already has actuals.

… and all you are trying to do is to modify resource IDs in line with a new dictionary you have created.

Let us see if we can find a fix for this problem.

Before you proceed you obviously need to set up your new resource dictionary and create a table cross-referencing old and new resource ID's.

1. Go to Resource tab in project settings and make sure the setting in the Resource Assignment section below is checked:

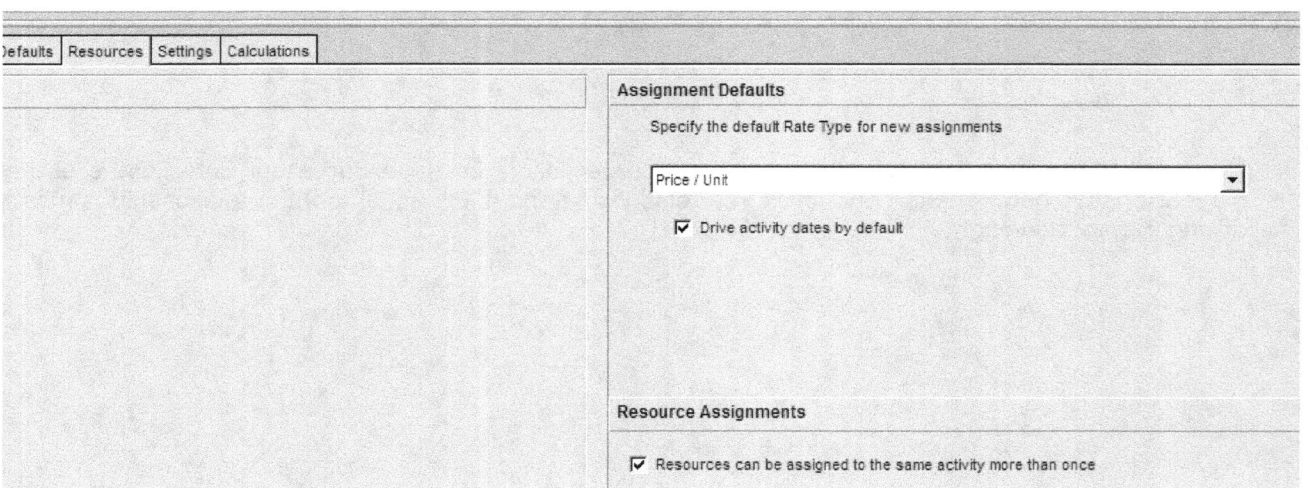

2. Open your project, go to File > Export > Spreadsheet

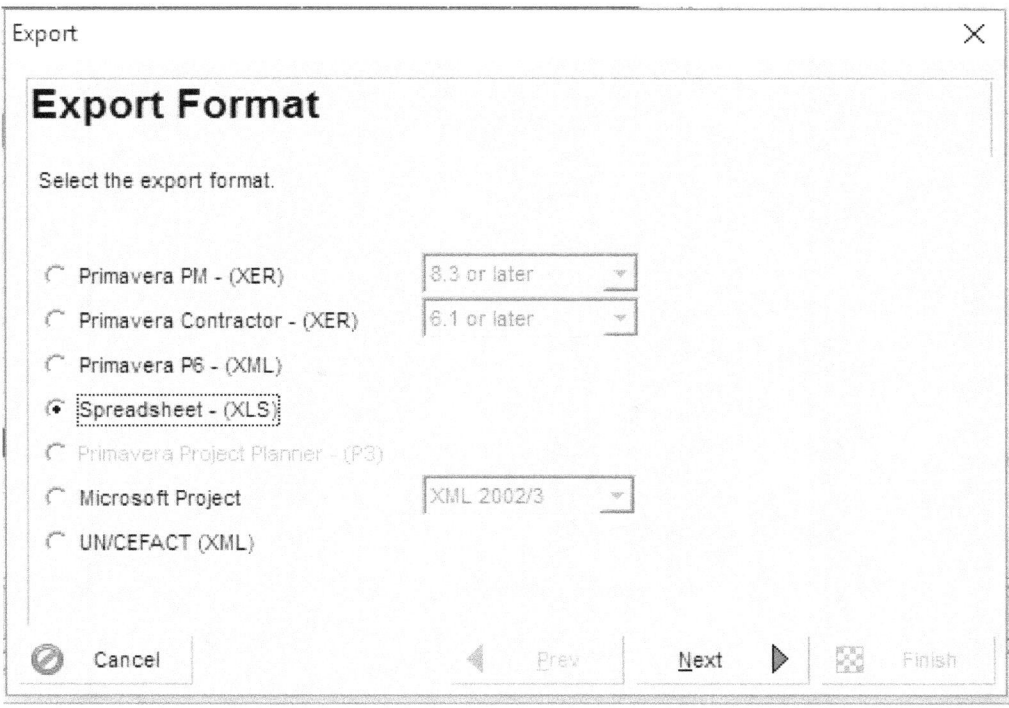

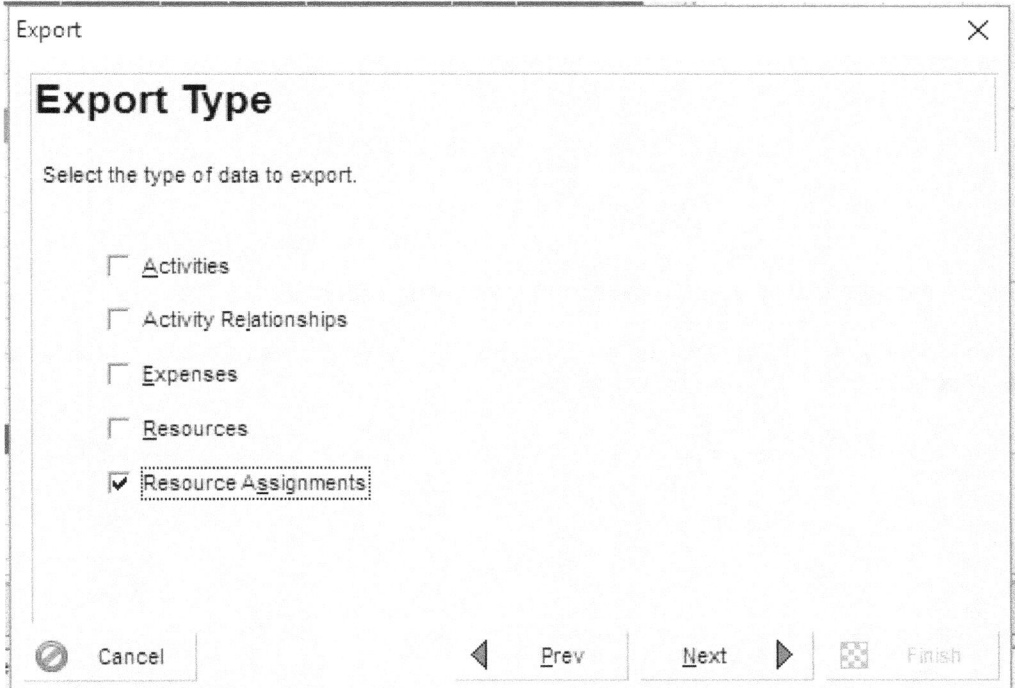

3. Create an export template with the following columns:

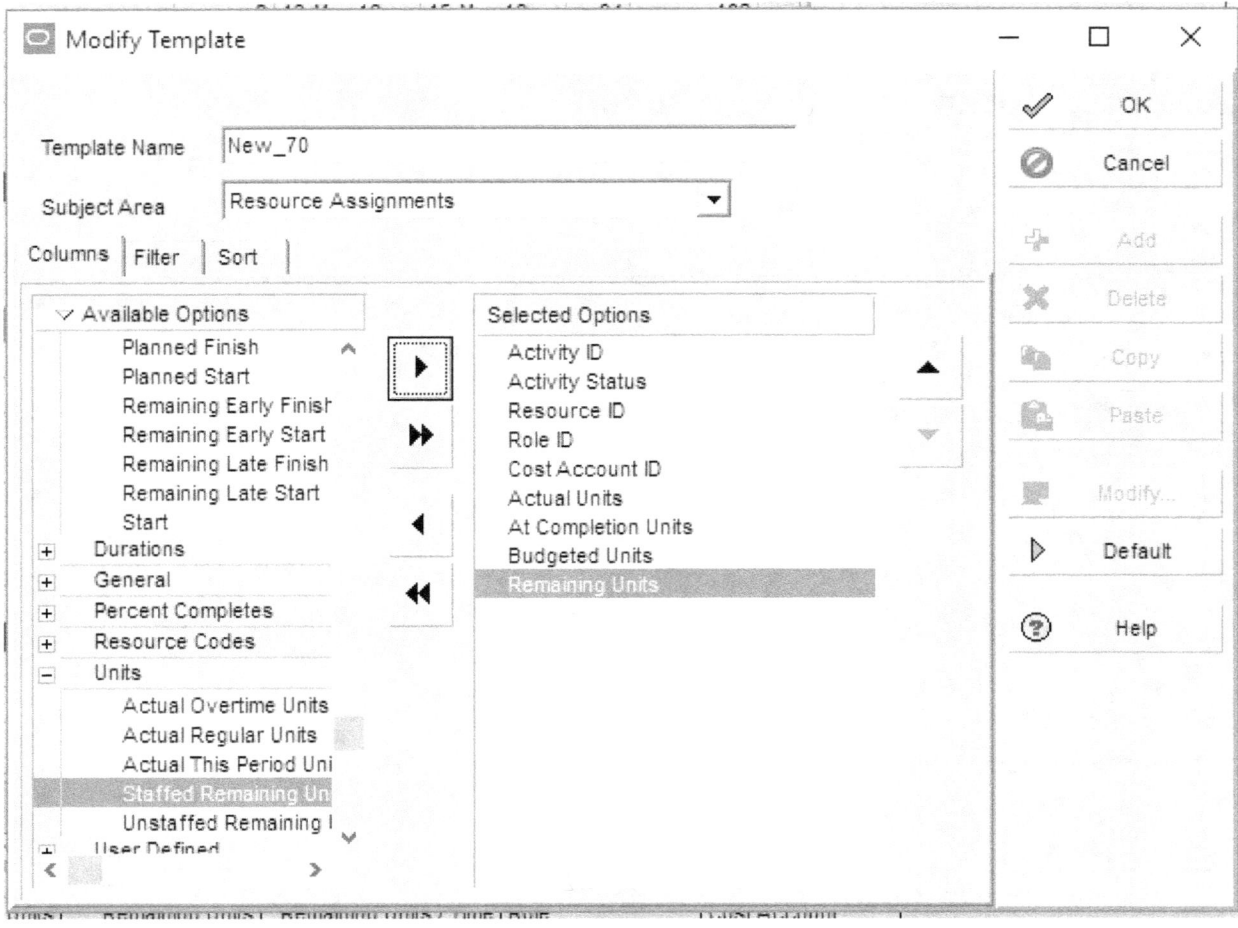

4. Run your export

5. Copy your cross-reference table under a new tab in the resulting export file

6. Delete all the rows where no changes will be necessary and keep only rows on which you want to replace old resources with resources from your new dictionary

| task_id | TASK_status_code | rsrc_id | role_id | acct_id | act_qty | total_qty | target_qty | remain_qty | delete_record_flag |
|---|---|---|---|---|---|---|---|---|---|
| Activity ID | (*)Activity Status | Resource ID | Role ID | Cost Account ID | Actual Units(h) | At Completion Units(h) | Budgeted Units(h) | Remaining Early Units(h) | Delete This Row |
| LNK013-0002 | Completed | PERM | | | 22 | 22 | 22 | 0 | |
| LNK013-0026 | In Progress | TREN1 | | | 4311 | 11000 | 11000 | 6689 | |
| LNK013-0032 | In Progress | BCKFIL1 | | | 353 | 3300 | 3300 | 2947 | |
| LNK013-0034 | Not Started | SPLICE1 | | | 0 | 2961 | 2961 | 2961 | |
| LNK013-0036 | Not Started | TIEIN1 | | | 0 | 22 | 22 | 22 | |
| LNK013-0038 | Not Started | TEST1 | | | 0 | 396 | 396 | 396 | |
| LNK013-0040 | Not Started | POHO1 | | | 0 | 396 | 396 | 396 | |
| LNK013-0006 | Completed | CROSS1 | | | 1320 | 1320 | 1320 | 0 | |
| LNK013-0008 | Completed | CROSS1 | | | 792 | 792 | 792 | 0 | |

Say, you want to replace all resources in column Resource ID above with new ID's that you already have in the resource dictionary. In a new tab in the export file you should have a table similar to the one below:

Andrei Sannikov
Tip of the day

| Old | New |
|---|---|
| PERM | 70CT |
| TREN1 | 60EL |
| BCKFIL1 | 50PI |
| SPLICE1 | 40EQ |
| TIEIN1 | 30AR |
| TEST1 | 20ST |
| POHO1 | 10CO |
| CROSS1 | 00EW |
| CROSS1 | 80TYR |

7. Copy all rows you want to change and paste them under the section you have just copied:

| task_id<br>Activity ID | TASK_status_code<br>(*)Activity Status | rsrc_id<br>Resource ID | role_id<br>Role ID | acct_id<br>Cost Account ID | act_qty<br>Actual Units(h) | total_qty<br>At Completion Units(h) | target_qty<br>Budgeted Units(h) | remain_qty<br>Remaining Early Units(h) | delete_record_flag<br>Delete This Row |
|---|---|---|---|---|---|---|---|---|---|
| LNK013-0002 | Completed | PERM | | | 22 | 22 | 22 | 0 | |
| LNK013-0026 | In Progress | TREN1 | | | 4311 | 11000 | 11000 | 6689 | |
| LNK013-0032 | In Progress | BCKFIL1 | | | 353 | 3300 | 3300 | 2947 | |
| LNK013-0034 | Not Started | SPLICE1 | | | 0 | 2961 | 2961 | 2961 | |
| LNK013-0036 | Not Started | TIEIN1 | | | 0 | 22 | 22 | 22 | |
| LNK013-0038 | Not Started | TEST1 | | | 0 | 396 | 396 | 396 | |
| LNK013-0040 | Not Started | POHO1 | | | 0 | 396 | 396 | 396 | |
| LNK013-0006 | Completed | CROSS1 | | | 1320 | 1320 | 1320 | 0 | |
| LNK013-0008 | Completed | CROSS1 | | | 792 | 792 | 792 | 0 | |
| LNK013-0002 | Completed | PERM | | | 22 | 22 | 22 | 0 | |
| LNK013-0026 | In Progress | TREN1 | | | 4311 | 11000 | 11000 | 6689 | |
| LNK013-0032 | In Progress | BCKFIL1 | | | 353 | 3300 | 3300 | 2947 | |
| LNK013-0034 | Not Started | SPLICE1 | | | 0 | 2961 | 2961 | 2961 | |
| LNK013-0036 | Not Started | TIEIN1 | | | 0 | 22 | 22 | 22 | |
| LNK013-0038 | Not Started | TEST1 | | | 0 | 396 | 396 | 396 | |
| LNK013-0040 | Not Started | POHO1 | | | 0 | 396 | 396 | 396 | |
| LNK013-0006 | Completed | CROSS1 | | | 1320 | 1320 | 1320 | 0 | |
| LNK013-0008 | Completed | CROSS1 | | | 792 | 792 | 792 | 0 | |

I would highlight the new section to avoid confusion.

8. Use lookup formulas to replace the Resource ID's in the highlighted portion and add letter "D" (for delete) in the last row in the non-highlighted section:

| task_id<br>Activity ID | TASK_status_code<br>(*)Activity Status | rsrc_id<br>Resource ID | role_id<br>Role ID | acct_id<br>Cost Account ID | act_qty<br>Actual Units(h) | total_qty<br>At Completion Units(h) | target_qty<br>Budgeted Units(h) | remain_qty<br>Remaining Early Units(h) | delete_record_flag<br>Delete This Row |
|---|---|---|---|---|---|---|---|---|---|
| LNK013-0002 | Completed | PERM | | | 22 | 22 | 22 | 0 | D |
| LNK013-0026 | In Progress | TREN1 | | | 4311 | 11000 | 11000 | 6689 | D |
| LNK013-0032 | In Progress | BCKFIL1 | | | 353 | 3300 | 3300 | 2947 | D |
| LNK013-0034 | Not Started | SPLICE1 | | | 0 | 2961 | 2961 | 2961 | D |
| LNK013-0036 | Not Started | TIEIN1 | | | 0 | 22 | 22 | 22 | D |
| LNK013-0038 | Not Started | TEST1 | | | 0 | 396 | 396 | 396 | D |
| LNK013-0040 | Not Started | POHO1 | | | 0 | 396 | 396 | 396 | D |
| LNK013-0006 | Completed | CROSS1 | | | 1320 | 1320 | 1320 | 0 | D |
| LNK013-0008 | Completed | CROSS1 | | | 792 | 792 | 792 | 0 | D |
| LNK013-0002 | Completed | 70CT | | | 22 | 22 | 22 | 0 | |
| LNK013-0026 | In Progress | 60EL | | | 4311 | 11000 | 11000 | 6689 | |
| LNK013-0032 | In Progress | 50PI | | | 353 | 3300 | 3300 | 2947 | |
| LNK013-0034 | Not Started | 40EQ | | | 0 | 2961 | 2961 | 2961 | |
| LNK013-0036 | Not Started | 30AR | | | 0 | 22 | 22 | 22 | |
| LNK013-0038 | Not Started | 20ST | | | 0 | 396 | 396 | 396 | |
| LNK013-0040 | Not Started | 10CO | | | 0 | 396 | 396 | 396 | |
| LNK013-0006 | Completed | 00EW | | | 1320 | 1320 | 1320 | 0 | |
| LNK013-0008 | Completed | 00EW | | | 792 | 792 | 792 | 0 | |

9. Make a copy of your project and import this file into this copy. If you are satisfied with the results, import it into the original.

Andrei Sannikov
Tip of the day

13-Mar-19 14:52

## How to demote a code from Global to EPS and from EPS to Project

We all know that activity codes can be easily promoted from project to EPS and from EPS to global (assuming you have the necessary rights, of course). This appears to be a one-way street, though – it does not look like you can demote a code from global to EPS or from EPS to project, at least not with standard P6 tools - you can of course break into the xer file with specialized software and manually demote a code but it is not something I would recommend to anyone who does not have an expert knowledge of P6 algorithms.

Let us see if there is a way to short cut the standard process.

1. Open your project > Go to Enterprise > Activity codes > Project > Modify > Add

Put in the name of the global code you intend to demote and set Max Length to 32 characters, which is always a good practice.

2. Go to the Global code dictionary and open the above code that we are going to demote

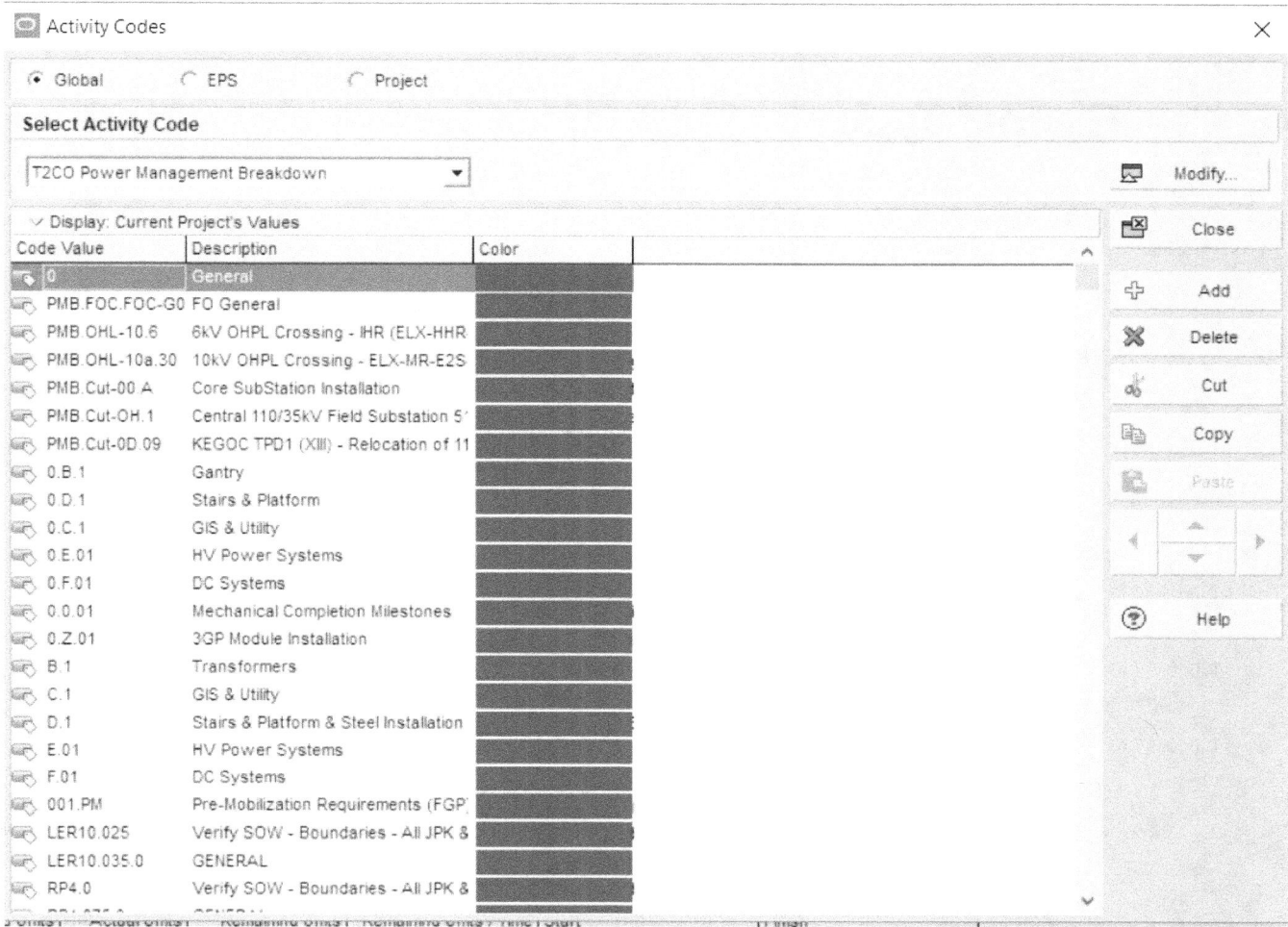

3. Press Ctrl A > Copy

4. Go back to the Project codes > Modify > Find the code we created in Step 1 > Click Close > Click Paste

5. Close the activity codes window, go to File > Export > Spreadsheet XLS > Next > Check Activities box

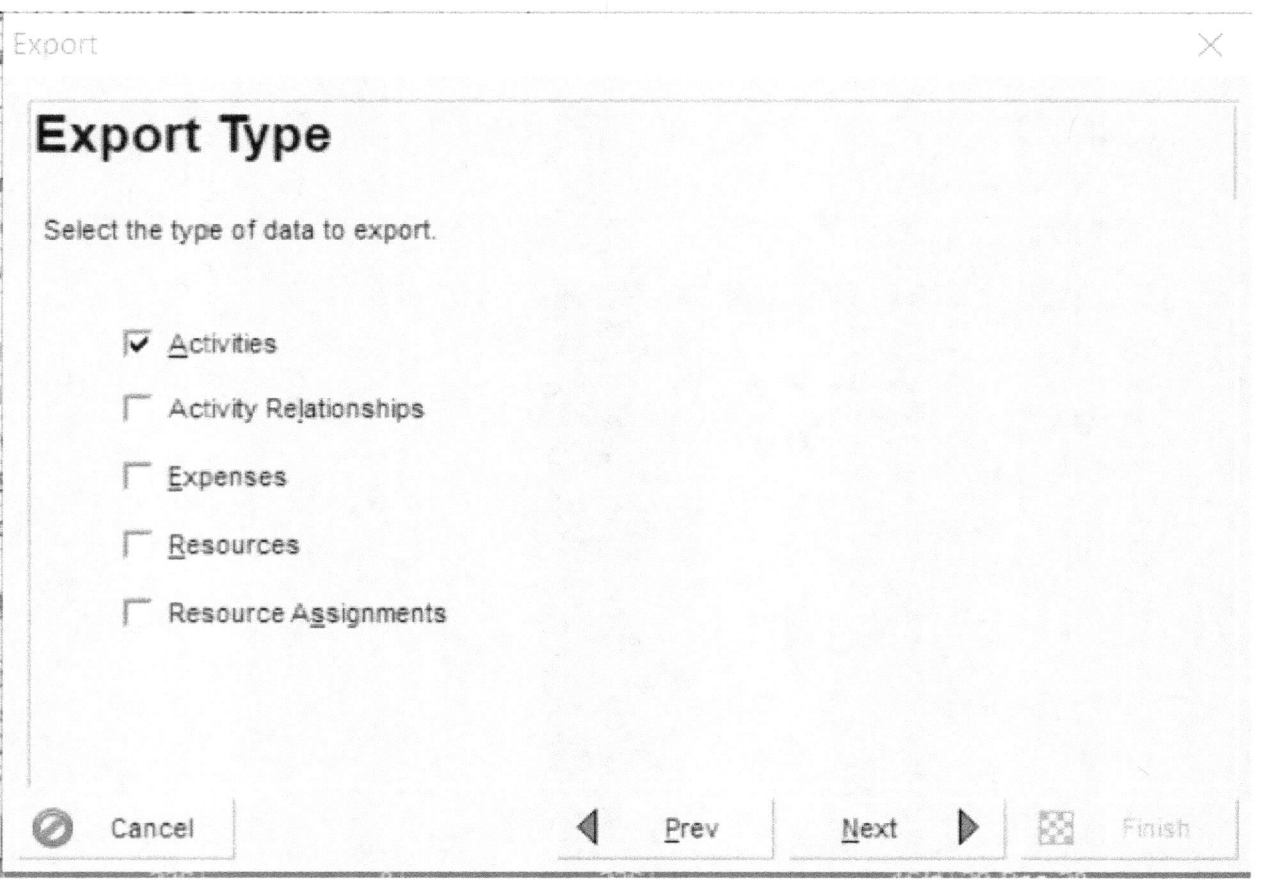

6. Click Next twice and when you get to the Select Template window click Add and set up a template with the columns below:

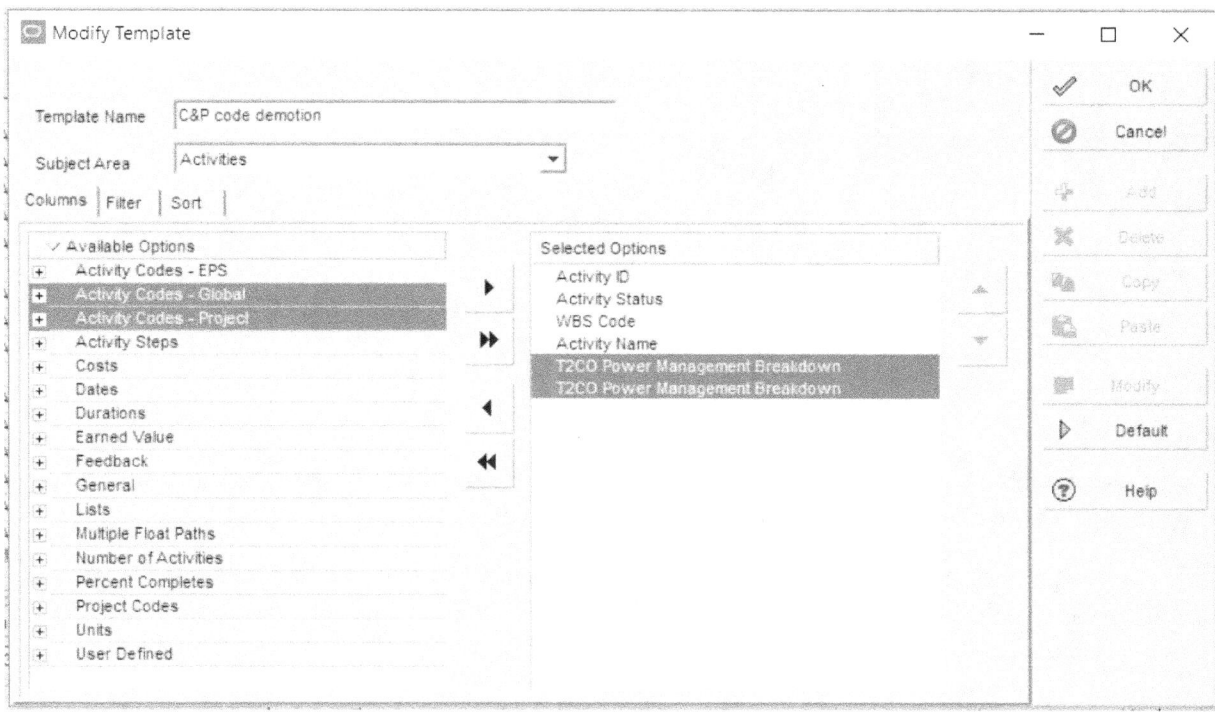

You have probably guessed that I pulled one of the codes highlighted above from Activity codes – Global and the other from Activity codes – Project field

7. Run the export, go to the resulting spreadsheet and make all values in Column F equal to Column E (in our example):

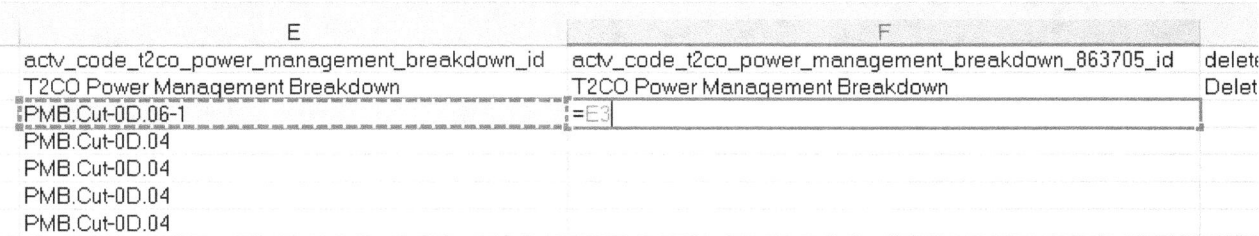

8. Save/close the spreadsheet and import it back into your schedule
    a. To speed up the import process it is recommended to convert column F to values and delete column E. You can also delete Activity name column prior to import.

9. Once your import is completed, go back to your schedule and display both codes (Global and Project) in two separate columns.

| ish | T2CO Power Management Breakdown* | T2CO Power Management Breakdown |  |
|---|---|---|---|
| an-23 | | | |
| an-23 | | | |
| an-23 | | | |
| an-23 | | | |
| ay-20 | | | |
| un-19 | INI | INI | |
| Jul-19 | INI | INI | |

Note: it might be a good idea to modify the name of the project code at this stage (I added * at the end in the example above) so you know which code is in which column.

10. Make sure the column with the Project code is fully populated (things sometimes go wrong with Excel imports) and once you are happy with the results go to the column with the global code (right column in our example) and use Fill down function to remove it from your activities.

Notes:

a) If this particular global code is used only by your project, you can of course delete it from the global dictionary. Make sure this is indeed the case before doing so.

b) If you have layouts that involve several projects DO NOT demote any of the global codes these layouts are organized by as such layouts would not work in this case.

c) If necessary, you can now promote this new project code to EPS.

02-Nov-19 17:43

# How to set up a filter for a period in the future

We all know how to create filters for look-ahead schedules – start or finish within the given range + activities in progress. But imagine you need to filter in a specific period in the future, say, from Feb 1, 2020 to Mar 31, 2020 – you will need to include activities that are scheduled to start or finish within this range (that's the easy part) + add activities that will continue throughout this period i.e. will start before Feb 1 and finish after Mar 31.

1. Add a new filter and create the following conditions (Any of the following):

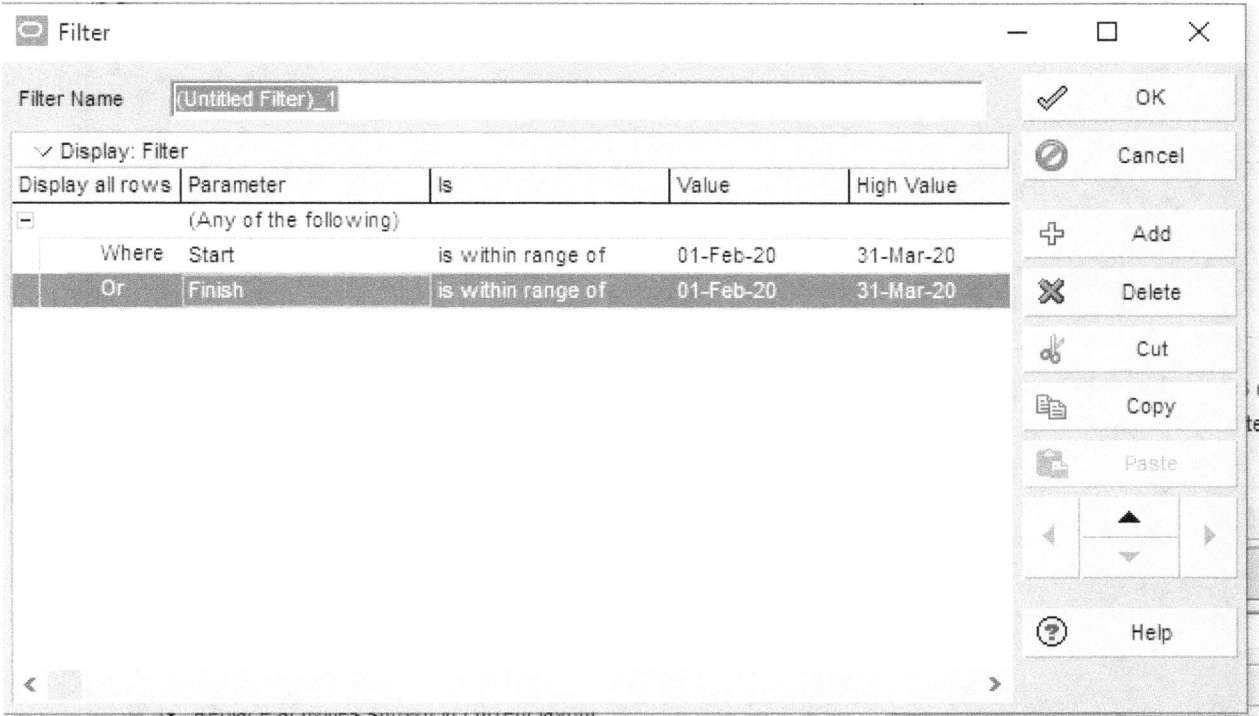

2. Click on Add twice, then click on the Shift right arrow

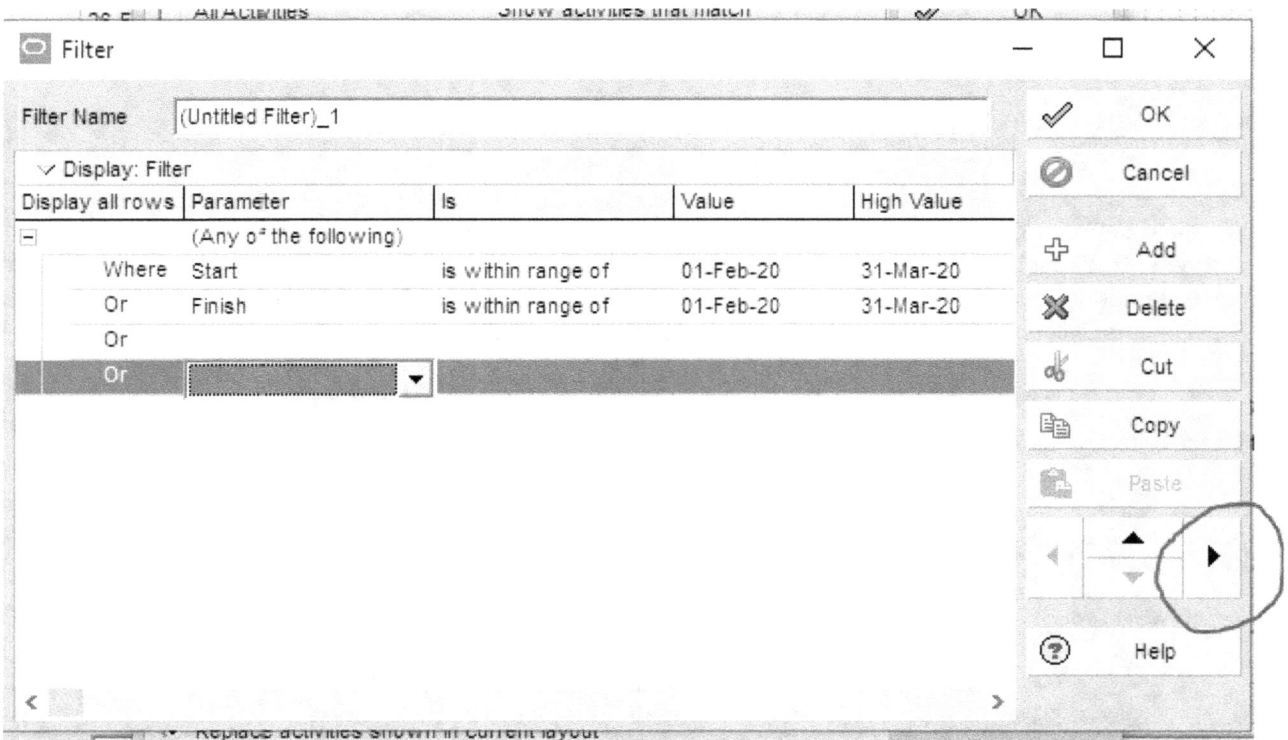

3. Choose All of the following in the second level filter we have just added:

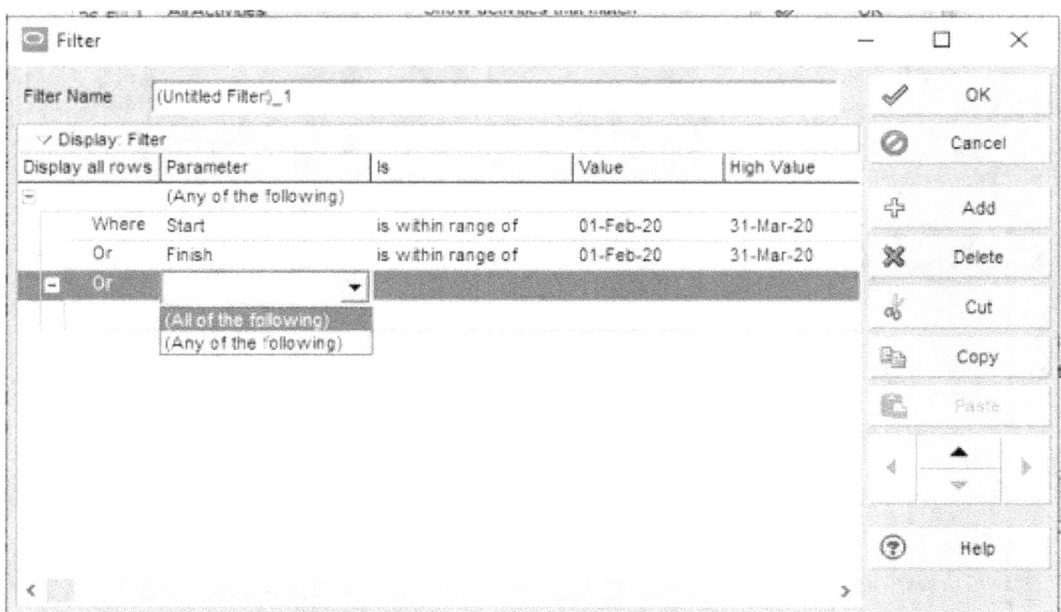

4. Finish your filter as follows:

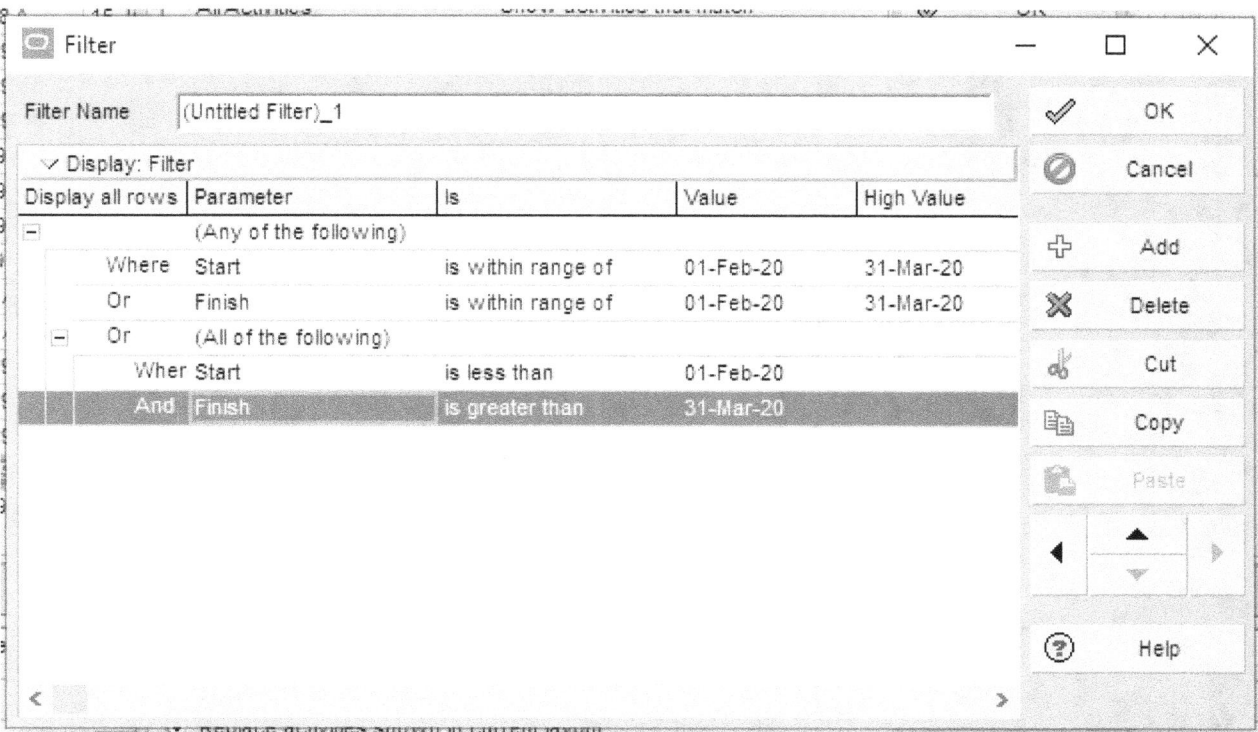

When you apply it to your schedule it will pick up all activities that are scheduled to start or finish between these dates + activities that will start before Feb 1 and finish after Mar 31.

| Start | Finish |
|---|---|
| 25-May-19 A | 24-Feb-20* |
| 25-May-19 A | 17-Mar-20* |
| 01-Jun-19 A | 19-May-20* |
| 08-Jun-19 A | 13-Feb-20* |
| 10-Jun-19 A | 06-Feb-20* |
| 11-Jun-19 A | 06-Feb-20* |
| 08-Jul-19 A | 10-Mar-20* |
| 17-Jul-19 A | 08-May-20* |
| 19-Aug-19 A | 21-Apr-20* |
| 19-Aug-19 A | 19-Feb-20* |
| 24-Aug-19 A | 07-Apr-20* |
| 20-Sep-19 | 10-Feb-20* |
| 01-Oct-19 | 19-Mar-20* |
| 08-Oct-19 | 26-Feb-20* |
| 14-Oct-19 | 31-Mar-20* |
| 24-Oct-19 | 19-Mar-20* |
| 06-Nov-19 | 04-Jul-20* |
| 22-Nov-19 | 24-Apr-20* |
| 30-Nov-19 | 20-May-20* |
| 03-Dec-19 | 05-Mar-20* |
| 25-Dec-19 | 23-Feb-20* |
| 01-Jan-20 | 07-Feb-20* |
| 24-Jan-20 | 12-Aug-20* |
| 06-Feb-20 | 09-Apr-20* |

Andrei Sannikov
Tip of the day

18-Feb-24 15:10

## How to link your schedule to a progress tracking system.

Planners usually need to reconcile the earned and budget hours and quantities with the progress reports generated by the project progress tracking system. In most cases this alignment is done manually, which could be a very time-consuming task.

Progress systems are typically much more detailed than the project schedules with multiple progress entries corresponding to a single schedule activity, and, in theory, one could create a lookup table mapping every progress system entry to an Activity ID. In fact, many progress systems contain an Activity ID field that can be populated by the project planners. This is a common practice on some projects, however, there are two fundamental issues with this approach: (a) this system requires constant maintenance as new line items are being added to the progress data base and (b) one line item in the progress file can be broken down into multiple rules of credit (ROC) or steps (from staging to acceptance), whilst in the schedule these steps might correspond to individual tasks. Since you are limited to one Activity ID per line item in the progress database, you won't be able to map all these steps to appropriate activities without additional user-defined fields, very complicated Excel functions and extensive maintenance. Let's see if we can simplify and automate this process to some extent.

First, you need to make sure that both the schedule and the progress system contain a series of common fields/codes such as Work Pack numbers, System numbers, Prime disciplines/Resources, Work Stage definitions (e.g., construction, pre-commissioning) etc.

As an example, let's look at piping activities in a Systems Completion schedule that we need to map to an ROC based progress system. There are a few rules that we need to follow to make this mapping as painless as possible:

- When you setup and load your schedule with labor hours and quantities, make sure each resource you use corresponds to a prime discipline identified in the progress database.
- Each activity must correspond to a well-defined rule of credit in the progress base, e.g., cable pulling, termination, glanding or a combination of several ROC's e.g., "Termination & Glanding."
- Each of the common fields mentioned above must be set up as a code in P6 and added as a field to the progress base.

1. Copy an Excel export from your progress measurement system into your mapping file.

2. Say, you have installation, testing and reinstatement activities in your schedule, and some budget/earned hours and quantities (installation) appear as individual rows for each line, and some (testing, reinstatement) are shown in columns as rules of credits.

3. Create an aid-memoir above your mapping table, which will show where the data you need is located as in the example below for easy reference:

| | |
|---|---|
| Piping | I:I |
| Testing and Cleaning | K:K |
| Testing budget hrs | BK:BL |
| Testing earned hrs | BS:BT |
| Reinstatement budget hours | BM:BN |
| Reinstatement earned hours | BU:BV |
| pre-commissioning | DE |
| System | Q:Q |
| WHRS (Total Budget hours) | AB:AB |
| EWHRS (Total Earned hours) | AF:AF |
| BUDGET QTY | AA:AA |
| INSTALLED QTY | AD:AD |
| ISBL | E:E |

ISBL in this example is the name of the area we are pulling the data for.

Say, we need to pull all budget hours for our pipe installation activity in system XYZ, all entries appear as individual line items in our progress base, our prime is Piping, and we need to summarize total budget hours across our progress base for this system excluding Testing and Cleaning and Pre-commissioning. The SUMIFS function will look as follows:

=SUMIFS('UPR10'!AB:AB,'UPR10'!I:I,$B$1,'UPR10'!DE:DE,"<>pre-commissioning",'UPR10'!Q:Q,A19,'UPR10'!E:E,$B$13,'UPR10'!K:K,"<>Testing and Cleaning")

Where: our prime description is in cell B1, area name is in cell B13, system numbers are in column A. The rest of the formula should be self-explanatory based on the table included in item 3 above.

Andrei Sannikov
Tip of the day

The formula for quantities will be similar, with references to column A:A where budget quantities are located:

=SUMIFS('UPR10'!AA:AA,'UPR10'!I:I,$B$1,'UPR10'!DE:DE,"<>pre-commissioning",'UPR10'!Q:Q,A39,'UPR10'!E:E,$B$13,'UPR10'!K:K,"<>Testing and Cleaning")

When you are done, copy the formulas down and you will have a table with budget and earned hours and quantities for all your systems:

|  | Piping installation hrs | | Piping qty | |
| --- | --- | --- | --- | --- |
|  | Budget | Earned | Budget | Earned |
| 1-11-A7-P30 | 5,068 | 4,690 | 612 | 576 |
| 1-12-A7-P10 | 2,757 | 1,630 | 29 | 20 |
| 1-12-A7-P20 | 3,435 | 1,326 | 92 | 35 |
| 1-12-A7-P30 | 2,090 | 1,168 | 80 | 46 |
| 1-12-A7-P31 | 0 | 0 | 0 | 0 |
| 1-13-A7-P10 | 7,571 | 5,213 | 99 | 62 |
| 1-14-A7-P10 | 37,085 | 31,338 | 781 | 559 |
| 1-14-A7-P20 | 69,696 | 53,726 | 1,880 | 1,270 |
| 1-14-A7-P30 | 51,263 | 49,167 | 1,203 | 1,107 |
| 1-14-A7-P40 | 1,447 | 667 | 214 | 85 |

The testing and reinstatement hours in our progress base are shown in columns as rules of credit of testing and cleaning activities. Since testing budget hours are in columns BK and BL, we will use the following formula to add them up for each system and exclude pre-commissioning:

=SUMIFS('UPR10'!BK:BK,'UPR10'!I:I,$B$1,'UPR10'!DE:DE,"<>pre-commissioning",'UPR10'!Q:Q,A38,'UPR10'!E:E,$B$13,'UPR10'!K:K,$B$2)+SUMIFS('UPR10'!BL:BL,'UPR10'!I:I,$B$1,'UPR10'!DE:DE,"<>pre-commissioning",'UPR10'!Q:Q,A38,'UPR10'!E:E,$B$13,'UPR10'!K:K,$B$2)

As in the previous example, we use references to prime "Piping" in B1, area in B13 and we also need subprime "Testing and Cleaning" in B2.

When you are done, copy the formula down and you will have a table similar to the one below:

|  | Testing hrs | | Testing qty | | Reinstatement hrs | |
|---|---|---|---|---|---|---|
|  | Budget | Earned | Budget | Earned | Budget | Earned |
| 1-46-A7-DM10 | 183 | 99 | 171 | 90 | 149 | 78 |
| 1-47-A7-IA10 | 350 | 75 | 652 | 137 | 286 | 61 |
| 1-47-A7-TA10 | 178 | 46 | 181 | 54 | 146 | 37 |
| 1-48-A7-N10 | 315 | 86 | 323 | 109 | 258 | 71 |
| 1-48-A7-N20 | 0 | 0 | 0 | 0 | 0 | 0 |
| 1-60-A7-FW10 | 0 | 0 | 0 | 0 | 0 | 0 |
| 1-60-A7-FW20 | 0 | 0 | 0 | 0 | 0 | 0 |
| 1-60-A7-FW30 | 15 | 15 | 16 | 16 | 12 | 12 |
| 1-60-A7-FW31 | 45 | 44 | 50 | 31 | 37 | 20 |
| 1-62-A7-DLH10 | 508 | 28 | 486 | 19 | 416 | 16 |

Create a tab for each discipline that you have in your schedule and populate them in a similar fashion.

4. Now we need to transfer this data into P6.
Go to the activities view, filter in, say, your piping activities, select what you need with your mouse, right click > Assign > Resources and choose appropriate labor and material resources.

5. After assigning these discipline resources you will need to export a resource assignment spreadsheet that can be populated with budget and earned units in the mapping file we have set up. Since system numbers and discipline codes will be our criteria for the SUMIFS functions we will be using, we need to add these fields to the export template. However, when you create your resource assignment export template, you will notice that activity codes are not among the available options. Let's see how we can bring them in.

Open P6 and go to Enterprise > User Defined Fields > Activities and either create Systems and Discipline (Prime) UDF's with text data type or pick up a text UDF from the list of available UDF's, if you don't have the necessary rights.

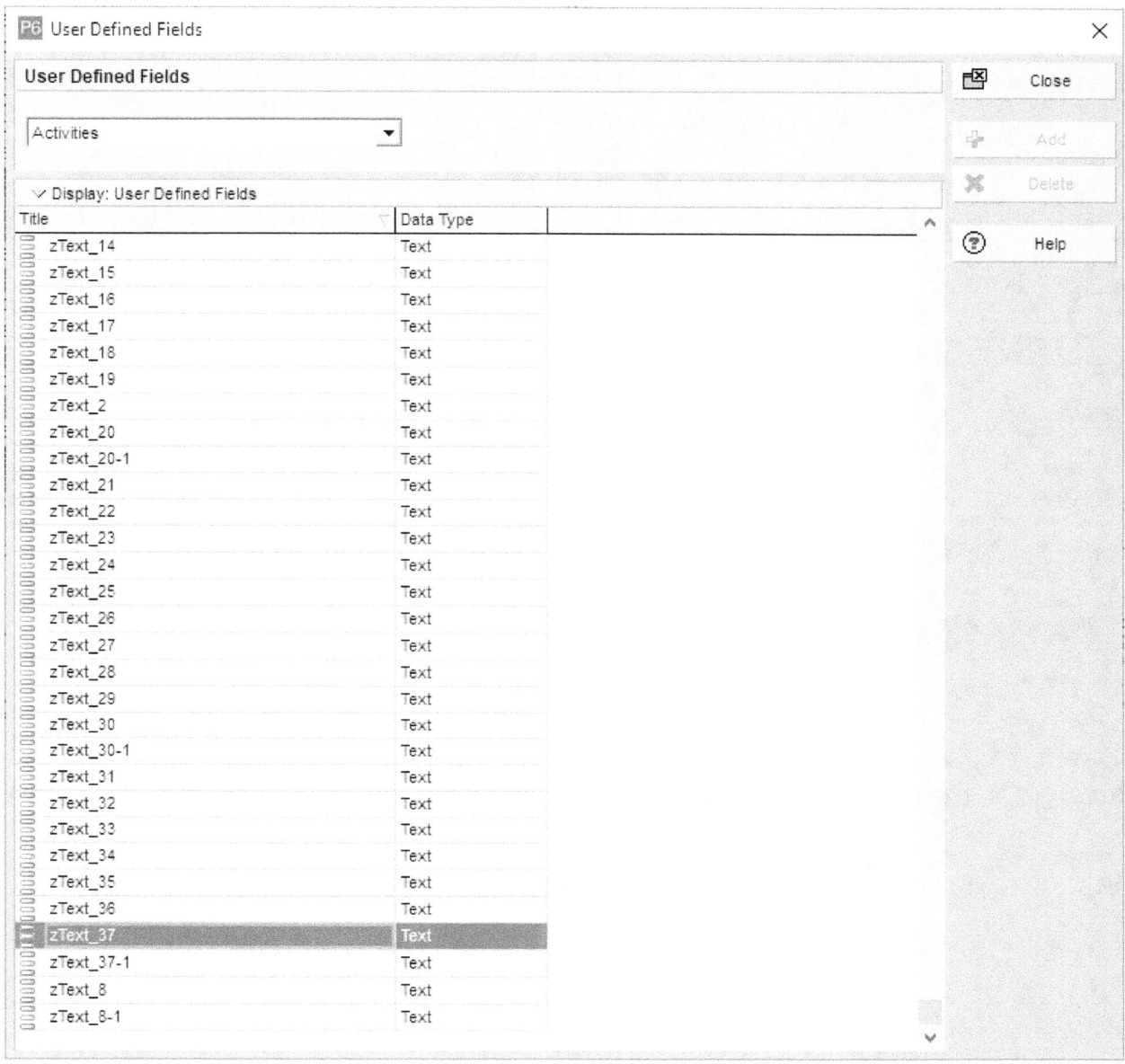

Go to Resource assignments section of the UDF menu and do the same.

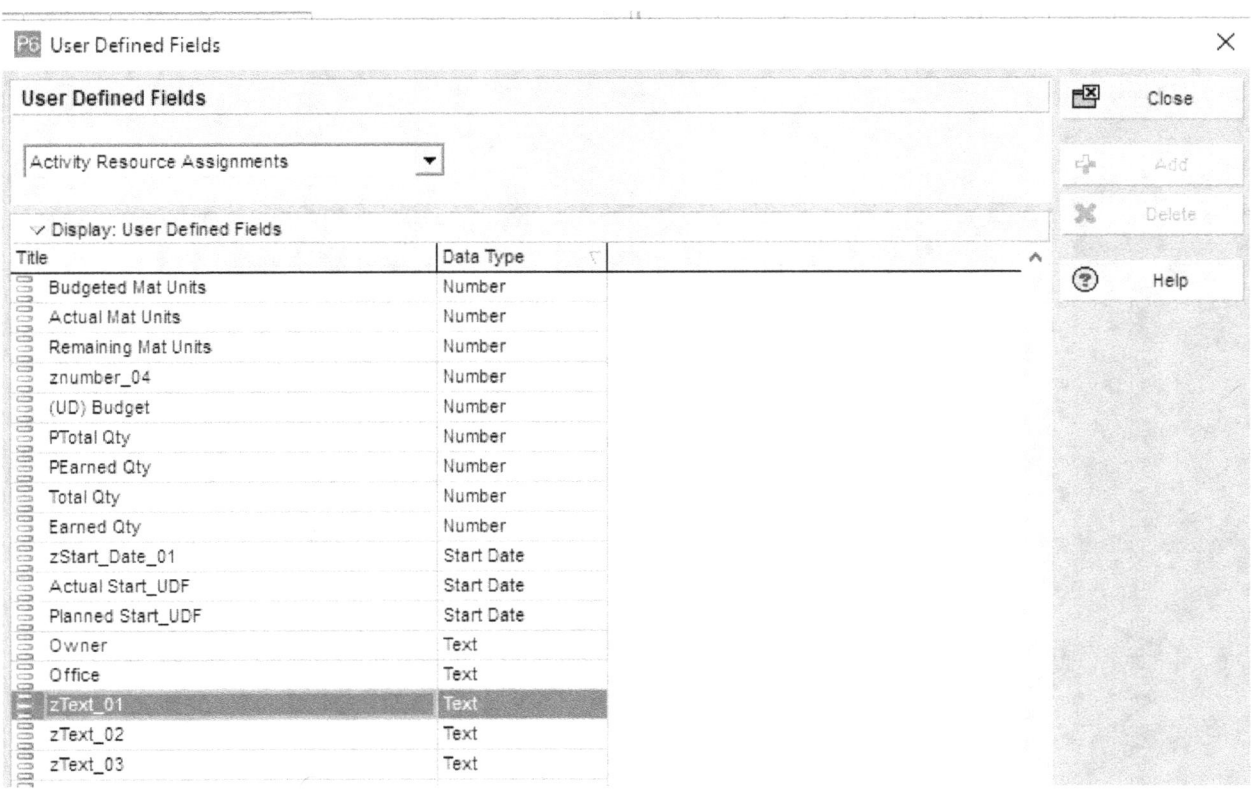

Run a global change to copy system numbers to an activity UDF of your choice, zText_37 in this example:

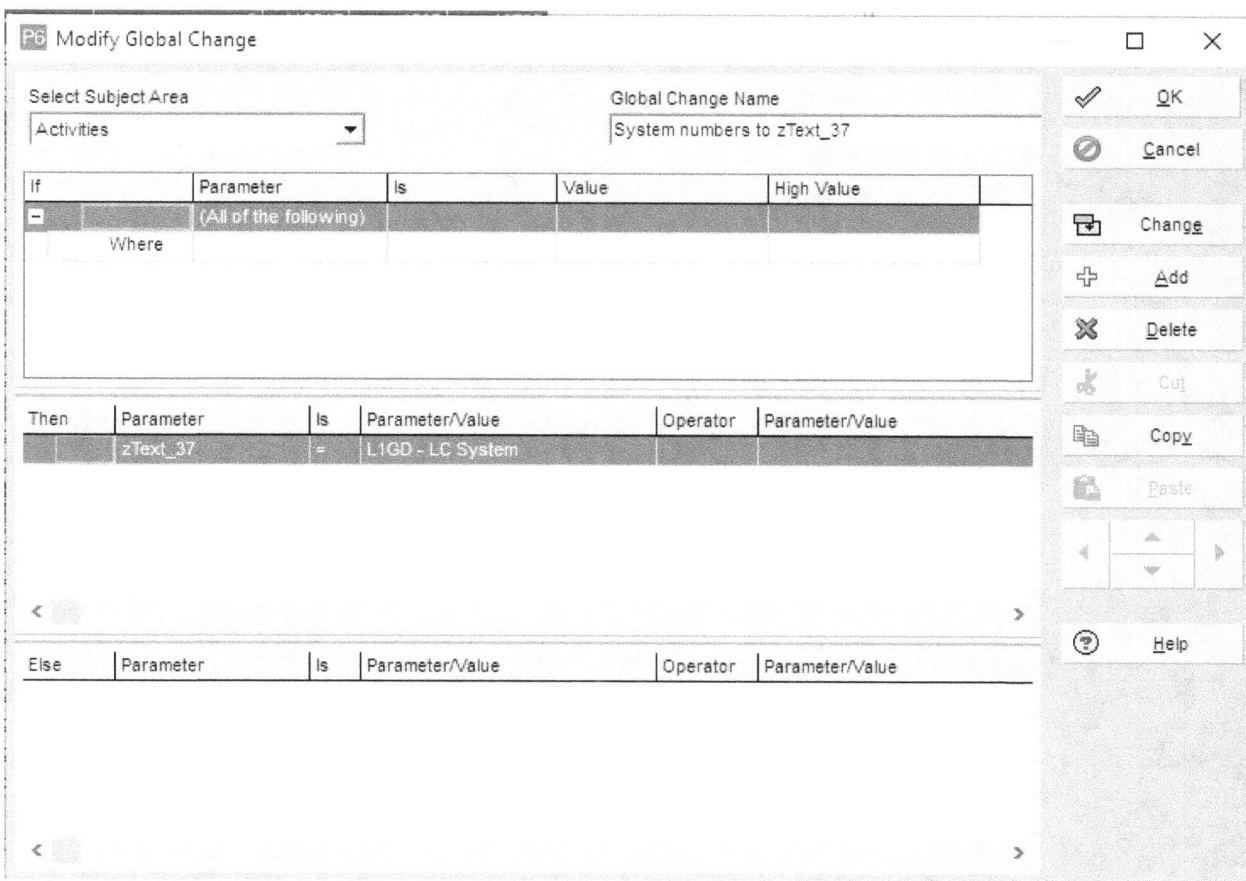

Then run another global change to copy system numbers from the above activity UDF to a resource assignment UDF:

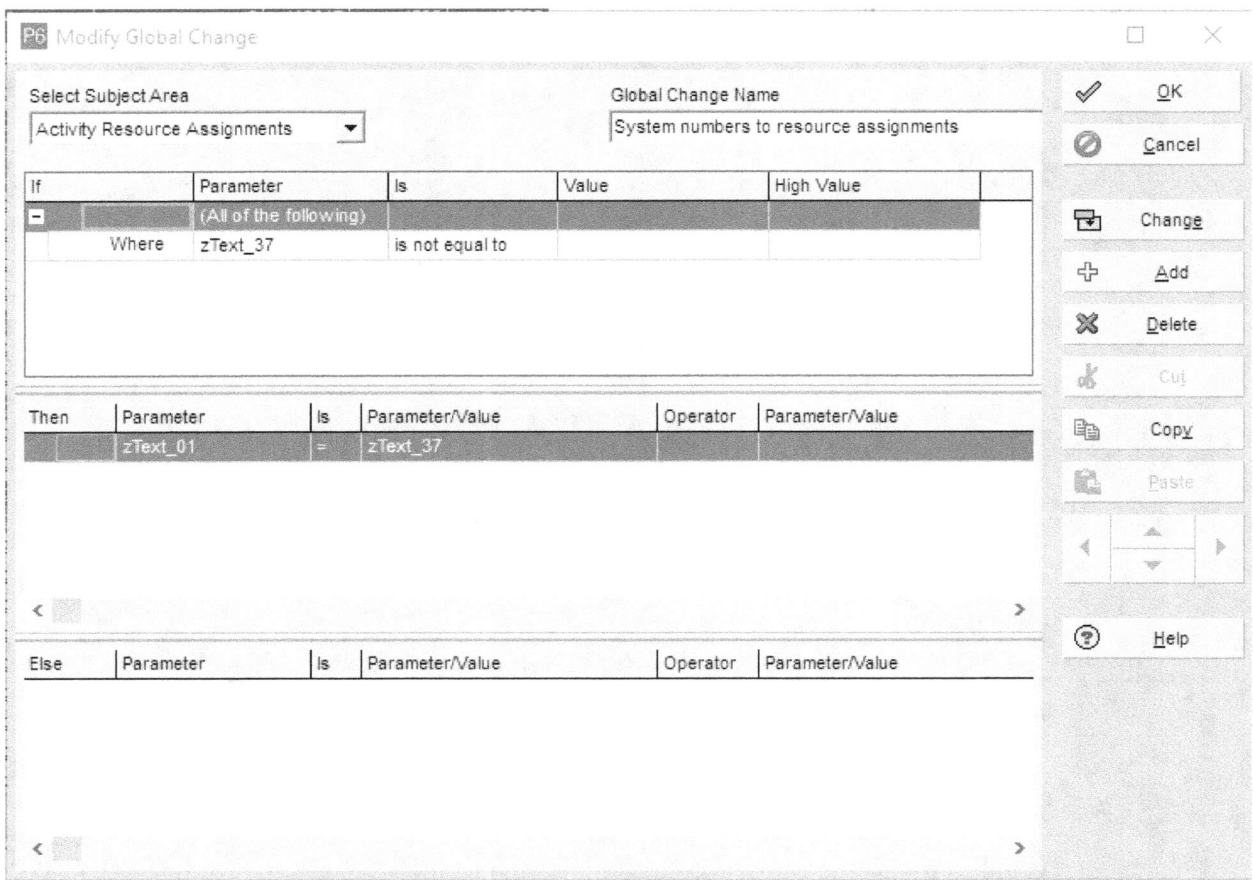

Repeat this operation for the discipline/prime codes you intend to use in your mapping.

Note: Activity UDFs are available in the Activity User Defined menu of the Modify Template dialogue shown in Step 6 below, the advantage of creating Resource Assignment UDFs is the ability to add new entries directly in the Resource Assignment spreadsheet as new activities are being added for import.

6. Go to File > Export > Spreadsheet (XLSX) > Resource Assignment > Select your project and create an import template with the following fields:

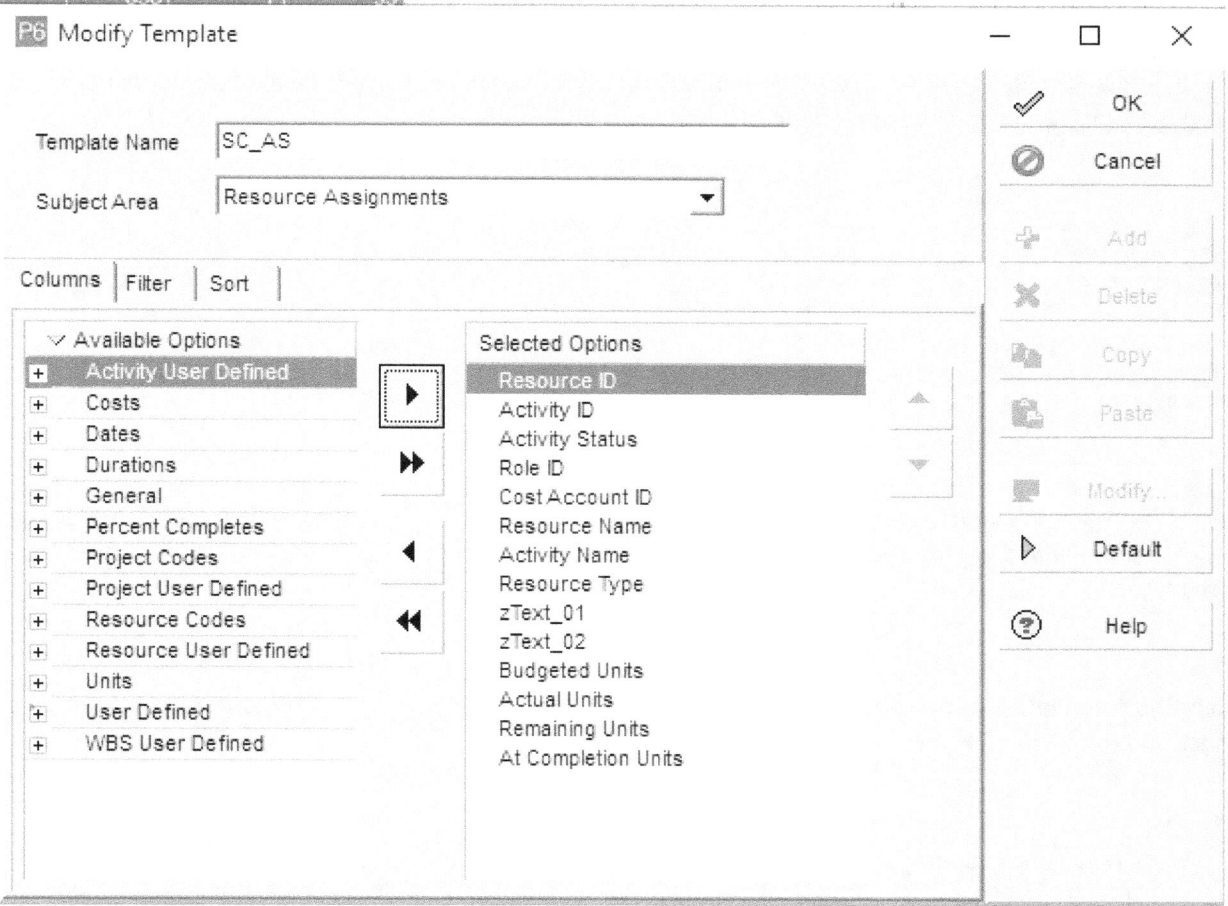

Where: zText_01 is the UDF with system numbers we have created in Step 5 above; zText_02 is the UDF with discipline codes we will be using for our mapping.

The resulting spreadsheet will look like the one below:

Andrei Sannikov
Tip of the day

In the example above PI is our code for pipe installation activities, PT for testing. In Step 3 above we have pulled all budget and actual hours and quantities for both installation and testing in separate columns, all you need to do now is to filter in, say, "Labor" and "PI" to summarize pipe installation hours for each activity resource assignment using a SUMIFS function like the one below:

| | A | B | C | D | E | F | G | H | I | J | K | |
|---|---|---|---|---|---|---|---|---|---|---|---|---|
| 1 | rsrc_id | task_id | rsrc__rsrc_n | task__task_name | rsrc_type | user_field_393 | user_field_395 | target_qty | act_qty | remain_qty | total_qty | del |
| 2 | Resource ID | Activity ID | (*)Resour | (*)Activity Name | (*)Resource Typ | zText_01 | zText_02 | Budgeted Un | Actual Units(l | Remaining Early Units(l | At Completion Units(h) | Del |
| 30 | UNSN_50 | 5C-1-14-A7-P43-PI | Piping | 1-14-A7-P43 - Piping installation | Labor | 1-14-A7-P43 | PI | 29.028 | 27.991 | 1.037 | =SUMIFS(Piping!B:B,Piping!A:A,TASKRSRC!F30) | |

Where:

B:B is the column in which we summarized all pipe installation hours for each system in the Piping worksheet; A:A is the column with System numbers in the Piping worksheet and cell F30 contains the system number we are mapping to.

Copy the formula down and proceed to the next discipline code and/or resource type to map, say, pipe testing hours and quantities.

7. When your mapping is complete for all your resources and prime disciplines, go back to the file we exported from P6 in Step 5 above, delete all the data, paste your mapping worksheet as **values**, save/close and import into P6.

NB:

a) Before attempting any imports, it is very important to back up your data so you can reinstate your original resource-loading (if you had one) in case something goes wrong. To do it, export your entire export assignment data like we did in Step 6 above and either rename the exported file or save it in a different folder as P6 always overwrites export files without any prompts. If you notice any issues with resource-loading after importing due to mapping errors etc., you can easily reinstate the original resource-loading by importing this file.

b) Sometimes P6 increases remaining durations of completed activities when you import remaining hours or quantities on them. To spot and correct such instances, always save a copy of your project, and assign it as a baseline prior to import. If you add "Variance - BL Project Finish Date" column and hit F9 after import, you will see if any of the activities have been impacted and will be able to make the necessary corrections.

c) Sometimes work is progressed out-of-sequence, in which case P6 will add actuals and actualize the start date on future activities. Make sure you filter in such activities and adjust the actual start dates and relationships, if necessary, to avoid issues with out-of-sequence logic covered in detail in other chapters of this book.

Andrei Sannikov
Tip of the day

25-Feb-24 9:59 AM

## How to change week start day in weekly resource exports

On most projects labor hours and quantities are exported from P6 with the weekly timescale and it is very important to make sure week start days are aligned with your project weekly cutoff periods. Week start day in P6 is an admin setting and most companies choose to keep the default one i.e., Week starting on Monday especially if they have multiple projects operating on different workweek calendars. Week starting on Monday works well for projects working on a 5-days calendar. However, when your site works 6 or 7 days a week, things start getting complicated if your weekly progress cutoff is Friday. The first week of your resource export will include only one or two days and, sometimes, planners need to redistribute the exported data manually to achieve a more realistic labor profile. Let's see if we can align the week start date with our weekly cutoff calendar without changing any of the admin settings.

1. Set up an Excel spreadsheet, with daily and weekly tabs. Add daily and weekly timescales under both tabs starting at the date following your data date, the example below is for the Friday cutoff:

| B | C | D | E | F | G | H | I | J | K | L | M | N | O |
|---|---|---|---|---|---|---|---|---|---|---|---|---|---|
| 30/Dec/23 | 31/Dec/23 | 01/Jan/24 | 02/Jan/24 | 03/Jan/24 | 04/Jan/24 | 05/Jan/24 | 06/Jan/24 | 07/Jan/24 | 08/Jan/24 | 09/Jan/24 | 10/Jan/24 | 11/Jan/24 | 12/Jan/24 |
| Sat | Sun | Mon | Tue | Wed | Thu | Fri | Sat | Sun | Mon | Tue | Wed | Thu | Fri |

| B | C | D | E | F | G | H | I | J | K | L | M | N | O |
|---|---|---|---|---|---|---|---|---|---|---|---|---|---|
| 30/Dec/23 | 06/Jan/24 | 13/Jan/24 | 20/Jan/24 | 27/Jan/24 | 03/Feb/24 | 10/Feb/24 | 17/Feb/24 | 24/Feb/24 | 02/Mar/24 | 09/Mar/24 | 16/Mar/24 | 23/Mar/24 | 30/Mar/24 |
| Sat | Sat | Sat | Sat | Sat | Sat | Sat | Sat | Sat | Sat | Sat | Sat | Sat | Sat |

2. Add the following formula to the weekly tab under the first date of your timescale in the first row where you intend to have your data:

=SUMIFS(Daily!$B4:$RP4,Daily!$B$1:$RP$1,">="&Weekly!$B1,Daily!$B$1:$RP$1,"<"&Weekly!$C1)

Copy it across the entire worksheet.

3. Go to User preferences and change the setting for time-distributed data under the resource-analysis tab as follows:

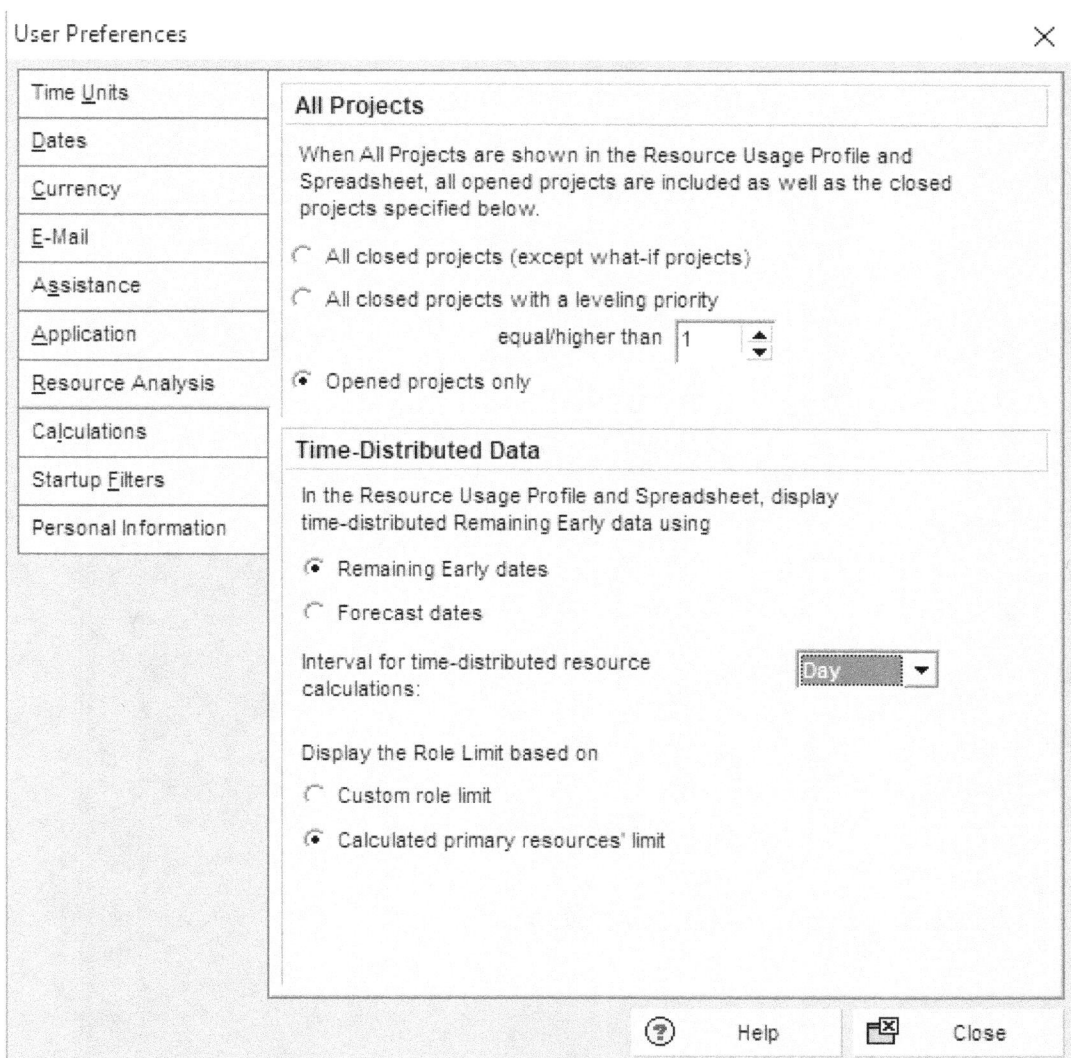

4. Go to the resource assignment view in P6, right click on the time scale and change it to daily:

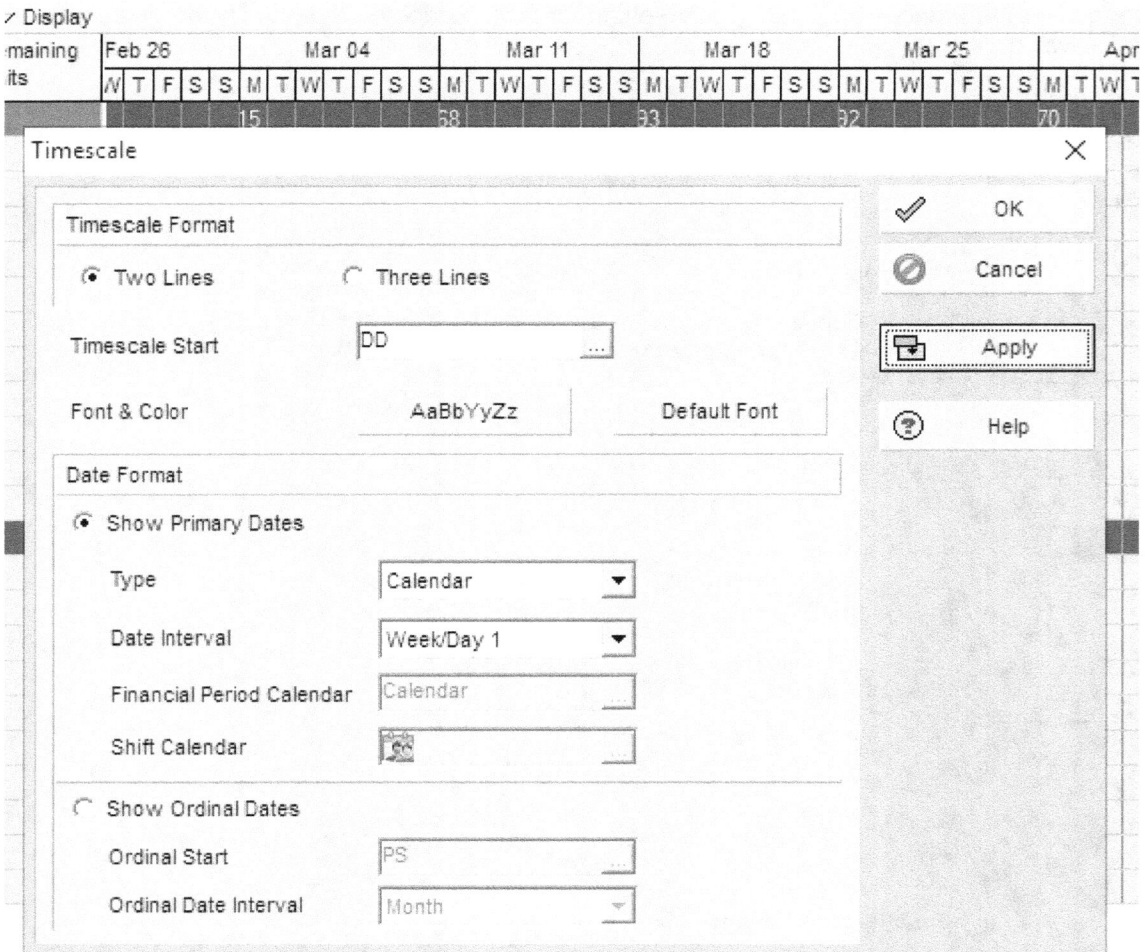

5. Copy/paste the resulting spreadsheet into the Daily tab:

| Paste daily resource assignment dump here | 24/Feb/24 | 25/Feb/24 | 26/Feb/24 | 27/Feb/24 | 28/Feb/24 | 29/Feb/24 | 01/Mar/24 | 02/Mar/24 | 03/Mar/24 |
|---|---|---|---|---|---|---|---|---|---|
| | Sat | Sun | Mon | Tue | Wed | Thu | Fri | Sat | Sun |
| L1GC _ Reporting Area L2.5: 2AA200  LNG Process Train 2 | | | | | | | | | |
| L1GD - LC Subcontractor: K054  K054 - Painting | 61 | 61 | 61 | 61 | 61 | 61 | 61 | 61 | 61 |
| Resource ID Name: UNSN_81  Paintings & Coatings | 61 | 61 | 61 | 61 | 61 | 61 | 61 | 61 | 61 |
| L1GC _ Reporting Area L2.5: 2TA100  LNG Process Train 1 | 48 | 48 | 48 | 48 | 48 | 48 | 48 | 48 | 48 |
| L1GC _ Reporting Area L2.5: 2AA200  LNG Process Train 2 | 13 | 13 | 13 | 13 | 13 | 13 | 13 | 13 | 13 |
| L1GD - LC Subcontractor: K055  K055 - Painting & Insulation - Pipe & Equipment | 1673 | 2033 | 2033 | 2033 | 2090 | 2090 | 2096 | 2029 | 2064 |
| Resource ID Name: UNSN_81  Paintings & Coatings | 326 | 326 | 326 | 326 | 383 | 383 | 383 | 383 | 383 |
| L1GC _ Reporting Area L2.5: 2TA100  LNG Process Train 1 | 244 | 244 | 244 | 244 | 301 | 301 | 301 | 301 | 301 |
| L1GC _ Reporting Area L2.5: 2AA200  LNG Process Train 2 | 81 | 81 | 81 | 81 | 81 | 81 | 81 | 81 | 81 |
| Resource ID Name: UNSN_82  Insulation | 1347 | 1707 | 1707 | 1707 | 1707 | 1707 | 1713 | 1646 | 1681 |
| L1GC _ Reporting Area L2.5: 2TA100  LNG Process Train 1 | 953 | 1313 | 1313 | 1313 | 1313 | 1313 | 1319 | 1252 | 1287 |
| L1GC _ Reporting Area L2.5: 2AA200  LNG Process Train 2 | 394 | 394 | 394 | 394 | 394 | 394 | 394 | 394 | 394 |
| L1GD - LC Subcontractor: K077  K077 - Supply & Install Architectural Components for SB Buildings | 1212 | 1310 | 263 | 257 | 174 | 174 | 174 | 174 | 174 |
| Resource ID Name: UNSN_30  Buildings & Architectural | 1212 | 1310 | 263 | 257 | 174 | 174 | 174 | 174 | 174 |
| L1GC _ Reporting Area L2.5: 2TA100  LNG Process Train 1 | 1120 | 1221 | 175 | 169 | 86 | 86 | 86 | 86 | 86 |
| L1GC _ Reporting Area L2.5: 2AA200  LNG Process Train 2 | 93 | 89 | 88 | 88 | 88 | 88 | 88 | 88 | 88 |

Andrei Sannikov
Tip of the day

Your daily data will be converted into weekly under the weekly tab with the week starting on Saturday.

| | 24/Feb/24 | 02/Mar/24 | 09/Mar/24 | 16/Mar/24 | 23/Mar/24 | 30/Mar/24 | 06/Apr/24 | 13/Apr/24 | 20/Apr/24 | 27/Apr/24 | 04/May/24 |
|---|---|---|---|---|---|---|---|---|---|---|---|
| | Sat | Sat | Sat | Sat | Sat | Sat | Sat | Sat | Sat | Sat | Sat |
| L1GC _ Reporting Area L2.5: 2AA200 LNG Process Train 2 | 0 | 0 | 0 | 0 | 0 | 0 | 0 | 0 | 0 | 0 | 0 |
| L1GD - LC Subcontractor: K054 K054 - Painting | 427 | 427 | 453 | 455 | 263 | 119 | 131 | 140 | 140 | 140 | 140 |
| Resource ID Name: UNSN_81 Paintings & Coatings | 427 | 427 | 453 | 455 | 263 | 119 | 131 | 140 | 140 | 140 | 140 |
| L1GC _ Reporting Area L2.5: 2TA100 LNG Process Train 1 | 336 | 336 | 336 | 336 | 144 | 0 | 0 | 0 | 0 | 0 | 0 |
| L1GC _ Reporting Area L2.5: 2AA200 LNG Process Train 2 | 91 | 91 | 117 | 119 | 119 | 119 | 131 | 140 | 140 | 140 | 140 |
| L1GD - LC Subcontractor: K055 K055 - Painting & Insulation - Pipe & Equip | 14048 | 15457 | 16867 | 18245 | 21223 | 23779 | 26365 | 31023 | 34111 | 31988 | 30722 |
| Resource ID Name: UNSN_81 Paintings & Coatings | 2453 | 2753 | 2852 | 2816 | 2471 | 2420 | 2322 | 2014 | 2255 | 2164 | 1542 |
| L1GC _ Reporting Area L2.5: 2TA100 LNG Process Train 1 | 1879 | 2182 | 2261 | 2206 | 1853 | 1731 | 1284 | 806 | 758 | 666 | 283 |
| L1GC _ Reporting Area L2.5: 2AA200 LNG Process Train 2 | 567 | 567 | 591 | 610 | 616 | 689 | 1038 | 1208 | 1498 | 1498 | 1259 |
| Resource ID Name: UNSN_82 Insulation | 11595 | 12705 | 14015 | 15430 | 18753 | 21359 | 24044 | 29008 | 31856 | 29825 | 29178 |
| L1GC _ Reporting Area L2.5: 2TA100 LNG Process Train 1 | 8837 | 9948 | 11260 | 12669 | 15992 | 17966 | 18331 | 20682 | 19140 | 16397 | 13263 |
| L1GC _ Reporting Area L2.5: 2AA200 LNG Process Train 2 | 2758 | 2758 | 2758 | 2758 | 2758 | 3392 | 5713 | 8326 | 12722 | 13428 | 15912 |
| L1GD - LC Subcontractor: K077 K077 - Supply & Install Architectural Com | 3564 | 1238 | 2082 | 2561 | 1780 | 702 | 561 | 504 | 490 | 404 | 307 |
| Resource ID Name: UNSN_30 Buildings & Architectural | 3564 | 1238 | 2082 | 2561 | 1780 | 702 | 561 | 504 | 490 | 404 | 307 |
| L1GC _ Reporting Area L2.5: 2TA100 LNG Process Train 1 | 2943 | 612 | 1178 | 1342 | 784 | 293 | 251 | 266 | 246 | 157 | 77 |
| L1GC _ Reporting Area L2.5: 2AA200 LNG Process Train 2 | 622 | 626 | 905 | 1220 | 997 | 406 | 310 | 238 | 238 | 242 | 230 |

Notes:

a) You can add formulas in column A of the weekly tab to autofill the resource/area descriptions from the Daily tab where you will be pasting your data

b) As you move your data date, you will need to change your timescale, so it starts after your Data Date. It would be easier to hide unnecessary columns rather than deleting them to avoid #REF errors and the need to rewrite all the formulas. You can then paste your resource export into a separate spreadsheet and transfer the data into the daily-to-weekly conversion file.

Andrei Sannikov
Tip of the day

26-Feb-24 1:09 PM

## How to place Completion Milestones after their predecessors when sorting by Finish

I am sure all of us have noticed that completion milestones do not always appear where we want them to be i.e., after their predecessors.

In the screenshot below one Mechanical Completion milestone is in the right spot, the other is not – for no apparent reason:

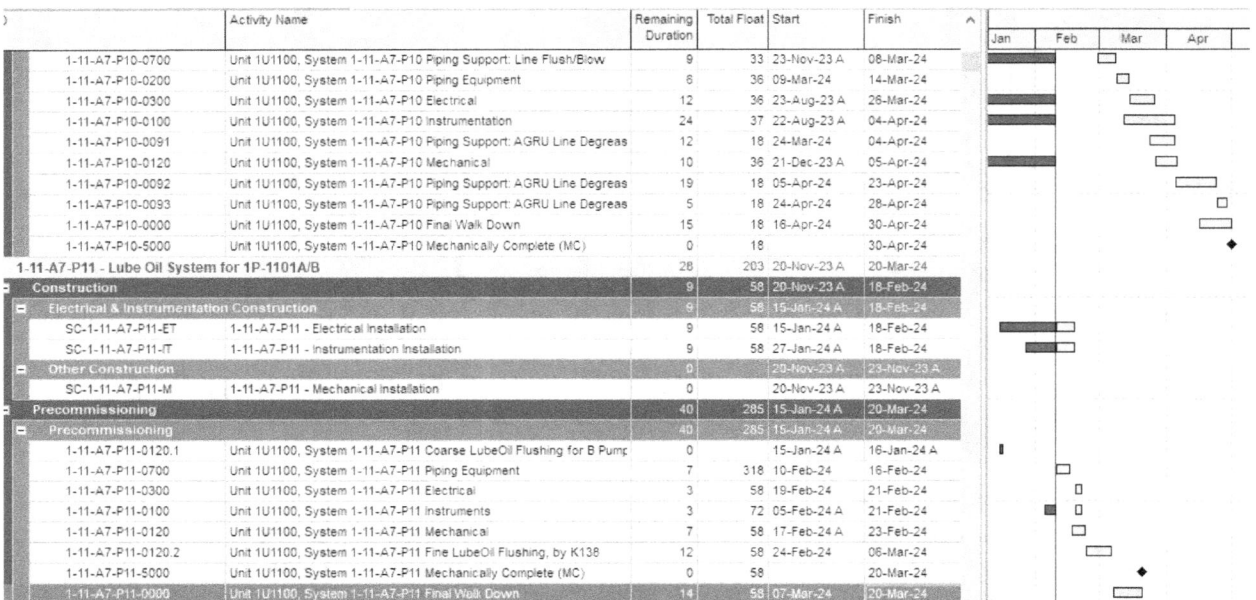

I have tried to investigate why some of the finish milestones behave differently from others but failed. Seems like a rather irritating glitch that some planners address by adding a lag of 1 day or less, which will, obviously, work but might require adjustments of other durations. On the other hand, if we print or view somebody else's schedule, we should not be messing around with their logic.

Let's see if we can find a different solution to this problem.

Open your schedule, go to Group and Sort and click on Sort button:

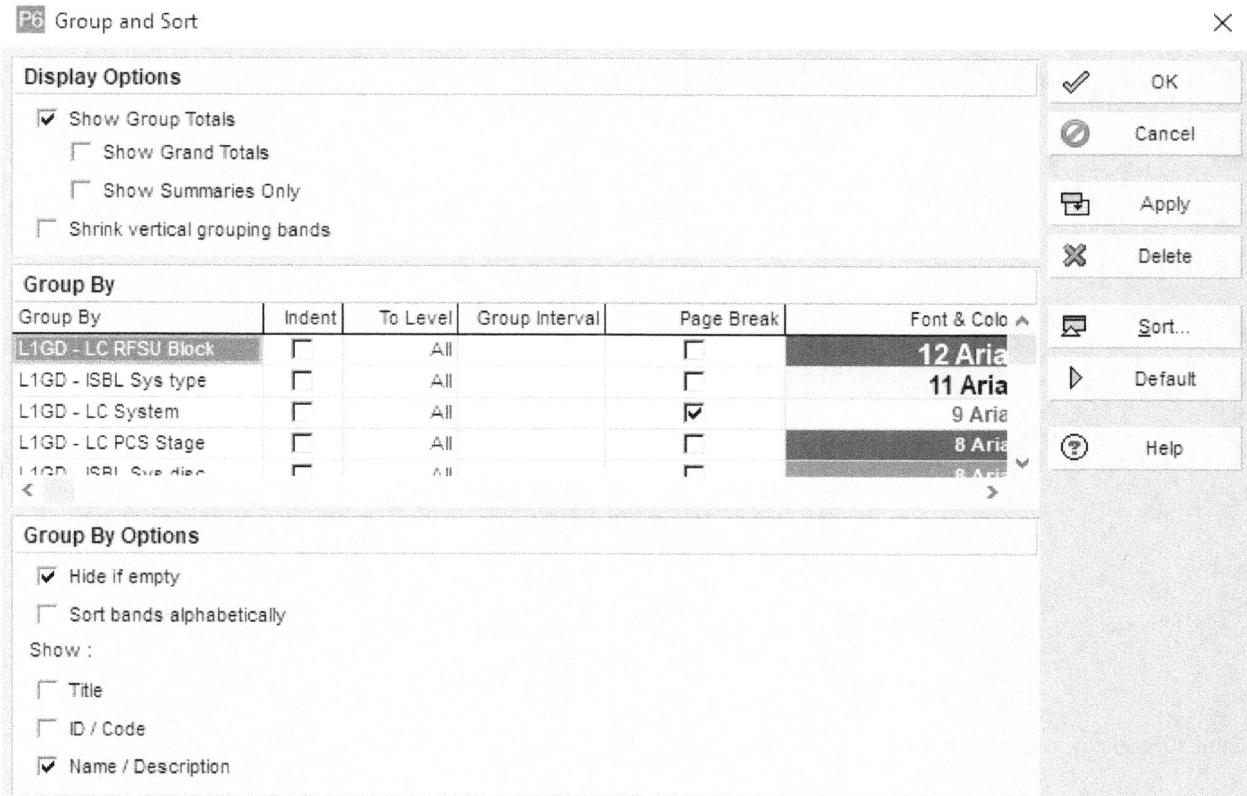

In the Sort window add sort by Start underneath sort by Finish as shown below:

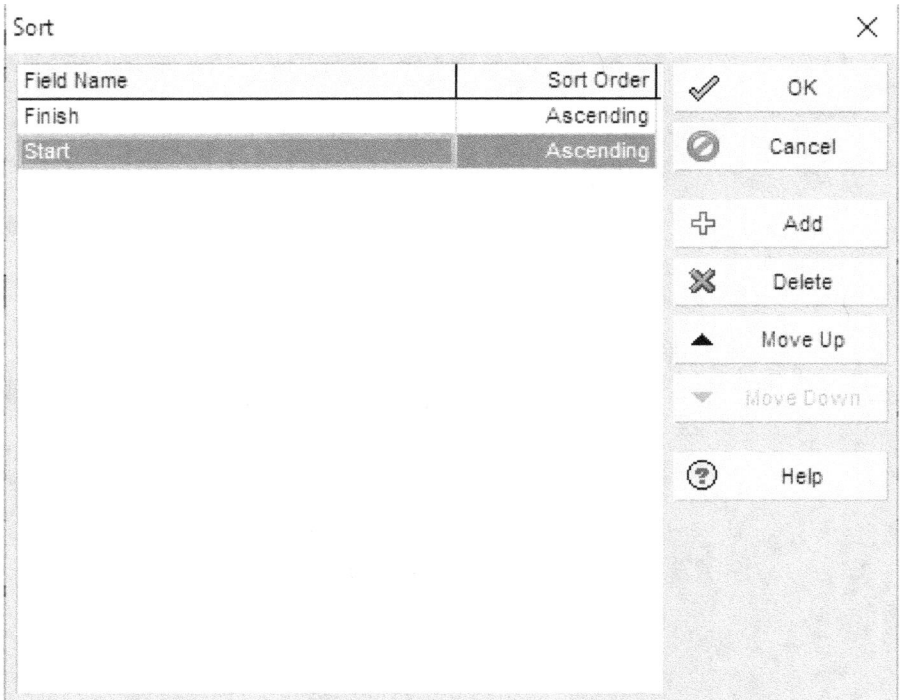

Click OK to close both windows and save your layout.

This should fix the problem:

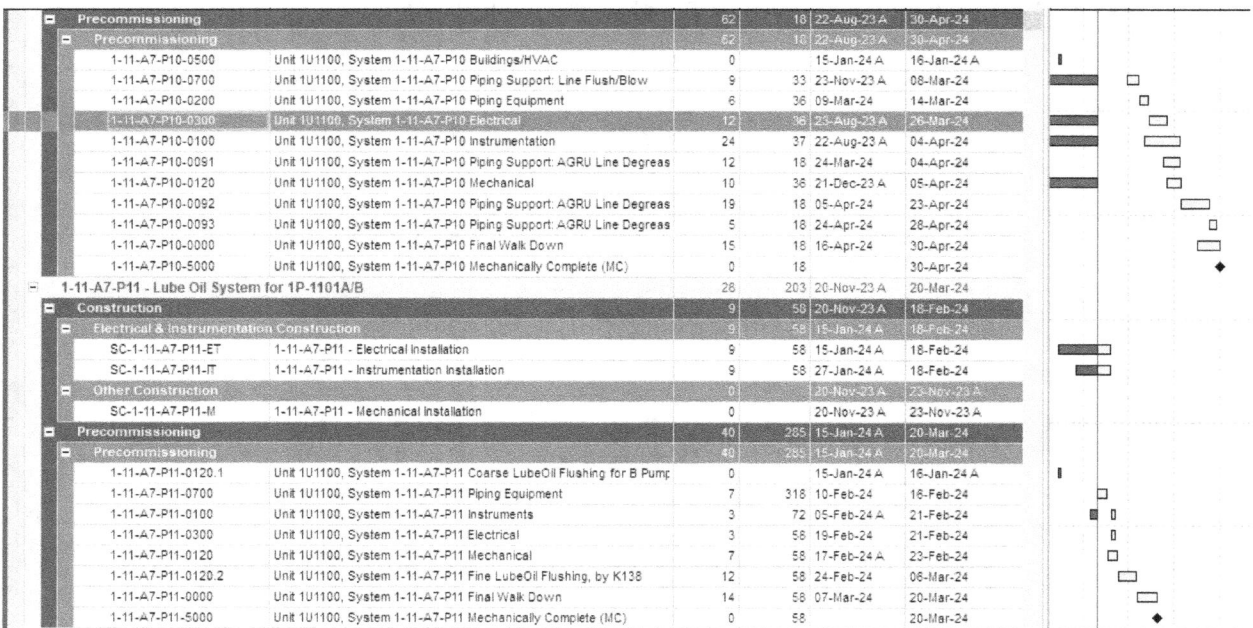

Andrei Sannikov
Tip of the day

12-Mar-24 10:15 AM

# How to import contractors' schedules into your master plan

On a typical projects contractors produce detailed L4/L5 schedules that need to be incorporated into a higher-level master plan. This process can be automated to some extent using Excel import functions described in detail in my earlier tips. To update your master plan with contractors' schedule information you can export some of the following fields:

- Remaining durations,
- Actual start and finish dates,
- Start/Finish on or after constraints.
- User defined fields
- Budget, actual, and at completion hours and quantities,

And export them into our master plan. To do that, you have a couple of options.

## Option 1

When your contractor is willing to add a few things to their schedule.

To make sure this import is as accurate and easy as possible try to do the following:

- If all or some of the activities you are updating using this import technique correspond to multiple activities in the contractor's schedule, ask your contractor to create LOEs summarizing them and assign them to the same calendar you use in your schedule.
- Make sure Contractor's schedule activities that correspond to individual activities in your master plan are on the same calendar.
- Ask your contractor to add a user defined field (UDF) containing activities IDs in your schedule corresponding to activities you will be importing.
- If you intend to import hours and quantities from the Contractors schedule as described below, you will need to ask your contractor to add a UDF with your activity IDs to all activities summarized by LOEs mentioned above and add a code that you can use to exclude them from the activity import.

When all this is done, we can proceed to the actual import.

1. Import your contractor's schedule, then export it inro Excel with the following export template:

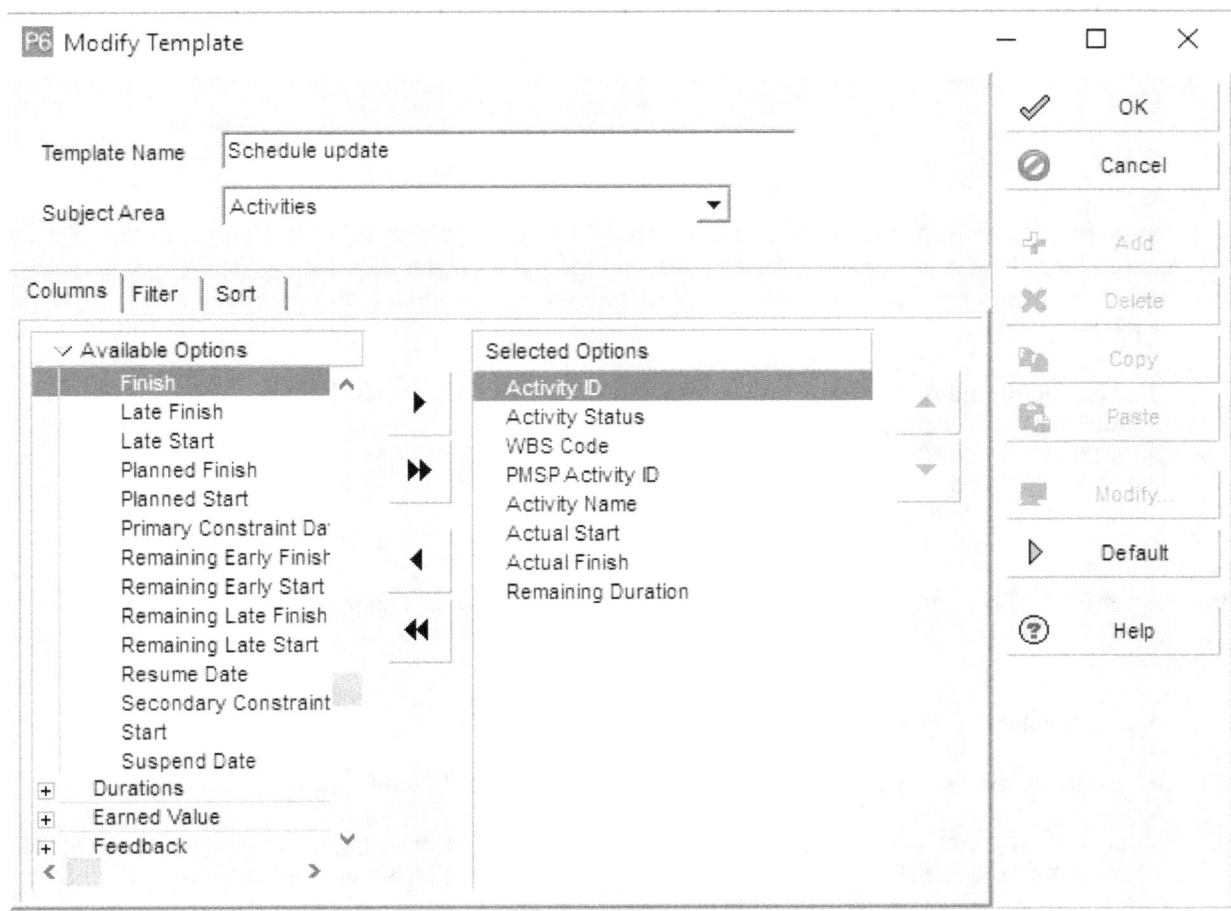

Where PMSP Activity ID is a UDF we asked our contractors to populate with corresponding activity IDs from our master plan.

Notes:

a) You can also add any other UDFs your contractor is using to store information you want to transfer into your project such as number of ITRs, remaining punches, notes etc. If you do include such UDFs into your data transfer exercise, make sure you add corresponding UDFs of the same data type (text, number, start/finish date or integer) to the export file that you will run from your master file in step 3 below.

b) There might be other data fields you would like to transfer from the contractor's schedule into yours e.g., physical percent complete or activity suspend dates. You can try to include them into the export file, however, fields marked with (*) in front of the field name like in the example below, cannot be imported:

| task_code | status_code | wbs_id | task_name | calc_phys_complete_pct | suspend_date | act_start_date | act_end_date | remain_drtn_hr_cnt | delete_record_flag |
|---|---|---|---|---|---|---|---|---|---|
| Activity ID | Activity Status | WBS Code | Activity Name | (*)Physical % Complete(%) | (*)Suspend Date | Actual Start | Actual Finish | Remaining Duration(d) | Delete This Row |

2. Complete the export of the contractor's schedule.

3. Open your master plan and export it into Excel using the template below:

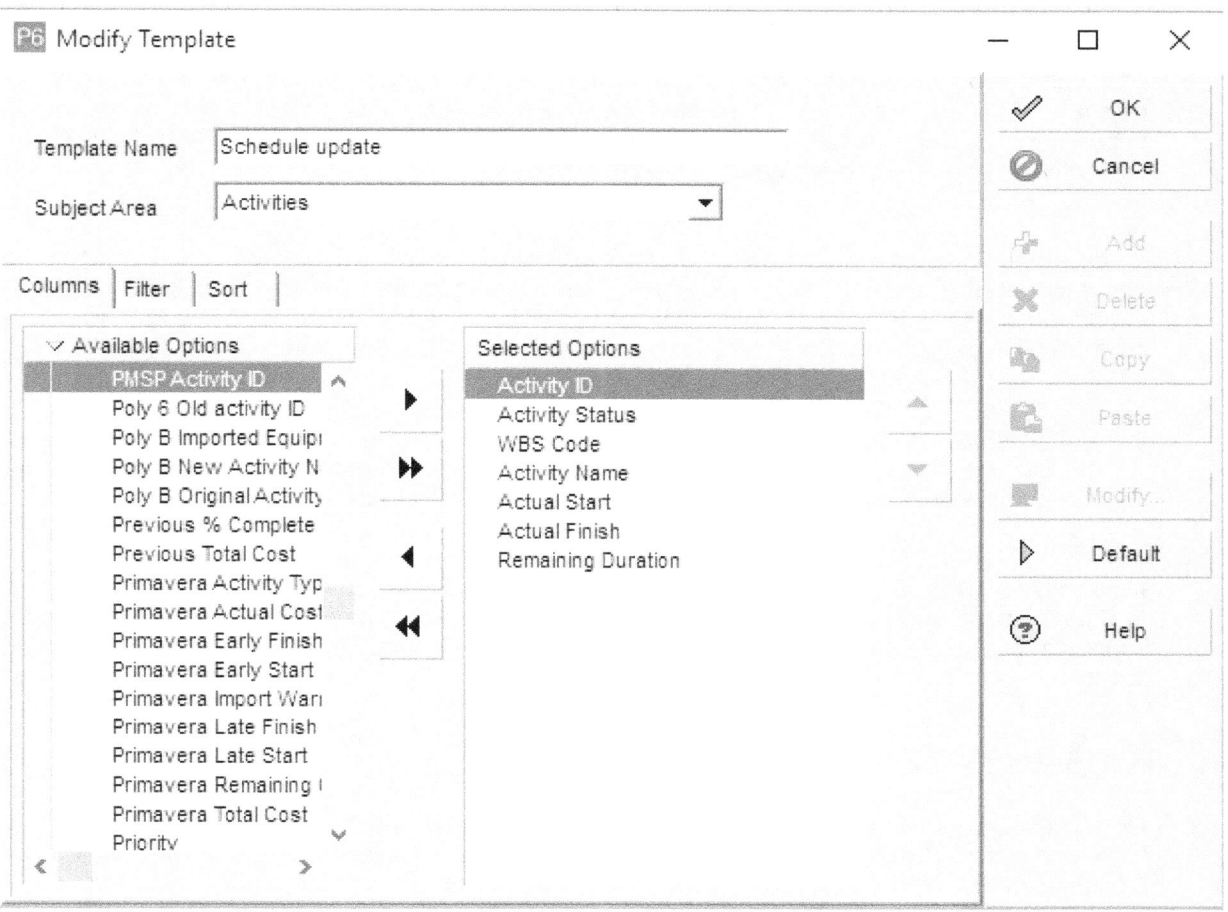

4. Copy the TASK worksheet from the Contractor's schedule export into your master plan export file. Since your master plan export file already contains a worksheet named TASK, the contractor's schedule export will be added as TASK(1), let's rename it to CONTRACTOR for clarity.

5. Use a lookup formula of your choice to transfer the data you need from the CONTRACTOR tab to the TASK tab using the UDF with Activity IDs (PMSP Activity ID in our example) as your reference.

6. Replace all formulas with values in the TASK tab (Ctrl A > Ctrl C > Paste Values) and delete the CONTRACTOR tab.

7. Save/close the file and import it back into your master plan.

Notes:

a) You will notice that P6 always includes the Activity Status and WBS code field that you cannot remove from your export template. When you add an actual start or finish date to your file for import, activity status will be updated automatically during import, and you don't need to change it in the Excel file.

b) Although we don't need the WBS column for our import operation, make sure you don't accidentally delete it. If the WBS column is absent in the import file, your entire WBS will be wiped out during the import process. If this happens, you can reinstate by exporting Activity IDs and WBS fields from a backup copy of your schedule and importing it into your master.

c) If you are OK with using start on or after constraints on your activities, you can add "Start" field to the contractor schedule export template and Primary Constraint and Primary Constraint Date fields to the export template in your master file. Activities you will be importing this constrained date to will have "Start on or after" in the Primary Constraint field and the date from the Start field in the CONTRACTOR tab.

   a. Finish constraints on Finish milestones can be imported in a similar fashion – add "Finish" field to the contractor schedule export template and use "Finish on or after" the Primary Constraint field and the date from the Finish field in the CONTRACTOR tab.

d) Imports do not always go as planned and it might be a good idea to make a copy of the file you exported in Step 3 above and save it in a backup folder. If you are not happy with the results of your contractor's schedule import, you can easily reverse all the changes by importing this backup file into your master project.

To import the actual and budget/at completion hours/quantities:

8. Go to Resource Assignment export and create a template similar to the one below, keep in mind that the UDF with your activity ID's will appear in the Activity User Defined section at the top of the Available Options menu:

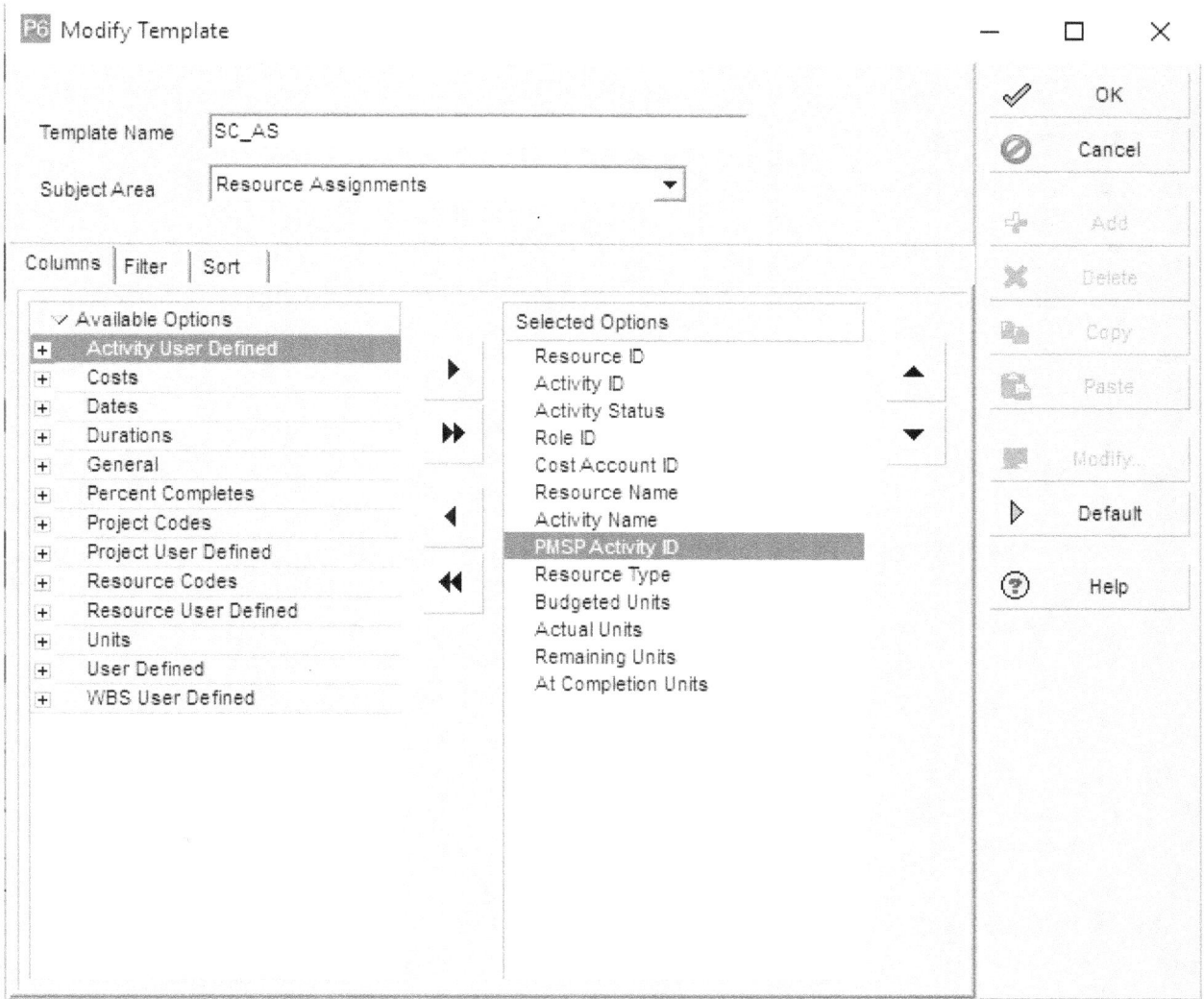

9. After exporting resource assignments from your contractor's schedule, open your master plan and run an Excel export of resource assignments using a similar template but obviously without the UDF highlighted above:

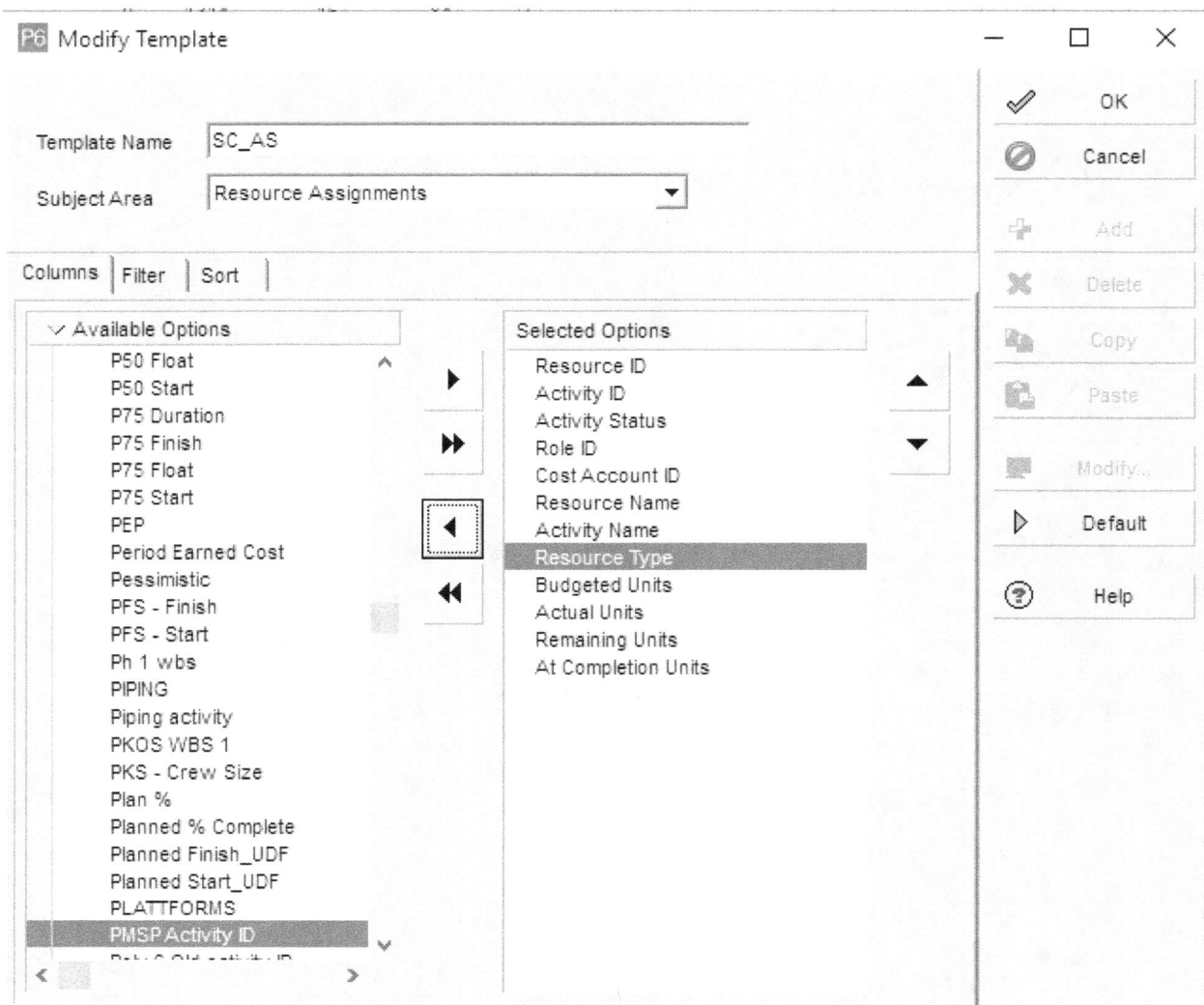

10. Copy the TASKRSRC worksheet from the Contractor's schedule export file we created in Step 8 above into the file you have exported from your master plan and repeat steps 5, 6 and 7 to transfer the data you need between the contractor's schedule and your master plan.

Notes:

a) Since you will most likely have multiple activities in the contractor's plan corresponding to a single activity in your master schedule you will need to use the SUMIFS function to transfer resource assignment values between the two schedules.

b) Keep in mind that the resource IDs in the two schedules might be different and you might want to create a lookup table to match them up.

Andrei Sannikov
Tip of the day

## Option 2

Your contractor is not willing to make any changes to their plans and you need to use their schedule "as is".

1. Create a lookup table in Excel matching activity IDs in the contractor schedule and your master plan.

2. Import your contractor's schedule, then export it inro Excel using the following export template:

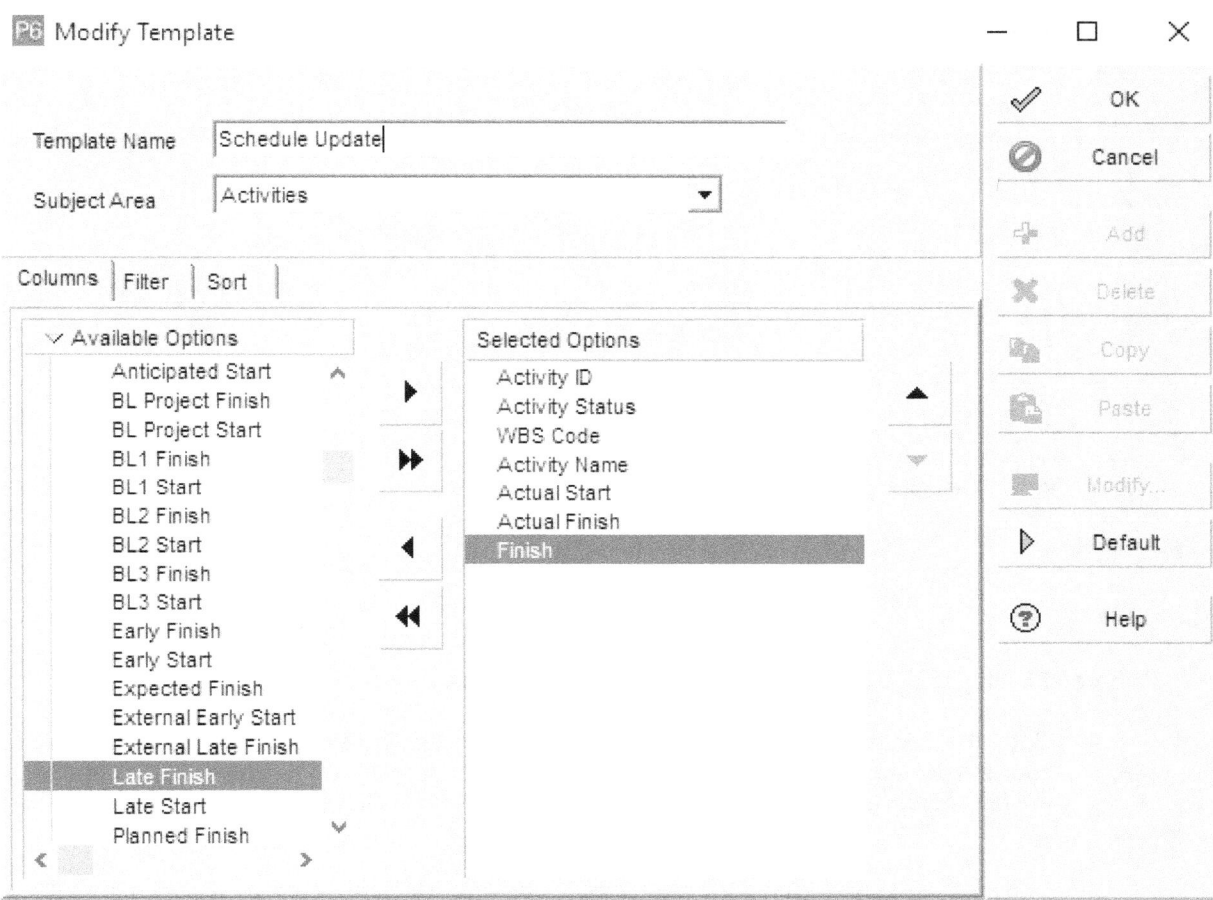

3. Export your master plan into Excel using the following template:

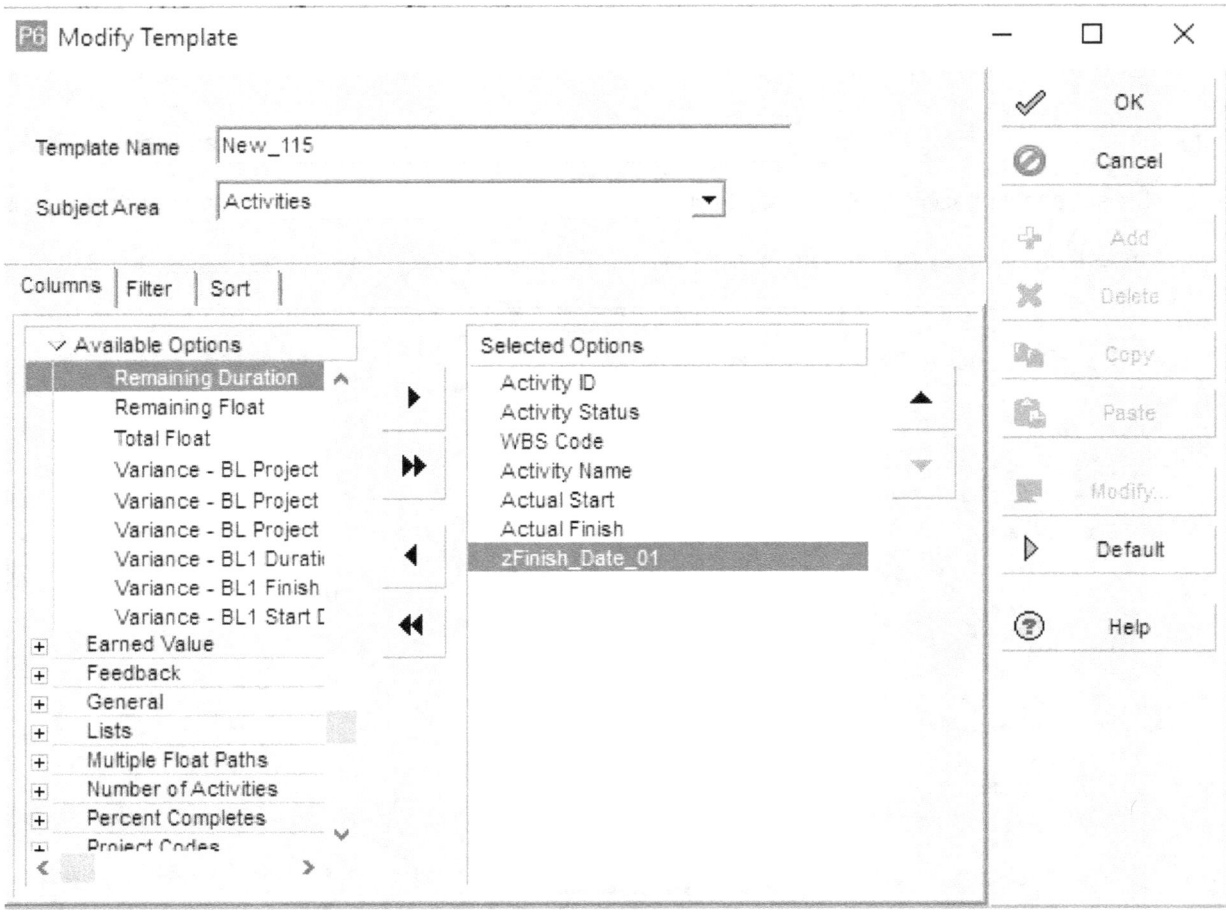

Where zFinish_Date_01 is a Finish date UDF we will need to calculate the remaining durations.

4. Copy the TASK worksheet from the Contractor's schedule export into your master plan export file. Since your master plan export file already contains a worksheet named TASK, the contractor's schedule export will be added as TASK(1), let's rename it to CONTRACTOR for clarity.

5. Copy the worksheet with the lookup table we created in Step 1 above into the same file.

6. Go to the CONTRACTOR worksheet and insert a column next to the Activity ID field. Use a lookup formula to populate it with you master plan activity IDs from the lookup table. You can delete the Activity Status and the WBS Code columns in the **CONTRACTOR tab** as we will not need them.

7. If your Activity IDs are in column B in the CONTRACTOR worksheet and the actual start dates are in column C you can use the following formula to pull in the actual start dates: =IF(MINIFS(Contractor!C:C,Contractor!B:B,TASK!A3)=0,"",MINIFS(Contractor!C:C,Contractor!B:B,TASK!A3)) on the first line of the TASK worksheet and copy it down

8. For the Actual Finish dates use =IF(MAXIFS(Contractor!D:D,Contractor!C:C,TASK!A3)=0,"",MAXIFS(Contractor!D:D,Contractor!C:C,TASK!A3))on the first line of the TASK worksheet and copy it down.

Note: We need these formulas to make sure the function does not return 0 values from empty cells in the CONTRACTOR worksheet.

9. Filter out all lines with actual finish dates in the TASK worksheet and use the function =IF(MAXIFS(Contractor!E:E,Contractor!C:C,TASK!A3)=0,"",MAXIFS(Contractor!E:E,Contractor!C:C,TASK!A3)) to populate the zFinish_Date_01 column

10. If you intend to import constrained start dates from your contractor's schedule, follow the instructions under Note c) in Option 1 above.

11. Replace all formulas with values in the TASK tab (Ctrl A > Ctrl C > Paste Values) and delete the CONTRACTOR tab.

12. Save/close the file and import it back into your master plan.

13. Go to Tools and set up/run the following Global Change

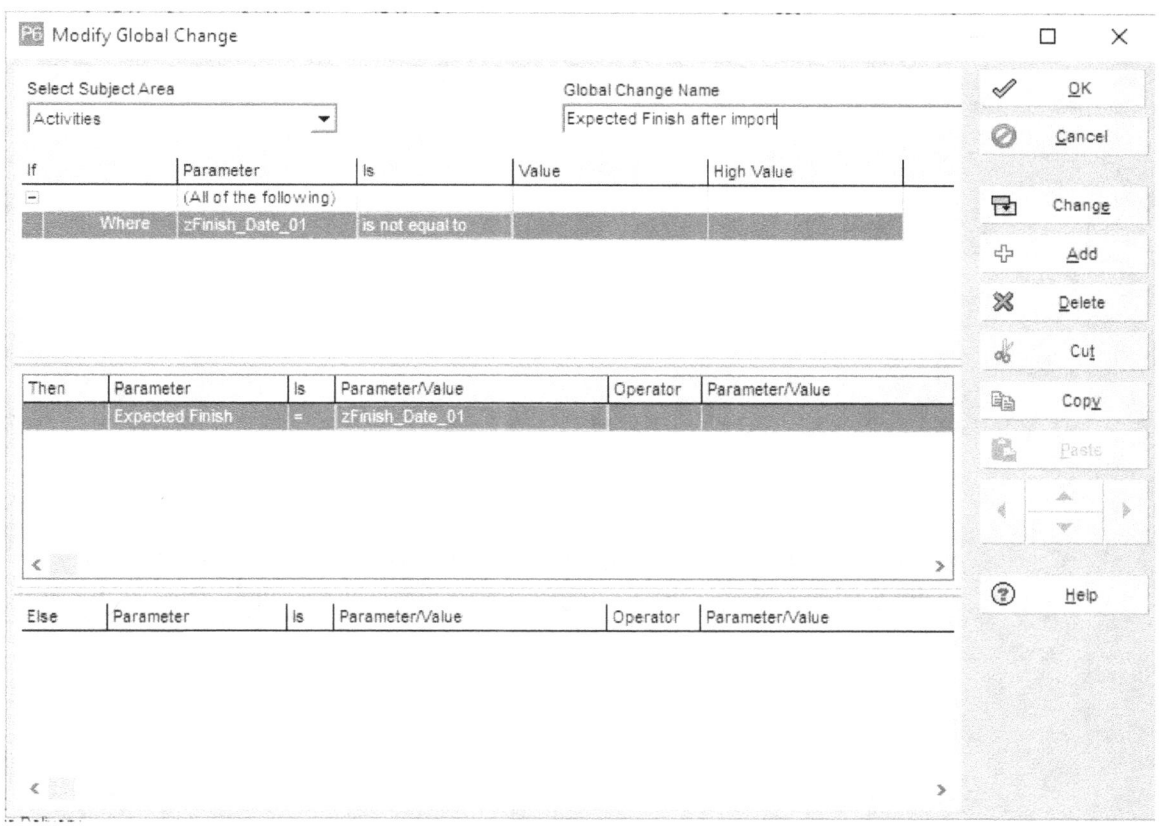

14. Schedule your project. If necessary, remove the Expected Finish dates by filtering them in and using the Fill down function.

15. The process of importing hours and quantities will be similar to one described under Option 1 above, the only difference being that instead of using a UDF with your master schedule activity ID's you will need it to bring them in from the lookup table we set up in Step 1 above.

Andrei Sannikov
Tip of the day

21-Apr-24 01:15 PM

## How to identify all UDFs and activity codes used in a schedule

When you receive a schedule from a contractor or inherit a large network from a colleague it might be important to understand which User Defined Fields (UDF) and activity codes it has been loaded with so you can setup appropriate layouts and filters. P6 lets you view activity codes loaded on a particular activity under the Codes tab in the activity details section but not in the entire network and there is no easy way to determine which UDFs are used on an activity, never mind in the whole schedule.

To view all UDFs and Activity codes assigned in a schedule and their respective types consider the following.

1. Export your schedule as an xer file or use the xer file you have received.

2. Go to this xer file in your File Explorer, right click > Open with > Notepad.

3. When the file opens, press Ctrl + F and type UDFTYPE in the search window. This will take you to the UDF block of the xer file, which will look like the one below:

```
UDFTYPE
udf_type_id    table_name    udf_type_name       udf_type_label    logical_data_type
128            TASK          user_field_128      Gate Status       FT_STATICTYPE    N
129            TASK          user_field_129      Qty (UDF)         FT_TEXT N
130            TASK          user_field_130      UDF - Cwp         FT_TEXT N
131            TASK          user_field_131      BL-Battery Limits(UDF)    FT_TEXT N
137            TASK          user_field_137      Remarks FT_TEXT N
138            TASK          user_field_138      CWA(UDF)          FT_TEXT N
140            TASK          user_field_140      ALTRAD CRITICAL   FT_TEXT N
142            TASK          user_field_142      CheckMark         FT_STATICTYPE    N
143            TASK          user_field_143      Comments          FT_TEXT N
144            TASK          user_field_144      AREA    FT_TEXT N
145            TASK          user_field_145      Text 01 FT_TEXT N
146            TASK          user_field_146      IWP (UDF)         FT_TEXT N
357            TASK          user_field_357      Previous Actual Date    FT_START_DATE    N
358            TASK          user_field_358      Scope - UDF       FT_TEXT N
370            TASK          user_field_370      Units   FT_TEXT N
886            TASK          user_field_886      UDF - System No:  FT_TEXT N
933            TASK          user_field_933      IWP (UDF 2)       FT_TEXT N
1056           TASK          user_field_1056     MIlestone (Sys)   FT_TEXT N
1057           TASK          user_field_1057     Modification      FT_TEXT N
1269           TASK          user_field_1269     Equipment Reference    FT_TEXT N
```

4. Now you can copy and paste this list into a text file and use the UDF descriptions in the udf_type_name column to find and display them in columns or use in filters or sorts. The UDF type is indicated after "FT_ " – text, indicator, number, integer, cost, start or finish date.

5. Activity codes can be found in a similar fashion. Press Ctrl + F in the xer file opened in Notepad and type ACTVTYPE in the search window.

6. This will take you to the Activity codes block, which will look like the one below:

```
ACTVTYPE
actv_code_type_id    actv_short_len  seq_num  actv_code_type     proj_id  wbs_id  actv_code_type_scope  export_flag
205      10    201      SCOPE                              AS_Global
206      10    202      EXSCOPE                            AS_Global
1222     7     73957    Priority                                   AS_Global
1307     21    73954    Work Package                               AS_Global
1308     25    73956    System                             AS_Global
1309     25    73951    Work Area                                  AS_Global
1310     25    73952    CWP                                AS_Global
2057     7     73953    CWA                                AS_Global
2345     7     300      AREA/UNIT         675                      AS_Project
2346     15    0        CWP       675              AS_Project
2347     25    400      PRIME DISCIPLINE  675                      AS_Project
2348     20    100      IWP       675              AS_Project
2349     50    500      Discipline        675                      AS_Project
2350     40    600      REMARKS   675              AS_Project
2351     25    700      CONTRACT          675                      AS_Project
2352     7     503      PARTITION         675                      AS_Project
2353     15    502      Indirect Labor    675                      AS_Project
2354     7     501      CHECKING          675                      AS_Project
2355     20    301      Milestone Description   675                AS_Project
2356     7     1        Battery Limits    675                      AS_Project
2357     7     73955    Area Priority                              AS_Global
```

7. Now you can copy and paste this list into a text file and use the Activity code descriptions in the actv_short_len column to find and display them in columns or use in filters or sorts. Activity code type is indicated after "AS_ " – Project, Global or EPS.

8. Close the xer file **without saving it**, especially if prompted to do so, as it would corrupt the file and make it unsuitable for future imports.

Andrei Sannikov
Tip of the day

22-Apr-24 04:21 PM

# How to link your schedule to a systems completion database

When we work with systems completion schedules, we are often asked to include information from the project systems completion database: outstanding punch list (PL) items, check sheets or inspection and test records (ITRs). Different companies use different types of systems completions databases, however, all of them have a few things in common – they track outstanding completions items by system/subsystems and discipline and have Excel export capabilities. To setup an automatic transfer of this information into your schedule, consider the following:

1. Create or select the User Defined Fields (UDF) you will be using to display the required numbers from your systems completion database with Integer as the data type.

2. Go to File > Export > Spreadsheet (XLSX) > Activities and set up an export template with the following fields:

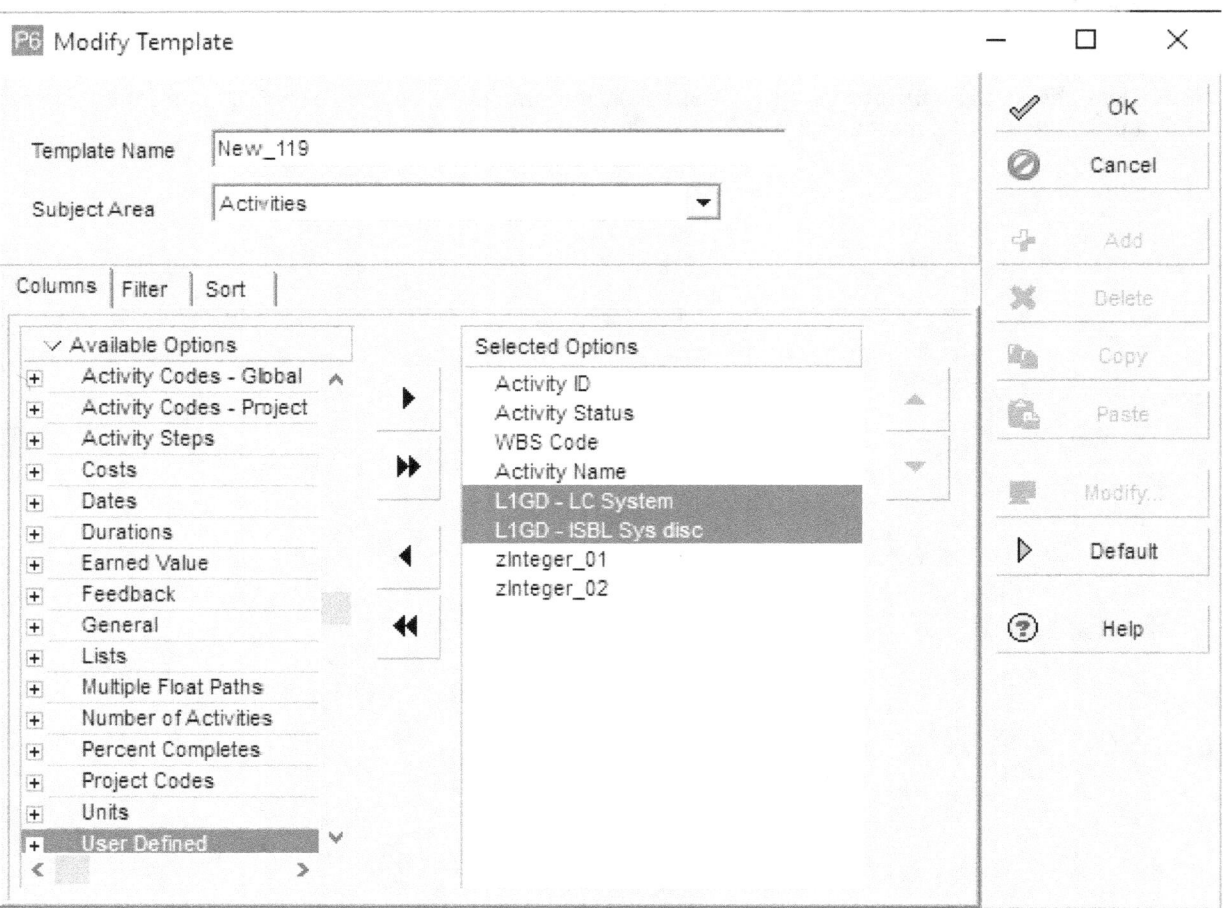

Andrei Sannikov
Tip of the day

The two entries highlighted above are system and discipline codes that I have in my system, the last two entries are Integer types UDF we will be using to pull outstanding PL items and ITRs from our systems completion database.

3. Export your project and copy the TASK tab of the resulting file into an Excel spreadsheet. Delete the columns you don't need and rearrange the remaining ones as necessary – I prefer to have my system numbers in column A, Activity IDs in column B etc.

4. Go to your Systems completion database and run a report containing, as a minimum, systems, disciplines, outstanding ITR and PL counts, ITR/PL types (typically A for construction, B for pre-com etc.) and your project/operation center code, if you have more than one in your system. Export to Excel and copy into the same spreadsheet under a separate tab. We will name this tab "ITR" for clarity.

5. Go to the TASK tab, Insert a column next to the Discipline code and assign discipline definitions from your Systems Completion database corresponding to P6 discipline codes like in the example below:

| Activity ID | Activity Name | L1GD - ISBL Sys disc | ITR Discipline |
|---|---|---|---|
| SC-0-00-A7-SS10-ET | 0-00-A7-SS10 - Electrical Installation | E | Electrical |
| SC-0-00-A7-SS10-IP | 0-00-A7-SS10 - Pipe Insulation | INS | Insulation |
| SC-0-00-A7-SS10-M | 0-00-A7-SS10 - Mechanical Installation | M | Mechanical |
| SC-0-00-A8-SS10-ET | 0-00-A8-SS10 - Electrical Installation | E | Electrical |
| SC-0-00-A8-SS10-IE | 0-00-A8-SS10 - Equipment Insulation | INS | Insulation |
| SC-0-00-A8-SS10-M | 0-00-A8-SS10 - Mechanical Installation | M | Mechanical |
| SC-0-60-A2-FW60-ET | 0-60-A2-FW60 - Electrical Installation | E | Electrical |
| SC-0-60-A2-FW60-IT | 0-60-A2-FW60 - Instrumentation Installation | I | Instrumentation |
| SC-0-60-A2-FW60-IP | 0-60-A2-FW60 - Pipe Insulation | INS | Insulation |

Note: If you have more than one activity in each discipline (e.g., pipe installation and hydrotest), add ITR Discipline definition against only one activity and leave it blank (or put n/a) for the rest of them to avoid double counting:

| Activity ID | Activity Name | L1GD - ISBL Sys disc | ITR Discipline |
|---|---|---|---|
| SC-0-60-A2-FW60-PI | 0-60-A2-FW60 - Pipe Installation | P | Piping |
| SC-0-60-A2-FW60-PT | 0-60-A2-FW60 - Pipe Testing & Reinstatement | P | n/a |
| SC-0-60-A2-FW70-PI | 0-60-A2-FW70 - Pipe Installation | P | Piping |
| SC-0-60-A2-FW90-PI | 0-60-A2-FW90 - Pipe Installation | P | Piping |
| SC-0-60-A2-FW90-PT | 0-60-A2-FW90 - Pipe Testing & Reinstatement | P | n/a |
| SC-0-64-A2-CC12-PI | 0-64-A2-CC12 - Pipe Installation | P | Piping |
| SC-1-11-A7-P10-PI | 1-11-A7-P10 - Pipe Installation | P | Piping |
| SC-1-11-A7-P10-PT | 1-11-A7-P10 - Pipe Testing & Reinstatement | P | n/a |
| SC-1-11-A7-P20-PI | 1-11-A7-P20 - Pipe Installation | P | Piping |
| SC-1-11-A7-P30-PI | 1-11-A7-P30 - Pipe Installation | P | Piping |
| SC-1-11-A7-P30-PT | 1-11-A7-P30 - Pipe Testing & Reinstatement | P | n/a |

6. Use the COUNTIFS function to populate the ITR UDF field (zinteger_01) we have included in our export template. In the system I am using construction ITRs are called "A1" and outstanding ones can be "Incomplete", "In progress" or "Re-opened", therefore, I will need the following formula in the zinteger_01 column to capture all of them:

=COUNTIFS(ITR!A:A,TASK!A12,ITR!L:L,TASK!G12,ITR!M:M,"Incomplete A1",ITR!T:T,"YOC")+COUNTIFS(ITR!A:A,TASK!A12,ITR!L:L,TASK!G12,ITR!M:M,"Re-opened A1",ITR!T:T,"YOC")+COUNTIFS(ITR!A:A,TASK!A12,ITR!L:L,TASK!G12,ITR!M:M,"In-progress A1",ITR!T:T,"YOC")

Where:

System numbers are in columns A in both TASK and ITR tabs.

Discipline definitions are included in column G in the TASK tab and in column L in the ITR tab.

Column M in the ITR tab contains ITR categories.

YOC is the operation center code I need to filter in only ITRs related to my area.

7. PL items we will include in the zinteger_02 column appear as numeric values against each outstanding ITR, and we will need a different function to sum them up – SUMIFS:

=SUMIFS(ITR!Q:Q,ITR!A:A,TASK!A12,ITR!L:L,TASK!G12,ITR!M:M,"Incomplete A1",ITR!T:T,"YOC")+SUMIFS(ITR!Q:Q,ITR!A:A,TASK!A12,ITR!L:L,TASK!G12,ITR!M:M,"Re-opened A1",ITR!T:T,"YOC")+SUMIFS(ITR!Q:Q,ITR!A:A,TASK!A12,ITR!L:L,TASK!G12,ITR!M:M,"In-progress A1",ITR!T:T,"YOC")

Where:

Outstanding PL counts are in column Q in the ITR tab.

The rest of the parameters are the same as in step 6 above.

8. To complete the automation setup, go back to P6 and run another Activities export to Excel with the following template:

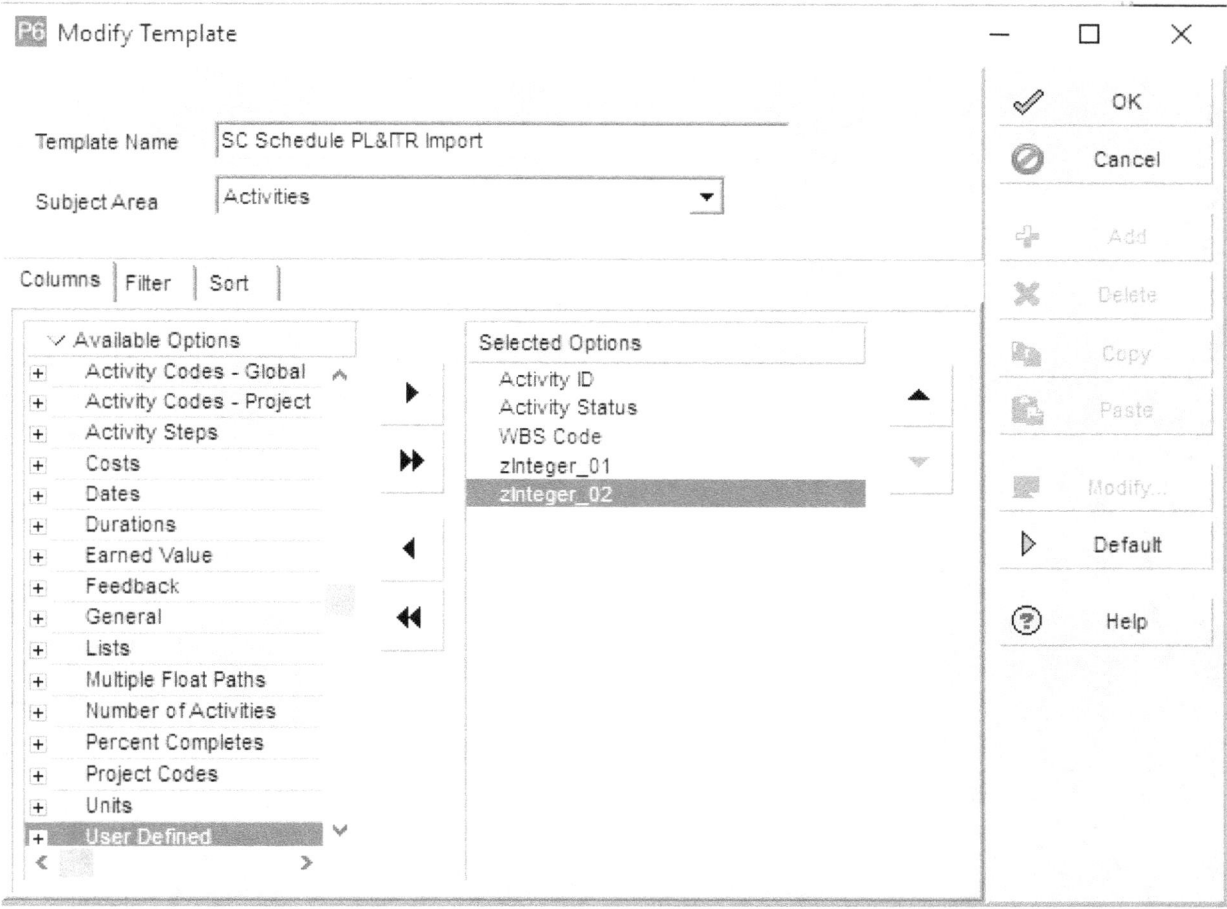

9. Copy the TASK tab from the exported file into the spreadsheet we created earlier – let's call it the bridge file for clarity - it will be added as TASK (2). Delete the Activity Status column. If your schedule is based on WBS, **DO NOT delete** the WBS column – otherwise, your WBS will be wiped out after import.

10. Use a lookup function of your choice to populate the zinteger_01 and zinteger_02 columns from the TASK tab.

Andrei Sannikov
Tip of the day

11. Go back to the file we exported from P6 in step 8 above and delete all data in the TASK tab.

12. Go to the TASK (2) tab in the bridge file, select all (Ctrl + A), copy and paste as values in TASK tab of the exported file. Save, close, and import back into P6.

13. Add the zinteger_01 and zinteger_02 columns to your layout in P6 and rename them to Outstanding ITR and Outstanding PL respectively.

14. Going forward, all you will need to do to update the ITR/PL counts in your schedule is paste a new ITR/PL dump from the systems completion database into the ITR tab of the bridge file and repeat steps 11 and 12 above.

Andrei Sannikov
Tip of the day

02-May-24 04:27 PM

# What to do if P6 does not let you de-actualize an activity start date

After earned hours are imported from Excel, sometimes, you will notice actual start dates on the right-hand side of the data date on activities that have been progressed out of sequence. To avoid issues associated with out-of-sequence logic you will obviously need to filter in such activities (Actual start date greater than DD), move these actual start dates to the left of the data date and adjust the logic if necessary.

In some cases, you might need to change the actual units back to zero and de-actualize the activity start date e.g., when you notice an error.

In the example below, the actual labor units are equal to 0 and we obviously need to change this activity status to "Not Started":

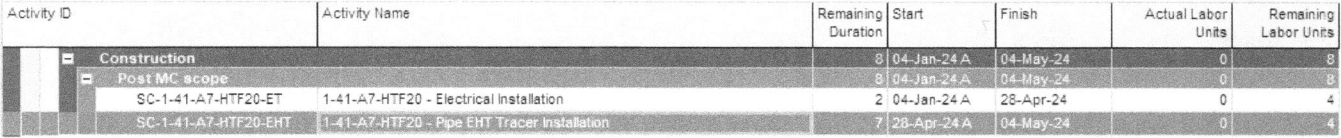

However, when you try to uncheck the Started checkbox the following message pops up:

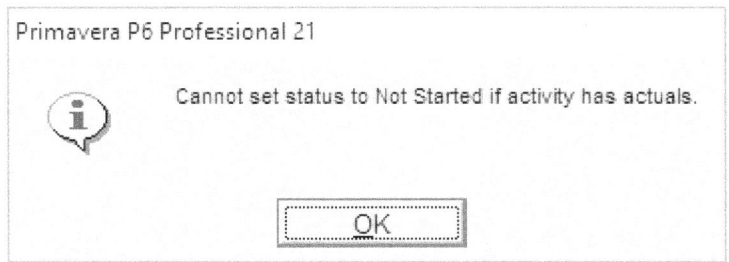

You go to the Resources tab, see that the actual labor units are equal to zero, and try to reset them to zero manually by typing "0" in the Actual Units column:

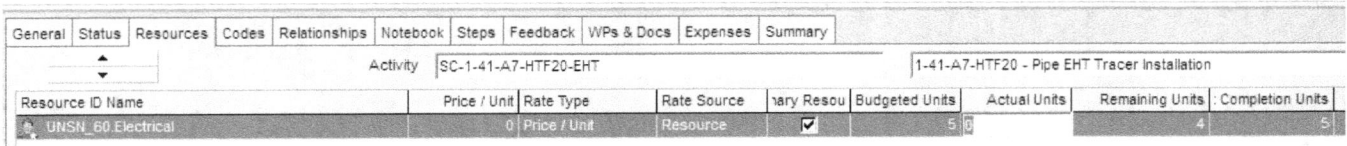

It does not help - when you uncheck the Started checkbox, you get the same message.

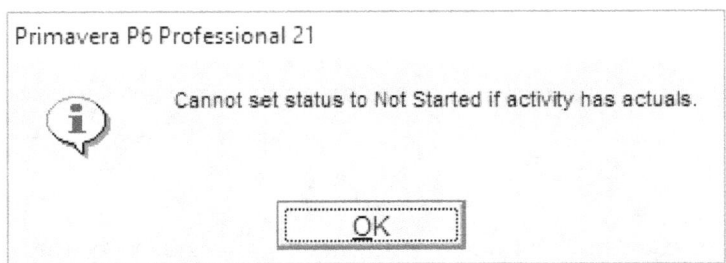

Here is the solution:

1. Go to Edit > User Preferences > Time Units and set Decimals to "2":

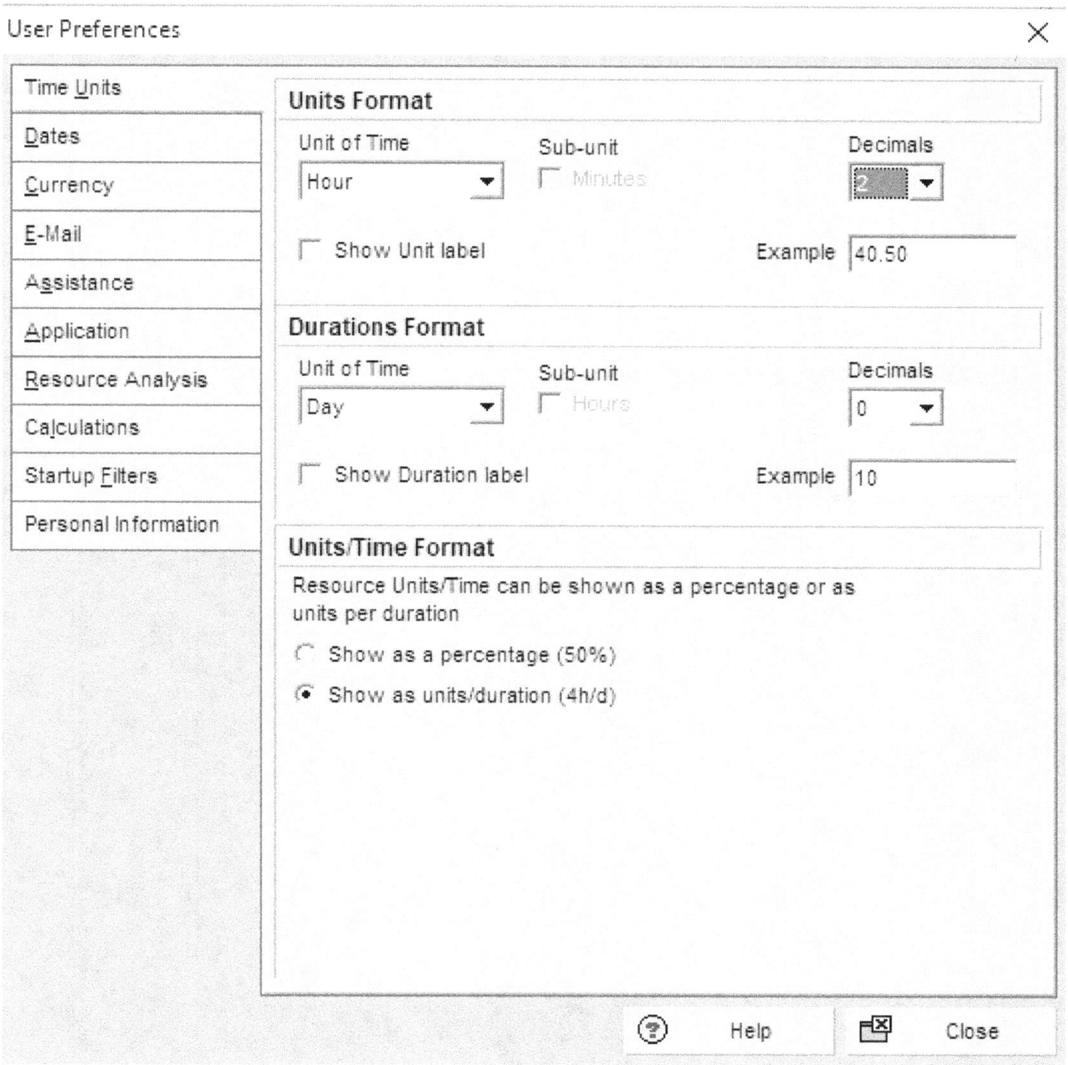

2. Go back to the Resource tab in the Activity detail window:

| Resource ID Name | Price / Unit | Rate Type | Rate Source | ıary Resou | Budgeted Units | Actual Units | Remaining Units | : Completion Units |
|---|---|---|---|---|---|---|---|---|
| UNSN_60.Electrical | 0 | Price / Unit | Resource | ☑ | 4.83 | 0.48 | 4.34 | 4.83 |

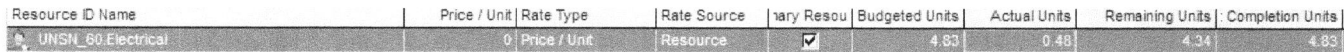

As you can see, the actual units on this activity were rounded to zero but are higher – 0.48.

3. Reset them manually to 0, go to the Activity status tab and uncheck the Started checkbox. You will get the usual prompt:

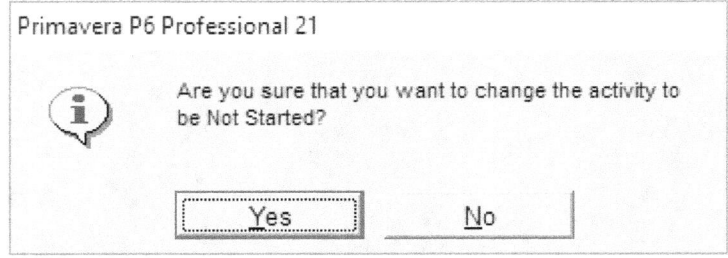

…and will be able to change the activity status.

You can now reset the decimals back to 0 in the User Preferences.

Andrei Sannikov
Tip of the day

05-May-24 04:07 PM

## How to reinstate deleted activities from a baseline

If you accidentally delete one or several activities from your schedule they can be reinstated from a baseline where these activities are still present. You can reinstate activity ID/name, resource assignments, actual start and finish dates, WBS, durations, EPS and Global activity codes, UDFs, constraints and logical links. Pretty much everything, except for Project activity codes and activity Suspend and Resume dates. Obviously, you would need to use this method only if you have made multiple changes or closed your project after this deletion and the Undo function is no longer available.

1. Go to Project > Assign baseline to make sure the baseline you will be reinstating from is not assigned as a User or the Project baseline.

2. Go to Project > Maintain baseline and restore this baseline. It will be restored in the node where you working project is located.

3. Open the restored baseline.

    a. If you use Project activity codes, it might be a good idea to locate the activities you are planning to reinstate, open the Codes tab in the Activity Details window and take a screenshot of the code assignments. As mentioned above, EPS and Global activity code assignments will be transferred electronically, Project activity codes will need to be re-assigned manually after the import (or you can use the tool described in the second part of this tip if you are reinstating multiple activities). Skip this step if your schedule is based on EPS and Global activity codes only.

    b. If your activities have Suspend and/or Resume dates, you can either take a screenshot of those in the Activity Details window or display them in columns and copy/paste into Excel – they will need to be re-entered manually.

4. Go to File > Export > Export Format > Spreadsheet – (XLSX) > Next and choose the following types of data to export:

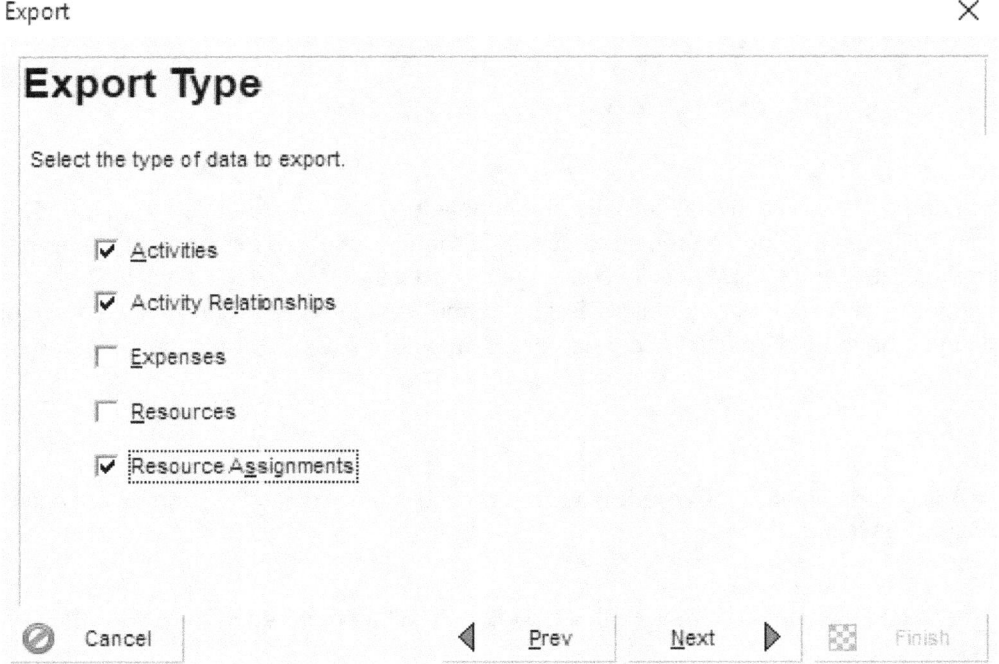

5. Click Next, select your project and click Next – this will open the Select Template dialogue. Click Add, rename if necessary, and click Modify.

a) Choose "Activities" in the Subject Area and setup a template with all or some of the following fields depending upon their use in your schedule:

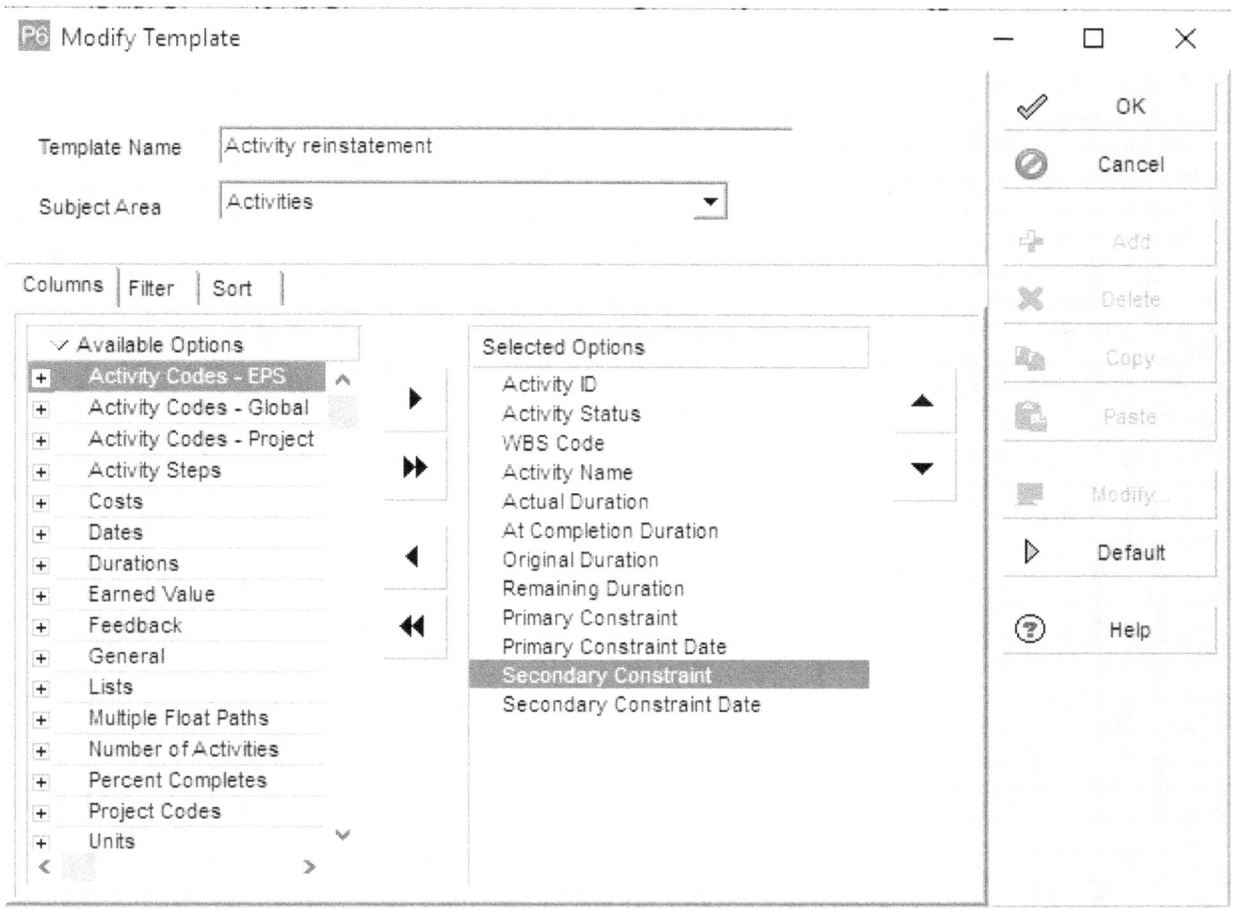

Add EPS and Global codes your activities are assigned to. If your activities have multiple code assignments and your system has a reasonable number of EPS and Global codes, it might be easier to add all of them to your export template – P6 will ignore unassigned codes during import.

Add all User Defined Fields you are planning to transfer.

Go to Filter and set up a filter to include activity IDs you are planning to reinstate.

> b) Choose "Resource Assignments" in the Subject Area and setup a template with the following fields:

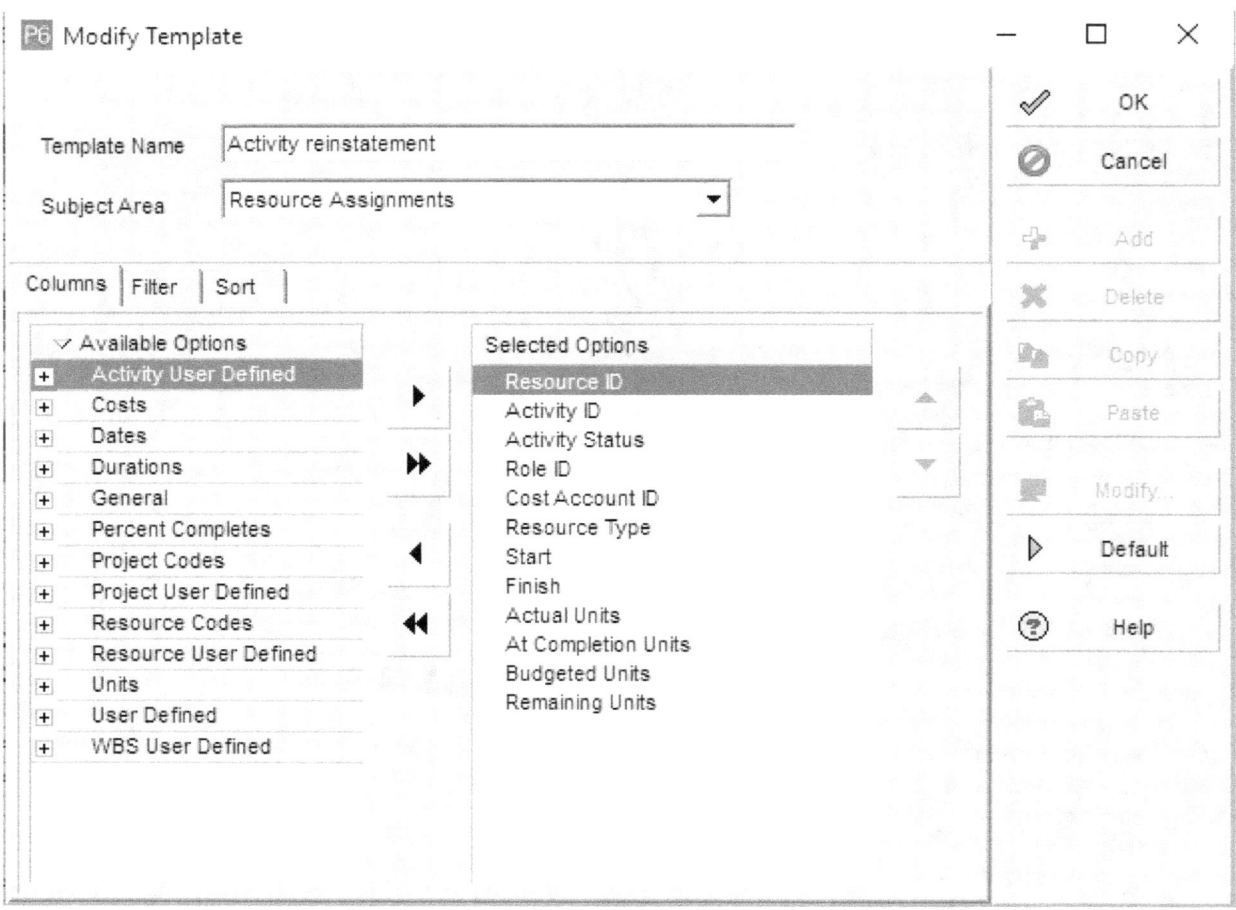

Add all User Defined Fields you are planning to transfer.

Go to Filter and set up a filter to include the names of the activities you are planning to reinstate. Unfortunately, P6 does not have an option to setup a resource assignment filter based on Activity IDs and if your activity names are rather generic you might need to export all resource assignments and delete what you don't need in Excel after export.

    c)   Choose "Activity Relationships" in the Subject Area and setup a template with the following fields:

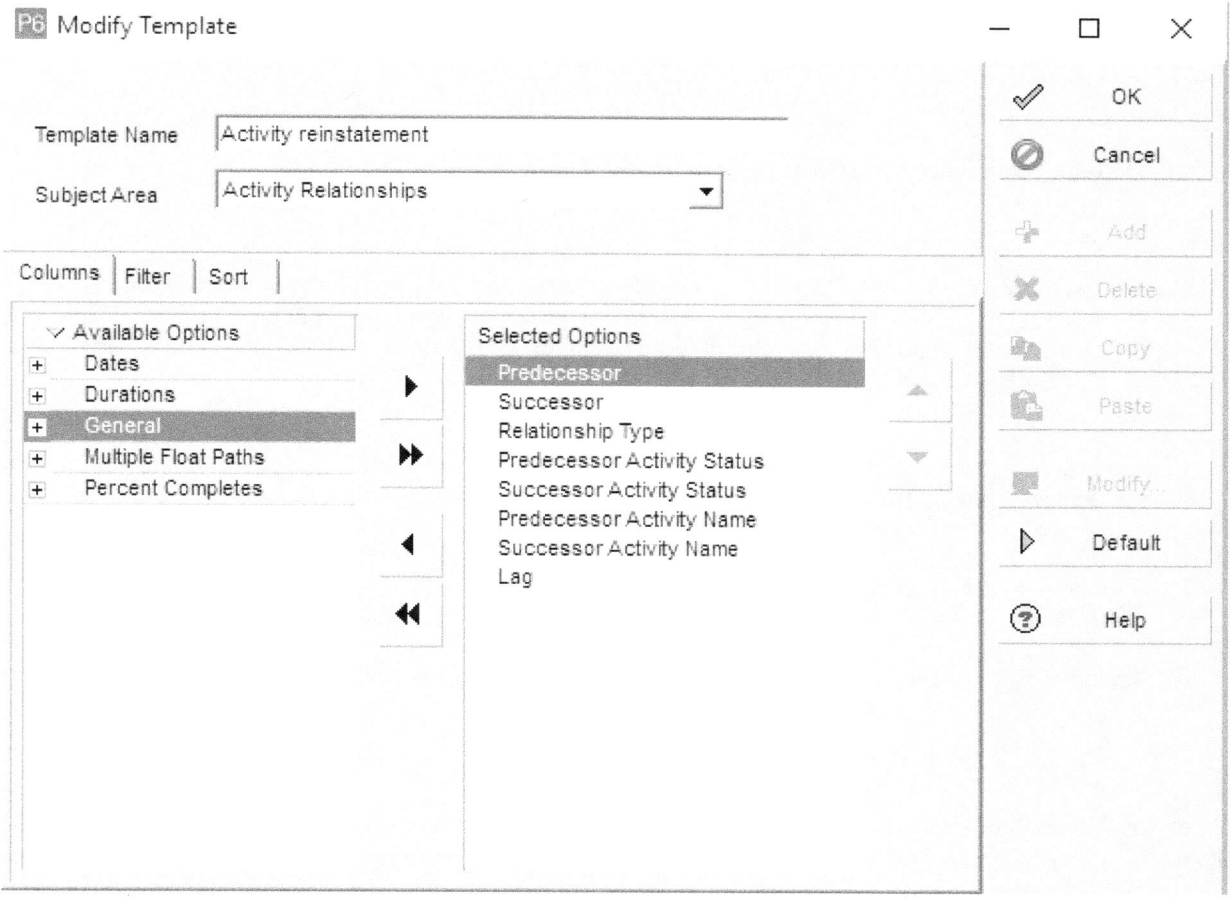

6. Click OK to save your template and export your project.

7. There will be four tabs in the resulting file:

   a) Go to tab TASK and make the following change in the wbs_id (WBS Code) column:

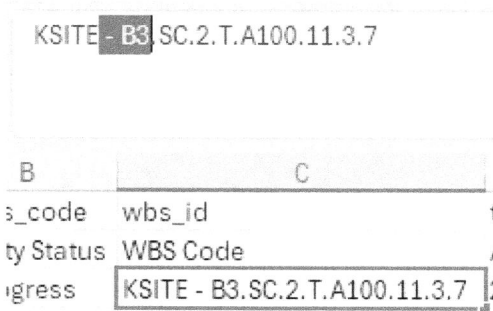

Andrei Sannikov
Tip of the day

Delete the characters after Project ID highlighted above, which are "space"-"space" and the baseline number – B3 in our example.

Delete the status_code (Activity Status) column.

    b) Go to tab TASKPRED, apply filters to all columns and filter in the IDs of the activities you are reinstating in the pred_task_id (Predecessor) column. Highlight the filtered in rows. Repeat the same in the task_id (Successor) column. Filter out highlighted rows, delete the rest of the lines and remove all filters.

8. If you did not set up a resource assignments filter in Step 5.b) above, go to the TASKRSRC tab, filter out the activity IDs you are reinstating, delete the rest of the lines and remove all filters.

9. Save, close, and import the file into your project.

10. Assign Project activity codes and add activity Suspend and Resume dates, if necessary.

The method described above is intended for reinstatement of a relatively small number of activities without or with a limited number of Project Activity codes, however, if you have deleted multiple activities and your schedule is built on Project Activity codes you might need another tool to restore their assignments on reinstated activities. Consider the following:

1) After completing Step 9 above, open the restored baseline.

2) Go to File > Export > Export Format > Spreadsheet – (XLSX) > Select Activities > Select your project and setup the following Export template:

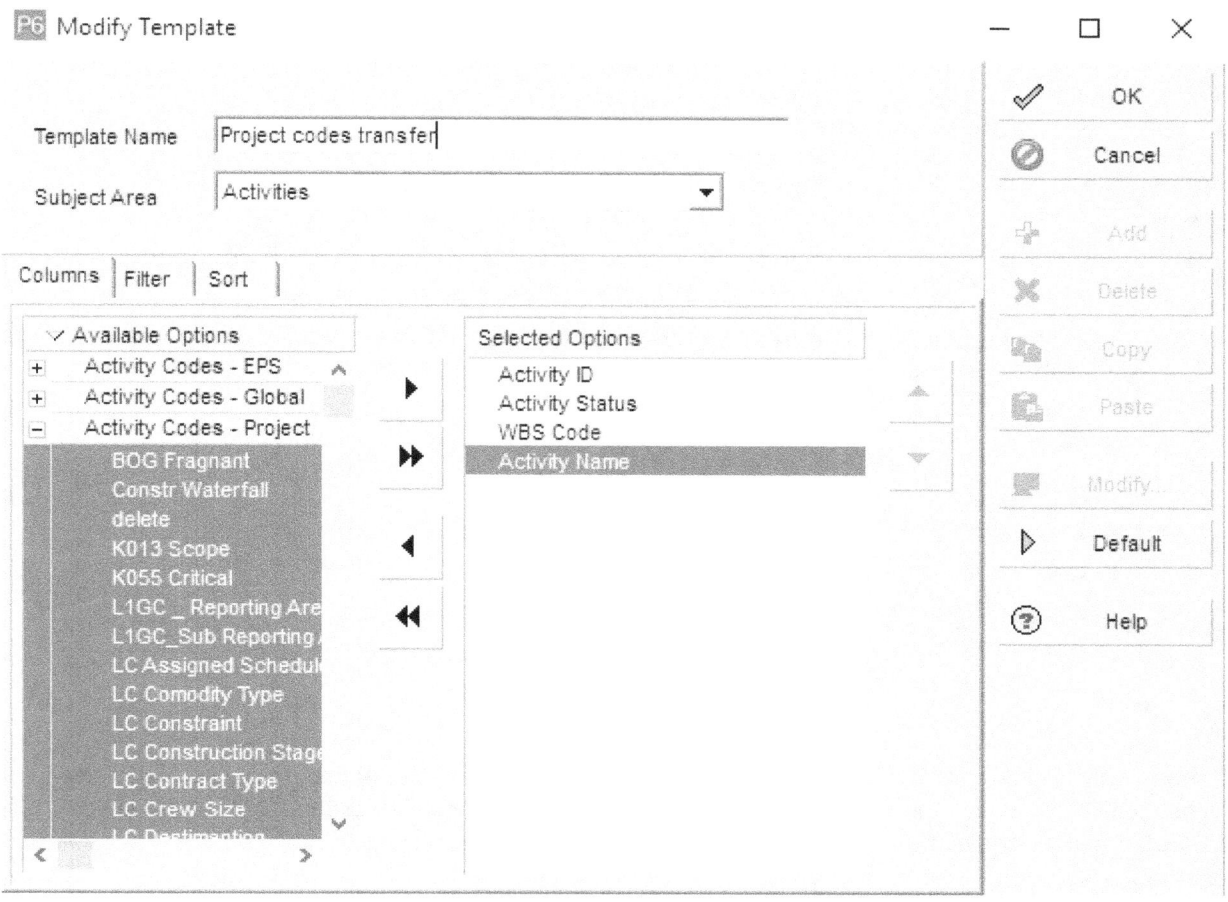

Add all Project codes or the ones you need and export your project in Excel. It will be saved in your system as XXXX – B3-Activities.xlsx, where XXXX is your project ID.

3) Go back to your working project and run an Excel export using the template we set up in Step 2) above. It will be saved in your system as XXXX-Activities.xlsx, where XXXX is your project ID.

4) Open the TASK tab in the XXXX-Activities.xlsx file, filter out activities you have reinstated from the baseline, delete the rest of the lines and remove all filters.

5) Copy the TASK tab from XXXX – B3-Activities.xlsx to XXXX-Activities.xlsx. It will appear as TASK (2).

6) If you are confident that the Project Activity codes in the restored baseline are identical to the Project Activity codes in your working project, you can use a simple lookup formula shown below in cell E3 of the TASK tab. Copy it down and across all columns:

| | A | B | C | D | E |
|---|---|---|---|---|---|
| | | | | fx | =XLOOKUP($A3,'TASK (2)'!$A:$A,'TASK (2)'!E:E,"") |
| 1 | task_code | status_code | wbs_id | | task_name | actv_code_l1gc_reporting_area_l25_66297_id |
| 2 | Activity ID | Activity Status | WBS Code | | Activity Name | L1GC _ Reporting Area L2.5 |
| 3 | EKC-0035-N300-03-080 | Completed | KSITE.SC.1.G.N300 | | Section 2: | 1GSWCN |

7) If your restored baseline was created sometime ago and the Project Activity code fields have changed, you might want to use a different Excel function, like the one below, to avoid any surprises:

| | A | B | C | D | E |
|---|---|---|---|---|---|
| | | | | fx | =INDEX('TASK (2)'!$E$3:$N$10298,MATCH($A3,'TASK (2)'!$A$3:$A$10298,0),MATCH(E$2,'TASK (2)'!$E$2:$N$2,0)) |
| 1 | task_code | status_code | wbs_id | | task_name | actv_code_l1gc_reporting_area_l25_66297_id |
| 2 | Activity ID | Activity Status | WBS Code | | Activity Name | L1GC _ Reporting Area L2.5 |
| 3 | EKC-0035-N300-03-080 | Completed | KSITE.SC.1.G.N300 | | Section 2: | 1GSWCN |

This formula will look up the code descriptions in Row 2 and return code values in corresponding code columns against activity IDs in column A. Copy it down and across all columns. Check the results – if you see #N/A in a code column, it means that that this code has been deleted from your working project. Delete this column from the TASK tab.

8) Select all cells in the TASK tab (Ctrl + A), paste Values.

9) Delete the TASK (2) tab, save, close your XXXX-Activities.xlsx file and import it into your working project.

## Attachment – Planners' Frustration Corner

My personal collection of project related quotes that took me some 25 years and seven major projects to compile…

1. Expensive but slow.

2. Save money at all cost.

3. There is nothing more permanent than temporary.

4. The advantage of not planning is that failure comes as a complete surprise rather than being preceded by moments of uncertainty and worry.

5. Schedules are prone to slippage.

6. The great thing about schedules is their ability to show what management wants to see.

7. Sinking as planned.

8. Teamwork is a lot of people doing what I say!

9. If I wanted it tomorrow, I would have waited until tomorrow to ask for it!

10. Contractor's definition of tomorrow: not today.

11. The basic principle of Russian roulette consists in repeating the same thing and expecting a different outcome.

12. Doing it right is not an excuse for not meeting the schedule.

13. If you take 2 taxis you don't get to the airport any sooner.

14. What do doctors and pipeliners have in common? Both bury their mistakes…

15. Initial estimates are built on the premise that their magnitude will be inversely proportional to the probability of project approval.

16. The client dreams, the manager promises, the contractor lies, the planner takes the blame.

17. It's not the end of the world but you can see it from here!

18. There are lies, damn lies and progress.

19. Never underestimate the power of very stupid people in large groups.

20. The number of victories that can be claimed in a reporting period is inversely proportional to the criticality of the selected targets.

21. Our ultimate goal is to finish this project before they find an alternative energy source.

22. Planners for management are like dictionaries: useful when you need them but anyone would do.

23. Every good plan must have an exit strategy.

24. The best joke for God is a detailed description of your future plans.

25. Our plan is to start when we can, where we can, with all resources we can find and to finish as soon as we can.

26. For every complicated problem there is always a simple neat solution, which is usually wrong.

27. If you don't know where you are going any road will take you there.

28. What can go wrong will.

29. Here it does not matter who was right, it matters who is left.

30. Safety first! said the accountant and started his budget cuts.

31. You are allowed to think as long as you think correctly.

32. It does not matter how they vote, it matters how we count (Joseph Stalin)

33. Alternative reality is when the contractor is lying, and we know that he is lying, and he knows that we know that he is lying but everybody nods seriously and takes notes.

34. The sooner you get behind the schedule the more time you will have to make it up.

35. Work expands to fill and exceed time available for its completion.

36. No project would have started if the truth had been told about cost and time scale.

37. Dates in the calendar are closer than they appear.

38. If you want a truck load of bricks, ask for two.

39. There are two types of planners: those who don't know and those who don't know they don't know.

40. If everything is going exactly as planned, something somewhere is going massively wrong.

41. The most important management skill is the ability to convert yesterday's lies into tomorrow's reforecast.

42. If I had the money, design, manpower and materials I would not need you.

43. What is the difference between Contractor's schedule and a broken clock? A broken clock shows the correct time twice a day…

44. We tried our best you know the rest…

45. Artificial intelligence will never be a match for natural stupidity.

46. What we lack in physical progress we make up for in progress reporting.

47. No initiative goes unpunished.

48. Mechanical completion is achieved when all the remaining construction scope has been successfully classified as punchlist items.

Andrei Sannikov
Tip of the day

49. When addressing his superiors every subordinate shall assume a cheerful and stupid appearance in order not to embarrass the management by his intelligence (Peter the Great, decree of December 9$^{th}$, 1709)

50. The circus has left town, the clowns have stayed behind...

51. Changes in reporting requirements do not have to make sense as long as they provide management with the illusion of leadership and control.

52. Today is worse than yesterday but better than tomorrow.

53. It is dangerous to be right when management is wrong.

54. The rules here are hard but they are applied selectively.

55. We do not change the dates until we miss them.

56. Incorrect data is readily available, correct numbers can be provided upon request.

57. Teamwork is a concept invented by management to share the blame more efficiently.

58. Overall progress is like the mean body temperature of all the patients in a hospital: average of highs and lows equals normal.

59. The easiest way to ensure that a schedule is approved is to have it reviewed by someone who has no idea what he is looking at.

60. The worst possible schedule delay is a delay that cannot be blamed on somebody else.

61. Contractor shall not be held responsible for the Company's action, or lack of action, resulting from any assumption that Contractor intends to perform any of the construction activities in accordance with its schedule.

62. A schedule is a tool used to create a professionally looking justification for essentially predetermined results.

63. Dreaming, after all, is a form of planning.

64. Common sense is not that common.

65. Every complicated problem can be explained in simple, easy-to-understand, wrong terms.

66. The answer to every question here depends on who wants to know.

67. If at first you don't succeed, parachuting is not your sport.

68. When your plan meets the real world, the real world wins.

69. Anything is possible if you don't know what you are talking about.

70. The definition of a milestone completion changes as the result of diminishing probability to finish on time.

71. This project is a race against time and time is winning.

72. The best proven recipe for being on schedule is a carefully balanced mix of inflated durations, overestimated budgets and vaguely defined milestones accompanied with a good story to facilitate their approval in the baseline plan.

73. When it comes to increasing the Project's percent complete no schedule mitigation is as effective as a major reduction in the remaining scope of work.

74. The impact of future budget cuts is best mitigated by well-targeted inflation of the estimates in the areas where such cuts are anticipated to occur.

75. Generation of random dates is an alternative planning method commonly used in areas where lack of schedules, and the resulting data gaps, would otherwise unsettle project management and cause interruptions in its decision-making process.

76. A minor deviation from project reporting rules can generate more progress than any schedule recovery measure.

77. Planned progress curve can either support schedule requirements or meet management expectations. Choose one.

78. A well-targeted re-evaluation of the rules of credit, applied to completed work, can generate enough progress to create the impression of a schedule recovery.

79. Productivity is best managed by inflating budget labor hours to the limits required to achieve the desired productivity factors.

80. Planners are expected to comply with all scheduling directives from senior management and accept full responsibility for any errors or omissions resulting from them.

81. Reporting of unverified contractors' progress is unacceptable, unless it is substantially higher than the percent complete calculated by the Company progress tracking system.

82. The most efficient schedule mitigation technique consists in timely revision of planned finish dates in the areas where negative progress trends are being observed or anticipated.

83. Risks associated with expression of opinion can be mitigated by limiting all discussions with senior managers to enthusiastic appreciation of their own ideas on the subject.

84. Employees thrown under the bus must accept this measure as an integral part of the work processes designed to protect the reputation of their line manager.

85. Sometimes that light at the end of the tunnel comes from the headlamp of an approaching train.

86. Safety is our top priority as long as key production and schedule targets are being met.

87. A detailed schedule is a document that the manager does not read, the client does not need, and the contactor does not follow.

88. Schedule delays are often driven by lack of management interest in its detail.

www.ingramcontent.com/pod-product-compliance
Lightning Source LLC
Chambersburg PA
CBHW082203220526
45470CB00010B/3030